ABOUT THE AUTHOR

Dr. Anne Wad has been a researcher and a professor in the Criminal Justice field for over 30 years. She currently holds a position as a Provost/CAO in a University, and Director of Research at another university. She holds an Ed.D. in Educational Leadership and a Ph.D. in Public Safety Leadership/Criminal Justice. Her research interests are in Criminology, Victimology, and the Human Services. She is married to Wesley Wade. She is an artist, writer, researcher, professor, and university administrator.

GENDERED JUSTICE: FEMINIST PERSPECTIVES ON LAW AND ORDER

GENDERED JUSTICE: FEMINIST PERSPECTIVES ON LAW AND ORDER

GENDERED JUSTICE: FEMINIST PERSPECTIVES ON LAW AND ORDER

Dr. Anne Wade

SOCIETY Publishing

www.societypublishing.com

Gendered Justice: Feminist Perspectives on Law and Order

Dr. Anne Wade

Society Publishing
4164 Lakeshore Road
Burlington, ON L7L 1A4
Canada
www.societypublishing.com
Email: orders@arclereducation.com

ISBN: 978-1-77956-459-7 (Hardcover)

TABLE OF CONTENTS

LIST OF FIGURES

LIST OF TABLE

PREFACE

Gender justice encompasses a broad and comprehensive approach aimed at protecting individuals from abuse and discrimination, particularly focusing on empowering those who have historically been marginalized or subordinated, often women. This concept asserts that women should not only be participants but should actively influence decision-making processes across various spheres, including in family dynamics and societal issues. It emphasizes that both women and men should collaboratively engage in seeking fair and practical solutions to these challenges. Rather than adhering to outdated stereotypes and roles traditionally prescribed by patriarchal norms, gender justice advocates for a more inclusive and equitable framework. It challenges the notion that gender roles should be narrowly defined and controlled by societal expectations, particularly those established by dominant groups. Gender justice is grounded in the belief that every individual, regardless of gender, should have equal opportunities to contribute to and benefit from societal advancements.

This perspective supports the idea that women, as well as men, possess fundamental rights and should be recognized as autonomous agents capable of influencing their own destinies. Gender justice calls for a transformative approach that goes beyond mere participation, aiming for substantial change in how both genders are perceived and valued in various contexts. It envisions a society where gender equality is not just a theoretical concept but a lived reality, ensuring that everyone has the freedom and capacity to pursue their goals and contribute meaningfully to their communities.

This book, "*Gendered Justice: Feminist Perspectives on Law and Order*," explores a range of issues at the intersection of gender, law, and justice through ten comprehensive chapters.

Chapter 1 introduces the foundational concepts of gendered justice, setting the stage for an in-depth examination of how feminist perspectives influence legal and societal understandings of justice. It outlines the importance of integrating gender considerations into discussions about law and order.

Chapter 2 covers the historical context of gender and law, tracing the evolution of legal systems and their impact on gender relations. It highlights how historical precedents have shaped contemporary legal frameworks and gender dynamics.

Chapter 3 presents feminist legal theory, exploring its foundations and developments over time. This chapter examines key feminist theories and their contributions to reshaping legal thought and practices.

Chapter 4 addresses the gendered nature of crime and punishment, investigating how gender biases influence both criminal behavior and the penal system. It discusses the disparities in how different genders are treated within the justice system.

Chapter 5 focuses on sexual violence and its treatment within the legal system. It analyzes the challenges and shortcomings in addressing sexual violence and advocates for reforms to better support survivors.

Chapter 6 covers reproductive rights and legal frameworks, exploring how laws affect reproductive health and autonomy. It discusses key legal battles and ongoing issues related to reproductive rights.

Chapter 7 examines gender, family law, and custody issues, investigating how family law intersects with gender concerns. This chapter highlights the impact of legal decisions on family structures and gender roles.

Chapter 8 looks at the experiences of women in the criminal justice system, including issues of representation, treatment, and systemic biases that affect women involved in the justice system.

Chapter 9 explores LGBTQ+ rights and legal challenges, addressing the legal struggles faced by LGBTQ+ individuals and the evolving legal landscape in relation to LGBTQ+ rights.

Chapter 10 concludes with an analysis of race, gender, and the law, discussing how intersecting identities affect legal outcomes and justice. This chapter emphasizes the need for a nuanced understanding of how race and gender intersect in legal contexts.

This book will serve students, scholars, and practitioners in law, gender studies, and social justice. It is particularly valuable for those interested in feminist legal theory, gender justice, and the impact of legal systems on marginalized communities.

–Author

Chapter **1**

Introduction to Gender Justice

Contents

INTRODUCTION

Gender inequality and disparities are still widespread worldwide, making gender justice—like racial justice—a crucial issue in today's society. It manifests itself in a variety of ways, such as institutional and social discrimination, lack of access to resources for healthcare and education, economic hardship, and systematic prejudice. Gender inequality still presents a barrier to women seeking equal opportunities in all spheres of life, despite global efforts to address the issue. As SAHR, we think that the path to gender justice must include awareness-raising, education, and advocacy. The idea of gender justice encourages all genders to fully realize their rights and opportunities. It aims to achieve equality in terms of rights, obligations, and opportunities between men and women as well as between different gender identities. It is a comprehensive strategy that guarantees that women and other gender minorities can fully exercise their human rights and tackles the underlying causes of gender discrimination.

1.1. OVERVIEW OF THE STATE OF GENDER JUSTICE

The equitable treatment of all genders, guaranteeing that people have equal rights, opportunities, and access to resources irrespective of their gender identity, is known as gender justice. Its foundation is the idea that a person's ouldn'tshould not restrict their ability to fully engage in social, political, economic, or cultural life. Gender justice addresses the underlying systemic injustices that sustain violence and discrimination against people based solely on their gender. It goes beyond formal equality, which concentrates only on equal treatment under the law. The acknowledgement of the historical and current marginalization of women and gender minorities, such as transgender, non-binary, and gender nonconforming individuals, is fundamental to the cause of gender justice. Patriarchal norms, which value men and masculinity, as well as institutional and legal frameworks that were formerly created by and for the benefit of men, frequently serve to perpetuate this marginalization. Destroying these institutions and changing cultural norms are necessary to achieve gender justice and build an inclusive society where everyone can prosper.

It is the collective responsibility of all spheres of society, including businesses, individuals, governments, and civil society, to achieve gender justice. It necessitates modifications to public policies, legal reforms, and cus. In order toTo confront and alter discriminatory norms and practices, education and awareness-raising are essential elements. Gender justice also calls for the people who are most impacted by gender inequality to actively participate in the decision-making processes that determine their course in life.

1.1.1. Gender-Based Violence

Women and gender minorities are disproportionately affected by gender-based violence, which is a widespread and deeply ingrained problem worldwide. It has multiple manifestations, such as sexual harassment, domestic abuse, and human trafficking. It stems from power imbalances and social norms that support gender inequality. Domestic violence is one of the most common types of gender-based violence, frequently taking place inside intimate relationships. It includes mistreatment that is financial, emotional, psychological, and physical as well as a climate of fear and control that robs victims of their freedom and dignity. Economic dependence, a lack of legal protections in many situations, and societal expectations that normalize male dominance and female subservience make women and gender minorities especially vulnerable to domestic violence.

Another prevalent instance of gender-based violence is sexual harassment, which can happen in a variety of contexts such as public places, workplaces, educational institutions, and online forums. It involves unwelcome and improper sexual advances, remarks, inappropriate jokes, or actions that put the victim in a hostile situation. The pervasiveness of ss a reflection ofreflects ingrained gender norms that reduce women and gender minorities to nothing more than objects of sexual desire. Sexuaious consequencesprofound consequences that include psychological distress, lost career opportunities, and a strengthening of gender inequality. Women and gender minorities are disproportionately affected by gender-based violence, which also includes human trafficking, a serious violation of human rights. Traffickers take advantage of weak people, frequently by force, deception, or coercion, and expose them to different kinds of exploitation, such as forced labor and sexual slavery. The majority of victims of human trafficking worldwide are women and girls, primarily because of conditions like poverty, illiteracy, and discrimination based on gender that make them susceptible to exploitation. Gender minorities, in particular transgender people, frequently experience additional layers of marginalization and discrimination, making them highly vulnerable to human trafficking.

These violent acts have terrible effects that cause long-term harm to one's body, mind, and emotions. In addition to physical injuries, victims frequently struggle with anxiety, depression, post-traumatic stress disorder (PTSD), and other mental health problems. Because gender-based violence perpetuates cycles of poverty, inequality, and social instability, its effects on society are equally profound. Moreover, it impedes the social and economic advancement of countries and communities, as well as efforts to attain gender equality.

A multifaceted strategy is needed to address gender-based violence, including legal reforms, awareness campaigns, victim support services, and the challenge of cultural norms that normalize or condone violence. Legal safeguards, such as those that make sexual harassment, domestic abuse, and human trafficking crimes, are crucial, but they also need strong enforcement systems. Campaigns for public awareness and education are also very important in modifying the attitudes and actions that support gender-based violence. For victims to heal and start over, support services such as counseling, shelters, and legal aid are essential. In the end, attaining gender justice and guaranteeing that no one has to live in fear or violence depends on tackling gender-based violence.

1.1.2. Reproductive Rights and Justice

One of the main tenets of gender justice is the ability to obtain reproductive healthcare, which includes contraception, abortion, and maternal care. This right, which is closely related to more general concerns of autonomy, equality, and human rights, is necessary for people to be able to make educated decisions about their bodies, health, and futures. Access to reproductive healthcare is essential for people's empowerment and general well-being because it gives people—especially women and members of gender minority groups—control over their reproductive lives. However, laws, policies, and social norms that aim to control and limit reproductive choices frequently contest and restrict this right, creating serious health and social disparities.

One of the most important aspects of reproductive healthcare is contraception, which helps people plan their families, avoid unplanned pregancies, and guard against STIDs. People can select the contraceptive method that best fits their needs and circumstances by having access to a variety of methods. However, marginalized groups, such as low-income women, adolescents, and gender minorities, are disproportionately affected by barriers to contraception access, such as cost, lack of availability, cultural stigma, and restrictive policies. These obstacles not only impair people's autonomy but also raise the risk of poverty, unplanned pregnancies, and maternal death.

Another essential component of reproductive healthcare is accebortion, which enables people women to end a pregnancy in a safe and authorized manner. Protecting the health and lives of expectant mothers, especially in situations involving rape, incest, or other health risks, requires the right to an abortion. Despite its significance, abortion is still heavily regulated and politicized in many nations, with some even enacting complete bans or severely restrictive laws. Due to these limitations, people are forced to seek out risky, illegal abortions, which increases their risk of serious health consequences, such as death, serious injury, and long-term reproductive harm. Furthermore, restrictive abortion laws exacerbate already-existing health disparities by disproportionately harming marginalized communities, such as the poor, people of color, and those residing in rural areas. For moms and babies to be healthy and happy, prenatal, delivery, and postnatal care are all essential components of maternal care. The risk of complications duri pregnancy and childbirth hasis decreased, maternal and infant mortality rates are lowered, and healthy early childhood development is supported when access to high-quality maternal care is available. But there are still gaps in access to maternity care, especially in low-income and rural areas where there may not be enough infrastructure for proper healthcare. The intersectional nature of disparities in reproductive healthcare is further highlighted by the fact that systemic racism and discrimination in healthcare settings can result in worse maternal health outcomes for women of color.

Achieving gender justice requires fighting laws that limit eproductive healthcare. In order toTo advocate for reproductive rights, one must confront social and economic obstacles that keep people from exercising their right to procreate and challenge laws and regulations that restrict access to abortion, contraception, and maternal care. This entails encouraging thorough sex education, making sure healthcare is available and affordable, and battling stigma and discrimination against people who seek reproductive healthcare. In the end, maintaining and enhancing access to reproductive healthcare is crucial to guaranteeing that everyone has the freedom and chance to make decisions about their bodies and lives that are informed and unaffected by violence, discrimination, or coercion.

1.1.3. Gender Pay Gap and Economic Inequality

Gendered economic inequality, or the differences in income and opportunities between the sexes, is a serious global issue that impedes economic progress and sustains systemic injustice. Gender wage gap, or the ongoing difference in pay between men alem in this area. Generally speaking, womenWomen are paid less for similar work. Women are overrepresented in lower-paying industries and professions due to occupational segregation; discrimination in compensation, hiring, and promotion policies; and the devaluation of work traditionally done by women, such as domestic work and care giving. These factors interact in a complex way to cause this disparity. An additional factor contributing to income inequality is the fact that women are less likely to hold leadership positions and frequently encounter obstacles to career advancement, even when they acquire comparable levels of education and experience as men.

The feminization of poverty, a phenomenon in which women experience poverty at a disproportionate rate relative to men, is another important component of gender economic inequality. Women are more likely than men to work in casual, part-time, or low-paying jobs that provide little in the way of benefits, security, or career advancement. This is just one of the many factors contributing to this. Women also frequently take on the majority of unpaid care responsibilities, such as childrearing and elder care, which restricts their ability to pursue higher-paying professions or paid employment. Because it prevents women from accessing opportunities for education, job training, and income generation, this unequal burden of unpaid labor is not only economically undervalued but also contributes to the cyclical nature of poverty. Social and legal structures that perpetuate gender inequality make women's economic vulnerabilities even more severe. For example, in many parts of the world, women's access to financial resources—such as credit, property, and inheritance rights—is restricted, which limits their capacity to accumulate wealth and become financially independent. onomic opportunities are further restrictedrestricted, and their marginalization is exacerbated by discriminatory social norms and practices, such as early marriage and gender-based violence.

It takes extensive legislative interventions and cultural transformations to address the wage gap and the feminization of poverty. The implementation of equal pay legislation, the promotion of pay transparency, and the encouragement of women to assume leadership positions are all necessary components of the fight against the wage gap. Women can also succeed in higher-paying, traditionally male-dominated fields by addressing occupational segregation through targeted policies, education, and training. It is critical to aand rebalance unpaid care labor in order toto counteract the feminization of poverty. Soc nets, such as paid time off and child carechildcare, should also be easily accessible to encourage women to participate in the workforce. Dismantling societal and legal constraints that prevent women from accessing opportunities and resources is also necessary for the economic empowerment of women. This includes fighting detrimental gender norms that limit women's freedoms and choices, protecting women's property rights, and increasing access to financial services. When women are able to contribute fully and equally to society, families, communities, and economies as a whole benefit from achieving gender economic equality, which ultimately serves as both a matter of justice and a catalyst for greater economic prosperity.

1.1.4. Gender Identity and Expression

Gender justice is fundamentally based on the rights and recognition of transgender, non-binary, and gender non-conforming people. These rights include equal access to healthcare, protection from discrimination, and legal recognition. Social norms that uphold rigid ideas of male and female and favor binary gender identities present these individuals with considerable obstacles on a regular basis. Legal recognition is essential to affirm transgender and non-binary people's identities and enable them to live authentically and with dignity. This includes the freedom to modify the gender marker on identification documents, such as driver's licenses, birth certificates, and passports, without having to go through onerous bureaucratic procedures or intrusive medical requirements. Ensuring that gender identities are respected in all spheres of life—from housing and social services to work and education—is another critical aspect of legal recognition.

Gender nonconforming, non-binary, and transgender people also face discwhen it comes to healthcare access. In order toTo match their physical attributes with their gender identity, these people frequently need gender-affirming care, such as hormone therapy, surgeries, and mental health support. However, barriers to receiving this kind of care often include insurance not covering the full cost of treatment, a lack of skilled providers, and discriminatory healthcare policies. Furthermore, the healthcare system may harbor prejudice and stigma against transgender and non-binary people, which could result in subpar or harmful care. It will take extensive reforms to ensure that these people have equitable access to healthcare. These reforms include financial barrier removal, policy implementation that forbids discrimination in medical settings, and training healthcare providers on gender-affirming care.

Safeguarding the rights of individuals who identify as transgender, non-binary, or gender nonconforming requires protection from discrimination. Gender identity and expression are grounds for discrimination in a number of spheres of life, such as public accommodations, housing, work, and education. People who identify as transgender or non-binary frequently experience harassment, violence, and exclusion; these acts not only violate their human rights but also negatively affect their mental and physical health. Legal safeguards, such as the adoption and implementation of anti-discrimination legislation that specifically cogender identity and expression, are required to stopstop, and remedy this kind rimination. Legal actions are necessary, but societysociety's attitudes also need to change in order to accept and value gender diversity and dispel the myths and prejudices that encourage violence and discrimination.

Addressing the intersectional nature of the experiences of transgender, non-binary, and gender nonconforming people is also necessary to achieve true recognition and equality for them. Many people experience discrimination that is made worse by factors related to their identity, including socioeconomic status, race, ethnicity, sexual orientation, and disability. When it comes to addressing the complex issues that people who are at the intersections of multiple marginalized identities face, an intersectional approach to gender justice acknowledges these issues and seeks to provide inclusive and equitable solutions.

1.1.5. Political Representation and Participation

The attainment of inclusive governance and genuine democracy is impeded by the inadequate representation of women and gender minorities in political institutions and decision-making procedures. Women and gender minorities, despite making up a sizable portion of the population, are frequently marginalized in political arenas, which prevents a diversity of viewpoints and experiences in policymaking. These groups have historically been excluded from power due to systemic and historical injustices, which are the root cause of their underrepresentation. Gender stereotypes, institutional biases, and social norms all play a part in maintaining male-dominated political environments where women and gender minorities have lower chances of being appointed to leadership roles, elected to office, or having their opinions heard during crucial decision-making processes.

This underrepresentation has a significant effect. Policies and laws may not adequately address the unique needs and concerns of women and gender minorities if they are not represented in political institutions. It's possible to ignore or provide insufficient attention to problems like economic inequality, access to healthcare, reproductive rights, and gender-based violence. In addition, the marginalization of these groups is sustained and existing power disparities are reinforced by the lack of representation. To create just and efficient policies that benefit the entire community, inclusive governance—where political institutions reflect the diversity of the populace—is crucial. It guarantees that the specaced by women and gender minorities are taken into accountconsidered, as well as the interests of all citizens, regardless of gender.

There are many different obstacles that prevent women and gender minorities from participating in politics. There are structural barriers that restrict their ability to run for office and win elections, including unfair voting procedures, restricted access to political networks, and insufficient funding for campaigns. Furthermore, women and gender minorities are discouraged from pursuing careers in politics by social and cultural norms that see politics as a male domain. These groups are further discouraged from engaging in politics by gender-based violence, harassment, and intimidation, which fosters a hostile environment that limits their capacity to support governance.

Comprehensive approaches to removing these obstacles and fostering an inclusive political climate are necessary to advance the political representation of women and gender minorities. Gender quotas and reserved seats are examples of electoral reforms that have been successful in raising the representation of women in politics across numerous nations. By ensuring that women are more heavily represented in political institutions, policies that are more sensitive to the needs of women and gender minorities will be made, and women will be held more accountable for their actions. Building the capacity of women and gender minorities to engage in politics effectively requires not only quotas but also efforts to support and train them in leadership, political campaigning, and governance.

1.1.6. Human Rights and Gender Justice

In order to question and change the norms that support gender inequality in politics, cultural change is also required. Campaigns for public awareness, instruction, and media representation can all contribute to a change in public opinion that will support and encourage more women and gender minorities in positions of leadership. In addition, political organizations and parties need to make a commitment to inclusivity by advocating for laws that take gender equality into account, fighting prejudice, and making sure that every member has an equal chance to participate in decision-making.

Gender justice covers a wide range of topics, including safety from violence and discrimination, as well as access to healthcare, education, employment, and political participation. These problems are not isolated; rather, they intersect with and exacerbate broader human rights issues such as social exclusion, poverty, and racial inequality. For instance, gender-based violence violates the fundamental human right to live free from coercion and harm. The rights of women and gender minorities to life, security, and bodily autonomy are seriously jeopardized by violence, including sexual harassment, domestic abuse, and human trafficking. Gender justice is also crucial to the advancement of social and economic rights. The feminization of poverty and the global gender pay gap serve as stark reminders of the deep-rooted gendered nature of economic inequality. Systemic barriers, such as unpaid caregiving obligations, discriminatory laws, and limited access to financial resources, prevent women and gender minorities from fully participating in the economy. To achieve greater economic justice and reduce global poverty, gender-just policies—such as parental leave, equal pay laws, and social safety nets—must address these issues.

Gender justice and wider human rights also depend on political representation and participation. The democratic ideal of equal participation is undermined and the scope of inclusive governance is restricted by the underrepresentation of women and gender minorities in political institutions. It takes inclusive governance—where a range of opinions are respected and heard—to develop policies that represent the interests and rights of all people. Therefore, ensuring gender parity in political and decision-making processes is essential to democratic governance, human rights, and gender justice.

Global movements for social justice and equality, includi disability rights, and LGBTQ+ rights, are closely associatedstrongly associated with the fight for gender justice. The understanding that people encounter several, overlapping types of discrimination—known as intersectionality—highlights how intertwined these battles are. For instance, discrimination against women of color, LGBTQ+ people, and women with disabilities is frequently compounded and cannot be completely addressed by focusing only on gender. Therefore, the struggle for gender justice needs to be intersectional and inclusive, recognizing and addressing the various forms of oppression that different groups have experienced.

1.2. INTERSECTIONALITY AND GENDER JUSTICE

Feminist theory, research methodology, and platform for social justice action are all embodied in intersectionality. It is predicated on the idea that individuals have multiple, complex identities that are shaped by their past, present, and interactions with power structures. By highlighting the various forms of discrimination and disadvantage that arise from the combination of identities, intersectional analysis seeks to reveal multiple identities. It attempts to address the ways in which systems of discrimination such as racism, patriarchy, class oppression, and others produce disparities that define women's relative positions. It considers social, political, and historical contexts in addition to acknowledging the distinctive personal experiences brought about by the fusion of various identities.

The concept that social relations involve multiple intersecting forms of discrimination is known as intersectionality. This implies that an individual may simultaneously encounter multiple types of discrimination, including ableism, racism, and sexism. For instance, discrimination against a Roma woman may be motivated by her ethnicity as well as her gender. Gender equality benefits from intersectionality because it clarifies the ways in which various types of discrimination interact to worsen inequality. Our attempts to advance gender equality may have less of an impact and may even make things worse for some of the most marginalized women if we ignore intersectionality. A project that seeks to empower women, for example, might ignore the unique needs and challenges that Roma women face, which could exacerbate their marginalization.

1.2.1. Intersectionality: Key to Tackling Gender Inequality in the Workplace and Beyond

The LGBTQ+ community, individuals with disabilities, members of racial, ethnic, and cultural minorities, and other underrepresented groups must all be central to an intersectional feminist approach if we are to truly advance equity and inclusion in the workplace. It is only feasible to recognize and address structural inequalities by taking into account the unique characteristics and connections of the struggles and experiences that these groups face. Too frequently, the experiences of white, cis, heterosexual, middle-class or upper-class women are still presented as the "universal experience" when it comes to discussions about gender equality, especially when it comes to work and leadership. In order to advance past this, the conversation must shift from an intersectional to an intersectional, meritocratic point of view. In this way, the depth of the innumerable structural barriers impeding the professional advancement of women in general and women from marginalized groups in particular can be comprehended.

The literature highlights that the experience of women who face multiple intersectionalities at work is more precarious, despite the fact that women from all backgrounds report feeling invisible in professional settings. For example, non-white women experience unique challenges in feeling like they "belong" in the workplace because they are members of both gender and racial minorities, finding themselves at the intersection of gender and race. Black and brown women's careers are shaped by numerous needs and challenges that reflect global structural inequality, particularly in countries outside of Africa. For decades, they have been identified as the group that, in comparison to their white counterparts, faces greater precariousness in work relationships and fewer opportunities for social mobility. They have encountered discrimination in the workplace based on both gender and race since the start of their careers. Additionally, the underrepresentation of women in leadership roles and the lack of suitable professional growth opportunities further impede their career progression, perpetuating existing inequalities.

Research suggests that black women frequently experience high levels of stress, insecurity, low self-esteem, fear of vulnerability, marginalization, silencing, and objectification. These conditions can impair mental health, make them invisible, cause them to feel inadequate and unauthentic, and hinder their ability to advance in their careers. Furthermore, they frequently refrain from speaking up or voicing their opinions when decisions need to be made, but when they do, they are also less frequently regarded as having leadership qualities. As a result, the decision of whether to confront racism, sexism, and other unfavorable circumstances or to ignore them marks the career of black and other non-white marginalized women, and this decision can be extremely stressful. Daily negotiating these dynamics and constantly having to choose between confronting and ignoring barriers takes time and energy away from other behaviors like networking and job-related activities that could lead to promotions. Racial battle fatigue is the term used to describe the social, physical, and psychological reactions to stress that non-white individuals have when they are in primarily white institutions and work environments.

Due to the fact that people who openly "transgress" gender norms are the targets of both explicit and implicit forms of aggression, including verbal abuse, name-calling, cruel jokes, derogatory remarks, and criticism, many LGBTIQIA+ people—especially those who identify as transgender or belong to gender diverse groups—face comparable obstacles. Evidence suggests, for instance, that trans people frequently face a variety of challenges, including transphobia, financial hardships, limited or nonexistent access to opportunities for education and employment, and daily humiliations like problems using a restroom that corresponds with their gender identity and challenges changing their name and gender on official documents. Furthermore, transitions between genders frequently occur during the working years, and these times are typically marked by a lack of appropriate organizational support and accommodations for their unique needs.

Thus, it is important for those working on gender inequality research and policy to consider the particular requirements intersectionality places on the workplace and other settings. In addition to specific strategies to embrace diversity as a whole, it is imperative to develop targeted solutions to overcome these barriers, such as laws to encourage organizations to hire more trans and gender diverse people. Gender has to be "decolonized" in order to give underrepresented voices a platform and the ability to speak freely. Observing how frequently minorities gather at the table to talk about what works and what doesn't for them is one way to observe decolonization in the field of policy-making. In order to decolonize academia, it would be necessary to address issues like how many academics from marginalized groups are valued and acknowledged for their contributions, and how much of our research questions place intersectionality at the center of the idea for the study?

By bringing attention to the racism, phobias, discrimination, and microaggressions that members of marginalized groups frequently experience, we can help decolonize society by increasing awareness of these problems. Understanding feminism as a means of dismantling all kinds of privilege, oppression, and domination that work in tandem with sexism and gender biases—such as racism, classism, colonialism, heterosexism, ethnocentrism, white supremacy, ageism, and ableism—will help gender equality initiatives present a multicultural and critical perspective and push intersectionality to the forefront of all discussions. Furthermore, those who are part of privileged groups should also make a commitment to bringing the intersectionality discussion to the table; it shouldn't be the minority who does so.

Even though there have been many structural advancements over the years, there are still a lot of oppressive mechanisms to get rid of, and doing so will take a lot of effort and time because social structures and norms take time to adjust. In order to address these issues, it is essential to develop inclusive settings, affirmative action guidelines, and targeted initiatives that advance diversity and equity in all contexts. Rather than merely trying to fit people into preconceived boxes of existence that bear no resemblance to the reality of their lived experiences, we are looking for ways to question the structuring systems of oppression through the discussion of and pursuit of specific solutions to the needs of people in all of their intersectionalities.

1.2.2. Intersectionality in a Global Context

The intersections of social classifications have been a topic of discussion in the European Union (EU) over the past few decades. These social categories were up for discussion prior to Crenshaw's definition of intersectionality. Rather than remaining distinct, the lines separating the categories of gender, race, and class have blurred to form a multifaceted intersection of race that now encompasses factors like sexual orientation, religion, and ethnicity. These intersections are known as the concept of multiple discrimination in the UK and the EU. There is disagreement over whether the EU's non-discrimination law still proactively focuses on the appropriate inequalities, despite the fact that it was passed to address these various intersections. Intersectional categories have also been contemplated outside the EU. In the book Analyzing Gender, Intersectionality, and Multiple Inequalities: Global, Transnational, and Local Contexts, the writers make the following claims: Chinese migrant workers (Chow, Tong), sex workers and their clients in South Korea (Shin), Indian widows (Chauhan), as well as Ukrainian migrants (Amelina) and Australian men of the new global middle class (Connell), all bear the scars of patriarchy and traditional gender and family assumptions. According to this text, there are a lot more places where people experience discrimination globally than what Crenshaw initially included in her definition.

Chandra Mohanty addresses global women's alliances as intersectionality in a global setting. She disagrees with western feminist theory, particularly its treatment of global women of color and women from the third world in general. She contends that although third world women are perceived as a homogeneous group, their experiences of oppression are shaped by their history, geography, and culture. This is how western feminists write about women in the global South; they ignore the overlapping identities that are part of the global South's feminism dynamic. Mohanty challenges how colonialism and the US's history of colonial power structures are performed in terms of intersectionality and relationality, as well as how to collaborate across identities. Feminism in India discusses how Indian women practice feminism within social structures and the ongoing effects of colonization, which are different from those of Western and other non-western countries. This lack of homogeneity and intersecting identities is evident in this area.

Christine Bose expands on this, describing a global application of intersectionality that seeks to disentangle particular inequalities from particular institutions while demonstrating the intersectional effects these systems produce. Using this method, she creates a framework for analyzing gender inequality across national borders. This approach differs from the one Mohanty was referring to, which does two things: it treats inequality at the national level as a monolithic entity and only makes distinctions between the global North and South. This takes the form of the meeting point of national histories, gendered disparities in education and property education, and global dynamics such as migration, economics, and violence with regional dynamics.

The way the law treats intersectionality is a problem on a worldwide scale. There is a clear problem with intersectionality in the UK's laws protecting worker's rights. The Equality Act 2010 lists the following as "protected characteristics": age, disability, gender reassignment, race, religion or belief, sex, and sexual orientation; marriage or civil partnership; pregnancy and maternity; and maternity. As combined or dual discrimination, Section 14 prohibits direct discrimination based on up to two combined grounds. Nevertheless, because the government considered this section to be too "complex and burdensome" for businesses, it has never been implemented. Due to the UK court's explicit decision to not consider intersectional discrimination in their proceedings, this shows a systematic disregard for the challenges that intersectionality presents.

When an intersectional framework is ignored, bad things can happen. According to the African American Policy Forum (AAPF), there is one instance in which the abusive citizen spouses of immigrant women endanger their lives. The authors of A primer on intersectionality contend that battered women, who frequently faced the risk of deportation or serious injury or death, were not given any special treatment under previous immigration reform, which required spouses who immigrated to the US to marry American citizens and remain lawfully married for two years before they were eligible to receive permanent resident status. They go on to say that advocates for a variety of causes, such as more equitable immigration laws and support for victims of domestic abuse, had not previously taken into account the unique difficulties that many immigrant women encounter.

Marie-Claire Belleau makes the case for strategic intersectionality as a means of promoting collaboration between ethnically diverse feminisms. She references various national-cultural (nat-cult) groups that generate different forms of feminism. Belleau argues that, through strategic intersectionality, the differences between nat-cult feminisms are neither essentialist nor universal, but should instead be understood as resulting from socio-cultural contexts. She uses the Québécois nat-cult as an example to illustrate her point that many nat-cult groups contain infinite sub-identities within themselves. Belleau also claims that there are countless ways in which different feminisms can cooperate by using strategic intersectionality, and that these partnerships can help bridge gaps between dominant and marginalized groups. Moreover, these nat-cult feminisms' performances are not essentialist; rather, they are tactics.

1.2.3. Transnational Intersectionality

Critics of postcolonial and transnational feminist thought argue that intersectionality is a WEIRD (Western, Educated, Industrialized, Rich, Democratic) society-derived concept that over generalizes the experiences of women. Postcolonial feminists have endeavored to modify Western interpretations of intersectionality, which presume that every woman faces identical forms of racial and gender oppression. The term transnational intersectionality was introduced by Shelly Grabe as a way to conceptualize intersectionality more broadly. In the context of empire building or imperialist policies defined by historical and emerging global capitalism, Grabe wrote, transnational intersectionality places importance on the intersections among gender, ethnicity, sexuality, economic exploitation, and other social hierarchies. Attention to multiple forms of resistance and complex, intersecting oppressions is encouraged by postcolonial and transnational feminists alike. According to Vrushali Patil, transborder constructions of racial and cultural hierarchies should be acknowledged by intersectionality. Regarding the state's influence on the formation of identity, Patil states: "Our analyses will remain tied to the spatialities and temporalities of colonial modernity if we do not problematize the nation and its emergence via transnational processes and ignore cross-border dynamics."

1.2.4. Social Work

Intersectionality advocates in the social work field contend that service providers will be less helpful to different populations, including victims of abuse who are disabled or who report domestic violence, if they do not consider intersectionality. Intersectional theory holds that because of the history of racially motivated police brutality, women of color benefit little from the practice of domestic violence counselors in the US encouraging all women to report their abusers to the police. Instead, these counselors should modify their counseling for women of color. There are more abusers and more victims of domestic abuse for women with disabilities. In these situations, abuse is committed by personal care attendants and health care workers, and women with disabilities have fewer options for leaving the abusive environment. When it comes to the intersectionality of women and disability, there is a silence principle that perpetuates a societal denial of the prevalence of abuse among the disabled and often results in the abuse being disregarded when it is discovered. The over-protection of disabled individuals and the expectations placed on disabled women to engage in promiscuous behavior present a paradox. This causes impaired people to have less autonomy and to become socially isolated, which puts disabled women in situations where abuse may happen more frequently or repeatedly.

1.2.5. Situated Intersectionality

A theoretical framework that can encompass various forms of inequality simultaneously (ontologically) but entangled (concretely) was proposed by migration researcher Nira Yuval-Davis as a way to build on Crenshaw's framework. This concept of situated intersectionality is based on a dialogical epistemology that can include differentially located situated gazes at these situations. As noted by Reilly, Bjørnholt, and Tastsoglou, Yuval-Davis does not adopt a universalism that rejects diversity, but rather shares Fineman's critical stance regarding the essentializing and fragmenting aspects of identity politics. Although it avoids a universalist viewpoint that minimizes differences, this strategy stays critical of the fragmentation and essentialism in identity politics, in line with Fineman's criticisms.

1.2.6. Implementation within Organizations

Intersectionality practices can be applied differently in various organizational contexts. Five distinct conceptualizations of intersectionality were identified by Christoffersen within the framework of the UK charity sector. In policy domains, generic intersectionality was noted. Here, intersectionality was understood to mean crafting policies that serve the interests of all people, not just specific groups. Concern for issues affecting the majority of marginalized groups was pan-equality. Multi-strand intersectionality made an effort to take into account various groups when reaching decisions, but it infrequently saw the groups as overlapping or concentrated on problems specific to one group. Diversity within regarded one primary form of identity—for example, gender—as paramount while sporadically considering other aspects of identity, with the latter forms of identity occasionally perceived as subordinate to the former. No identity was deemed to be more significant than another in the intersections of equality strands, which examined the intersection of identities. It was occasionally believed that by addressing the most marginalized identities, the system would inevitably benefit everyone. According to Christoffersen, there are interpretations of intersectionality that are additive, meaning that disparities can be subtracted from or added to one another.

1.2.7. Gender Intersects with Race, Class, Sexuality, and Disability

Gender intersectionality with race, class, sexual orientation, disability, and other identities presents marginalized groups with particular and complex challenges that shape their experiences of oppression in ways that cannot be explained by a single identity lens. The term "intersectionality" refers to this idea that different types of privilege and discrimination overlap, interact, and compound each other, creating unique and frequently more severe forms of injustice and inequality for people who live at the intersections of multiple marginalized identities. For example, analyzing a Black woman's gender or race in isolation will not provide a complete understanding of her experiences. Instead, in addition to other variables like her socioeconomic status or sexual orientation, the discrimination she experiences is a result of both her gender and race. Intersectional discrimination can appear in a number of contexts, such as the workplace, the criminal justice system, education, and healthcare. For instance, racial biases that undervalue their labor in addition to gender make women of color more susceptible to wage discrimination. Likewise, LGBTQ+ people who identify as people of color or who have disabilities frequently experience higher rates of violence and discrimination from both inside and outside of their communities.

Another important component that interacts with gender to exacerbate disadvantages is class. Education, healthcare, and economic opportunities are frequently inaccessible to low-income women and gender minorities, especially those who belong to racial or ethnic minorities. These obstacles stem not only from economic disparities but also have a strong connection to institutionalized discrimination based on race and gender. For instance, due to both racial biases and economic barriers, impoverished women of color may have limited access to high-quality healthcare, including reproductive health services. The dynamics of oppression are complicated further by sexuality. People who identify as LGBTQ+, particularly those who are also women, people of color, or disabled, face particular difficulties that are frequently disregarded by civil rights or mainstream feminist movements. They may face prejudice and marginalization from both the larger community and their local communities, which makes their fight for acceptance and equality especially difficult. Particularly for transgender people and queer women of color, the intersection of gender and sexuality frequently results in greater rates of mental health problems, financial instability, and violence.

To the intersectional experiences of oppression, disability adds a new dimension. A disability can prevent disabled women and gender minorities from participating fully in society, finding work, or attending school. It can also lead to ableism, which further discriminates against these groups. When disability interacts with other marginalized identities, like race or sexual orientation, these difficulties are exacerbated and result in heightened susceptibility and marginalization. To address the entire range of oppression and inequality experienced by marginalized groups, it is imperative to comprehend intersectionality. Policies and advocacy initiatives run the risk of maintaining or escalating inequality if they ignore the ways in which gender is entwined with issues of race, class, sexual orientation, and disability. For there to be true social justice, the fight for equality and human rights must take an intersectional perspective that recognizes and tackles the many interconnected systems of oppression and makes sure that the experiences and voices of those who live at these intersections are heard.

1.2.8. Sexual and Reproductive Health and Rights (SRHR)

A vast range of topics related to sexual health are essential to human rights, autonomy, and well-being on an individual basis. It covers things like having access to thorough sexual education, having rights regarding one's sexual orientation protected, and continuing the fight against harmful practices like Female Genital Mutilation (FGM). Sexual health includes a positive and respectful view of sexuality and sexual relationships in addition to the absence of illness or dysfunction. This strategy is directly related to more general concerns of gender equality and human rights, and it necessitates the capacity to have enjoyable and safe sexual experiences free from coercion, discrimination, and violence. One of the main pillars of sexual health is having access to thorough sexual education.

Along with advice on consent, relationships, and communication, this education should include factual, age-appropriate information about human sexuality, reproduction, contraception, and Sexually Transmitted Infections (STIs). People, especially young people, are better equipped to make decisions about their sexual health and well-being when they have comprehensive sexual education. Additionally, it dispels damaging gender stereotypes and norms, advancing equality and respect in interpersonal relationships. Unfortunately, access to this kind of education is restricted by political, religious, and cultural barriers in many parts of the world. This results in stigma, misinformation, and an increased risk of STIs, sexual assault, and unplanned pregnancies. Sexual health also revolves around rights related to sexual orientation. One of these rights is the ability to express one's sexual orientation without worrying about prejudice, violence, or retaliation. For LGBTQ+ people, sexual health rights include being protected from hate crimes and other forms of violence, having access to healthcare services devoid of prejudice, and having their relationships recognized legally.

Sexual orientation discrimination can result in serious health disparities because LGBTQ+ people may choose not to seek care out of fear of stigma or may receive subpar care from medical professionals who are not trained to meet their needs. Destroying these obstacles and fostering an inclusive atmosphere where everyone, regardless of sexual orientation, can get the care and support they require are necessary to ensure sexual health for everybody.

Another vital component of sexual health is the battle against harmful practices such as Female Genital Mutilation (FGM). FGM is a practice that violates girl's and women's human rights since it involves removing all or part of an external female genitalia for non-medical purposes. In certain communities, it is a deeply ingrained cultural practice that is frequently used to regulate women's sexuality, uphold gender norms, and preserve social harmony. FGM has serious aftereffects, such as persistent pain, infections, difficult childbirth, and psychological trauma. Legal actions, education, community involvement, and support for survivors are all part of the effort to end FGM. In addition to being a matter of health, addressing FGM also involves gender justice because it entails taking on the social norms and power structures that support violence against women and girls.

1.2.9. Workplace Equality

The absence of discrimination is the most fundamental aspect of workplace equality. Laws and definitions are created in various nations to combat discrimination. For instance, the U.S. It is prohibited by law to discriminate against a job applicant or employer based on their race, color, religion, sex (including pregnancy, gender identity, and sexual orientation), national origin, age (40 years of age or older), handicap, or genetic information, according to the Equal Employment Opportunity Commission.

The Commission goes on to state that it is unlawful to take adverse action against a worker who reports discrimination, makes a charge, or assists with an inquiry into or litigation involving discrimination. Nevertheless, workplace equality is more than just the lack of discrimination. In order to give every employee the opportunity to advance their careers, businesses must also treat all employees equally. In practical terms, this could mean ensuring that certain employees aren't passed over for additional training and that retreats and workshops aren't too costly for lower-paid staff members.

1.2.9.1. How to Achieve Equality in the Workplace

In order to understand how workplace equality actually works, businesses must first make a firm commitment to change and conduct a thorough assessment of their current setup. Companies can improve equality by looking at their books. One of the most prevalent workplace issues is the gender pay gap. Are all the laws pertaining to employment equality being respected? Are there any obvious issues? They can also promise to be open and honest about the pay for each position and to stop basing hiring decisions on the prior salary of candidates.

Senior management needs to pay close attention to the job requirements when it comes to hiring staff and promoting equality. If a company is discriminating against certain groups, it can be discovered by taking the time to ask these kinds of questions. Are there any that discourage or actually prevent certain groups from applying? Are certain qualifications, like work in a traditional office or education, weighted significantly higher than other types of experiences? The third strategy for attaining equality is to promote a secure workplace. It should be the responsibility of a trained human resources department to ensure that all hiring, firing, and other employee interactions adhere to the law and do not incite animosity. The role of HR is to support each employee and hold the company accountable. It should be secure and comfortable for employees to visit HR with concerns. No worker should ever experience fear of facing reprisals as a result of filing a complaint.

1.2.9.2. Equality in the Workplace – a Willingness to Learn and Grow

There is more to equality than merely not discriminating against people based on their gender, sexual orientation, or race. Equality in the workplace is a dedication to introspection and transformation. While there will never be a perfect workplace, the best ones are those that foster growth and learning. There should be as little conflict as possible when addressing issues of discrimination or equality. Diversity ought to be viewed as a strength rather than a hindrance or something unworthy of recognition. Workers ought to experience respect and being heard.

1.3. SOCIAL JUSTICE AND GENDER JUSTICE

Although the concept of social justice has been a catalyst for social revolutions worldwide since ancient times, it is still a relatively new theme in the field of social science. Since upholding justice is a state's top priority, it must be considered from a wider angle. Actually, the core of this doctrine is derived from the concepts of equality and liberty that human beings value most. In a broad sense, social justice refers to the distribution of the material and moral benefits of social life. It signifies a development model and a progressive idea. Justice—social, economic, and political—is promised by the Indian Constitution, notably in the Preamble and the section on the Directive Principles of State Policy. In popular discourse, the phrase "social justice" typically refers to the integration of the social, economic, and political facets of justice in society. It also means rearranging social life so that the material and ethical gains from social work benefit the majority rather than a small, privileged class in order to uplift marginalized groups within society and to foster a sense of group solidarity.

A completely different perspective on development is required, one in which distribution and growth are integrated into the same process and social barriers such as prejudice and discrimination based on gender, caste, language, religion, or ethnicity are methodically broken. For us in India, development with social justice must entail this. In order to forge a new course for development, it is crucial to prioritize both development and dignity for the underprivileged. All citizens cannot be granted dignity by political democracy or economic equality alone. In actuality, the two must coexist with social equality. Providing for the economic, social, and political dignity of all Indian citizens is the ultimate goal of development with social justice.

1.3.1. Theoretical Outline of Social Justice

In opposition to rigid, structural divisions of wealth and social status, the liberal model is grounded in individualism and is predicated on a commitment to social mobility and a flexible pattern of inequality. N. MacCormic argues that social justice begins with everyone's equal well-being. R. A. Pinker emphasized that the nature of equality and the standards by which inequality may be judged as just or unjust are not the only issues that social justice addresses. Social justice is particularly required for the most disadvantaged members of society, according to D. Miller, who contends that inequality is pervasive and becomes an absolute evil. Contrary to liberal-utilitarian justice, liberal-egalitarian justice is thought to be characterized by John Rawls's concern for the welfare and equality of all people, especially the most disadvantaged. Distributive justice is argued to be absolutely necessary. Rawls emphasized the equal distribution of all social primary goods, including income and wealth, liberty and opportunity, and the foundation of self-respect, unless an unequal distribution would benefit the least advantaged.

There is a lot of discussion in this context regarding how to view the idea of justice in a hierarchical society. In this context, it is worthwhile to examine

Ambedkar's contribution. He had the vision that social justice could be achieved through the extension of political democracy to the social and economic spheres. His conception of social justice is essentially the same as that of John Rawls, who included the concept of difference—in Ambedkar's case, the principle of special treatment—into his theory of distributive justice.

(a) **Liberal Approach:** With its roots in collectivism, the socialist model of justice shows a stronger commitment to social equality and community. Justice exists where there is no injustice, according to socialists of all stripes. The main grievance shared by all socialists is the unfair treatment of laborers, peasants, the poor, the unemployed, the destitute, and so forth within the framework of society as a whole and the capitalist system in particular. Marxists believe that in class societies, justice is always determined by class—justice for the capitalists, and injustice for the workers. Therefore, only in a society without classes can Marxists find justice. For them, justice is not just about just laws; it is about just laws that come from just societies; justice is not just about being social or economic; it has socio-economic implications as well. Since the democratic socialists are democratic and socialists, they believe that justice can be found in a just society and just order. Democratic socialism aims to protect citizen's socioeconomic rights in addition to their democratic rights and civil liberties, which is a challenging combination to achieve. This would make the perfect social justice plan, if it could be implemented.

(b) **Socialist Approach:** The socialist model of justice is rooted in collectivism and exhibits greater support for social equality and community. With socialists of all shades, justice exists where there is no injustice. The chief concern of all the socialists has been injustice meted out to the workers, peasants, poor, unemployed, the lowly and so on in the system that exists in the society in general, and the capitalistic one in particular. For the Marxists, justice in the class societies is always a class justice, justice for the capitalist and conversely injustice for the workers. Hence the Marxists find justice only in classless society. For them, justice is not merely just laws, but also just laws emanating from just society; it is merely economic or social in nature, but also socio-economic in its ramifications. The democratic socialists are both socialists as well as democratic, and therefore, for them, justice exists in just order and in a just society. Democratic socialism seeks to provide for democratic rights and civil liberties as well as socio-economic rights of citizens – a difficult combination indeed. If this could be achieved, it would serve as an ideal scheme for social justice.

(c) **Subaltern Approach:** The subaltern approach considers any group within society that has been marginalized due to factors such as age, gender, caste, class, race, religion, language, or culture belong to the class of subalterm groupings. Due to several societal norms and limitations, they are essentially positioned in a subordinate role. They belong to marginalized, oppressed, and exploited groups. Social justice for the underprivileged is a demand of the subaltern perspective on justice. It calls for the simultaneous achievement of two goals: (a) the abolition of all forms of discrimination; and (b) the provision of special care to achieve social equality. The subaltern viewpoint on justice encompasses social, cultural, educational, and even psychological aspects in addition to economic ones.

(d) **Feminist Approach:** According to feminist critiques of justice, women are not entitled to the same opportunities as men because of biological and natural differences. These discriminatory practices have their roots in the social structures that have harmed women. The position regarding women's status needs to be reevaluated, contested, and altered considering the growing social consciousness against various forms of injustice in society. Feminist theory and activism do, in fact, advocate treating women's status and gender inequality as major political concerns. Every school of feminism focuses on the reasons behind and solutions to women's oppression, inequality, and subjugation. Women are viewed as inferior to men, and as such, they are forced to endure suffering throughout their lives. Women are oppressed, subjugated, and helpless because of male dominance. From a feminist standpoint, justice necessitates running away from women's internalization of female gender and the resulting low self-esteem, apathy, and helplessness.

The feminists contend that in addition to equal rights that men inherit, communalization of household and childcare responsibilities is also necessary. They further argue that male superiority must be eliminated, patriarchal culture must be destroyed, gender socialization must be ingrained, and women's liberation from male oppression must be actively pursued. The feminists believe that since justice is inherently male-structured, the law cannot be neutral in conflicts between men and women. Among other things, the feminist vision of justice calls for the abolition of all forms of male dominance, the equality of rights, the fusion of the public and private domains, and the development of new, largely non-patriarchal forms of politics, society, and culture. Accordingly, a feminist perspective on justice demands that women's entire development be ensured, including improvements to their health and education as well as an appropriate share of social and political power as well as economic space.

1.3.2. Theoretical Outline of Gender Justice

Gender justice is frequently associated with emancipatory initiatives that push for legislative changes that strengthen women's rights or advance women's interests in social and economic policy. Nonetheless, there is seldom a clear definition of the term, which is frequently used synonymously with concepts of gender equity, women's rights, women's empowerment, and gender equality. The definition and implementation of gender justice are complicated by its distinctive components, which transcend related ideas of justice in terms of race or class. However, to gain a comprehensive understanding of gender justice, it is possible to analyze three distinct conceptions of the concept.

(a) **Gender Justice as Entitlements and Choice:** Rooted in liberal feminist political philosophy, this approach starts from a central feminist political conundrum: because oppressed women have been socialized into accepting their circumstances, it may be difficult for them to propose a gender justice model that challenges male privilege. The agency of women can be hindered by social and familial norms, which force them to prioritize the needs of others over their own and limit their ability to think and act independently. Feminist political philosophers have discussed what minimal social, economic, and even psychological conditions women might be able to refuse or renegotiate the social arrangements in which they find themselves in response to this conundrum of women's complacency in their own social and economic subordination. Martha Nussbaum, who modified Amartya Sen's capabilities approach, has expounded on these minimum capabilities approach in the most detail. What people can truly do and be are their capabilities. This strategy has drawn a lot of criticism in addition to the issue of the political difficulties associated with implementation, especially considering national resource constraints. Anne Phillips, a liberal feminist political philosopher, makes a serious argument that the capabilities approach is fundamentally driven by neo-liberal goals. She argues that Nussbaum's capabilities approach retreats from the profound challenges of the struggle for human equality, not only between women and men but also across social groups within and between nations, because it concentrates on the bare minimum requirements. Indeed, the capabilities approach's material focus retreats from equal rights to fundamental entitlements and ignores end-state absolute inequalities.

(b) **Gender Justice as Absence of Discrimination:** In 1999, the Convention on the Elimination of All Forms of Discrimination Against Women (CEDAW) was established, marking the first formal attempt to establish principles of gender justice. The convention defines gender justice as the absence of discrimination based on gender. This method, which requires states to forbid discrimination under CEDAW, may be called a "negative liberties" strategy. Establishing broadly applicable justice principles and applying them as impartially as possible is the foundation of European legal tradition, which is where CEDAW fits in. Those who oppose legal systems contend that because of the illusion of impartiality, significant and deeply ingrained biases will remain hidden. That CEDAW lacks effective enforcement mechanisms is, nevertheless, the most frequent criticism leveled at it. Considering that it depends on state parties to monitor the wrongdoings they personally perpetrate.

(c) **Gender Justice as Positive Rights:** This optimistic view of gender justice is a component of the modern rights-based perspective on development. After the global wave of democratization at the end of the 20th century, rights-based approaches emerged in the 1990s. They are predicated on the knowledge that political and legal institutions are critical to the advancement of economic growth. They specifically highlight the connection between the expression of both individual and group preferences (voice) and the actions taken by the state, and they work to define the fundamental rights that people have the right to demand from it. They signify an understanding of how power dynamics influence the results of policies and the necessity of a legal framework and fundamental accountability in order to promote human development and allow people to maximize their fundamental abilities and resources. For gender justice projects, understanding politics and governance is essential because it can be applied to women's relationships with men. It also recognizes that social, economic, and political institutions must be held accountable to women, which entails dismantling institutionalized patriarchal power structures. Women's interests can be impeded by power imbalances.

More ground has been gained for gender equality claims in the political and civil rights spheres than in the economic sphere, where neo-liberalism has provided less support. Social, cultural, and political rights tend to be formulated as relative and culturally specific, to be realized gradually, while political and civil rights are typically seen as absolute and non-negotiable, because they can force resource-constrained states to provide concrete entitlements. Critics have pointed out that the rights-based framework is associated with a particular western liberal republican approach to political democracy and constitutionalism, and that it is a tool of Western cultural imperialism. Even worse, some critics suggest that it is just another step in the growth of capitalist markets, with human rights serving as a springboard for changes to governance structures intended to bring domestic economies into the international marketplace. As well as being extremely evasive when it comes to identifying the agents required to satisfy rights claims and the extent to which they should do so, rights-based approaches have also been characterized as being unworkable and deceptively simple to implement. According to the major current viewpoints on gender justice, gender justice is the elimination of disparities between men and women that lead to women being subservient to men, as well as the provision of redress where necessary. It is possible that these disparities stem from how opportunities and resources are distributed, which allows people to develop their social, political, economic, and human capital. Alternatively, they might reside in ideas about human dignity, individual autonomy, and rights that deprive women of their bodily integrity and their ability to make decisions about their lives. Thus, agency, or the capacity for decision-making, is paired with control over and access to resources in gender justice.

1.3.3. Violence: A Societal Analyses

The serious issue of violence against women demands quick response. Domestic violence is just one type of violence. Women are always vulnerable to mistreatment, including rape and mental and sexual harassment. In addition to being the targets of individual violence, women and children are still the victims of both natural and man-made disasters. Thus, women are targeted first by famines, cyclones, earthquakes, worker struggles, poverty and debt, radicalism, casteism, and regional fanaticism. Women still live in a vulnerable environment. Not only does she frequently experience physical abuse from outside her home, but she also experiences it within. Recent years have seen significant legal reforms in India aimed at preventing violence against women. Within the context of feudalism, caste, and religion, men etched their honor and the honor of their community on the bodies of their women, leading to the emergence of sexual violence. Thus, it was believed that maintaining and desecrating male honor and caste or religious identity, respectively, meant either defending a woman's chastity or sexually abusing her. Throughout the late 1980s and beyond, there were frequent episodes of caste and religious rioting, with women frequently at the center of the unrest as victims or focal points for aggressive declarations of relig. Working with the rural poor, dalits, adivasis, and riot victims, feminists perceived sexual violence as a particular, gendereda, gendered form of authority dedicated to upholding an unjust and hierarchical social structure. They emphasized that patriarchal disputes over identity and power, oppression and resistance, were fought out on the bodies of women. Despite all the talk of women's empowerment and security for marginalized women, there is a clear increase in sexual harassment. Sexual harassment has turned into a threat for today's working women, and most victims choose not to disclose their experiences to the public.

Paradoxically, the advancement of society has weakened the status of women both at home and at work. Even though women have entered traditionally male-dominated fields like politics and the civil service, their working conditione far from ideal in the Indian context. When it comes to treating women equally at home and at work, Indian men still have a waysway to go. Every day, someone reports some incident of sexual harassment that occurred in a hospital, academic institution, or secretariat. Sexual offenses against we harassment and violence towards them, are unquestionably rising. It is necessary to conduct epidemiological studies in order toto determine the etiology, nature, range, and forms of this pathology as well as its pathogenesis. It's important to determine the steps that must be taken to address this phenomenon. Health professionals are not receiving enough sensitive and appropriate training to identify and treat this issue on a medical, legal, and psychological level. They lack the knowledge and resources necessary to provide legal counsel and advice.

1.3.4. Gender, Human Rights, and Role of Governance

Women were not given the necessary opportunities to participate in the nation's mainstream governance system under the democratic system. Thanks to constitutional amendments that reserve 33% of local government seats for them, Indian women have recently been able to feel a sense of the public and an active part of it. There are a lot of women in every panchayat these days. While many of them are shy and serve as alibis for their husbands or brothers, the fact that they are expected to be present and have the authority to decide on matters pertaining to the village has allowed the more outspoken women to take part in the democratic process. If the local government system persists, it is plausible that women's perceptions of their identities, roles, and responsibilities will gradually change in the near future. The ideologues of the women's movement contend that a greater and more active role for women in national governance is necessary to address many of the current problems with the Indian political system, including the nation's rising political violence.

Not every political issue facing India will be resolved by the proposed Women's Bill, one of which is the creation of a fair system of representation for a society that is highly inequitable, multiethnic, and multicultural. But most democracies nowadays are dealing with that issue. The women were persuaded by the intricacy, difficulties, violence, and additional requirements that they could never advance through the current nomination process and that they require some form of coercion, such as quotas and reservations. Women's bills under the UPA-II government were not properly discussed or passed by the Rajya Sabha because of patriarchal and non-serious pulls and pressures. The public's support and widespread advocacy for women's political participation and empowerment have not changed men's views toward women's growing roles in society. Although they agree in theory, they struggle to let go of the patriarchal way of thinking. This frequently manifests as a fear of losing male dominance, which is justified by asserting that men are better than women in terms of experimental knowledge, physical prowess, and general understanding of gender justice. Numerous violent incidents that occurred during the election campaign and in their operations have been made public. Some female candidates were denied permission by men to submit their nominations, citing the belief that women belong solely in the home. In some instances, the villagers had accused them of having relationships with men and had attempted to dissuade them from competing or emerging victorious. It's not uncommon to harass women and expose them to various forms of character assassination and rumors. Many SC women experienced discrimination and humiliation; their ability to preside over panchayats was especially called into question. Some women experienced violence even after they were elected.

When the illiterate female members try to finish their work, even the officials seem to make fun of them. In particular, the officials frequently try to discourage elected women because they don't feel comfortable with them. The male opposition members frequently threaten and file no-confidence motions against the female chairpersons in their collusion with them. Numerous female pradhans have expressed that the men would not put up with a woman leading them. Political parties have threatened members, and there have also been cases of members being sexually abused by close relatives or even government officials. As a result, it appeared that the women had more issues after the election than they did when they were just housewives. Positive changes also occurred at the same time, such as women eschewing the purdah/goonghat veil system, sitting with men, becoming more mobile, demanding the right to speak, and protesting against injustices done to them. Not just women but also a large number of men have fully endorsed women's reservations. They think that reservations have improved women's awareness in the community, allowed them to leave the four walls of their homes, and changed social attitudes.

They are also respected and given voice in meetings because they are women in many places. Some men even find value in women's functioning because they perceive some sincerity and significance in the words that they express. Numerous women in elected office have talked about how they prioritize the needs and activities of women's development, supporting them in their fight for rights against domestic abuse, dowry extortion, property disputes, and alcoholism. However, a lot of people were unable to take significant action because of a lack of sufficient financial and political power, family roles and responsibilities, patriarchal social norms, and family controls. Therefore, it is necessary to further reinforce political empowerment—especially at the local and rural levels—with support mechanisms like informational campaigns and capacity-building initiatives. if the goal of this empowerment process is to ultimately result in greater justice for women. More than half of the Indian population will continue to be denied the concept and rights of citizenship in the absence of such gender justice and equality. The rights that the Constitution affords all citizens, regardless of gender, caste, or class, will continue to be fabricated. The Preamble's solemn commitment to economic, political, and social justice will be shown to be untrue, especially when it comes to women. This is the most important promise made.

1.3.5. Human Development and Gender Justice

Strong objections have been made to the concept of development. The concept of development, which was the most recent of all, is closely related to the concepts of modern industrialism, nation-state, and scientific worldview. It was said that they had all done things that were detrimental to women. It is argued that they have widened the gap between rich and poor and taken away women's control over family and community resources. Those rights and powers were meant to have been assumed by the contemporary state and its agencies. In a similar vein, the criticism highlighted how the large industrial complexes conflict with the interests of women. The world of technology and technical complexes works against some of the fundamental qualities and interests of women. Thus, the currents of feminism and environmental activism combined to form a potent critique that became known as eco-feminism.

The Green Revolution in India has been cited by some feminist writers as a prime illustration of how development was detrimental to womeGreen Revolution point out that its benefits were not distributed equally and that the emphasis on new technologies actually increasedincreased inequality between men and women. Additionally, this shift led to monoculture farming, which reduced crop diversity and increased reliance on the market, making life more difficult for women than it had been previously. Monocultures are also more susceptible to pests, droughts, and other environmental factors, resulmental hazards such as elevated soil salinity and decreased local food security, which began to affect people's lives. In the midst ofDuring these changes, women suffered significantly. Domestic violence, particularly against women and children, increased. In the regions affected by the Green Revolution, there has been a rise in alcohol consumption and domestic violence. A serious concern is the widespread practice of female foeticide in some of India's comparatively more developed states, such as Punjab, Haryana, and Gujarat.

REFERENCES

1. Akbari, M. (2021). Forced sterilization of Indigenous women: An act of genocide or policing women's bodies? *York University Criminological Review, 3*(1), 1–23. https://csri.journals.yorku.ca/index.php/default/article/view/113 (accessed on 9 October 2024).
2. Chaib, F. (2019). Uneven access to health services drives life expectancy gaps: WHO. *World Health Organization.* https://www.who.int/news/item/04-04-2019-uneven-access-to-health-services-drives-life-expectancy-gaps-who (accessed on 9 October 2024).
3. Corradi, L. (2021). Intersectional alliances to overcome gender subordination: The case of Roma/Gypsy Traveller women. *Journal of International Women's Studies, 22*(4), 152–166. https://vc.bridgew.edu/jiws/vol22/iss4/11 (accessed on 9 October 2024).
4. Guerrero, J. M. A. (2003). 'Patriarchal colonialism' and indigenism: Implications for Native feminist spirituality and Native womanism. *Hypatia, 18*(2), 58–69.
5. Laboucan-Massimo, M. (2018). Climate justice must include gender justice. *David Suzuki Foundation.* https://davidsuzuki.org/climate-justice-must-include-gender-justice/ (accessed on 9 October 2024).
6. Scully, P. (2005). Malintzin, Pocahontas, and Krotoa: Indigenous women and myth models of the Atlantic World. *Journal of Colonialism and Colonial History, 6*. https://doi.org/10.1353/cch.2006.0022.
7. Smith, A. (2016). Heteropatriarchy and the three pillars of white supremacy: Rethinking women of color organizing. In *Color of Violence: The INCITE! Anthology* (pp. 66–73). INCITE! Women of Color Against Violence.

Chapter **2**

Historical Context of Gender and Law

Contents

INTRODUCTION

The intricate historical fabric of the relationship between gender and the law reflects broader societal perspectives on gender roles and equality. Legal systems have historically reflected patriarchal structures, elevating male dominance and placing women in subservient positions. Women were frequently viewed as property rather than independent persons in ancient societies like those in Greece and Rome. For example, Roman law established that women were subject to the authority of their male guardians, which could be their husbands or fathers.

This legal subordination included marriage, property rights, and even individual liberty. Laws in Europe throughout thesMiddle Ages continued to uphold and reflect patriarchal values. This dynamic is exemplified by the English common law concept of coverture, which severely restricted a married woman's rights and liberties by combining her legal identity with her husband's. In general, women were not allowed by law to enter into contracts, own property on their own, or take part in court proceedings without their husband's approval.

These conventions started to be questioned during the Enlightenment, when philosophers like Mary Wollstonecraft fought for the equality and rights of women. Incremental legal reforms were implemented in the 19th and early 20th centuries, frequentlofbecause of broader social changes and women's suffrage movements. The United States, for instance, achieved a major legal milestone in the fight for gender equality when the 19th Amendment, which gave women the right to vote, was passed in 1920. However, because social and legal barriers continued to exist, this progress was uneven and frequently contested.

Feminist movements and larger civil rights agendas spurred a more determined push for gender equality in legislation in the second half of the 20th century. The United States passed landmark laws like the Equal Pay Act of 1963 and the Civil Rights Act of 1964 to combat gender discrimination in the workplace and other settings. Global norms for gender equality were also established by international agreements such as the Convention on the Elimination of All Forms of Discrimination against Women (CEDAW).

The gender-related legal landscape is still change ofdespite these advancements. Gender identity, reproductive rights, and the intersection of gender with race and class are examples of issues that bring attention to ongoing discussions and the need for ongoing legal reform. The historical trajectory shows a slow but steady march toward equality, reflecting broader changes in society and the continuous difficulty of eliminating ingrained gender prejudices in the legal system.

2.1. THE HISTORICAL RELATIONSHIP BETWEEN GENDER AND LAW

The historical relationship between gender and the law shows how societies have viewed and implemented gender equality and roles. Laws have shaped and reflected societal attitudes toward gender from the dawn of civilization to the present, frequently upholding patriarchal norms while also gradually advancing toward greater equality. This intricate interaction demonstrates how, over time, legal frameworks have played a crucial role in both upholding and challenging gender inequality. The intricate and dynamic interaction between legal frameworks and societal perspectives has characterized the historical relationship between gender and law. The journey represents broader shifts in social norms and values, moving from antiquated legal codes that enshrined gender inequality to modern legal frameworks striving for gender equality. Even though there has been a lot of progress, there is still more work to be done in terms of reform and vigilance before there can be true gender equality. The legal environment is always changing due to both current issues and historical precedents, which highlights how dynamic and enduring the fight for gender justice is.

(a) **Ancient Civilizations and Early Legal Codes:** Gender inequality was ingrained in ancient societies' legal codes, which frequently reflected the patriarchal structures in place at the time. For example, one of the oldest known legal codes, the Code of Hammurabi from ancient Babylon (c. 1754 BCE), established significant legal distinctions based on gender. Women's rights were often restricted compared to men's, and they were regarded as legal dependents of their male guardians. Severe penalties were typically imposed on women found guilty of adultery, underscoring the emphasis on female chastity and the control exerted over women's sexuality. Similar restrictions on women's participation in public life and politics existed in ancient Greece. The majority of Athens' women's ro domesticdomestic, and their legal rights were restricted. Their legal identities were frequently absorbed into those of their male guardians, and they were unable to own property on their own. On the other hand, women in Sparta had comparatively greater freedoms, such as the ability to own property and be in public, but these were still within the larger framework of a society that ultimately valued male authority. Roman *patria potestas*, which granted male heads of household significant control over their family members, further entrenched gender roles. Under Roman law, women had limited rights regarding property and legal matters and were legally subordinate to their fathers or husbands. Roman legal doctrines like *coemptio* and *manus* demonstrated the belief that a woman's legal power was essentially transferred from her father to her husband upon marriage, reinforcing the gender hierarchy of the time.

(b) **Medieval and Early Modern Europe:** In Europe during the Middle Ages, patriarchal standards were still reflected in and upheld by legal systems. During this time, the idea of coverture—which has its roots in English common law—was very common. According to Coverture, a married woman becomes her husband's legal identity, making her legally invisible and reliant. The ability of women to own property, make contracts, and participate in independent legal proceedings was severely restricted by this doctrine. Women's autonomy was severely restricted, and their legal status was primarily determined by their relationships with men.

Gender norms began to change in the early modern era, but change came gradually and unevenly. Traditional gender roles faced intellectual and philosophical challenges during the Reformation and Enlightenment periods. Though significant legislative changes remained scarce, intellectuals such as Mary Wollstonecraft started to advocate for women's equality and rights. Although many other legal and societal barriers continued, the Married Women's Property Act of 1882 in England signaled a significant change by allowing married women to own property independently of their husbands.

(c) **19th and Early 20th Centuries:** Gender law underwent significant transformation in the 19th and early 20th centuries. Significant legislative changes were brought about by the growing women's suffrage movements and the larger social reform movement. The United States' suffrage movement resulted in the 19th Amendment, which gave women the right to vote, being passed in 1920. While this was a significant step in the right direction, not all legal disparities were immediately addressed. In the United Kingdom, women over thirty who satisfied specific property requirements were granted the right to vote by the 1918 Representation of the People Act, and women and men were granted equal voting rights by the 1928 Equal Franchise Act. The recognition of women'tical agencyagencies underwent a substantial shift as a result of these legislative changes. Gender discrimination continued in other legal domains, such as employment and education, despite these developments. Equal pay, professional opportunities, and legal protections remained unattainable for women. The gradual and frequently contested nature of legal reforms addressing these issues reflected a broader societal resistance to completely deconstructing deeply ingrained gender norms.

(d) Mid-20th Century to Present: A more determined effort to achieve gender equality was made in the middle of the 20th century, propelled by feminist movements and larger civil rights agendas. Historic laws like the Equal Pay Act of 1963 and the Civil Rights Act of 1964 attempted to address systemic discrimination against women in the workplace and other domains in the United States. The Equal Pay Act sought to end salary differences between men and women doing the same work, while the Civil Rights Act forbade discrimination based on sex in employment and education. Global guidelines for gender equality were established in 1979 by the Convention on the Elimination of All Forms of Discrimination Against Women (CEDAW), which also offered a framework for nations to evaluate and enhance their women's rights legal frameworks. Several countries changed their laws and policies in response to CEDAW's adoption, which represented a major commitment to combating gender discrimination globally. Additional legal developments occurred in the later half of the 20th century and the early 21st century, such as the inclusion of sexual orientation and gender identity in anti-discrimination legislation. The case of *Obergefell v. Hodges*, a 2015 ruling by the US Supreme Court, which made same-sex marriage legal across the country, was a major step toward recognizing and defending LGBTQ+ rights in the legal system.

But despite these developments, problems still exist. Concerns about things like gender-based violence, workplace discrimination, and reproductive rights still exist. The pursuit of gender equality is made more difficult by the intersectionality of gender with race, class, and other social factors, which highlights the need for continued social and legal reforms.

2.1.1. Historical and Political Journey of Women Laws/Gender Laws

Gender equality and women's rights have been greatly enhanced by social, cultural, and political movements. History demonstrates how society has evolved gradually over time and how social reform movements have infused equality and liberty into our consciousness. The international community and policymakers have correctly recognized the need for a more egalitarian society where women's rights are protected with the passage of time, the end of monarchy and feudalism, and the arrival of democracy in politics. This political consciousness, along with a shift in people's perspectives brought about by education, has significantly helped to address the social norms and traditions that have historically placed women in a subordinate role. As a natural next step, laws have evolved to reflect this evolution, giving rise to gender laws that aim to empower and emancipate women (Figure 2.1).

Figure 2.1. *Political Journey of Women Laws.*

https://blog.ipleaders.in/wp-content/uploads/2020/10/gender-equality-638x375.jpeg.

2.1.2. Historical Background of Gender Laws

It is implied by gender equality that girls and boys, as well as women and men, have access to the same opportunities, resources, rights, and protections. It is not necessary for women and men, or girls and boys, to be identical or to receive the same treatment.

In society, there are many different kinds and degrees of gender bias and inequality. It has persisted for centuries, leading nations all over the world to enact laws aimed at lessening this injustice by means of positive discrimination and affirmative action.

There are disparities in the workplace when it comes to pay, benefits, sexual exploitation, etc., at home (spousal abuse, unequal work distribution), iext of a marriagemarriage, property rights, health and education, entrepreneurship, credit availability, and a plethora of other domains.

They therefore needed legal protection as part of the effort to lessen these disparities and create level playing fields. However, the road was not as simple because men, who wished to keep women in subjection, controlled women's lives to a great extent (though this is still the case to some extent).

Perhaps one of the first known movements supporting women's rights was started by the Shakers, an evangelical sect known for rigorous celibacy and gender segregation. They were advocates for gender parity. The second half of the 18th century saw the growth of this movement in America, which implemented gender equality. Following World War II, movements for gender equality ntum. A number ofSeveral conventions that support gender equality have been adopted by the UN and other international organizations.

The unequal social structure views women as commodities and properties of men, favoring sons over daughters. The status of women in society hased as a result ofbecause of unfair property and inheritance laws, pervasive social beliefs that women are inferior, illiteracy, inadequate health care, neglect, an uneven power structure, workplace discrimination, harassment by husbands and in-laws, and numerous other unfair practices. In the absence of legal backing and affirmative action, it was evident that their social standing would not improve.

2.1.3. Salient Features of Gender Laws

Until both men and women have the will to change it from within, gender inequality in India will continue to be a social problem. Women have the right to equal treatment just like men do. No one can be treated differently because of their race, color, caste, creed, religion, or sexual orientation.

However, because patriarchal society has historically discriminated against women, the nation has passed a number of laws to support them and combat injustice. The country's supreme law is the Constitution. Articles 14 and 15 guarantee equality and prohibit discrimination against Indians based on their sex, among other things, and are the provisions in this article that protect the rights of women. Regardless of gender, Article 16 ensures equal opportunities in public employment. Additionally, this article contains a proviso that permits the State to take affirmative action for women, including assigning seats and positions to them in government. In order toTo give women more political voice and empowerment, the 73rd and 74th amendments to the Constitution guarantee that seats in local bodies, both urban and rural, be reserved for them. Article 51A guarantees women's dignity by imposing an obligation on all citizens to abstain from actions that diminish women's worth.

The nation's numerous gender laws have attempted to address social norms that have oppressed women. These behaviors stem from long-standing social norms and traditions that have viewed women as less valuable than men and have taken advantage of them all of their lives. Women have been taken advantage of in the workplace, at home, and elsewhere. Both appropriate health care and education have been denied to them. Additionally, they have been denied equal opportunities at work, including pay disparities and subpar working conditions. Additionally, they have denied property rights. There have always been threats to their safety when they are not at home. Finding her a groom is still challenging in the absence of dowry. Women nationwide endure the most horrific crimes and atrocities, including rape, molestation, sexual abuse, domestic abuse, and immoral trafficking.

1. Socio-legal status of women in modern

Unquestionably, women play a crucial role in building naequently, the societysociety places great importance on their empowerment. Over the past few centuries, there have been significant changes in the status of women in India. Women are involved in many facets of life, including politics, sports, literature, education, and other fields. In India, women have occupied prominent positions.

However, it must be acknowledged that a sizable portion of women continue to live lives of deprivation and oppression. Women's status in society haproved as a result ofbecause of their aspirations, desire for success in life, education, participation in political and social movements that support women's rights, and—most importantly—societal changes. Affirmative action policies, enabling legislation, and court rulings have all attempted to address the disparities and enhance the lives of women. Therefore, the advancement of women in society has likely been facilitated by the application of law and justice more than any other factor.

Since the country's independence, women have been empowered and given security against injustice and crimes against them through social welfare programs, laws focused on women, and other initiatives.

The Immoral Traffic (Prevention) Act, 1956, the Dowry Prohibition Act of 1961, the Protection of Women from Domestic Violence Act of 2005, the Sexual Harassment of Women at Workplace (prevention, prohibition, and redressal) Act of 2013 and other laws have been enacted in addition to constitutional provisions to address various forms of injustice against women. In the Indian Penal Code (1860), Section 498A was added to prohibit cruelty against women. Similar to this, severe penalties have been added under Section 326A of the IPC to stop acid attacks. The Factories Act has been modified to offer improved working conditions. The Equal Remuneration Act of 1976 prohibits discrimination against women based on their sex and guarantees equal pay for male and female employees. Women who become pregnant and give birth are guaranteed stable employment and wages under the Maternity Benefit Act of 1961.

It is not a fact, though, that these broad legal and social reforms have significantly improved the status of women. One cannot interpret the law in a vacuum. It must be read in conjunction with society, and one must comprehend the social order. Old beliefs, a lack of education, a lack of confidence, and a lack of empowerment are all to blame and must be seriously addressed.

For instance, dowries are rarely reported. Both sides give their approval. As the father of a woman, the bride's father feels compelled to accept this because of his financial situation and perceived lower social standing. As such,y. Despite the fact thatEven though section 498A of the IPC (cruelty against married women) serves as a potent deterrent, many of the people who cause dowry deaths escape punishment. Settlements outside of court occur frequently. In exchange for money, the victim's father frequently consents to end the case because he believes it will help him marry off his other daughter(s).

Comparably, even though domestic abuse and marital rape are also forms oft women, the majority ofmost of these incidents go unreported. Women are also disadvantaged by the legal provision that does not classify forced sexual activity between a husband and wife who are older than fifteen as rape.

Because women are financially dependent on their husbands and would face their wrath if they went to the police, domestic violence cases are also not reported. Here are a few instances. We have a lot more to givenstrate that a number ofseveral crimes against Indian women have their origins in the country's socioeconomic structure and long-standing social customs.

As a result, despite legal protections and supportive policies, these crimes are difficult to eradicate, especially among the society's poor and marginalized groups. Modifying the social structure is a challenging endeavor. Law cannot be read in a vacuum or be used to just address one type of wrongdoing. in the general public'spublics actives in particular areare crucial. The main problems that require attention are empowerment, economic advancement, and education. To further improve the socio-legal status of women, all legal provisions must be implemented correctly, promptly, and strictly.

2.1.4. How Gender Laws have Evolved Through Judicial Pronouncements

Because they understood that laws must adapt and change to reflect a changing society, the drafters of the constitution made sure it was a flexible document rather than a rigid one. Following independence, numerous laws and rules were passed, along with some significant rulings that altered the trajectory of society. A handful of them also concentrated on gender issues, aiming to better the lives of women and other marginalized groups. Certain rulings have established new guidelines and expectations for behavior and conduct, putting an end to criminal activity.

The courts have also considered the rights of sex workers and women who have experienced sexual abuse. In this petition, respect and equal rights for sex workers are demanded. The Supreme Court ruled that because sex workers are forced to work in this industry by poverty rather than choice, they should receive the same treatment as other members of society. Although society perceives them as unsavole ought to make an efforttry to comprehend their viewpoint and refrain from disparaging them. They are entitled to the same respect as individuals in other professions. The state governments were instructed by the court to act in their best interests, create plans that work for them, and raise public awareness of this matter.

In India, domest is pervasive. In order toTo address this problem, the Indian government passed the Protection of Women from Domestic Violence Act in 2005. The act recognized mental, verbal, and financial abuse in addition to physical violence as forms of domestic abuse. The law primarily established safeguards for those who have been abused at home. Numerous other laws, such as the Factories Act and the Dowry Prohibition Act, have also been drafted with the advancement and development of women in mind.

As a result, the judiciary has recognized the injustice and plight that women experience in a variety life and has made an efforttried to address these issues by formulating rules and regulations and giving directives to the relevant authorities. These have led to the creation of laws that prioritize women.

(a) **Incidents of Violence Against Women:** Women have always been the targets of abuse, both sexual and physical. We read about such incidents in newsps channels on a daily basisdaily. Usually, women commit these crimes because they are viewed as the weaker sex. There is inequality in every aspect of life. In patriarchal India, men are viewed as the head of the household, in charge of women and household matters. Past customs such as Sati and child marriages afflicted the nation until laws were passed outlawing them. These days, the most common crime womene.

Women in today's societytoday face a variety of forms of violence, including rape in marriage, acid throwing, female infanticide and feticide, honor killings, deaths due to witchcraft, and domestic abuse. Women are treated with disdain and denigrated because of the internalized misogyny that permeates our society. They are not provided with their fair share of resources, such as early access to education and instruction in societal gender norms.

Because divorce is not socially acceptable and because financial difficulties take precedence over other factors, married women continue to stay in abusive marriages. Women are expected to function in accordance with the wishes of their male counterparts and are not taught how to be independent. It is important to address social norms and practices that view women as less valuable than men, as well as a lack of education. It will be difficult to stop violence against women until it is stopped.

(b) **What to Learn from the Women's Rights Movement in the USA:** The United States saw the emergence of women's liberation and rights movements in the 1800s. Since that feminism promotes gender equality, they are also known as the feminist movements. The original movement was centered on the freedom to vote and to possess property. The second wave of women's rights movements emerged in the 1960s and 1970s, with a focus on combating various social stigmas and promoting personal freedom and equality of opportunity. These feminist movement's third wave concentrated on social, economic, and cultural issues. From the early 1990s until the end of 2010, these movements took place. Also, their only platform during the campaign was increased political representation. The fourth wave, which promoted intersectional equality and the use of online resources, began to emerge around 2012. These movements demonstrate how social and political uprisings can result from years of oppression; when injustice becomes intolerable, people band together to fight it. It also demonstrates the necessity of teamwork and unity in order to accomplish goals. Every politically and socially conscious citizen of a nation must put pressure on the government to alter society.

(c) **Critical Analysis:** Since gaining its independence, India, the biggest democracy in the world, has supported women's affirmative action. The framers of the constitution understood that as long as inequality persists, women's suffering will not end. They realized that in this context, formal equality would be useless. Substantial equality is needed, which would address and attempt to rectify the fundamental causes of discrimination. Women's welfare has thus received special attention under the Fundamental Rights, Directive Principles, and Fundamental Duties. Given that there have never been equal opportunities for men and women, we must acknowledge that the equality provisions of the Indian Constitution are insufficient. One cannot treat the unlike like the same. Article 15(3) has therefore made special provisions for women in recognition of their vulnerability and lack of opportunities. Based on the theory of protective discrimination, the Indian judiciary has made numerous precedent-setting rulings to make sure that the laws are put into practice rather than just remaining on paper.

2.2. INCLUDING HOW LEGAL SYSTEMS HAVE HISTORICALLY MARGINALIZED WOMEN AND GENDER MINORITIES

Laws have been used to maintain and reinforce social hierarchies, as evidenced by the historical marginalization of women and gender minorities within legal systems. This marginalization has been present in many cultures and historical periods, taking many different forms, from overt legal discrimination to more covert structural inequality. Knowing this historical background helps to clarify the systemic basis of gender-based discrimination as well as the continuous difficulties in achieving social and legal justice.

2.2.1. Ancient and Medieval Legal Systems

Legal systems were created specifically to marginalize women and uphold patriarchal standards in many ancient societies. For instance, women's legal status was severely restricted in ancient Greece. Women in Athens were not allowed to participate in politics or public life. They were not allowed to own property on their own or conduct legal business without their guardian's consent because they were regarded as the legal dependents of their male guardians, who were typically their fathers or husbands. Women were effectively made economically dependent and legally invisible by this legal system, which served to further solr social inferiority.

Similar toLike this, the idea of *patria potestas*—which gave male heads of households considerable control over family members—incorporated the subordination of women in Roman law. Roman law regarded women as the property of their male guardians and granted them few legal and property rights. For instance, the legal theory of *coemptio* allowed the legal authority over a woman to be transferred from her father to her spouse upon marriage. This system prolonged women's economic and legal dependence on men while simultaneously restricting their autonomy.

Women's legal marginalization was equally ingrained in medieval Europe. The common law English concept of coverture explained how married women's legal identities were absorbed into those of their husbands. A married woman could not enter into contracts, own property on her own, or take legal action without her husband's approval under coverture. This theory strengthened women's marginalization within the legal system and institutionalized their reliance on their husbands for both financial and legal support.

2.2.2. Early Modern and 19th Century Developments

While there were some changes in gender norms during the early modern era, there were still substantial social and legal barriers in place. Traditional gender roles started to be questioned by new concepts about individual rights and personal autonomy that emerged during the Reformation and Enlightenment periods. Although feminists and other thinkers like Mary Wollstonecraft pushed for women's equality and rights, significant legislativere slow to come about.

A number ofSeveral important legal changes were brought about in the 19th century by the rise of women's suffrage movements and larger social reform agendas. Seneca Falls Convention of 1848, which called for equal rights and women's suffrage, was a turning point in the American women's rights movement. Women still had to overcome subsial and legal barriers in spite ofdespite these initiatives. Traditional gender norms were frequently upheld by the legal system, and reforms were regularly opposed.

An important development came about in England in 1882 when the Married Women's Property Act was passed, enabling married women to own property apart from their husbands. Nevertheless, many legal obstacles continued to exist, and this reform did not immediately address all aspects of gender inequality. After the 19th Amendment was passed in 1920, women in the US were granted the right to vote, but their opportunities and freedoms were still restricted by other legal discrimination.

2.2.3. Mid-20th Century to Contemporary Challenges

A more determined effort to achieve gender equality was made in the middle of the 20th century, propelled by feminist movements and larger civil rights programs. Historic laws like the Equal Pay Act of 1963 and the Civil Rights Act of 1964 attempted to address systemic discrimination against women in the workplace and other domains in the United States. Title VII of the Civil Rights Act outlawed sex-based discrimination in the workplace, and the Equal Pay Act sought to do away with pay gaps that existed between men and women who did the same job.

Globally, combating gender discrimination gained traction with the 1979 ratification of the Convention on the Elimination of All Forms of Discrimination Against Women (CEDAW). CEDAW created thorough guidelines for gender equality and offered nations a framework for assessing and revising their laws pertaining to women's rights. After the convention was adopted, many nations changed their legal systems as a sign of their commitment to combating systemic gender discrimination.

Notwithstanding these developments, problems remained, and new kinds of marginalization appeared. For instance, the fight for reproductive rights emerged as a major concern, with discussions about abortion and access to contraception illuminating the ongoing social and legon to women's autonomy. The Roe v. Despite the historic Roe v. Wade decision of 1973, which made abortion legal in the US, reproductive rights still face formidable political and legal obstacles. Roe v. Wade was overturned June 2024. This overturning made abortion illegal and was then left up to the states to make a decision as to what they will allow case by case.

Legal frameworks that acknowledge gender identity and sexual orientation have brought attention to persistent issues of marginalization. The case of Obergefell v. The Hodges ruling from 2015, which made same-sex marriage legal in the US, was a major victory for LGBTQ+ rights. Nonetheless, there are still legal and social obstacles that LGBTQ+ people and gender minorities must overcome, such as discrimination in the workplace, the healthcare system, and public services.

2.2.4. Intersectionality and Ongoing Inequality

Understanding the intricacies of marginalization based on gender requires an understanding of intersectionality. The concept of intersectionality acknowledges the connections between discrimination based on gender and other categories such as race, class, and sexual orientation. This viewpoint shows how social and legal structures can exacerbate inequality, creating special difficulties for people who experience multiple forms of marginalization.

For instance, racial and gender discrimination against women of color frequently affects their ability to obtain legal protections, healthcare, and employment opportunities. Similarly, discrimination against transgender people occurs not only because of their gender identity but also because of their race, socioeconomic status, and place of residence. It is still very difficult for the legal system to deal with these interlocking forms of discrimination. The marginalization of women and gender minoritiesthroughout history is a reflection ofreflects larger societal attitudes and power structures.

The development of legal frameworks shows both advancement and continuing difficulties, ranging from antiquated legal codes that institutionalized gender inequality to modern campaigns for gender justice. Even though there have been great strides, gender-based discrimination still exists, which emphasizes the noing reform and awareness. In order toTo effectively address the complexities of gender inequality, one must have a deep awareness of historical contexts as well as a persistent commitment to achieving true justice and equality for all people.

REFERENCES

1. Acemoglu, D., Autor, D., & Lyle, D. (2004). Women, war and wages: The effect of female labor supply on the wage structure at midcentury. *Journal of Political Economy, 112*(3), 497–550.
2. Alesina, A., Brioschi, B., & La Ferrara, E. (2016). Violence against women: A cross-cultural analysis for Africa. *Harvard Mimeo.*
3. Alesina, A., Giuliano, P., & Nunn, N. (2013). On the origins of gender roles: Women and the plough. *The Quarterly Journal of Economics, 128*(2), 469–530.
4. Bertocchi, G. (2011). The enfranchisement of women and the welfare state. *European Economic Review, 55*, 535–553.
5. Bertocchi, G., & Bozzano, M. (2015). Family structure and the education gender gap: Evidence from Italian provinces. *CESifo Economic Studies, 61*(1), 263–300.
6. Cowan, R. S. (2003). The transformation of gender roles in the 20th century: Implications for legal studies. *Law and Society Review, 37*(2), 315–340.
7. Friedman, L. M. (2006). The evolution of gender and the law in the United States. *Journal of American History, 92*(4), 1337–1356.
8. Ginsburg, F. D. (2002). Gender, law, and the politics of reproduction. *Annual Review of Anthropology, 31*, 219–242.
9. Giuliano, P. (2015). The role of women in society: From pre-industrial to modern times. *CESifo Economic Studies, 61*(1), 33–52.
10. Tong, R. (2009). *Feminist Thought: A More Comprehensive Introduction.* Routledge.

Chapter **3**

Feminist Legal Theory: Foundations and Evolutions

Contents

INTRODUCTION

The evolution of feminism in general and feminist legal theory in particular were linked. The women's movement fought for political rights such as the right to vote among many other early rights. A few of the early tactics, like Sojourner Truth's argument for equal treatment because she had "ploughed and planted" similarly to a man, hinted at ideas of equality that would later become significant legal theories. Feminist legal theory was frequently preceded by feminist political action. Legal scholars did not develop distinct branches of feminist legal theory until the late 1970s and early 1980s, despite feminist lawyers pushing courts to address gender inequality in the 1960s and early 1970s.

There are numerous variations of feminist legal theory, some of which overlap. However, two elements are shared by all the theorieionobservation aan aspiration. Feminists first acknowledge that men have shaped the world and that as a result, they hold greater privileges and power shares. The rather obvious (though unspoken) fact that almost all public laws in the history of existing civilization were drafted by men is emphasized by all feminist legal scholars. If men have always had an advantage due to American law, then this news should not be shocking. Second, all feminists think that there should be political, social, and economic equality for men and women. Although feminists agree that equality is a goal, they don't agree on what equality means or how to get there.

3.1. EQUAL TREATMENT THEORY

Equal treatment theory, sometimes known as "liberal" or "sameness" feminism, emerged in the early 1960s, marking the beginning of the first wave of feminist legal theory. The foundation of equal treatment theory is the idea of formal equality—that is, the idea that women should have the same rights as men—which served as the impetus for the suffrage movement. The theory was based on liberal political and philosophical ideals that support individualism, rationality, equal citizenship, and equal opportunities in public life. The principles of equal treatment were straightforward: a woman should not be treated differently by the law than a man in a similar situation. Furthermore, judgments made by the law regarding specific women shouldn't be based on generalizations about women in general—even those that are supported by statistics.

The early attempts to achieve women's equality of treatment had two objectives. First, equal social and political opportunities—such as equal pay, employment, and access to public benefits—had to be secured. The second was to repeal laws designed to keep women out of the public eye and protect them. Such protective laws have included restrictions on women's employment hours and career choices. Equal treatment theorists emphasized the similarities between men and women and used this as the foundation for demanding equal employment and financial advantages, possibly in part as a response to the historical treatment of women as special protection recipients.

In the 1970s and 80s, groups like the League of Women Voters, the National Organization for Women, and the American Civil Liberties Union (ACLU) prevailed in a number of Supreme Court cases that broke down barriers for women to participate in the economy, own property, and earn a living. The ACLU established the Women's Rights Project (WRP) in the 1970s to pursue legal action against sex discrimination. Following the lead of future Supreme Court Justice Ruth Bader Ginsburg, the WRP pursued formal equality using the same tactic as the pioneers of the civil rights movement. The WRP maintained that women and men were not legally different in any way, arguing that women had to prove they were "similarly situated" rder toto be granted equal treatment under the Constitution. In the 1971 case of Reed v. Reed, they were successful in persuading the Supreme Court that laws favoring male relatives over female relatives as administrators of a decedent's estate were unconstitutional because both sexes were equally qualified to administer estates. After two years, in Frontiero v. In an amicus brief, Richardson, the WRP contended that female military personnel should be entitled to the same family benefits as their male counterparts. The military benefits policy that assumed all wives of servicemen were financially dependent on their husbands was declared unconstitutional by the Supreme Court in the Frontiero case. However, the same presumption did not apply to the husbands of service women. Justice Brennan noted that "our Nation has had a long and unfortunate history of sex discrimination" in his opinion for the Court justified by a "romantic paternalistic" mindset that, in reality, placed women in a cage rather than on a pedestal."

Initially, the WRP employed a strategy of using male plaintiffs to contest laws that appeared to favor women, at least on the surface.rity ofmost judges were men, WRP lawyers reasoned that the best way for them to perceive discrimination was if they could imagine themselves as potential victims. The tactic yielded inconsistent outcomes. The Court maintained a law exempting widows from property taxes, but not widowers. Because the state tax exemption was "reasonably designed to further the state policy of cushioning the financial impact of spousal loss upon the sex for which that loss imposes a disproportionately heavy burden," the Court concluded that it was an appropriate equalizing measure for the discrimination that women face in the labor market. However, based on the alleged higher traffic-safety risks posed by underage males, the Court overturned a law that forbade the sale of low-alcohol beer to females under the age of eighteen and males under the age of twenty-one. The Court rejected the stereotype that young men were more reckless than young women when the state provided only flimsy empirical evidence of a correlation between gender and driving while intoxicated (0.18% of females and 0.02% of males between the ages of eighteen and twenty-one were arrested for driving under the influence).

Ginsburg's strategy in the equal treatment cases was strong because it took aim at the idea that "natural" distinctions should be used as justification for different legal treatment. She demonstrated how many of these distinctions were socially constructed and how different roles for men and women were dictated by social norms. She further contended that discrimination based on these unchangeable biological distinctions between the sexes warranted a higher standard of judicial review if they distinguished the sexes.

The formal equality strategy was largely successful in removing overt obstacles to equal treatment in the late 1970s and early 1980s. The Supreme Court determined that both the statute requiring husbands alone to pay alimony and the congressman's decision to fire a female administrative assistant due to her sexual orientation violated the equal protection guarantee. Potential jurors could not be turned away by law firms because they were women, and nursing schools could not turn away prospective students because they were men. However, in certain instances, the Court allowed women to recover benefits like additional Social Security allotments as recompense for the disadvantages they face in the me equalEqual treatment theory has greatly increased women's access, especially to work and education. Its reasoning was widely accepted and simple to comprehend. The fact that the plan focused on specific cases of inequality and only sought gradual change contributed to its popularity wi publicpublic. However, this indicated that the theory was mild, logical, and progressed slowly. Additionally, rather than focusing on the more contentious area of individual behavior, equal treatment lawsuits continued to target public policies and practices like taxes, alcohol sales, and education.

The theory of equal treatment recognizes the norm or reference point of male experience. Women can only be considered equal to the extent that they share the same circumstances as men. This symmetrical approach has a flaw in that it disadvantages women on matters pertaining to pregnancy, childbirth, and property division during a divorce because of its emphasis on similarity. A second group of theorists responded by contesting the equal treatment framework and claiming that women's rights ought to be established independently of male norms. It was on this premise that cultural feminism emerged.

3.2. CULTURAL FEMINISM

The theory of cultural feminism, also referred to as "difference theory" or, less favorably, "special treatment theory," contends that substantive equality does not always follow from formal equality. The sameness model was criticized by cultural feminists as being biased towards men and only assisting women in demonstrating their similarities to men. There was insufficient formal equality of opportunity to produce equal outcomes. Women were harshly judged by society for not fitting the masculine norm. If gender-neutral lawto accountconsider the diverse experiences and viewpoints of women, they may be used to suppress women. This theory highlights the distinctions between men and women, regardless of whether those distinctions are due to biological variations associated with childbearing or cultural variations evident in interpersonal interactions. Cultural feminists point out that many organizations, like the workplace, have policies that disadvantage women because they are largely based on experiences that are dominated by men. For example, under the voluntary-quit rules of unemployment compensation, people (mainly women) who quit their jobs due to work-family conflicts are usually not eligible to receive benefits. Female plaintiffs frequently receive damage awards discounted by anticipated work absences during the childrearing years because damages in most tort cases are based on anticipated losses of future earning capacity. Though battered women live in constant fear of domestic abuse, they are unable to predict when their partner will attack because traditional criminal law self-defense rules require an immediate threat before allowing a defense.

Cultural feminists contend that women shouldn't be forced to conform to male norms and that men and women shouldn't be treated equally when there are pertinent differences between them. Rather, they advocate for a notion of legal es into accountconsiders the biological and cultural distinctions between men and women. According to some cultural feminists, women's connections are derived from both their biological and cultural heritage. According to them, women are "essentially connected" to humanity through an ethic of care and to other humans through the physical connections of sexual activity, pregnancy, and breastfeeding. Therefore, the issue with legal theory is that it treats people as unique, physically unconnected, and different from one another, which makes it "essentially and irretrievably masculine."

Educational psychologist Carol Gilligan's "different voice" research served as a foundation for cultural feminist theory in the legal field. Gilligan contested the widely accepted psychological theory, linked to Lawrence Kohlberg, which held that higher moral development stages were associated with the application of abstract notions of justice and rights. She developed the idea that boys and girls acquire moral reasoning in distinct ways. Boys are taught to value abstract moral principles, rights, autonomy, and individualism, while girls are taught to value empathy, compassion, maintaining harmony, and a sense of community. Boys develop into men who reason with "an ethic of justice," which values abstract rights, regulations, and autonomy; girls grow into women who reason with "an ethic of care," emphasizing connections and relations with other people.

Supporters of special treatment advocated for a model that emphasizes differences between the sexes, regardless of whether those differences are biological or cultural. These differences include variations in care giving duties, reproductive functions, and even emotions and perceptions, such as how women view sexual harassment, rape, and other aspects of reproduction. Cultural feminists contend that when one sex is harmed by significant differences between men and women, those differences should be recognized and legally compensated. They have supported workplace accommodations for women, such as flexible work schedules or special maternity leaves. The reasonable woman standard, which gives the harassed female plaintiff the option to ask the jury to consider her claim from a woman's perspective rather than a person's (possibly male) perspective, is one example of the female-centric standards in the law that cultural feminists have pushed for.

Gilligan's methodology has drawn criticism from certain feminists who argue that it is anecdotal, subjective in characterizing traits as masculine or feminine, and relies too heavily on a small sample of privileged subjects. Some of these critics argue that there are more differences among women than there are between men and women, and they dispute the notion that there are many differences along gender lines. Some claim that social policies that highlight differences will serve to further entrench gender stereotypes. Although there hasn't been much empirical backing for Gilligan's findings, she has addressed these methodological criticisms and received support from others. Surprisingly, though, the general acceptance of her theories has not been affected by these criticisms.

Cultural feminism celebrates women's differences rather than merely identifying them: "To their credit, cultural feminists have reidentified these differences as women's strengths, rather than women's weaknesses." For the cultural feminist, women's art, craft, narrative ability, critical eye, ways of knowing, and hearts are all redefined as things to be celebrated. Legal scholars contended that this distinctly feminine approach to moral and legal reasoning had been ignored, or at the very least, discounted, in the legal system. To put it another way, "Vive la différence!." Gilligan's writings were cited by feminist legal theorists in their arguments for reevaluating several enduring legal precepts. For example, citizens are not required by traditional tort law, which respects individual autonomy, to help strangers in need, even if they are able to do so without endangering themselves. It is legal to watch a blind person cross the street without having to give them a warning in almost all states. It's not pleasant, but it's also not agonizing. Feminist legal scholars promoted the establishment of tort duties to protect strangers who are in danger by arguing that the law should promote social obligations of care. Genderneutral custody standards, according to some cultural feminists, have hurt women, who tend to plan their lives around caring relationships. Some have argued for less confrontational, more collaborative legal practices, such as increasing the use of mediation in place of litigation. In general, cultural feminists advocated for a shift away from the rights model that is geared toward men and for a stronger integration of an ethic of care into the law.

The main complaint against cultural feminism is that it only values women who conform to traditional social roles. Women's stereotypical association with domesticity is reinforced by cultural feminism, which celebrates qualities associated with women, such as empathy, nurturing, and caring. The fact that it portrays women as needing extra protection is another issue. Protectionist laws have historically placed women "not on a pedestal, but in a cage," as the Supreme Court noted."

The "equal treatment–special treatment" or "sameness-difference" debate centers on which model—formal equality or the celebration of difference—leads to greater fairness. Maternity and maternity leave are a major point of contention for cultural feminists and proponents of equal treatment theory. California Federal Savings and Loan Association v. was a 1987 Supreme Court case. Guerra ("Cal Fed"), depicts the respective stances of the two factions. A California law in Cal Fed mandated that employers give unpaid maternity leave to women for a maximum of four months, but it did not mandate leave of absence for other temporary disabilities. On opposing sides of the dispute, equal treatment theorists and cultural feminists submitted "friend of the court" briefs. Equal treatment theorists claimed that because the state law denied similar leaves to employees with other temporary "disabilities," employers were in violation of federal Title VII provisions. These groups included the Women's Rights Project of the ACLU and the Legal Defense and Education Fund of NOW. They argued that the way pregnant women were treated differently contributed to the misconception that laws protecting working women were necessary. The Coalition for Reproductive Equality in the Workplace (CREW), a cultural feminist organization, supported the state law by arguing that pregnancy accommodations would advance Title VII's goal of workplace equality and that biological differences between men and women justified different leave policies. The group claimed that, in the absence of the statute, women were forced to choose between having children and maintaining job security—a choice not imposed on men."

Thus, proponents of equal treatment theory argued that pregnancy ought to be treated similarly to other disabilities, to which cultural feminists countered that a policy specific to pregnancy was both constitutional and reasonable, given that pregnancy is a special condition that only affects women. The California pregnancy disability leave statute allows both men and women to have children without losing their jobs, the Supreme Court said in upholding the state law.

The sameness and difference camps tried to come together in favor of the Family and Medical Leave Act (FMLA) after the Cal Fed debate. However, recent research highlights the persistent gap between cultural feminist organizations and equal treatment. The FMLA, for instance, is a case in point. Although the statute "accommodates women's caretaking, protection that gives them a measure of job security but at the same time preserves employer's incentive to prefer male employees," observers have noted that, in reality, "only mothers take leave." Requiring paid family leave is one way to address this issue, as it would lessen the disincentive for men to take on primary care giving duties.

The assimilation model, which highlights the similarities between men and women, and the accommodation model, which emphasizes their differences, are the two models that theorists continue to disagree overwhich one better fostersfoster true equality. The arguments over things like custody rules that favor the "primary caregiver" (or whether that presumption discriminates against men), the parent track, which allows working parents to work part-time so they can spend more time with their children, and whether the formal equality principles that underpin sharp drops in maintenance (alimony) result in poverty for nonworking mothers are still being discussed. Certain feminists have attempted to go beyond the dichotomy between equal treatment and special treatment by challenging fundamental institutional frameworks and the societal beliefs that support them. Joan Williams, for instance, questions whether the "ideal worker," someone who can work full-time plus overtime and doesn't have to take care of children, needs to be the standard for the workplace. Theorists have acknowledged that while different treatment "is a double-edged sword permitting unfavorable as well as favorable treatment against an historical background of separate spheres ideology," equal treatment presents challenges by ignoring real differences. "When does treating people differently emphasize their difference and stigmatize and hinder them on that basis, and when does treating people the same become insensitive to their differences and likely to stigmatize or hinder them on that basis?" is the question that law professor Martha Minow believes sums up the difference dilemma.

3.3. DOMINANCE THEORY

Since both equal treatment theorists emphasize how similar women are to men and cultural feminists celebrate how different women are from men, dominance theory rejects the sameness/difference debate and diverges from it. It notes that both theories used the male standard as the primary benchmark: "Under the sameness standard, women are measured according to our correspondence with man, our equality judged by our proximity to his measure," whereas "under the difference standard, we are measured according to our lack of correspondence with him." The aim of dominance theory is freedom from men; the aim of equal treatment theory and cultural feminism is equality between men and women.

Instead, dominance theorists emphasize how men and women have different levels of power. Dominance theory, also known as radical feminism, was first proposed by Catharine MacKinnon in 1979 and is centered on the power dynamics between men and women. According to dominance theory, male dominance patterns are to blame fces women face as a result ofbecause of sex discrimination in the workplace, politics, and family spheres. According to this theory, most social institutions and a complex system of cultural beliefs s idea that men are privilegedprivileged, and women are subordinate. Together with other social institutions, the law contributes to the construction of women as inferior, dependant, and sex objects. Laws that contribute to women's oppression include those that prohibit abortion excessively, lack regulations on sexual harassment and pornography, and fail to adequately address violence against women, according to dominantheory, in particular, offered offered an alternative viewpoint on various forms of violence against women and children, including rape, intimate partner abuse, sexual harassment, and child pornography. For example, a Toronto police officer's 2011 observation that "women should 'avoid dressing like sluts" in order to "not be raped" sparked a nationwide grassroots protest movement known as SlutWalk, which included events in Canada, India, Singapore, Mexico, Finland, Germany, South Africa, and many American cities. Since equality theories "failed to address the patriarchal structures of power that led to and perpetuated" these experiences, they were ill-suited to address them. Patriarchy refers to the authority or dominance of the fathers. It is a set of political and social norms where men oppress and take advantage of women. Complex patterns of force, social pressures, and societal norms, rituals, and customs all contribute to the subordination. Not only does this dominance happen in interpersonal relationships, but it is also reinforced by the main societal institutions.

Men dominate women in the family because they are the "heads of the household." Extreme dominance is what domestic violence is. This dominance is accepted because those who commit acts of violence against women often receive light sentences from the criminal justice system. There is a gendered division of labor in the workplace, with women being assigned to lower-status positions with lower pay. Dominance theorists have illustrated how laws, written by men for the most part, contribute to the continuation of male dominance. For example, even in cases of violence, a rape victim must demonstrate that she did not consent in the majority of states. For instance, women who are compelled to resign from their jobs due to family obligations (like not being able to care for their children) are not eligible for unemployment insurance benefits.

Men should be superior in all spheres of life, including politics, education, work, and religion, according to a set of beliefs that both establish and maintain patriarchy. "A political structure that values men more than women," is what it is. Women are reduced to being second-class citizens. Catharine MacKinnon describes the ways men are dominant and privileged:

Male physiology defines most sports; male needs define health and auto insurance; male perspectives and concerns define quality in scholarship; male experiences and obsessions define merit; male objectification of life defines art; male military service defines citizenship; male presence defines family; male incompatibilities—wars and rulerships history; male genitalia definesdefine sex; and male physiology defines most sports.

The legal system upholds these demeaning portrayals of women as protected speech, despite the media's dehumanizing portrayals of women that treat them like property. Stereotypes force women to conform to expectations that dictate how they should behave—presenting themselves as submissive and feminine, taking on an excessive amount of childcare, housework, and elder care. Patriarchy grants men authority over women's lives, sexuality, and freedom of reproduction. Men's sexual dominance and women's sexual submission are aspects of patriarchy. In this society, men's desires and satisfactions are the main focus of sexuality. Women always fear being raped or subjected to sexual abuse. They discover how to leverage their sexuality as a tool for success. In the workplace, women are not regarded as professional peers but rather as objects of attraction. From fashion advertisements to pornography, women are portrayed as commodities or objects for sexual gratification.

The antipornography ordinance that Andrea Dworkin and Catharine MacKinnon proposed in 1983 established a cause of action for sex discrimination against pornography that depicted women as "presented as sexual objects" and "the graphic sexually explicit subordination of women, whether in pictures or in words."

Men are also shaped by patriarchy when it reinforces traits linked to conventional notions of masculinity, teaching them to shun closeness and suppress their feelings. Socialization to stereotypical gender behaviors specific to their sex occurs for both men and women. In addition to being subjugated like women, men who act in ways that defy conventional notions of manliness and exhibit effeminate behavior are viewed as threats to masculinity and frequently face consequences for their transgressions.

Promoting heterosexuality and discouraging same-sex relationships are two ways to uphold the established patriarchal system. "Compulsory heterosexuality" is enforced by laws, such as the former "Don't Ask, Don't Tell" policy of the military, as well as by much subtler forms of cultural indoctrination, such as the widespread use of "faggot" among high school boys (which is still very popular today) and the male fear of everything pink. Politicians are more adept than most at recognizing our unconscious pull toward the dominant male. Thus, California governor Arnold Schwarzenegger made fun of those who opposed his party's economic platform at the 2004 Republican National Convention by referring to them as economic "girlie men."

Women who reside in patriarchal societies are susceptible to internalizing the values of the majority. They might seek out, select, and even take pleasure in caregiving or dependent relationships. According to MacKinnon, "women value care because men have valued us based on the care we provide for them." Because their existence is defined in relation to men, women think in relational terms. This psychological subtype of oppression is known as "false consciousness." Joining women-only groups and discussing their experiences with housework, sexuality, caregiving, and menial jobs is one way MacKinnon suggests women engage in "consciousness-raising" to bring attention to oppression and expose this system of internalized beliefs. Through this process, women will increase collective knowledge about their experiences of oppression and make visible to themselves and each other the small injustices that arise daily as a result of male privilege.

The notion of false consciousness—that women are incapable of making their own decisions—has been criticized by other feminists as being "infuriatingly condescending," and consciousness-raising as a solution is unworkable since sharing personal experiences does not guarantee political solutions. The idea that all women have the same experience—that is, that of victims—is known as "gender essentialism," and it has been criticized for being a feature of dominance theory. Furthermore, detractors of dominance theory claim that it undervalues the experiences of women as mothers and incorrectly "universalize[s] the experience of white women as the experience of all women, ignoring differences of race, class, and ethnicity." However, the theory has had a significant impact on legal thought, especially when it comes to rape, sexual harassment, and pornography.

3.4. ANTI-ESSENTIALISM

3.4.1. Critical Race Fem.inism

Several legal theorists, mostly lesbians and women of color, expressed dissatisfaction in the mid-to-late 1980s, claiming that feminist legal theory ignored their issues and experiences. White feminists who are traditional overlook significant racial and ethnic distinctions among women by focusing solely on gender. They claimed that feminist legal theory overindulged in the requirements of well-off White women. Certain generalizations concerning women's experiences were made by mainstream feminists (e.g., all women experienced subordination, or women are generally more nurturing and compassionate than men). Lesbians and women of color were silenced in the name of commonality by the phenomenon known as "feminist essentialism," which holds that "a unitary, 'essential' women's experience can be isolated and described independently of race, class, sexual orientation, and other realities of experience."

"Anti-essentialists," who oppose essentialism, contend that marginal perspectives are more useful in understanding discrimination than those from the center of an oppressed group's membership (that is, from the perspective of women who identify as white, middle-class, and heterosexual). Put differently, discrimination operates differently based on the combination of an individual's personal traits. All women, from Taylor Swift to Rosa Parks, are undoubtedly impacted by sexism. But what actually predicts how people will treat you is the intersection of traits like sex, race, wealth, and sexual orientation.

Legal doctrines pertaining to rape, sexual harassment, and domestic violence, according to critical race feminists, fail to sufficiently address discrimination based on the intersections of these categories. For instance, the requirement in employment discrimination that a black woman identify as a woman or a member of a racial minority and assert that the discrimination is based on race or sex ignores the ways in which sexism and racism are intertwined. Poor women of color face a "triple" disadvantage in the labor market due to issues with income, sex, and race. Compared to other populations, immigrant women experience intimate violence at higher rates. Additionally, they lack access to shelters, legal representation, and support services when facing deportation threats. Compared to white men and women, men of color face more prosecutions, convictions, and harsher sentences. Since formal guarantees of equality accept existing measures of merit, such as one-dimensional standardized tests and traditional employment credentials, critical race theorists reject formal equality as meaningless.

People display multiple consciousnesses, which is another insight of critical race feminism suggested by the various categories of human identity.

A person can be in multiple relationships or roles at once and can move easily between them. Examples of these roles include lesbian, student, bank teller, daughter, and possibly mother. Due to the diverse range of roles, individuals can experience oppression at various pressure points and, with practice, start to comprehend it from viewpoints other than ts capacity, known as "multiple consciousnessconsciousness," by law professor Mari Matsuda, is more than just "a random ability to see all points of view, but a deliberate choice to see the world from the standpoint of the oppressed," in Matsuda's words."

The ability for outsiders to use formal legal discourse without losing their empathetic understanding—their consciousness—of oppression makes multiple consciousness crucial to the study and practice of law. With this line of reasoning, attorneys can consider laws that go beyond the strict doctrines that now exist but do not recognize their client's helplessness. For example, they can consider tort damages for hate speech against people of color, comprehend the needs of same-sex clients seeking adoption, or even imagine reparations for slavery. The idea that many laws are not neutral or objective, as they pretend to be, but rather are means of upholding traditional power relations, is the foundation of critical race feminism. This movement originated in the critical legal studies field. For instance, those who have been the targets of violent hate speech are not permitted to file a lawsuit for damages under traditional First Amendment law. Law has contributed significantly to the maintenance of racial and gender hierarchies by permitting the demonization of women and people of color.

Critical race feminists occasionally use narrative scholarship or a more intimate style of storytelling to illustrate how various forms of oppression affect the lives of people of color. Most women do not have the same experiences as women of color. Telling "stories" is one approach to incorporate minority perspectives into legal analysis. These narratives, or personal stories, expose readers to issues and feelings that members of the majority group might not have otherwise given much thought to.

One year, while Patricia Williams, a law professor, was shopping for Christmas in New York City, a white teenager who was chewing bubble gum declined to press the buzzer to let her in to a Benneton store. Professor Williams later explored the social connections between race, sex, crime, and commerce in a well-known essay. According to Adele Morrison, stories of lesbian victims of intimate partner abuse are told. However, because the batterers are also female, the safe house admits them. Anthony Alfieri, a law professor and former legal aid attorney, talks about a conversation he once had with a woman who was applying for food stamps. He learned from the woman's account not only of her legal need but also of her pride and sense of dignity in raising foster and biological children. Stories, parables, chronicles, and narratives are effective tools for dismantling mindset, which is the collection of assumptions, conventwisdom, and common understandings that servesserve as the backdrop for political and legal discourse, as noted by Richard Delgado. The goal is to have the law recognize these outsider's experiences.

The theory that races are biological phenomena is contested by critical race theorists. Of course, affirmative action policies would be rendered ineffective as a tool in the quest for equality if biological variations between racial groups resulted in intrinsic performance disparities. Additionally, it supports the Bell Curve theory that claims academic tests are a measure of "merit." It categorically defends racism as a harmless byproduct of naturally existing differences. The concept of race itself poses many difficulties. Without a doubt, biology and evolutionary history play a major role in the development of many racial characteristics, including skin color, hair type, facial features, and other physical characteristics. However, biologists do not identify subtypes among human races. The lines dividingdividing between different human races have, in fact, frequently changed over time and between societies. In this sense, race could be seen more as a social construct—a set of values pertaining to a person's unique set of physical traits. Because of this process of social construction, the negative and inferior connotations associated with different races are also products of society. The biological perspective on race justifies current opposition to transracial adoption and has recently resulted in laws that forbid interracial marriage. This critique of biological race has been expanded upon by critical race feminists to show how laws and legal judgments are still influenced by it. They have demonstrated how this genetic race belief affects surrogacy decisions made by courts, which see black women serving as gestational surrogates as little more than breeders. They have also shown how pregnant women of color who use drugs are more likely than white women to face drug-related charges as well as charges related to abuse, neglect, or endangerment of children.

According to critical race feminists, liberation can result from a legal approach that acknowledges "that differences are always relational rather than inherent." They also stress the usefulness of narrative or storytelling as an instrument. Making sure the stories of oppression are told—"speaking truth to power"—is a first step toward equality because legal cases always start with human stories.

3.4.2. Lesbian Feminism

The focus of lesbian legal theory is the legal challenges faced by individuals who identify as lesbian, gay, bisexual, or transgender (collectively, "LGBT"). Some lesbian feminists claimed that sexual orientation is more about politics than desire starting in the 1970s. Lesbian theorists argued against the stereotype of LGBT individuals as abnormal by citing data from sexuality studies that demonstrated the range of sexual orientations and the frequency of same-sex inclinations. Legal scholars who identify as gay or lesbian have enumerated the fundamental civil rights that are denied to non-heterosexuals by the government. These rights include the ability to marry, serve openly in the military (under the "Don't Ask, Don't Tell" policy), adopt, and work in any job without facing discrimination.

The mainstream feminist movement has long disregarded lesbian feminists and their concerns since Betty Friedan, the president of the National Organization for Women at the time, denounced them as the "lavender menace" in the 1970s. This marginalization is an illustration of the more common practnant subgroups excluding subordinates in order toto gain acceptance for themselves. Lesbian feminists, according to other theorists, have ignored the impact of laws on transsexuals, paid little attention to the voices of poor lesbians and gays, and excluded gay men and bisexuals from their analyses.

Early theorists of lesbian and gay law made connections between sexism and heterosexism clear. They demonstrated how stereotypical notions of masculinity called for the separation of the sexes, the suppression of feminine characteristics in men, and the marginalization, abuse, and demonization of people who were thought to be sexually abnormal. This served to elevate heterosexuality above all other forms of sexuality and to reinforce the superiority of "masculinity over femininity." They outlined the legal sanctions meted out to lesbians and gay men, clarifying that these sanctions stem from social interpretations of gender that validate only conventional family structures (e.g., Ward, June, Wally, and the Beave). Gay and lesbian legal theorists have tried a variety of arguments to break free from the oppression, subordination, and exclusion. These arguments have included communitarian (highlighting the humanity of all people) and constitutional (debating whether gays and lesbians are a suspect class deserving of heightened scrutiny under the Equal Protection Clause).

Lesbian feminists in the legal field may have different concerns than straight feminists; the former may be battling for child custody, while the latter may be attempting to get male partners to take on more childcare duties. State exclusions from basic benefits, family arrangements, and employment rights that straight people take for granted have a multitude of effects on lesbian's day-to-day lives. Disclosure of your sexual orientation may serve as grounds for dismissal from your job if you identify as gay or lesbian. Same-sex marriage is currently legal in most states, but not all of them. As a result, some same-sex partners do not have the same rights to custody, adoption, insurance, or property as heterosexual couples. There are 1,049 federal laws, according to the General Accounting Office, where marriage is a prerequisite for receiving certain "benefits, rights, and privileges." Gays and lesbians have therefore put a lot of effort into their campaigns and legal battles for marital equality.

Regarding the biological basis of sexual orientation, some legal theorists have written. They have referred to scientific data regarding the genetic and biological roots of sexuality, such as the findings of Simon LeVay's autopsy study, which showed that heterosexual men's hypothalamus was twice as large as that of homosexual men; twin studies, which indicate that there is a 50% chance that one twin is gay; and studies demonstrating the high failure rate of gays and lesbians undergoing "conversion therapy" or "reparative counseling" in an attempt to change their sexual orientation. These scientific results have been utilized by lesbian, gay, bisexual, and transgender (LGBT) legal theorists to support their claims that, similar to racial and gender classifications, sexual orientation ought to be viewed with suspicion and subject to closer constitutional scrutiny if it has a significant biological impact. Others, such as law professor Sam Marcosson, contend that sexual orientation is "constructively immutable"—that is, a trait that is immutable for "all relevant legal and political purposes"—and ask how a legal blame system can be justified if sexuality has biological roots even in cases where it results from social construction. The point is that, although not entirely biological, sexual orientation must be regarded as something that goes beyond free will because, like religious orientation, it is so strongly linked to personal identity. LGBT people require protection from discrimination under the constitution because the social connotations associated with sexual orientation are so strong in upholding a social class that is deemed undesirable. Lesbian and gay legal theory's organizational framework is somewhat reminiscent of the feminist legal theory's sameness/difference controversy. Some proponents of formal equality theory have attempted to demonstrate how LGBT couples are devoted partners and devoted parents, just like the heterosexual "ideal." They aim to show that sexual orientation is not the only factor in LGBT identity and that it shouldn't have any social or legal ramifications. Difference theorists, also known as anti-subordination theorists in this context, question how society has wrongly labeled sexual nonconformists as deviants while criticizing the heterosexual norm. However, given that one definition of equality is treating people in similar circumstances equally, it may not be shocking at all that discussions of equality frequently come back to ideas of sameness and difference.

3.5. ECOFEMINISM

Women's complex and varied relationships with society and the natural world are described by ecofeminism. Since its inception in the 1970s, ecofeminism has blossomed into an astounding variety of forms, with focuses on everything from international human rights to spiritualism to economics. The most current and possibly most promising iteration of ecofeminism highlights the connections between environmental degradation and human oppression (racism, sexism, and so forth). The analysis starts with the same premise as all of ecofeminism: the connection between the oppression of women and the destruction of the natural world. According to this perspective, the root cause of both environmental degradation and sexism is a mistaken dualism in Western thought that prioritizes the human mind and spirit over the natural world and its functions. This dualism subjugates both nature and women because Western culture frequently identifies the masculine with mind and spirit (science, reason, Descartes) and the feminine with the natural world (sex, instinct, Mother Nature). An explanation for everything from the nation's fixation with damming rivers to the pope's disapproval of premarital sex has been offered for this hierarchy, which dates back to Adam.

In an approach reminiscent of cultural feminism, most ecofeminists advocate fd respect for feminine, "nature-based" values in order toto counteract the dominance of masculine ideals. Some ecofeminists contend that the emphasis on the male/female duality is excessiveore coordinated campaign against oppression as a whole isis more appropriate. This tactic reminds me of the domination theory. Many ecofeminists believe that the dynamics of control and separation that support environmental degradation and sexism also support other forms of oppression. This results in a complex examination of power abuse and sexism. According to Ellen O'Loughlin, ecofeminism must consider mor the ways that sexism and naturism are related in order toto combat the oppression of women and nature, as most women "experience [discrimination] in more than one way (that is, through the dynamics of racism, classism, heterosexism, and ageism, as well as sexism)."

Environmental philosophy has made positive contributions to society, such as valuing ecological ethics over human-centered utilitarianism, considering equitable access to natural resources, and appreciating aesthetics. Environmentalists use these concepts to guide their initiatives, such as the push to protect the Arctic National Wildlife Refuge for future generations rather than drilling there in the hopes of finding oil. These same ideas about the interconnectedness of all living things and the importance of community over the self are integrated into ecofeminism along with feminist ideas about inclusivity, respect, and empathy for others.

It is tempting to think of ecofeminism as merely an eco-friendly version of anti-essentialism. However, the ecofeminist perspective on compound oppression offers a novel perspective. First, the recognition that women and the natural world are oppressed in common is the central tenet of ecofeminism. This principle not only makes it conceptually impossible to avoid compound oppressions, but it also encourages the investigation of other forms of shared oppression. After all, removing the "esm" from ecofeminism is to undermine the concept as a wholeconcept.

Second, ecofeminism offers the ecological system metaphor for comprehending shared oppression. Actually, theThe idea of ecology gives us a picture that is almost poetic in order to help us understand many of the challenges that women encounter. Ellen O'Loughlin writes,

An ecologist cannot describe an ecosystem and its functioning by simply adding up the components of a pond. When considering an ecosystem, it is necessary to recognize that a fish in a pond and a fish in the ocean live in different, albeit possibly related, environments. Women are also in different places. Whether I work in an office or a field, the interplay of societal environmental factors determines at least some of what I do there, my niche.

The theory is particularly helpful in forming alliances amongst legal organizers because it places a strong emphasis on compound oppressions within an ecological framework.

The environmental justice movement, a grass-roots movement addressing environmental threats impacting the impoverished and people of color, has produced some excellent examples. Women make up the majority of those involved in and leading the Environmental Justice (EJ) movement in the United States. This was a grassroots movement that began at kitchen tables across the nation, where mothers would compare notes about the illnesses their kids were experiencing and link common illnesses to toxins leaching from landfills or contaminated well water. Therefore, EJ advocates focus on issues related to pollution that have an impact on families and kids, such as lead-based paint in older homes, drinking water contamination, or childhood asthma in inner cities that is made worse by air pollution. EJ advocates are adaptable partners who have teamed up with public health, mainstream environmentalists, and poverty attorneys. Love of justice—the dedication to oppose oppression in all of its forms—rather than a love of nature, though that may play a role, is what binds these groups together.

These new environmentalists are able to connect discrimination and contamination through the lens of social justice. Zoning laws that maintain the segregation of low-income single mothers and minorities are questioned by EJ advocates when national studies reveal links between neighborhood pollution and wealth or race. EJ advocates question pollution limits that were made strict enough to protect men but not women when the federal government advises women of childbearing age to reduce their intake of tuna due to mercury contamination.

After Kenyan activist Wangari Maathai won the Nobel Peace Prize in 2004 for inspiring thousands of African women to fight against poverty, deforestation, and authoritarian governments, the ecofeminist movement gained international traction. For women, each of these issues presented significant difficulties. For example, deforestation left rural communities without firewood, forcing women and girls to hike great distances in search of fuel for cooking. Furthermore, African women are disproportionately vulnerable to poverty and corrupt autocrats due to a multitude of legal and social traditions that restrict their ability to participate in the workforce and public life. A Nobel Committee representative explained that year's selection by saying, "We have added a new dimension to the concept of peace." Human rights, particularly those of women, the environment, and advancing democracy have all received special attention."

Maathai demonstrated ecofeminist principles through her involvement in the Green Belt Movement, which helped women plant over 40 million trees on community land, farms, and in the vicinity of schools and churches. The goal of this effort was to help reduce poverty for women by protecting the environment. The ecofeminist movement has enthusiastic and innovative American supporters, even though it seems to have the largest support outside of the country. Ecofeminists have fought for better healthcare for women, migrant farmworker's security, animal rights, and Native American's access to the environment in the United States.

3.6. PRAGMATIC FEMINISM

One of the main insights provided by pragmatic legal feminism is that contextual solutions are usually more helpful than abstract theories. The writings of classical philosophers like John Dewey and Charles Sanders Peirce, who understood that "truth is inevitably plural, concrete, and provisional," are a source of inspiration for feminist legal pragmatists. This indicates that pragmatics draw speculative conclusions and are aware that their realities are frequently imprecise and subject to revision. Legal pragmatists who identify as feminists critique universalism (e.g., all men rule women) of some other forms of feminist legal theories, placing more emphasis on the significance of perspective and context. They acknowledge that "the time and place where they occur" and "all observations are relative to a perspective." and the preexistingparty making the observation."

Generally speaking, pragmaticsPragmatics avoid abstractions because they believe that abstract ideas do not necessarily dictate practical solutions in the real world. As pragmatists, feminists see the law as a partial explanation for the results of specific cases, rather than as a source of answers. Realists understand that a lot of the arguments amongst feministsfeminists' center on varying perspectives of the best ways to achieve equality. They also acknowledge that people in oppressed groups frequently find themselves in a "double bind," with no way out if things go according to plan. For instance,

For instance, when we single out pregnancy for "special treatment," we worry that hiring managers won't want to work with women. However, women will lose their jobs if we do not give pregnancy special consideration. If we give women preferential treatment, we reinforce the outdated belief that they are inferior beings; if we don't, we stop women from growing more powerful in the real world.

Different methods or results might be required in different situations and eras. A lot of feminist topics are discussed in particular, concrete contexts. For instance, the question might be whether a certain law firm ought to implement a nonpartnership track in order to provide parents additional time to spend with their kids at home. Some feminists may worry that this will turn into a "mommy track," where female lawyers use it as a kind of second-class citizenship, sometimes even exclusively. A pragmatic feminist would see the parent track as the best option among less-than-ideal options—a means of broadening the options and helping some of the most affected individuals at that location and time reconcile work and family conflicts—rather than as the ideal result, which might be to change billable-hour requirements for all the lawyers in a firm. Pragmatic feminists search for context-specific solutions bderstand the risk of generalizations.

Pragmatism as a whole hashas been criticized by some for emphasizing the individual viewpoint, being ambiguous, and not being willing to commit to abstract theorizing. Law professor Jack Balkin makes light of the fact that "being a legal pragmatist means never having to say you have a theory." Finding a practical moral standard in the lack of a guiding theory is a significant challenge, though.

Think about, for instance, the ways in which the methods of a pragmatic feminist and an equal treatment theorist might differ. In certain tribal societies, land is typically only passable down to male heirs; however, customary practices require famivide unmarried daughters with a portion of their land in order toto care for them. An unmarried or divorced daughter with her own children to raise could argue for an extension of those rights to cultivation or occupancy, not because she should have the same rights as her brothers but rather because families have a duty to provide for all of their daughters. In this culture, the latter tactic has a far higher chance of succeeding than the former. Although this practical approach might result in a positive outcome in a particular instance, it might not contribute to theoretically satisfactory or long-lasting egalitarian outcomes: "This recognition of customary rights is not a real victory for long-term gender equality, however." It is based on the idea that women's rights to inherit property from their birth families are conditional. Daughters are only taken into consideration in special cases, suchthey choose not to marry or when their marriages end in divorce."divorce.

While pragmatism lacks strong beliefs, it may provide a better set of approaches to drawing conclusions, however tentative and incomplete they may be. Rather than offering specific legal solutions, feminist pragmatism makes more methodological recommendations. Because examining the realities of experience is a component of feminist methodology, pragmatic feminists look for truths in the details of women's everyday lives. Pragmatists thus believe that theories are constructed through personal experiences, and that theories must take into account the actual circumstances of a wide range of people.

3.7. POSTMODERN FEMINISM

The various feminist legal theories that we have been considering are like an endless variety of ice cream flavors. Some people love vanilla, while others prefer Rocky Road. However, rather than being a fixed flavor, postmodern feminist theory (and to a lesser extent pragmatism) serves as an interpretive tool. It resembles a scoop for ice cream.

Another attempt is presented by postmodern feminist legal theory to transcend the distinctions between sameness and difference. The comparative approaches of equal treatment ("women are like men") and cultural feminism ("women are not like men"), according to postmodern feminists, mistakenly presume that all women and men are essentially the same. This presumption is especially harmful and untrue when discussing men and women in terms of their ethnicity, socioeconomic status, or place of origin. Hence, postmodern feminist legal theorists reject the idea of a single truth and acknowledge that truths are multiple, liminal, and consequently connected to people's lived experiences, viewpoints, and places in the world.

Postmodern feminism rejects essentialism—the notion that all women have the same experiences or conditions—as do critical feminist theories and pragmatism. Yet postmodernists use a completely different degree of abstraction in their work. Postmodernists believe harmony is impossible, in contrast to anti-essentialists who believe truth can only be found in a harmony of many voices. Furthermore, truth—well, that's just a creation of your mind.

As the name suggests, modernism, an intellectual movement that disapproved of the Victorian art forms of realism in painting and narrative in literature, gave rise to postmodernism, an attempt to portray a less stylized, more immediate image of the human condition. The goal of modernists was to get to the core of the truth. In addition to rejecting conventional forms and styles, postmodernists also reject the idea of objective knowledge or experience. Postmodernists cast doubt on the idea of objectivity or truth itself. As Peter Schanck explains, "What we think is knowledge is always belief"—and "because language is socially and culturally constituted, it is inherently incapable of representing or corresponding to reality"—the postmodern perspective holds that knowledge can never be certain or empirically established. When the truth is stripped bare, all that's left is steam.

An initial step in postmodern analysis is the "deconstruction" method. French philosopher Jacques Derrida developed the concept of deconstruction in the 1960s and 1970s. It involves closely examining historical, artistic, or linguistic details to uncover underlying political messages and biases. Because language is inherently loaded with context-dependent explicit and implicit information, textual accounts are always encoding hidden messages. The Jim Crow South's "Whites Only" signs come to mind. Most people today would agree that the more important, covert message was about class power, despite some politicians' claims that the message was merely one of separation rather than subordination. The postmodern thesis asserts that power and the struggle to preserve it are all that exist in the end; justice, beauty, and truth are nonexistent. Every opera, treatise, or constitution has a foundation based on the geometry of power when you pull up the floorboards. There are hierarchies in every work, discussion, text, document, and language. Justice, or what passes for justice, is the property of the ruling class of the day, who define and mold it to suit their needs. Eventually, a new class will undoubtedly overthrow the old and impose its own interpretation of justice. (You get the idea if this makes you think of the French Revolution). Postmodernists must first recognize these power structures through deconstruction before using political action to overthrow them.

Postmodern feminists contest the modernist notion of an immutable rule of law by employing the instruments of deconstruction. Because laws are not neutral or unbiased because they are the product of political prejudices, reliance on them as well as on conventional legal procedures can serve to perpetuate inequality. Postmodern practices question a variety of subtle power structures, including those that exist between attorneys and their clients. These techniques aim to highlight the subtle ways in which power functions in interpersonal relationships.

Language, knowledge, and power are interconnected in ways that propagate gender norms in culture, as postmodernism demonstrates. Postmodernism is particularly interested in the formation and transmission of hierarchies in culture because it centers on oppression. Postmodernists propose that subtle and pervasive systems of speaking and acting (discourse and so-called discursive practices) are how we create and transmit hierarchies, such as gender oppression. As in the case of some previous protectionist laws that limited the number of hours that women could work to protect them from physically demanding labor, women may internalize the expectations of advertisements that present them as anorexically thin, perfectly coiffed, and skilled users of cleaning products.

Traditional gender identities are being rethought to become more fluid and less tied to biological sex or cultural norms, using the postmodern technique of comprehending the relationships between discourse and power. Postmodern feminists see gender as socially constructed, relative, experience-based, malleable, and contingent on context and time rather than natural, fixed, or objective. They emphasize that people are multi-identity and multi-role actors. Every day, there are differences in how gender is performed or presented (through, for example, attire, occupation, and demeanor). Take Judith Butler's postmodern analysis of how gender identity is "performatively constituted" by expressions as an illustration of how language shapes identities.

If I identify as a lesbian, I "come out" only to create an entirely new "closet." The "you" that I am speaking to now has access to a distinct opacity region. In fact, the opacity's location has only changed. The room, the den, the attic, the basement, the house, the bar, the university, or some other new enclosure—we are no longer in the closet, but into what now? What new unbounded spatiality? dot. Because being "out" only has meaning within that polarity, it always depends to some extent on being "in." Therefore, in order to continue being considered "out," being "out" needs to consistently produce the closet."

Postmodern analysis can occasionally resemble performance art more than legal critique, as in the example given in the paragraph above. Such "transgressive" rants, or riffs, are defended by claiming they are riffs of resistance. Postmodernists argue that by resisting conventional modes of speaking and writing, and by questioning the language of social relationships, they can counteract the implicit messages of inequality propagated by the prevailing culture. Maybe. Even so, it's challenging to identify and combat injustice if we can't even agree on what "out" and "in" mean. "Postmodernism as practiced often comes across as style—petulant, joyriding, more posture than position," as Catharine MacKinnon put it. "According to postmodernism, society exists only in your mind."

Postmodernism is not liberating or effective for some feminists. They contend that the stark realities of discrimination, intimate violence, and subordination that women have been working to document are undermined by the postmodern challenge to fundamental truths. They are concerned that the focus on different viewpoints will turn the realities of rape, sexual assault, prostitution, and harassment into just more "narratives." Furthermore, critics say that postmodernism operates at too a high a level of theory to be of political use:

Postmodernism holds that everything is a reading and that there are no facts, hence lies are impossible. It seems that there is no way to know if the Holocaust was a hoax, if women enjoy being raped, if Black people are less intelligent than White people due to genetics, or if homosexuals are child molesters. These factual things are ambiguous, contingent, dynamic, and open to interpretation, according to postminance theorists and postmodernists have also argued over whether or notwhether women have "agency"—the ability to choose to engage in sadomasochistic sex, for example. While a dominance theorist might reject the notion that S/M practices can ever be freely chosen or contend that any such "choice" is actually the result of false consciousness, the postmodern perspective sees S/M as "a potentially pleasurable and subversive sexual practice." This is but a small sample of the greater discussion surrounding postmodern methodologies. Postmodernism advises people to try to flee oppression by engaging in "subversive practices." It mobilizes people to oppose dictatorship and chauvinism, but it doesn't seem to care much about what true democracy or equality looks like. How will the oppressed know they are free once they have managed to free themselves and slip through the bars?

3.8. FEMINIST LEGAL METHODS

3.8.1. Unmasking Patriarchy

Legal feminists begin by posing a series of inquiries aimed at exposing the male prejudices concealed behind laws that are purportedly "neutral." This method, known as "unmasking," aids in identifying the effects that laws have on different genders. Feminist legal scholars first identify these effects before attempting to demonstrate that the conventional legal foundations are not set in stone and can be altered. According to Catharine MacKinnon, the approach presupposes that even the most routine parts of the law conceal "the substantive way in which man has become the measure of all things."

To start the process, Katharine Bartlett recommends asking what she calls "the woman question." In her words,

Asking the woman question refers to analyzing how the law ignores experiences and values that, for whatever reason, seem more typical of women than of men, or how the concepts and standards that are currently in place may be detrimental to women. The inquiry presupposes that certain aspects of the law may be "male" in a particular sense in addition to being nonneutral in general.

The woman's question is meant to highlight those characteristics, explain how they work, and offer suggestions for possible fixes.

Bartlett's explanation makes two inferences. Firstly, it is challenging to identify n the real world without having a thorough understanding of women's livedwomen's lived experiences. Feminist men already face discrimination. However, we all have distance to cover. Women's experiences differ depending on their class, age, race, and sexual orientation, sometimes in a very noticeable way. Developing the ability to empathize with others is a crucial skill for all feminists. Second, comprehending women's individual experiences aims to demonstrate how the unfair effects of the law "may be corrected." Corrective action typically entails enfranchisement, or the introduction of women's outsider experiences into the political or legal system. Enfranchisement can take place in less formal ways, such as seminars, protest marches, and demonstrations, or in more formal ways, such as the right to vote and the ability to organize at work.

As part of an empirical evaluation, the woman's question is meant to highlight the gender bias in laws that oar to be neutral. Questions about whether specific laws take into accountconsider the experiences of women, whether laws subtly favor one sex over the other, and whether social practices reinforce illegitimate gender stereotypes are important to ask. Mapping the proportion of men and women chosen for promotions at a specific company, recording the likelihood that mothers or fathers will obtain child custody in disputed cases, or compiling information regarding how boys and girls are treated in classrooms are a few examples of measuring the impact of gender. Because gendered biases in the law can also disadvantage men, the investigation's findings are not always in favor of women.

Feminists challenge the legal system's reliance on gender differences to allocate social benefits in an effort to reveal injustice through thorough investigation. There are two possible levels to this endeavor. First and foremost, feminists aim to demonstrate the empirical falsity of the widely accepted difference. At a second level, feminists acknowledge that there is a gender difference, but they object to the way that this difference is exploited to the detriment of women. How does all of this translate into the real world? Consider the case of Myra Bradwell, who was mentioned in the introduction and who tried in vain to follow her legal career despite the stereotype of women as "timidity and delicacy." Or Sally Reed, who disproved the notion that "only men can handle money" by opposing a law that gave preference to men for estate administration roles. These two instances illustrate the initial stage of unmasking, which disqualifies stereotypes based on factual accuracy.

Feminists aim to discredit, not the assumption of differences, but the assumption that differences justify burdening women relative to men when there are real underlying gender differences. The second stage of unmasking is this. Think about childbearing, which is a female-only experience. Women started protesting employee benefit plans, which excepted pregnancy covered nearly all potential disabilities, in the 1970s. Proponents of the policies contended that their exclusion was warranted because pregnancy leaves were more expensive than many other types of disability leaves. According to this perspective, the burden placed on women came from a real difference—the ability to become pregnant—rather than from the policy, which was merely a means of controlling costs. In fact, providing pregnancy leave while acknowledging that only women could use it would amount to giving women preferential treatment over men.

The feminist perspective holds that the argument is flawed because these disability policies are not grounded in gender-neutral principles. They recognize an employer's duty to an employee, who is presumed to be a man, and are founded on a set of moral and financial obligations. He might receive what the "typical man" needs for his bare minimum of peace of mind (disability leave for prostate cancer, weekends off to take care of his kids). Pregnancy leave and flexible work schedules during the week are "extras" that the "typical woman" requires to take care of her children. Men and women should be used as benchmarks, according to the second level of unmasking.

An effective substitute for simply placing the blame for social injustices on the victim is unmasking. Extensive social inequalities are best understood as structural issues that call for public, as opposed to private, solutions. Not because women were incapable of handling legal matters, but rather because of sexist attitudes that disregarded their abilities, women did not practice law in the nineteenth century. Not motherhood or working mothers are to blame for the uneasy balance between having children and making a living; rather, the male-dominated workforce is to blame.

This emphasis on institutional structural bias raises an important point from the second stage of the unmasking process: prejudice is real but not always deliberate. Consequently, even though it's possible that historically, employers have devalued motherhood, which is why there aren't any better pregnancy benefits today, this does not mean that every employer who chooses not to implement a better policy is being intentionally sexist. This is significant because there are laws against discrimination that only target deliberate discrimination, not institutional or unconscious discrimination. Ultimately, the unmasking process serves as a warning against assuming objectivity in almost any context involving human interaction. According to Martha Minow, feminists have uncovered the prevalence of "field after field of conceptions of human nature that treat women as 'other,' 'different,' 'deviant,' or baffling and take a male as the reference point." "Unmasking is the process of exposing the bias and partiality of laws, social structures, or fields of study. It takes a fresh understanding of social context to envision a different American society.

3.8.2. Contextual Reasoning

Feminists focus particularly on the social and personal histories of the parties involved, the parties' respective perspectives of one another, and the larger context when analyzing discrimination. The idea that actual people's everyday lives matter—that is, that "the personal is the political," as the bumper sticker puts it—is implicit in this vision. "[W]ho makes breakfast, who gets a paycheck, who gets whistled at in the street—all the experiences of daily life are a part of the distribution of wealth and power in society," writes Mari Matsuda, capturing this idea.

Some people think that women are more likely to be empirically linked to context and experience sensitivity. For years, feminists have used the realities of private life as a catalyst for social and legislative change that benefits women. Suffragettes maintained that granting women the ability to vote would enhance governance by enabling them to contribute their morality and unique perspectives to public debates. Concerned for families endangered by alcoholic husbands who wasted money and mistreated their spouses and kids, some feminists supported the temperance movement. More recently, feminists have documented the unjust and sometimes tragic consequences faced by women and children in domestic violence and divorce cases, which has led to often dramatic changes in the legal treatment of these cases. Accounts of firsthand experience are now common in legal scholarship, courtroom briefs, and even the opinions of judges.

3.8.3. Consciousness-Raising

ugh which people share their individual experiences with others in an attempt toto extract meaning or significance for the group as a whole is known as consciousness-raising. "The arts of human intercourse; the art of understanding other people's lives and minds, and the little arts of talk," as Virginia Woolf put it, are its catalysts. Through consciousness-raising, women start to see signs of larger societal oppression in what would otherwise seem to be isolated incidents of chauvinism or insensitivity. Through this exercise, participants can also more easily uncover unconscious prejudices and determine which personal contexts are best for examining issues. For example, a pattern of women's suffering and misfortune in the narrative makes participants doubt the purported objectivity of the laws. Women's stories disproved the idea that the law is impartial and fair. "Women who are currently told that strict enforcement of the legal guarantee of equal pay for equal work has created an abstract condition called 'equality' look at their own experience as underpaid workers and then redefine 'equality' as equal pay for work of equal value," says Mari Matsuda, providing a concrete example. Drawing broad conclusions about institutional oppression from individual observations validates the integration of the political and personal and grounds social theory in real-world experience. Furthermore, participants receive reassurance from sharing stories through consciousness raising that they are not alone or misguided in their observations. Instead, this kind of cooperation gives the group a feeling of unity and the ability to redefine "the meaning of women's social experience."

Many people associate consciousness-raising with small, interactive groups, such as knitting circles, book clubs, or exercise classes. However, the landscape has been greatly expanded by digital and broadcast media. Television hosts Oprah and Ellen, feminist and Jezebel blogs, and an endless supply of amateur confessionals on YouTube are all available to us. It's open to interpretation where to draw the lines between voyeurism, politics, entertainment, and discussion. However, that might be the tipping point for a movement that is so wary of nooks and entreaties to "fit in."

The fundamental principles of consciousness-raising are the same whether it is done in an official or informal setting, on a global or personal scale: acceptance of individual viewpoint, public significance of private life, and dedication to group engagement. Similar to contextual reasoning and the techniques for exposing patriarchy, the process itself is more important than the outcome. In and of itself, telling stories promotes "spiritual and humane values."

3.8.4. Pulling it Together

3.8.4.1. Telling a Story

We'll use an example to demonstrate how feminist strategies can unite into a legal movement. Consider Gloria, a single mother who recently moved into a rented home in her new city's industrial area. She works as a server at a nearby restaurant on an hourly basis. Marcus, her son, recently enrolled in the neighborhood elementary school. For the first few weeks, everything goes smoothly, but then bad luck strikes. By mid-autumn, Marcus starts having breathing issues. He can't catch his breatcoughs and wheezes. Theredays when Marcus's issue is so severe that he has tomust miss school. Gloria wouldwill have to forfeit a day's pay if she chooses to stay home from work to take care of Marcus. Marcus has asthma, the doctor says, and she gives him medication. It helps, but not always, so Gloria and Marcus continue to miss work and school because it can be difficult to find trustworthy childcare, particularly for a sick child. Gloria's women's Bible stud a conversation one day about children's health. Gloria finds out that a number ofseveral mothers in her neighborhood are also absent from school, frequently on the same days, due to asthma in their young children. Gloria looks up information about this issue online with the other moms. They search medical websites, read blogs about environmental justice, and share their findings on each other's Facebook pages. They discover that air pollution can greatly exacerbate childhood asthma attacks, which are at an all-time high. Gloria lives near a city power plant that releases some of the most annoying pollutants into the air every day. For local asthma sufferers, those chemicals can be dangerous in the right temperature and humidity conditions. There are additional hazards from other chemicals that the power plant emits. For example, there are new warnings regarding locally caught fish that state that all women of childbearing age should limit their diets to one fish meal per month due to mercury fallout from the plant, according to some evidence.

Some people write Gloria and the other mothers off as "nervous Nellies" or, worse, "hysterical housewives" when they complain to the operators of the power plant and state officials. A plant spokesman speculates that inadequate pest control, bad housekeeping, or incorrect medication use could be the cause of the kid's respiratory attacks. Regarding the fish warnings, the cost of providing people with clear instructions on how to protect themselves outweighs the sacrifice made because stricter regulations would significantly increase the cost to the state's power generato2. *Analyzing the Story*

This hypothetical but fact-based account raises a number ofseveral potential applications for feminist legal theory. Let's begin by exposing patriarchy and discussing Bartlett's "woman question." Gloria quickly discovers that the laws of employment do not offer much of a safety net when illness strikes a single-parent family. How does law in this situation "fail to take into account the experiences and values that seem more typical of women than of men"? Gloria's employer is not required by law to give her paid or unpaid time off while she takes care of her son. Her employer might not be able to provide the time off she took, and it could hurt her chances of getting promoted. Drop-in childcare for sick children is not guaranteed by any law or public program. Laws pertaining to health and insurance may not always guarans like Marcus receive inexpensive prescription medications avepreventive care. Gloria's cheap house was probably situated in close proximity tonear a hazardous power plant due to zoning and land use regulations, or the other way around. Environmental regulations allow pollution levels that are unhealthy for young women and children with asthma who consume fish. Gloria is finally written off as an overly sentimental woman by state representatives tasked with upholding health and safety regulations.

Several of these components clearly show a bias toward men. The remark about "hysterical housewives" purposefully uses stereotypes rather than reason to support its claim. Women are disadvantaged compared to men by the pollution standards that affect fish, though this bias imost likely unintentional. (Is it relevant?) However, further research is needed oninto some disparities. In and of itself, policies such as progressive zoning, childcare, affordable healthcare, paid leave, and pollution protection for children with asthma do not discriminate based on a person's sex. However, an outcome that is detrimental to women arises when we take into account that single parents are typically mothers, who shoulder the majority of leave obligations and childcare issues. Women are disproportionately affected by public health laws that affect children because they are more likely than men to care for sick children. Lastly, laws pertaining to land use and zoning that prioritize affluent neighborhoods over impoverished ones are more likely to negatively impact single mothers, who are a less affluent class than single fathers.

Contextualizing the legal issues follows the realization that Gloria's issues are a result of laws that are discriminatory against women. We have already partially completed this as part of the unmasking procedure. Knowing the demographics of single parents and primary caregivers, for example, was necessary to uncover the gendered effects of insurance policies and employment-leave policies. However, contextual thinking is not limited to this. Gloria uses her own specialized knowledge to connect pollution and illness—a connection that appears to have eluded even health officials—when she puts together the pieces of information surrounding Marcus's asthma, such as the nationwide spike in diagnoses, the correlation with specific weather conditions, and the evidence of other children missing school on the same days. Gloria and her fellow activists will be able to frame this "public health" issue as an ecological issue thanks to their shared understanding of the context, which could result in alliances with environmental advocates.

Finally, having friends helped Gloria's investigation. In this instance, the friendship came from a church group. Other feminist initiatives start in a bridge club, a yoga studio, or the parking lot of a local elementary school. The idea is that people gather to exchange insights, observations, and theories. A "big picture" is created by exchanging and sorting ideas, connecting women's everyday experiences with more significant political and economic forces. Political movements can emerge occasionally. Gloria moves from "me" to "us" and then, at last, to "we," making the crucial transition from object to subject. They discover that the laws that are upheld for us mold our everyday experiences, and that we have the power to alter the laws that do not serve us well.

REFERENCES

1. Baker, P., & Zeleny, J. (2009). Obama chooses Hispanic judge for Supreme Court seat. *The New York Times*, p. A1.
2. Batlan, F., Hradsky, K., Jeschke, K., Meyer, L., & Roberts, J. (2009). Not our mother's law school: A third wave feminist study of women's experiences in law school. *University of Baltimore Law Forum, 39*, 124–151.
3. Beauvoir, S. D. (1952). The second sex: Introduction. In S. K. C. R. McCann (Ed.), *Feminist Theory Reader: Local and Global Perspectives* (pp. 40–44). Routledge.
4. Case, M. A. C. (1995). Disaggregating gender from sex and sexual orientation: The effeminate man in the law and feminist jurisprudence. *Yale Law Journal, 105*, 1–105.
5. Chamallas, M. (2013). Chapter 2: Three generations of feminist legal theory. In *Introduction to Feminist Legal Theory* (p. 18). Walter Kluwer Law and Business.
6. Cohen, D. S. (2009). No boy left behind? Single-sex education and the essentialist myth of masculinity. *Indiana Law Journal, 84*, 135–188.
7. Collier, R. S. (2009). The fathers' rights movement, law reform, and the new politics of fatherhood: Some reflections on the UK experience. *University of Florida Journal of Law and Public Policy, 20*, 65–111.
8. Collinson, D. L. (1988). Engineering humor: Masculinity, joking and conflict in shop-floor relations. *Organization Studies, 9*, 181–199.
9. Connell, R. W., Hearn, J., & Kimmel, M. S. (2005). Introduction. In M. S. Kimmel, J. Hearn, & R. W. Connell (Eds.), *Handbook of Studies on Men and Masculinities* (pp. 1–34). Sage.
10. Cooper, F. R. (2009). Who's the man? Masculinities studies, Terry stops, and police training. *Columbia Journal of Gender and Law, 18*, 671–742.
11. Crenshaw, K. (1989). Demarginalizing the intersection of race and sex: A black feminist critique of antidiscrimination doctrine, feminist theory, and antiracist politics. *University of Chicago Legal Forum, 1989*, 139–167.
12. Dowd, N. E. (2008). Masculinities and feminist legal theory. *Wisconsin Journal of Law, Gender and Society, 23*, 201–248.
13. Eagly, A. H., & Karau, S. J. (2002). Role congruity theory of prejudice toward female leaders. *Psychological Review, 109*, 573–598.
14. Ehrenreich, N. (2002). Subordination and symbiosis: Mechanisms of mutual support between subordinating systems. *University of Missouri-Kansas City Law Review, 71*, 251–324.

15. Fineman, M. A. (2009). Introduction: Feminist and queer legal theory. In M. A. Fineman, J. E. Jackson, & A. P. Romero (Eds.), *Feminist and Queer Legal Theory: Intimate Encounters, Uncomfortable Conversations* (pp. 1–6). Ashgate.
16. Foschi, M., Wallen, A. S., Fuchs, D., & Tamkins, M. M. (1994). Gender and double standards in the assessment of job applicants. *Social Psychology Quarterly, 57*(4), 326–339.
17. Harper, M. C. (2010). The causation standard in federal employment law: *Gross v. FBL Financial Services, Inc.*, and the unfulfilled promise of the Civil Rights Act of 1991. *Buffalo Law Review, 58*, 69–145.
18. Harris, A. P. (2000). Gender, violence, race, and criminal justice. *Stanford Law Review, 52*, 777–807.
19. Heilman, M. E., Wallen, A. S., Fuchs, D., & Tamkins, M. M. (2004). Penalties for success: Reactions to women who succeed at male gender-typed tasks. *Journal of Applied Psychology, 89*, 416–427.
20. Hogue, M., & Lord, R. G. (2007). A multilevel, complexity theory approach to understanding gender bias in leadership. *Leadership Quarterly, 18*(4), 370–390.
21. Hollander, E., & Samons, D. M. (2003). Male menopause: An unexplored area of men's health. *Psychiatric Annals, 33*, 497–500.
22. Hulett, D. M., Bendick, M., Thomas, S. Y., & Moccio, F. (2008). Enhancing women's inclusion in firefighting in the USA. *International Journal of Diversity in Organizations, Communities and Nations, 8*(2), 189–208.
23. Kimmel, M. S. (2004). Masculinity as homophobia. In P. F. Murphy (Ed.), *Feminism & Masculinities* (pp. 182–199). Oxford University Press.
24. Kisthardt, E. S. (2007). Singling them out: The influence of the "boy crisis" on the new Title IX regulations. *Wisconsin Women's Law Journal, 22*, 313–337.
25. Satinoff, D. L. (1998). Sex-based discrimination in U.S. immigration law: The high court's lost opportunity to bridge the gap between what we say and what we do. *The American University Law Review, 47*, 1353–1392.
26. Sen, A. (2006). *Identity and Violence: The Illusion of Destiny*. Penguin Books.
27. West, R. (2018). Women in the legal academy: A brief history of feminist legal theory. *Fordham Law Review, 87*, 977–1008.

Chapter 4

The Gendered Nature of Crime and Punishment

Contents

INTRODUCTION

The relationship between gender, crime, and punishment is a complex and multifaceted issue that reflects broader societal norms and power dynamics. Historically, crime and punishment have been deeply gendered, with societal expectations and stereotypes shaping how men and women are perceived in relation to criminal behavior. Men have traditionally been viewed as the primary perpetrators of crime, particularly violent offenses, leading to a criminal justice system that is largely designed with male offenders in mind. This has resulted in harsher penalties for crimes typically associated with masculinity, such as violent crimes, while often overlooking or misinterpreting crimes where women are the primary offenders.

Women, on the other hand, have been stereotyped as passive, nurturing, and inherently less criminally inclined. When women do engage in criminal behavior, it is often perceived through the lens of these gender norms, which can lead to different outcomes in terms of punishment. For example, women may receive more lenient sentences due to perceptions of them being more reformable or because their crimes are seen as extensions of their roles as caregivers. Conversely, when women commit crimes that starkly contradict gender norms, such as violent crimes, they may face harsher judgments as they are seen as transgressing both legal and societal expectations.

Furthermore, the gendered nature of crime and punishment extends to the experiences of individuals within the criminal justice system. Women prisoners, for instance, often face conditions that fail to address their specific needs, such as those related to motherhood or reproductive health. Overall, the intersection of gender with crime and punishment reveals how societal constructs of masculinity and femininity influence the ways in which justice is administered and experienced. Understanding this dynamic is crucial for developing a more equitable criminal justice system that acknowledges and addresses these gendered disparities.

4.1. GENDER PERSPECTIVE OF VICTIMIZATION, CRIME, AND PENAL POLICY

Compared to men, women commit far fewer crimes. This holds true for almost all crimes, however there are somless commoncommon in terms of the involvement of women in the commission of particular crimes. Furthermore, since there aren't many crimes committed by women, a small increase in total numbers could result in an unexpectedly large increase. According to Heidensohn, women made up between 10 and 20% of all those involved in criminal proceedings in a number of European nations. However, historical research indicates that this share does not differ significantly from current levels, with rare exceptioomen's crimecrime rates stayed steady or even slightly decreased throughout the 20th century, despite an increase in overall crime rates. On the other hand, self-reported studies on delinquency have revealed that more girls than boys are reluctant to acknowledge that they have committed a crime. This resulted in the conclusion that there is a smaller gender gap, particularly when it comes to juvenile crime.

In addition, the rise in female arrests, convictions, and incarcerations—particularly for drug- and assault-related offenses—suggested that they are growing increasingly aggressive. Concerning the features of female criminality, women commit less serious crimes than men do, including minor traffic violations, prostitution, drug offenses, theft, handling stolen property, fraud, and forgeries.he majority ofmost women who commit crimes do so for the first time. There are very few women who could be classified as professional offenders.

Men are the most common perpetrators of violent crimes, so it makes sense that men are also the most common victims of violent crimes. This differs depending on the kind of violent crime, though. Homicide victims who are men are more prevalent than those who are women. The relationship between the perpetrator and the victim varies; women are more frequently killed by a current or past intimate partner, whereas men are more frequently killed by a stranger or acquaintance. "The likelihood of women becoming victims of specific types of victimization, like rape and domestic abuse, is significantly higher than that of men." Despite these variations, victimology explanations cannot be limited to the gender perspeg into accountconsidering other victimological factors, such as race and class, that affect the likelihood of victimization. In addition, it ike into accountconsider societal norms, broader social, political, and economic contexts, as well as variations in victimization rates among nations.

Many scholars focus on the court's penal policy from a gender perspective. While some academics contend that women have received preferential treatment over men, others draw attention to the fact that women commit fewer serious crimes overall, and particularly fewer violent ones. To help explain this potential difference is the idea that they are less likely to be recidivists. Although the proportion of women incarcerated is generally stable, certain countries have seen a greater increase in the proportion of women in prisons over the past few decades. There are several reasons why this increase is occurring. While some claim that women are becoming more violent and involved in crime in general, others point to changes in how formal social control is reacted to. There is a discernible difference between extra-legal and legal factors when it comes to sentencing disparities between genders.

For policymakers, each of these issues is crucial. Analysis of victimization and criminal offending reveals that these experiences frequently reflect gender expressions that need to be understood in relation to class and race. The criminological perspective is useful because it can shed light on the following topics: the true scope of crime and victimization; the significance of gender; victimization patterns not covered by the criminal code; and the effects and ramifications for victims. In order to prevent crime, create gender-sensitive criminal law legislation, and implement legal norms in the real world, policymakers should make use of this knowledge.

4.1.1. Gender and Crime

4.1.1.1. Crime Trends in Europe from Gender Perspective

Regarding gender, crime, and criminal justice in Europe, there are nine potential data sources, but none of them provide comprehensive information. Some people believe that the European Sourcebook on Crime and Justice Statistics (henceforth referred to as the "European Sourcebook") is the most trustworthy source, despite certain gaps. The data from it are therefore briefly presented in this section.

There are observable differences when it comes to the crimes that women commit in European countries. The proportion of female offenders per 100,000 people varies, ranging from at least 4% in Georgia to 26% in Greece, according to the most recent data available from the European Sourcebook for 2015 (police statistics). Germany, Luxembourg, Poland, and Austria have higher percentages of women than males. On the other hand, less than 8% of the total was found in Moldova, Azerbaijan, Albania, Croatia, and Montenegro. Data is available for fifteen European countries from 2006 to, 2015; eight of them exhibit a percentage increase in the share of women. In only two of these eight countries did the total number of perpetrators per 100,000 population increase concurrently. Other nations demonstrated a decrease in the number of offenders, either with or without notable fluctuations (Table 4.1).

Table 4.1. *ercentage of Women fFrom European Countries Among Offenders in 2015—Criminal Offenses: Total Offenders*

State	Total Offenders Per 100,000 Pop.	of Which % Women	State	Total Offenders Per 100,000 Pop.	of Which % Women
Albania	1178.6	7.9	Italy	1586.3	18.5
Armenia	364.4	12.2	Latvia	1169.9	12.5
Austria	2918.8	20.8	Lithuania	919.5	10.5

Azerbaijan	170.1	6.9	Luxembourg	5051.2	23.7
Bulgaria	566.8	13.4	Moldova	482.7	7.7
Croatia	1425.7	7.9	Montenegro	579.7	7.1
Cyprus	698.3	8.7	Netherlands	1784.3	16.3
Czech Republic	966.1	15.6	Poland	840.4	11.3
Finland	4788.1	18.6	Portugal	1803.1	20.2
France	1748.4	17.9	Serbia	694.5	10.9
Georgia	567.8	4.5	Slovenia	2191.9	18.6
Germany	2917.6	24.8	Spain	684.9	13.9
Greece	1022.5	26.2	Sweden	1796.5	20.9
Hungary	1004.4	16.3	Switzerland	1670.5	20.2
Iceland	1176.8	23.0	Ukraine	313.1	11.7
Mean	1335	15.0	Minimum	0	4.5
Median	1013	14.8	Maximum	5051	26

Source: European sourcebook of crime and criminal justice statistics 2021, sixth edition.

Example 1

There has been a noticeable decline in the reported female offender homicide rate between 2006 and 2015. While the average percentage of women reported as victims of homicide was 9% in 2006 and 13.1% in 2010, in all countries that provided data, this share was less than 1% in 2015. Conversely, a higher proportion of women than men experience physical harm (since this data is the most comprehensive, data was observed for both mild and severe forms of physical harm). Nearly fourteen (almost 80%) of the eighteen countries that provided data showed an increase during the observed period of 2006–2015, spanning at least two years.

Table 4.2. *Percentage of Women From European Countries Among Convicted Persons in 2015—Criminal Offenses: Total Offenders*

State	Total Offenders Per 100,000 Pop.	Of Which % Women	State	Total Offenders Per 100,000 Pop.	Of Which % Women
Albania	559	5.5	Latvia	481	11.8
Armenia	94	7.7	Lithuania	636	9.6
Austria	374	14.2	Luxembourg	1498	20.8
Belgium	1614	18.3	Netherlands	546	12.6

Bulgaria	386	8.4	Poland	684	10.3
Croatia	308	11.4	Portugal	597	12.2
Cyprus	6387	20.0	Serbia	494	9.2
Czech Republic	622	15.1	Spain	673	13.6
Finland	3321	20.8	Sweden	1095	17.3
France	864	10.1	Switzerland	1505	16.8
Georgia	406	6.3	Turkey	1971	5.4
Germany	911	19.8	Ukraine	222	11.6
Hungary	728	11.8	UK: England and Wales	2158	29.5
Italy	363	16.6	UK: Northern Ireland	1317	16.8
Latvia	481	11.8	UK: Scotland	1860	16.9
Mean	1014	13.8	Minimum	94	5.4
Median	622	12.6	Maximum	6387	29.5

Source: European sourcebook of crime and criminal justice statistics 2021, sixth edition.

The most recent conviction statistics data for 2015 that is currently available indicates that the mean percentage of women was 13.8%. Turkey had the lowest percentage share of women convicted (5.4%), while England and Wales had the highest value (29.5%) for the same year. More than 20% of women who were convicted were also found in Finland, Cyprus, and Luxembourg.

Example 2

The average percentage of women found guilty of killing someone varied from 7% in 2006 to 9.5% in 2015. Among the nations with the highest percentage of women convicted of homicide in 2015 were Austria and Finland (16%). The countries with the lowest percentage of women convicted of this crime were Albania (2.9%) and Turkey (2.6%). Fraud is another example of a crime. In 2015, Georgia had the lowest percentage at 0.4%, and Scotland had the highest percentage at 48.6%. The Czech Republic (34%), Germany (33.9%), Finland (33.8%), England and Wales (32.7%), and Switzerland (31.9%) all had high percentages as well (Table 4.2).

A lack of data preventsncomparison with police records for many countries. Several countries do not follow the trend, according to the data submitted by the countries; changes in conviction records do not correspond with changes in police statistics. Albania is a prime example of opposing trends, as the proportion of women with police records is rising while judicial statistics are falling. Similar trends can be seen in Sweden, where police statistics show a rise in the proportion of women while judicial statistics show a decrease. In Finland, however, there has been a decrease in the number of female police records and an increase in judicial records between 2006 and 2015. Poland provides an illustration of comparable patterns, with the percentage of women in both data sources consistently rising. Thus, there are no commonalities amongst European nations, even in the absenceoughthorough analysis. The assertions made in the literature regarding the widening gender gap should be taken with a grain of salt because they might only apply to the nations where the studies were carried out.

For instance, Jennifer Schwartz's study contained information on women who were reported and found guilty in the United States, Canada, the United Kingdom, Finland, Norway, and Sweden. The underlying premise of the study was that every level of the criminal justice system ought to account for the actual rise in female-perpetrated crime. The assault to homicide ratio and the arrest to incarceration case flow were examined by the author. This study concludes, among other things, that the UK is an anomaly when it comes to the rise in the proportion of female prosecutions. In Finland, Norway, and Sweden, the proportion of women remained largely unchanged. Thus, between 1997 and 2006, there was a consistent and significant increase (10%) in the United Kingdom but not in the Scandinavian countries. The auusionconcluded that this supports the theory of policy change rather than a real shift in the criminal behavior of women.

The trend of the percentage of women in the population and the trend of convicted people per 100,000 people do not always line up, according to judicial statistics data. It is necessary to take this into account before drawing any conclusions. It is plausible that extraneous variables may account for the variation in crime rates among males and females.

Example 3

In Germany, the percentage of women convicted increased between 2011 and 2015, but the percentage of all convicted individuals decreased during that same period. Similar circumstances were observed in Finland, Croatia, Finland and Wales, Poland, and England. In contrast, the situation in Albania is completely different, with a rise in the number of convicted people and a decrease in the proportion of women convicted.

The rise in female-perpetrated crime is typically explained in two ways in literature. The first perspective holds that as women's status and gender roles become more liberal, there is a corresponding rise in the number of criminal offenses. Due to these changes, women now have more opportunities and can commit crimes more frequently. Furthermore, it is asserted that women now exhibit "imitative male machismo competitiveness" ane freefreer to be assertive due to the "changing gender-role expectations." These changes have also been characterized as "masculinizing" female behavior. Adler promoted the masculinization thesis and forecast a rise in violent crimes by women, while Simon emphasized the need for greater labor market participation to increase the number of opportunities for crimes, particularly property and occupational ones. The opposing thesis, which focuses on economic marginalization, contends that as women's lives change, their economic standing deteriorates, divorce rates rise, and as a result, there are more single mothers, which raises the likelihood of female criminal activity. This could be explained by the fact that women are more reliant on the private sphere than men are in terms of both personal and economic standing. Family dynamics play a preventive role in women's involvement in criminal activity, particularly when it comes to traditional gender roles. Increased criminal activity may result from the deterioration of traditional family relationships and social control, which are features of social development, as well as potential stress and annoyance experienced besult ofbecause of their marginalized economic status. Women who are members of marginalized groups—like low-income women, members of ethnic minorities, and residents of chaotic urban areas—are undoubtedly the most impacted. The premise of economic marginalization is based on the observation that the majority of women who are convicted are disproportionately from the "underclass," far from being liberated. For instance, it is said of Russia that "there is a correlation between the rise in Russian women involved in criminal cases and the country's worsening socioeconomic conditions, rising rates of psychological disorders and issues with drug dependence, and a growing level of discrimination."

Different conclusions are indicated by the conducted studies results. It is noted that while improvements in women's status tend to lead to a decrease in violent crimes, particularly homicide, they also cause an increase in other types of crime, including property crimes, drug offenses, and fraud. Simon's 1963–1970 study examined the female recidivismenty fivetwenty-five nations and came to the conclusion that the highest increases were seen in those with more developed industrial and technological sectors. Results from a thirty-year study (1962–1995) pointed to a similar conclusion. According to the findings of this cross-national study, women are more likely to commit property crimes like theft and fraud in countries where they have greater levels of education, are more represented in the labor force, and have lower rates of fertility. The study, which examined women's crime statisnty seventwenty-seven European nations in 2006, reaffirms the significance of the liberalization thesis and how it affects the rise in property crimes like theft, fraud, embezzlement, and larceny. Reckdenwald and Parker, on the other hand, emphasize the significance of economic marginalization on female crime and attest to the fact that this element plays a role in explaining drug-related crimes, property crimes (particularly robberies), homicide in intimate relationship, and domestic abuse. Nevertheless, the authors came to the conclusion that economic marginalization has a different effect on drug-reery crimesrobberies than it does on domestic violence. In this case, power, social support, and resource scarcity all play major roles in creating pressure and frustration. Liberation and economic marginalization are intertwined, as demonstrated by Hunticut and Broidy. They discovered statistical evidence to support the idea that female conviction rates are impacted by economic marginality. Nevertheless, a positive correlation was found between female conviction rates and two emancipation variables (women in industry and age-dependency ratio).

It can be contended, nevertheless, that policy changes rather than behavioral shifts by women are the cause of the rise in criminal activity. Steffensmeier and associates. declare that the three components of policy change are as follows: a) the flexibility of definitions for violence, b) the breadth of offence categories, and c) the variation in the relationship between gender and violence based on behavior or item content. According to the first component, there is a great deal of latitude for citizens, law enforcement, and other officials to define violence. The second component suggests that broad behaviors are included in the definitions of crimes, such as simple and aggravated assault. Lastly, the third component suggests thas less of aless gender difference when less serious violent crimes are committed against an inmate in a private setting, with a lesser level of guilt.

It should be highlighted that the way that women and, particularly, young girls are portrayed in the media has a big influence on these shifting trends in the criminal justice system. According to Chesney-Lind, "whereas violence against juvenile girls represents a threat for a social order, when male juvenile violence increases, the media's response is 'So, wlse ishe fact thatEven though official data and victimization reports refute claims of a rise in female-perpetrated crime, young girls are frequently portrayed as "cruel," "mean," "sneaky," and "lying" in books, articles, and media.

4.1.2. Factors of Criminal Offending from Gender Perspective

Theoretical explanations in criminology, which did not consider the gender difference in theory, were influenced by the prevalence of male criminality. One of the reasons women's criminals are neglected in criminology is the low rate of female involvement in crime. However, as Smart points out, due to the nature of these offenses as well as the rarity of women's crimes, criminality among women has not been seen as posing as big of a threat to society as that of men. Women typically commit less serious crimes than men do. "Criminology is androcentric, shaped by male experiences and understanding of the social world," claim Daly and Chesney-Lind. Theories of crime that disregard the experiences of women as perpetrators or victims are shaped by these realities. Thus, the question of whether and to what extent men and women have different paths to crime arises.

The Pathway theory states that there are differences between how men and women enter the criminal justice system. A history of personal abuse, mental illness, substance abuse, economic and social marginalization, homelessness, and relationships are some of the factors that are more significant for female criminality.

Diverse paths of female criminality were identified by feminist criminology qualitative research. Daly's classification, which comprises five pathways, is one of the most frequently cited. (1) Women who harm others are those who experienced abuse or neglect as children. These women are labeled as "problem children," acting out and turning violent after consuming alcohol. This group is also prone to drug abuse and psychological issues; (2) battered women are those who are in violent relationships or have recently ended one; and (3) street women are those who are pushed out or who flee from abusive homes. They typically steal, commit prostitution, and commit drug-related offenses; (4) women with drug connections become addicted to drugs through their relationships with boyfriends or by selling drugs; (5) other women commit crimes out of greed or dire financial situations. Their offenses have nothing to do with drug abuse or living on the streets.

Pathways of harming and harmed men, street men, and drug-connected men were also identified, but 35% of the sample's male participants chose male-only pathways, per Daly. Men were divided into three categories: (1) "explosively violent men," who used violence to dominate or control others; (2) "bad luck men," who were either taken advantage of by other men or who reacted negatively to men who harassed them; and (3) "masculine gaming men," who committed crimes as a way to pass the time or show off their masculinity. Male's paths to crime did not fit this classification.

Russell and others. compared the paths taken by men and women to prison in their study, finding three common paths: (1) association with deviant peer groups or peer group affiliation; (2) harm and harming; and (3) economic motivation. On the other hand, two paths were designated exclusively for women: (1) victimization during adulthood and unhealthy personal relationships, and (2) naivety and dishonesty. Additionally, there were two categories of pathways driven by economic motivation: (1) economic, familial provisioning (women commit property crimes on average, and half of them are impoverished). Typically, they were financially dependent on their children and other family members, and (2) greed (limited to men).

With respect to gender perspective in the following text presents some of these crime factors on three different levels: individual, family, and social/ societal.

4.1.2.1. Individual-Levemakes

A number ofseveral initial arguments regarding the explanations for women's criminality, including the claim that women commit crimes because of their biological inferiority. According to him, female offenders are twice as deviant. First, because they are an exception when it comes to male offenders; and second, because women who commit crimes go against their natural tendencies. Such theories are out of date, but the question of biological influences is still important. Some believe that biological predispositions explain why men commit violent crimes in comparison to women. Nevertheless, a thorough examination of studies related to antisocial behavior that have been done in the fields of genetics, structural brain imaging, neuropsychology, psychophysiology, and hormones revealed that many of these risk factors are connected to criminal and antisocial behavior in both men and women. The Dunedin Multidisciplinary Health and Development Study, which examined heart rate and neurological abnormalities, was unable to find a statistically significant gender difference. Regarding potential distinctions, certain writers mention asymmetry in the brain. In the brains of antisocial girls, there is more frontal activn on the right thanthan on the left. Antisocial boys did not exhibit this. Moreover, premenstrual syndrome and menstruation may have an impact on female criminality. Among those who support this connection is Dalton. She investigated the relationship between menstrual cycle phases and criminal behavior using a sample of female prisoners. She came to the conclusion that nearly half of the sample's respondents had committed a crime either right before or during their menstruation. It has been investigated whether testosterone levels in males are associated with aggressive behavior, but the results emphasize the significance of mediating social factors.

Psychological theories offer additional explanations for female criminality in addition to the biological ones mentioned previously. For instance, Freud thought that women were less valuable than men. Pollak claims that women are more capable of manipulating than men, are inherently inconsistent, sly, and vindictive, while Thomas cultivates the myth of the manipulative woman. Regarding certain personality quirks, Dunedin's research indicates that there are no appreciable variations between male and female offenders concerning IQ, reading proficiency, challenging disposition, hyperactivity, or internalizing issues. Some people believe that women have lower crime rates because they develop their social cognitive skills earlier in life and have stronger pro-social abilities. Moreover, the lower involvement of women in crime may be explained by Gilligan's theory of moral development. This theory holds that women base their moral decisions on a "ethic of care," whereas men frequently base their decisions on an ethic of justice, which is a set of rules and principles. Women will think about the impact committing a crime would have on their dependent family members. It is possible for a woman to commit a crime if her needs—such as her need for food—outweigh the "immorality of crime."

Scientific findings on the relationship between mental illness and criminality are contradictory. There were no gender differences in psychiatric disorders among homicide offenders in a Finnish study. According to a meta-analysis comprising 62 completed studies, female prisoners did not exhibit a higher prevalence of mental illness than male prisoners. The study reveals that although women with personality disorders are not insignificant, they are more common in the prison population among men. Regarding antisocial and borderline personality traits, it is said that there are no appreciable variations based on gender for both victims and perpetrators of domestic violence. Nonetheless, other research indicates that a greater percentage of female offenders experience mental health issues due to higher levels of violence. The fact that there are more women in prison than men with mental health issues does not always indicate that this is a risk factor; rather, the higher proportions are a reflection of the prevalence of mental illness in the broader community. Alternatively, this might just be a response to being imprisoned.

Given that alcoh addiction is a factorare factors linked to numerous crimes, it is important to discuss addiction on an individual basis. For instance, there was no discernible gender difference in homicide offenders.

4.1.2.1. Family Level

The primary context for comprehending juvenile delinquency is the family environment. In this context, a number of factors stand out: poor parenting techniques; family disarray; low socioeconomic status; domestic violence; parental drug and alcohol abuse; and parental criminality. Is there a difference in how these factors behave depending on the juvenile's gender? Depending on the child's gender, different educational approaches are used. In general, daughters receive more lenient treatment than sons, but they are also subject to more c limitations in order toto prevent "bad things" from happening to them as they grow up. Heimer and De Coster stress that variations in juvenile violence between male and female adolescents rely on both the kinds and the extent of parental control. These authors contend that emotional attachment to families, which results in indirect control, is what will essentially shape "girls" understanding of violent definitions. On the other hand, boys will be more direcuenced by their parent'sparents' supervision and coercive discipline when it comes to their understanding of violent definitions. Hagan noted variations in the control over girls in patriarchal, matriarchal, and egalitarian households in his theory of power control. It is concluded that as egalitarian family structures take hold, young men's delinquent behavior will decline while femalwill rise as a result ofbecause of women gaining more power at home and at work.

Research indicates that exposure to criminal activity in the family and personal victimization are linked to juvenile delinquency. Girls find themselves in a different situation than men, who experience similar events for a shorter period of time before reacting. Individuals often internalize these issues by depressive, suicidal, and withdrawing from society. Following a number of unpleasant encounters, they become combative. Many girls run away from home, steal, or drop out of school to avoid being victims of abuse within the family. Russell along with others. underline that, compared to men, women are more likely to experience substance abuse, academic failure, and victimization as adults as a result of abuse and neglect during childhood. Men who had difficult childhoods were more likely to injure others, but women were more likely to internalize their trauma through substance abuse. Family disputes were previously believed to affect male juveniles mores, with the exception ofexcept for status offenses, where the opposite was believed to be true. But according to new research, aggressive girls experienced domestic abuse at the highest frequency. Studies generally show that girls experience abuse in families more frequently than boys do. Although there is a correlation between childhood victimization and subsequent violent behavior, empirical research yields different results. Asscher along with others. discover that, for males, any type of violent victimization was a predictor of violent offenses, but only physical abuse was a predictor of female violence. For males, sexual victimization was a stronger predictor of sex offenses. Research indicates that early exposure to intimate partner violence plays a significant role in the development of violent behavior later in life, for both men and women.

One of the things that could cause a woman to commit a crime is being victimized by a partner, as was previously mentioned in the pathways of female crime. Violence resistance is the term used to describe this kind of domestic abuse. Typically, female perpetrators are those who have experienced "intimate terrorism," which is defined as severe, one-sided violence, usually from male to female. Empirical research highlights that domestic violence has more serious repercussions (particularly physical injuries) for women, even though female partners also victimize men in situations other than self-defense. Women's violence frequently takes place in the backdrop of ongoing hostility and aggression. The literature ought to focus more on gay and lesbian couples, going beyond men who are abused by their female partners. The prevalence of domestic violence among same-sex partners is estimated t, possibly as a result ofbecause of the even greater reluctance of gay and lesbian victims to report that they have been harmed by a partner.

Example

Some estimates state that "many of the women prisoners were in violent relationships prior to their arrests, and the majority of them have experienced one or more forms of violence as children and adults." In the meantime, studies conducted over the last thirty years reveal that partner violence against a female perpetrator preceded 75% of all male victimizations in the context of partner homicide.

4.1.2.3. Social and Societal Level

Men and women are socialized into specific sex roles not only in the home but also in other social settings. These consist of peer groups, culture, and occupational structures. While cultural and societal norms and beliefs (such as gendered power relations, gendered behavioral expectations, and gendered inequality) would be considered a societal level, some authors characterize social networks as being at the social level. Bertrand claims that while "our culture is less tolerant of the foibles of young girls, it does condone and even expect a certain amount of acting out and aggressive behavior in young boys." Sutherland and Cressey emphasized that the gender gap in crime would be highest in nations where women are subject to strict supervision, like Algeria, and lowest in nations where women have the most freedom and equality with men, like Western Europe, Australia, Canada, and the United States. The disparity between crime committed by men and women depends on a number of factors, including age, community size, crime rate, and the social standing of the sexes within a country.

As a result, gender mainstreaming and behavior modification ought to be impacted by women's liberation. Women are primarily implicated in less complex crimes like embezzlement and fraud in white-collar and corporate crime. Contrarily, men are more likely to commit crimes like securities trading or restrictive agreements; as a result, women are underrepresented in higher positions within businesses and have fewer opportunities to commit these crimes. Men and women may have different reasons for committing crimes; although women may do so to meet personal or family needs, men may do so to elevate their status.

Example

One European study's findings indicate that, at least in terms of the typical incidence of white-collar crime (i.e., professional fraud), there is no distinction based on gender. The likelihood of a female committing an asset misappropriation crime is twice that of a male.

The results of the research, however, do not demonstrate that female offend Conversely, the majority ofmost female criminals have low socioeconomic status and come from chaotic social backgrounds. Even though a large percentage of women work, many of them are still economically marginalized and only work part-time or for low pay. For some of these women, turning to criminal activity might seem like the right course of action. As Smart notes, "the status of black and working-class women may actually have deteriorated, while middle-class women have benefited from changes in the labor market." An increasing number of women who are single mothers are facing worsening financial circumstances as a result of more frequent divorces.

The contribution made by feminist studies is also evident in the question of what makes men criminals—not because they are working-class, subservient, or immigrants, but rather because of theResearchers that looked intoinvestigated relationship, domestic, and rape violence came to the conclusion that men view these crimes as the pinnacle of masculinity. Critics of this viewpoint counter that masculinity is contingent on age, race, and class. It's likely that a crime will be committed if there is no way to exhibit masculinity through legal methods. Corporate crimes are just as much a part of proving one's manhood as street crimes. Although some authors explain women's crime in terms of doing femininity, others point out that it is necessary to question the explanations in terms of doing femininity or masculinity. Just as men can commit crimes because of their masculinity, the question is whether women commit crimes as a manifestation of their femininity. First of all, the idea that men's actions only represent "masculinity" and women's actions only represent "femininity" is limited to gender dualism and is a tautology. Secondly, disparities in gender ought to be combined with those pertaining to race, class, and age.associates. study a number ofseveral research findings and come to the conclusion that there is a repertoire of interacting class, race, and gender identities rather than a set "class," "race," or "gender" experience. Additionally, multiracial (multicultural) feminism is promoted by this intersectional approach. This viewpoint highlights the importance of distinctions based on class, race, sexual orientation, age, physical ability, and nationality just as much as gender. Other types of inequality that affect people in different ways and at different levels, both micro and macro, shouldn't take precedence over gender inequality. These assertions are supported by criticisms of the dominance approach, which holds that patriarchy affects all women equally. Rather, it is important to recognize the diversity that exists among women. This viewpoint provides an explanation for why some wealthy middle-class women choose to commit crimes, but not all marginalized women choose to commit crimes. The way a concrete person moves through various foion determines whether or notwhether th the law and whether or notwhether they achieve their goals or desires. Gender, race, and class can either improve one's standing in society or limit options. Men have more options than women, white people have more options than people of color, and the wealthy have more opportunities than the underprivileged.

4.2. CRIMINAL VICTIMIZATION FROM A GENDER PERSPECTIVE

4.2.1. Domestic Violence

The Council of Europe's Istanbul Convention, also known as CETS No. 210, was created to prevent and combat violence against women and domestic abuse. It was made available for signatures on May 11, 2011. Thirty-three of the forty-five countries that signed the convention ten years ago have ratified it. This treaty prohibits violence against women.

4.2.1.1. Definition

"Defined as any act, whether occurring in public or private life, that results in "physical, sexual, psychological, or economic harm or suffering to women, including threats of such acts, coercion, or arbitrary deprivation of liberty."

Combating men's violence against women is on the World Health Organization's agenda. Domestic violence is a recognized global public health problem, with one in three women having experienced it at some point in their lives.

In Europe, one in three women have been victims of physical or sexual abuse since they were fifteen, one in twenty have been sexually assaulted, one in two have experienced harassment online, and one in five have been stalked. Domestic violence is more common in nations with larger populations of people living in poverty, though this varies by country. The converse is also true: domestic violence rates are lower in nations with larger populations and higher socioeconomic status. Furthermore, Sub-Saharan Africa has the highest rates of domestic violence, while East Asia has the lowest rates. Moreover, recidivism rates for victims who have experienced repeated victimization range from 15 to over 40%.

Regardless of g or ethnicity, the majority ofmost studies conducted in Western societies depicabusers. Despite the fact thatEven though national laws may cause variations in the kinds of violence and behaviors, abusers are universal and more alike than different. The most frequent offenders of domestic violence can be categorized into one of two typologies: general violent and family only perpetrators. The first subtype is the abuser who is generally violent. This is the man who may lead a violent life and be involved in criminal activities. The second subtype of abusers targets only the victim and, in certain situations, other family members with violence. Other than that, they fit in with society fairly well. The primary distinction is that the typical violent abuser is more challenging to deal with because he disregards state regulations and so faces a higher risk of recidivism. The family only abuser, on the other hand, abides by the rules more strictly, which lowers the chance of relapse. However, if risk management is not implemented, both kinds run the risk of recidivism.

According to estimates, gender-based violence costs the EU 109 billion euros annually. The expenses are divided into three categories: lost economic output (11%); physical and emotional impact (48%); and health, social welfare, andstice (38%). A further 1.3% hashave been allocated to specialized services aimed at preventing violence, including counseling, support centers, helplines, and shelters. Not much money is spent on victim support and preventioenormous costs. The majority ofMany victims are female; it is an unwritten, vague law that women must willingly assist their sisters in need. States should not, however, rely on sisterhood as the cornerstone of the risk management required to assist and support women who have been subjected to severe violence. The core of the supportive work done to protect women is provided by Non-Governmental Organizations (NGOs). First and foremost, they must receive adequate funding; second, they cannot serve as the exclusive source of assistance for victims of domestic abuse. According to the Istanbul Convention and CEDAW, it is a state requirement. This varies between nations based on the administration of their welfare systems. Even in nations like Sweden, which have sizable welfare systems that are well-run, NGOs are underfunded by the government and must rely on the voluntary efforts of women to shield and assist victims of domestic abuse.

The ideal victim of domestic abuse is partially modeled by the victim support services offered. As a result, men's violence against women is now commonly associated with domestic violence. Six characteristics make up Nils Christie's theoral victims," which dates back todates to the mid-1980s. An ideal victim would be (1) weak; (2) engaged in a deferential project; (3) present in a proper setting; meanwhile, the perpetrators would be (4) "big and evil"; (5) unknown to the victim; and (6) strong enough to assert victimhood. Christie's theory thus states that a woman (weak), a mother (deferential project), somnon-violent, has no past historyhistory of substance abuse, works in a respectable field, or is a stay-at-home mother (in a legitimate place) would be the ideal victim of domestic violence. Her abuser is a man who carries out serious violent crimes ("big and evil") concurrently. She must also possess the strength to ask for and accept assistance (the ability to assert victim status). The majority of the support system is configured to meet this need. Obtaining support will be considerably more challenging if the victim is not the "ideal victim." Certain shelters, for example, cater exclusively to female victims and their small children. As a result, women who have a teenage son may not be permitted to remain at the shelter.

Furthermore, neither male victims of partner violence nor LGBTQIA+ victims of such violence can be adequately served by the support systems. It is even harder to report the crime if you're not the "ideal victim," because you don't think society could support or assist you. They may not be well received or taken seriously, which makes it harder for them to report the violence.

Due to the misconception that male victims of domestic abuse are uncommon, they do not receive the le victims. In actuality, violenceViolence against women is almost as common, even in cases of less severe forms that do not require hospitalization. An U.S. according to study estimates, between 23 and 29% of women report violent relationships with their male partners. Men's violence against women, on the other hand, is by far the most prevalent form of domestic violence when it comes to severe acts that require medical attention.

Sexual minorities are defined as "members of sexual orientations that are marginalized, such as LGBTQIA+ identities" by the Gender Equity Resource Center (2019) and are included in cases of domestic violence. Nonetheless, the scant literature on domestic violence among couples comprising sexual minorities primarily concentrates on same-sex couples, with findings indicating that domestic violence is just as prevalent, if not more so, in same-sex partnerships. In a national survey conducted in the U.S. According to the data, lesbian women experience victimization at rates between 43 and 48% higher than heterosexual women, while gay men experience victimization at a rate of 26%.

4.2.1.2. Sexual Crimes

Europe's crime statistics show that in 2009, the rate of sexual violence per 1,00,000 people ranged from 1.98 to 162.03; in 2018, it increased to 3.36 and 274.81. Liechtenstein's value was 23.61, which was the median. With rates above 158.13, England and Wales, Scotland, Northern Ireland, Sweden, and Iceland had the highest rates of sexual violence in 2018. Greece, Albania, Montenegro, and Cyprus had the lowest rates, all below 3.94. The median rate of rape victims in 2018 was 0.75, with men experiencing a range of 0.00 to 15.18. The median for women ranged from 1.91 to 147.63, with a median of 8 points. In addition, the median rate of sexual assault victims was 4.79, with men experiencing a range of 0 to 25.89. Women's rates ranged from 1.39 to 201.09, with a median of 25.65.

Example: The Nordic Paradox

Sweden (10.25 for men and 147.63 for women) and Norway (15.18 for men and 75.78 for women) have the highest rates of rape. Sweden has the highest rate of sexual assault for both men and women (25.89 and 201.09, respectively). Sweden also has the highest gender equality index value of 83.8, with the EU-28 average being 67 points. The Nordic paradox is, indeed, paradoxical: crime statistics show that the Nordic nations, especially Sweden, have the highest rates of gender-based violence alongside the highest gender equality index. A plausible explanation for this could be that the pursuit of gender equality disrupts traditional gender norms, potentially leading to increased male aggression. Another explanation might be that more victims are speaking out about gender-based violence, resulting in a rise in reports. However, many of the explanations support the existence of the paradox. More investigation is required to close this knowledge gap.

4.3. GENDER PERSPECTIVE IN RELATION TO PENAL POLICY

There is a common belief that the criminal justice system treats women less harshly than it does men. This "chivalrous" approach is evident in the way that penalties are applied. Additionally, it is present in criminal law, police responses, and the disparate treatment of males and females in correctional facicause of the text limit, the main focusfocus of this chapter is the court's penal policy. In addition to providing a European perspective on penal sanctions, this section of the chapter examines whether courts genuinely employ distinct methodologies when enforcing penalties against men and women.

4.3.1. Penalties and Sanctions on Women in Europe: Official Data

Regarding the first point, it is impossible to distinguish between men and women when it comes to the imposition of sanctions in Europe and their successful execution. Because of the disparities in information availability and regulations across the European region, the data available does not permit a comparative analysis. In any case, the European Sourcebook anil of Europe's Annual Penal Statistics—Statistics, which includes two reports on imprisonment and non-custodial sanctions and measures, respectively—are the primary sources of information on these subjects.

According to SPACE I and II, the progression of imprisonment and non-custodial sanctions imposed on women in the European context is as follows:

1. In terms of incarceration, SPACE I demonstrates that the numbers have not changed over the past few years, with 5% of the population being women and 95% of the population being men. The underrepresentation of women in correctional facilities is still a problem throughout Europe, despite regional variations. In 2020, Latvia had the highest rate (8.6%) among nations with a million or more residents, while Albania had the lowest rate (1.8%). Nonetheless, a rise in women's conviction rates throughout Europe starting in 2000 preceded this recent stabilization of the female incarceration rate. This is comparable to what is produced globally, as indicated by the most recent "World Female Imprisonment List" edition (2017). Specifically, starting in 2000, the proportion of women behind bars increased by 53% globally, while the same percentage for men inonly 20%. These numbers are in spite ofdespite the scant evidence suggesting a rise in the frequency or severity of female criminality. This is commonly referred to as a "criminal paradox." This trend can be explained by the verification of two factors: a rise in the severity of the penalties meted out by judges for crimes committed by women, and modifications to regulations raising the minimum sentence for a number of offenses. A few instances of the latter are modifications to public health. This primarily impacts female offenders, particularly those who are immigrants.
2. Regarding non-custodial penalties and measures, which the SPACE II views as probation agencies' purview, there is a discernible, albeit slight, disparity between the treatment of men and women. In 2019, the proportion of men serving non-custodial sanctions was on average 89%, for women was 11%. With the exception ofExcept for Greece and Serbia, the proportion of women serving these types of sanctions is actually higher than the proportion of women incarcerated (roughly 6% of the total population). These discrepancies could be explained by the less serious nature of the offenses as well as an estimated lower rate of recidivism among

women. In such cases, non-custodial measures might be considered more suitable.

The information presented in the European Sourcebook of Crime and Criminal Justice Statistics is in line with this data. The data also confirm that, at an average of 5%, the proportion of women incarcerated remains low. This ie overall pattern since tk'sSourcebook's 1996 debut. Actually, theThe modest shift in the percentage—from 4 to 9% in 2011 to 5 to 2% in 2016—along with a comparable pattern in the foreign population provide evidence of the relative stability of the prison population in Europe.

The data reveals the following percentages of specific crimes: the total number of convictions (both custodial and non-custodial) for women in 2015 was 13.8%; they were sentenced to prison for drug trafficking (8.5%), intentional homicides (9.5%), assaults (9.8%), rape (1%), sexual assaults in general (1.6%), robbery (6.15%), theft (15.8%), fraud (23.4%), cyber fraud (27.4%), document forgery (16.9%), money laundering (24.5%), corruption offenses (12%), and robbery (6.15%). Given that both the concentration of crimes against property and the low data pertaining to sexual offenses are comparable to prior years, it is expected that both will be low. Drug trafficking is portrayed as less serious than violent crimes (including killings and injuries), which signals a shift from crimes traditionally associated with women. Legislative changes that decriminalize crimes could be the cause of this. As a result, based on data from the European Institute for Crime Prevention and Control for the years 2010–2015, the analysis demonstrates concurrent progress for both categories of crimes.

Lastly, we can confirm that the recidivism rate is higher for men, at least as a general trend that goes beyond national differences, using data from the European Sourcebook 2021. This illustrates how the sexes differ in their criminal careers; men are more likely than women to be associated with violence.

4.3.2. Gender Differences in Sentencing

The first matter that needs to be addressed concerns the distinctions that courts make between presiding over cases involving male and female offenders. The research indicates that othetion to gender, should be taken into accountconsidered to account for the variations in conviction rates between men and women in Europe, the USA, and other countries. Therefore, the answer is neither positive nor negative.

Grühl, Welch, and Spohn provide a paradigmatic example of how gender plays a role in court decisions. According to the study's findings, adult women received softer penalties and were less likely to be imprisoned or placed in temporary detentioaution than men. They identified a number ofseveral factors that contributed to this situation, including: (1) Judge's perception of women as unique persons deserving of protection; and (2) Variations in female criminal behavior (fewer acts of violence and a lower rate of criminal activity are among mitigating factors). A victim's lack of defense can be exploited to commit crimes against life in a private setting, and other aggravating circumstances include the following: the existence of additional factors such as racial discrimination that could indirectly affect the sentence. The complexity of these differences cannot be explained by these assumptions alone. However, it offers a foundation for future research in an area that continues to yield pertinent information in order to guarantee that the criminal justice system treats all parties equally.

Given this complexity, the section outlines the primary conclusions in this regard by contrasting each research study's initial focus, its comparative variables, and its interpretation of the findings. The primary distinction between the approaches can be found in whether a perspective is grounded in a critical perspective or in a generalized version of court chivalry. Therefore, it is that the criminal decision is a reflection ofreflects societal gender stereotypes, particularly those that have a direct impact on familial relationships.

Given that thnt occurrence, numerous studies make an efforttry to explain the kind treatment that female offenders receive. Studies examining the impact of race and gender on sentencing for homicide in the United States can be cited. In homicide cases, it has been observed that men, young people, and repeat offenders receive lengthier prison sentences. Leiber and Peck's recent research demonstrated that women are 25% less likely than men to move on to the next phase of the criminal justice system, or the court. But misdemeanors are primarily linked to the potential for an advantage in terms of dismissal. If not, certain researchers draw the conclusion that women are more likely to be given a non-custodial sentence. Nonetheless, women are equally likely to serve the same amount of time in prison as men when given a sentence. The findings of these researchers, whose primary goals are to demonstrate how gender affects criminal responses and the assumption that female offenders should receive a general "gentlemanly and paternalistic treatment," could be categorized in accordance with the insights they provide regarding additional gender adjuvant factors. These are promoters of differences in sentencing:

4.3.2.1. Gender and Race

Numerous studies have examined how gender and race affect the criminal response. While the results of these vary, most come to the conclusion that Black women are more likely than Caucasian and Hispanic women to be sentenced to prison terms and to receive longer sentences. Black women serve a lesser proportion of the sentence imposed than Black men, but still a higher percentage than White and Hispanic women when it comes to the effective completion of the imprisonment.

4.3.2.2. Age

Women in older age groups are more likely to be sentenced to prison time, according to multiple studies. Conversely, other researchers contend that the reverse is true—that younger women are more likely than older women to be punished with parole rather than receiving no punishment at all, and that their conditions are positively correlated with parole's most frequent application.

4.3.2.3. Level of Education and Employment

Higher educated women are more likely to be sentenced to prison, according to some researchers, while other studies have found the exact opposite. This also holds true for employment.

4.3.2.4. Criminal Records

Women with criminal histories are more likely to be condemned, according to certain studies. Determining the severity and duration of the penalty also depends on this factor.

4.3.2.5. Type of Crime Committed

Many researchers have concentrated on demonstrating the correlation between the type of crime and the criminal response against women, not based on gender roles but rather on the generally lenient treatment of female offenders. Among these studies, the ones that demonstrated the response against drug-related offenses perpetrated by women were identified. According to some researchers, women are more likely to face the death penalty in certain situations even though they are not viewed harsher than men in this regard. This finding partially conflicts with findings from other studies that indicated women who committed drug-related or property-related crimes received better treatment than men did, but when they committed violent crimes, women were more likely to receive harsher treatment. Recent research appears to support the initial hypothesis that female offenders should receive better treatment when it comes to serious offenses. These, for instance, are the findings of a study that compared the punishments meted out to men and women who committed multiple homicides. This study would refute the following claims: (a) that women should receive preferential treatment based on the dynamics of the relationships between the offenders, placing women in a submissive role under men; and (b) that the most important factors influencing the severity of punishments are criminal histories and gender. This is the conclusion drawn from other research on the treatment of female sexual offenders; however, it violates social stereotypes about women's roles in sexuality and care giving, particularly with regard to victims who are children. Male sexual offenders in particular face harsher punishments than female ones. This gives rise to the presumption that women, regardless of the social and gender norms they break when committing crimes, are granted special court protection. Similar studies that challenge the il woman" support these findings, despite the fact thateven though sexual offenses are still largely associated with men and are not associated with negative stereotypes about female sexuality.

The intersectional approach advises considering the impact of each of these factors on vulnerability and inequality in addition to these findings. In order to account for the majority of the variations in the application of judgments and the assessment of related circumstances throughout the resocialization process, legal variables must be included. This approach challenges the gender perspective on the causes of violence against women. The previous explanation focused on a single axis of inequality and, at most, added isolated behavioral characteristics and individual variables (like age, race, or education level) and criminal histories. Two major risks of this gender-based analytic structure are highlighted by the intersectional perspective: the invisibility of differences between individual and structural features of people expressing conditions other than heteronormativity and disability; and the failure to challenge the notion that these differences could have different analytic values at different times (primarily because of changes in the law and to personal and affective circumstances in each rehabilitation process).

According to studies, criminal justice systems are gender institutions whose actions, by mirroring conventional ideas about how to treat men and women, reproduce and perpetuate gender inequalities. According to this interpretation, some writers claimed that women might face harsher punishment for breaking gender norms, regardless of the crime they committed. These days, the "evil woman theory," also referred to as "selective chivalry," holds that deference should only be extended to actions associated with female social roles. On the other hand, crimes that are seen as "male crimes" and that violate female gender roles would carry a heavier penalty. However, it is crucial to qualify this statement by pointing out that the patriarchal order's disparities are not only reproduced by the nature of crime, which is somewhat linked to gender roles, but also by the existence of a particular group or family framework. Studies on the impact on dependent individuals or children, studies on crimes involving a double deviation based on gender stereotypes, references to a gender-based assessment of culpability capacity, and the most recent advancements on the impact of gender equality in the enforcement of sentences all emphasize this idea.

4.3.2.6. Dependent Children

The outcomes vary on this. Mothers are more likely to be sentenced to longer terms of imprisonaccording to numerous studies. In contrast, the majority ofmost of the research found the exact opposite. The idea of family protection and the traditional role of women in the home—as caregivers, protectors, and facilitators of their children's education—are thought to be rooted in better treatment. The severity of the punishment appears to be connected to a breakdown in their role as a caregiver and to the expectation of unfavorable outcomes for dependent individuals and children resulting from jail terms. On the other hand, both men and women benefit from taking family obligations into account. A second study seems to support this theory as well, finding no difference in sentence length between individuals with and without children based on paternity or maternity. It did, however, demonstrate that the penalty had varying effects based on parental models that prioritized a particular gender. th their children before being arrested, in particular, were were more likely to be given a more lenient sentence; however, men's involvement in family responsibilities does not correlate in the same way. It appearsrity of the crime a mother commits determines whether or notwhether she violates social norms around gender roles. Courts view these kinds of behaviors as endangering the safety of the mother's dependents and children.

4.3.2.7. Crime is Considered as Double-Gender Deviance

It is true that in certain crimes, such as domestic crimes involving a woman as the victim, partner violence involving a man as the victim, and violent sexual crimes, a tougher treatment for female offenders has been observed, despite some studies showing better treatment for female offenders in serious crimes unrelated to female criminality. Regarding the last, the facts narrative has revealed an emotional viewpoint that promotes the idea of women as villains and unfeminine when contrasted with the same crimes committed by men.

4.3.2.8. Assessment of Guilt in Female Offenders

Research on the interpretation of female criminality emphasize that female offenders are viewed as victims of their own upbringing, environment, and fate. They will therefore probably receive a diagnosis of mental disturbance. Therefore, it is typical to find mitigating circumstances, such as increased remorse, greater willingness to cooperate with the clarification of the facts, and passive and helpful involvement during the commission of the crime by multiple individuals.

4.3.2.9. Influence of Structural Gender Equality

While this field's researchers have pointed out that this influence is negligible when it comes to explaining the individual sentences, certain structural variables showed significant effects for both men and women. This is true in nations where there is a greater proportion of women working; this is associated with a decrease in punitive measures. In turn, nations that have a greater percentage of women with university degrees also have a higher likelihood of using a custodial sentence.

We can confirm the need alize various factors under family or group criteria in order toto understand women's crimes, as well as the tendency to read this context from patriarchal stereotypes and asymmetries, by looking at this overview of various approaches and research that aimed to verify gender-based differences in sentencing.

It is also important to emphasize that these disparities do not appear to have been eliminated by the Sentencing Guidelines, which were used as tools to achieve greater judicial impartiality. This confirms that there is an inevitable margin of discretion in any interpretation process, one that judge's emotions, ideas, and logic may have an impact on in addition to prejudices and personal opinions.

4.3.3. Features in Criminal Treatment of Trans Offenders

In the United States, transgender women who have served time in prison account for 21% of the population, while transgender men, genderqueer individuals, aup 10%. They comprise only 5% of the adult population as a wholepopulation. This can be mainly explained by two factors: (1) increased social vulnerability due to discrimination in work, housing, identity documents, and social welfare; and (2) direct or indirect criminalization of this community as a result of family rejection, bullying, and discrimination in other areas of life. One clear illustration of this last point is the sexual labor sector, where trans women who identify as racialized typically work.

Generally, they receive inappropriate treatment during trial: they are frequently refused the right to have their preferred names; their guilt is attempted to be connected to "ambiguity" stemming from their identity; and they face unique difficulties in obtaining a specialized legal defense. This raises the likelihood of harsher punishment and pre-trial confinement (Lambda Legal's Survey). It is also established that those who commit sexual offenses stand to face harsher punishments. Sadly, there is very little research available on this topic. In order to enforce additional protective tools, it is therefore necessary to frame specific studies to evaluate their depth and extension within the criminal justice system.

Transgender inmates face a number of dangerous circumstances while incarcerated, including sexual assault, harassment, health issues, and general lack of respect. This has significant physical and psychological repercussions that harden; frequently, the custodial sentence is served in isolation to guarantee safety.

4.4. THEORIES OF PUNISHMENT

The pry under criminal law is punishment. It is a punishment meted out tomet by a convicted criminal by a court of law. A person's fundamental rights as a citizen are taken away from him when they are punished. The justification for acting in the same way is a breach of the law. A trial in accordance with due process of law is required to establish such a violation, and the state's authorized legal authorities must have carried out the deprivation.

To ensure that everyone has access to social, economic, and political justice and to preserve law and order in society, punishment provisions must be present. The Manu verse "Penalty keeps the people in restraint, penalty protects them, penalty remains awake when people are asleep, therefore the wise have regarded punishment may be a sourcusness" perfectly captures the significance of punishment.

In order forFor an individual to receive punishment, the offense for which they are found guilty must already be documented in the legal records, along with a corresponding penalty or punishment. Prior to the offense, a statute must be in effect in order for an off be subject to the liability imposed by it. The courts must apply a strictstrict interpretation to these statutes.

4.4.1. Deterrent

The deterrent theory refers to the act of rendering someone incapable of causing harm; it is applied as a cure through arrest. This process is referred to as incapacitation.

In the context of the Deterrent Theory of Punishment, the word "deter" refers to preventing someone from committing a crime. The main tenet of this theory is cited by Burnett, J. in his ruling: "Thou art to be hanged not for having stolen a horse, but in order that other horses may not be stolen." One way to better understand it would be to phrase it like this: "A man may be punished not only to ensure that crime is not committed, but also because he has committed an illegal act." Therefore, the goal of this theory is to discourage or stop criminals from trying to commit the same crimes or trying new ones in the future.

Thus, this theory can be said to set an example for bothoers and the entire society by creating fear through punishment in order toto deter crime. Supporters of this theory believe that if a criminal is given harsh punishment, it will raise public awareness of the harsh penalties meted out for some horrific crimes. As a result, people may become fearful of committing crimes and refrain from even considering them.

The deterrent theory, which centers on the goal of reducing crime rates in society, suggests that law is a social construct, which is consistent with the sociological school of jurisprudence. The foundation of contemporary deterrence in criminology was laid by social contract theorists such as Cesare Beccaria, Thomas Hobbes, and Jeremy Bentham. These theorists believed that a rational person would weigh the advantages and disadvantages of any action that might break the law, as well as the potential consequences, if the punishment was clear-cut, immediate, and harsh.

By looking at the theories of these great jurists, it can be said that the theory of deterrence is constituted of 3 major elements:

1. **Severity-** It refers to the severity of punishment being awarded to an offender. To restrict and rehabilitate the criminals it is important to include provisions of punishment and penalties in our legal framework. But at the same time, it is made sure that the rigidness of punishment granted should be proportionate to the severity of the offence being committed or else the objective of punishment to deter the criminals would be wasted.
2. **Certainty-** If anything wrong happens, the wrongdoer must be certainly punished. Philosopher Cesare Beccaria was of the option that to restrict a person from committing or repeating a crime, it must be certain in the mind of the culprit that his undesirable act will be punished.
3. **Celerity-** The attainment of provisions of punishment is made sure by the promptness in its implementation. The faster the prosecution takes place and punishment is imposed, the greater the impact it will have on deterring crime.

The deterrent theory is b on the idea that people should know and abide by the law regardless of whether they wereare aware of it. This idea is known as "Ignorantia Juris Non Excusat," which translates to "ignorance of law is no excuse." Because it doesn't addot causes of criminal behavior or how society treats him, it is criticized by a number ofseveral jurists who believe it to be ineffective in lowering crime.

4.4.2. Retributive

The oldest and most fundamental theory of punishment is retributive theory. founded on the doctrine known as Lex Talionis, which translates to mean "Tooth for Tooth, Eye for Eye, Limb for Limb, and Nail for Nail" in literal translation.

Sir John Salmond asserts that the goal of a retributive punishment is to exact revenge on a criminal for the harm they have caused to society. Accordingly, proponents of the retributivism theory contend that the wrongdoer ought to pay a price commensurate with the harm he has caused to a particular person or to society at large. Retributive theory guarantees that the punishment meted out must be commensurate with the severity of the injury that occurred, and it does not punish someone who has not yet committed a crime or who intends to commit one.

Supporters of this theory argue that by punishing criminals, we can better understand the suffering that their victims endure and the extent of immortality of their actions. Often referred to as the "Vengeance Theory," this type of punishment also serves to remind the populace that the government is in place to defend them and remove any unfair advantage that a criminal may have had when committing a crime.

It is important to ensure that severe offenses are punished with retributive measures, as this can prevent the emergence of strong, negative, or vindictive sentiments within the community. Furthermore, if there is no legal accountability for the approval of the death penalty, the state may have hegemony over it and utilize it as a tool of torture.

4.4.3. Prevention

Preventive theory, which is backed by proponents of utilitarianism such as Austin, Bentham, and Mill, aims to render criminals incapable of committing future crimes, regardless of how similar or different they may be. These jurists were persuaded by the theory because of its charitable bent.

It is imperative to adhere to the principle of "Justice denied is justice delayed" in order to guarantee the efficacy of preventive theory. The promptness factor is crucial because any kind of delay in the inquiry or investigation could make the punishment or function ineffective.

The idea is to change the offender temporarily or permanently in order to limit future danger. The way this is accomplished is by separating the offender from the rest of society, either permanently by giving them a life sentence or, in the most extreme of circumstances, by applying the death penalty. The deterrent theory and prevention theory are somewhat related. The former concentrates on stopping the offender from committing the crime, whereas the latter aims to deter society. Three dominant ways of advancing preventive punishment are:

1. by inculcating fear of punishment,
2. by incapacitating a criminal temporarily or permanently, and
3. by advancing reformative types of punishments that aim at restoring them as law-abiding citizens.

Penologists and jurists who oppose preventive punishment argue that because it doesn't deal with the underlying causes of criminal behavior, tactics like instilling fear in the minds of offenders or preventing them from committing crimes may not be successful in reducing crime rates. Particularly when it comes to minors and first-time offenders, as it could harden them even further and eliminate any chance of full rehabilitation.

4.4.4. Reformative

The foundation of reformative theory, also known as rehabilitative sentencing, is the idea that the goal of a state's penal system should be to reform the criminal through the approach of individualization and not by merely punishing him. This theory is based on the principle laid out by Mahatma Gandhi, the father of reformative theory, "Condemn the Sin, not the Sinner." This theory is predicated on the humanitarian idea that an individual who commits a crime does not automatically lose their humanity. This theory's proponents assert that treating an offender with compassion, tact, and love can help him become a law-abiding, orderly citizen.

The observation rendered in the Mohd case by Justice Krishna Iyer. Giasuddin v. This idea is summed up by the State of Andhra Pradesh: "Every saint has a past, and every sinner has a future." This theory holds that a person's physical or mental health, how society views him, and the circumstances and surroundings surrounding him are all related to their criminal behavior. Consequently, it happens as a result of the disagreemen the criminal's intent and character. The reformative theory views criminals as patients in light ofconsidering this. As a result, the state is required to work toward the offender's reform during his time in prison and ensure that he can live a life of dignity once his sentence has been served.

With regard to minors, it has been somewhat successful because of the parole, pardon, probation, sentence commutation, remand home, and other provisions. According to this theory, criminals can be transformed, and efforts can be made to re-educate and reform them by teaching them a certain trade, craft, or industry, or by educating them so they can go on with their lives normally once they are released from prison. The Lok Sabha passed a bill outlawing the death penalty in 1956, marking the beginning of attempts to carry out the reformative theory's objectives, though these have not yet been fulfilled.

Because punishment is more restorative than deterrent, reformative theory opposes penalization and harsh punishments intended to bring an offender back because doing so will only degrade the offender.

Opponents of the reformative theory contend that it takes an offender-centric approach and that, in many situations, relying solely on this type of punishment will be unjust to the victim, particularly in cases involving heinous crimes like rape or murder. While reformative punishments have shown efficacy when applied to juveniles and first-time offenders, they become ineffective and unworkable when applied to habitual offenders or when death sentences are involved. Furthermore, it needs a substantial investment, which those in poverty are unable to make.

4.4.5. Expiatory Theory

The expiatory theory of punishment, which is based on moral and ethical principles, holds that an offender's own repentance or expiration constitutes a form of punishment. This theory emphasizes atonement, reparation, repentance, and compunction as a conscience-oriented means of purifying one's heart.

One of the oldest theories of punishment still in use in Indian criminal law is the expiatory theory, which was highly regarded by the Manusmriti, an ancient Hindu legal commentary, as a method of punishment that emphasized the rehabilitation of offenders into members of society. The theory's application has become inadequate due to societal advancements, and relying solely on it for experimentation would be prohibitively expensive in terms of societal safety and security.

Expiatory Theory is based on the idea that "to pay for the sin committed" and is the opposite of the idea that a wrongdoer deserves to be pardoned and absolved if he repents completely of his wrongdoings. It is in favor of punishing wrongdoers who harm or cause any kind of loss to other people. Economical and compensatory forms of punishment are preferred over expiatory ones. It talks about the accused giving the victim compensation rather than subjecting the victim to physical harm as retribution.

Expiratory punishments can hardly be considered effective in bringing about any reformation in the criminal mentality of offenders in the current era of materialism and precedent, where every single being is just busy justifying their acts in one way or another. As a result, the punishments recommended by this theory may be sufficient to deal with minor and trivial offenses, but they are deemed unrealistic when it comes to the most serious ones.

4.5. GENDER AND DIFFERENT TYPES OF ORGANIZED CRIME

There are numerous guises and expressions of organized crime. In the following, we consider how applying a gender lens may help us better understand the gendered experiences of the men and women who affenses. What are the gender dimensions and considerations when it comes to some of the most commonly discussedmost discussed forms of organized crime: drug trafficking, smuggling of migrants, and trafficking in persons? Can some of the less explored forms and manifestations of organized crime, like trafficking in wildlife, cybercrime, and trafficking in cultural property, have a gender dimension?

4.5.1. Trafficking in Persons

The predominant perception of human trafficking is that it primarily affects women, particularly young, foreign women. Additionally, there is a propensity to confuse human trafficking with sex trafficking. Thousands of web pages, films, books, and a substantial corpus of official, grey, and scholarly literature detailing instances of sexual exploitation suffered by women and young girls can be found by condut online search for the term.

Nevertheless, we must take issue with these portrayals as knowledgeable informationinformation for consumers and enthusiasts for organized crime. We have to first determine how they define gender. The effects of human trafficking extend beyond women. In addition, it encompasses a wide variety of exploitation, not just sexual exploitation. Men who work in non-sex-related fields like conriculture are frequently the victims of human trafficking (Zhang, 2012). According to recent data, the majority ofmost victims of trafficking for sexual exploitation are women, while men make up over half of those trafficked for forced labor (UNODC (a), 2018). In contrast to other forms of exploitation, there are still relatively few victims of organ trafficking that have been identified. Approximately one hundred victims of organ trafficking were identted to UNODC between 2014 and 2017. Two thirds of them were men, and they were all adults. Although the majority ofmost victims found worldwide are trafficked for sexual exploitation, not all regions follow this pattern consistently. In sub-Saharan Africa and the Middle East, forced labor trafficking is the most frequently identified form; in Central and South Asia, forced labor trafficking and sexual exploitation are almost equally prevalent. We can learn more about how men and women deal with exploitative work conditions and the types of jobs that are more likely to result in exploitation by using an intersectional approach (UNODC (a), 2018).

We can better understand how crime representations frame or stereotype men and women from different cultures by critically analyzing them. For instance, a plethora of reports detail the experiences of Global South women who fall prey to sex trafficking. Although both men and women are affected by sex trafficking, stereotypes about women tend to paint them as excessively sensual and/or sexually repressed. They could also be described as easily duped, gullible, or incapable of making their own decisions. For example, reports and documentaries on sex trafficking have frequently portrayed Nigerian women as naive, ignorant, and under the control of their captors who have performed juju on them. As a result, the women are afraid to leave situations where they are being exploited or abusedk up the idea that misconceptions about women's involvement in organized crime need to be dispelled. The majority ofMost traffickers are still men, according to a sex-by-sex analysis of those who have reportedly been the subject of an investigation, been detained, charged, and/or found guilty of trafficking in persons. However, in 2016 there were more than 35% of the prosecution (out of 6,370 persons) and 38% of the convicts (out of 1,565 people) who were charged with human trafficking (Figure 4.1).

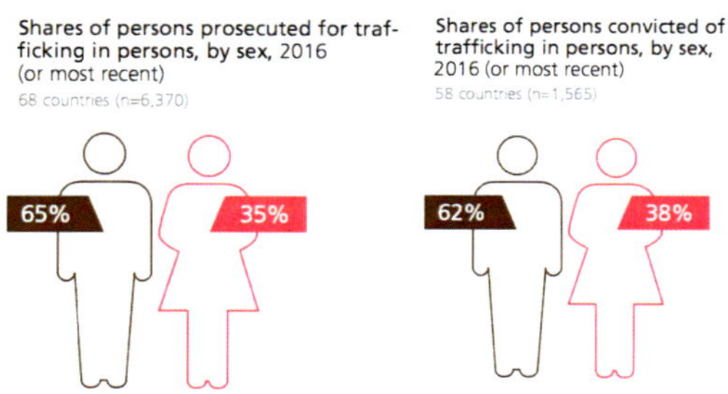

Figure 4.1. *Trafficking in Persons, Profile of Offenders.*

Source: https://sherloc.unodc.org/cld/uploads/images/education/tertiary/Modules/OrganizedCrime/figure_15.1_a.png.

https://sherloc.unodc.org/cld/uploads/images/education/tertiary/Modules/OrganizedCrime/figure_15.1_b.png.

Data on crime indicate that women are more likely than men to be involved in human trafficking (UNODC (a), 2018). As stated in the *UNODC Global Report on Trafficking in Persons*, 2012, the average percentage of recorded female offenders for all types of crimes is approximately 12% (of convictions), according to the United Nations Survey of Crime Trends and Operations of Criminal Justice Systems (2006–2009).

4.5.2. Smuggling of Migrants

Smugglers have a unique place in modern migration narratives. They are frequently depicted as Latin American, Black African, or Muslim men who take advantage of the weaknesses of migrants. In the media, they are frequently held solely responsible for the disappearances and deaths of migrants in transit, as well as the sexual assault of women.

It is true that men are disproportionately charged with smuggling migrants. Men make up roughly 70% of those found guilty of smuggling at the federal level in the United States, according to data from the US Sentencing Commission (US Sentencing Commission, 2017). However, this figure alone indicates that the remaining guilty, or about 30% of the total, are women. A closer examination of these numbers reveals that the majority of those found guilty of the crime are from the US-Mexico border region, where people typically live in areas with some of the highest rates of poverty in the country.

We can get a more comprehensive picture of the individuals who are involved in smuggling and the difficulties they might encounter by breaking down official data according to gender and place of residence. For instance, research by Victoria Stone-Cadena and Soledad Alvarez-Velasco (2018) revealed that a significant portion of the indigenous Quichua people of Ecuador are employed as smuggling facilitators. Their involvement in the market stems from a lengthy history of migration: many indigenous people were denied access to marketplaces where they could trade or sell their goods due to discrimination, and they also had restricted land rights. This made them more and more likely to choose to migrate overseas, mostly to the United States, learning about smuggling routes and techniques in the process.

Not only do we observe a market in Ecuador where smuggling operations are organized and/or facilitated by indigenous people as opposed to transnational organized networks. Additionally, we discover that smuggling is highly gendered, with tasks primarily being assigned based on traditional gender roles. While men lead groups through remote or isolated areas, keep an eye on migrants, and drive them through checkpoints, women provide room and board for migrants in transit and tend to those who become ill or injured during their travels (Sanchez, 2016). Adolescent men are quite active in the smuggling markets, according to research done by DHIA, a human rights organization in Ciudad Juarez, Mexico (2017); the International Organization for Migration in Alexandria, Egypt (2015); and Antje Missbach and Wayne Palmer in Indonesia (2016). Many of these young men turn to smuggling as a means of financing their own migration journeys, but for many more, engaging in smuggling is a means of fulfilling gender roles that they have been unable to exercise due to the dearth of employment and educational opportunities in their communities (Sanchez,

2018). Many of these young children claim that by engaging in smuggling, they are able to financially support their families, be acknowledged as the head of the household, and obtain access to social roles that are traditionally filled by men.

Because of this division of labor based on gender roles, women are disproportionately found guilty of smuggling in friends and family members. Comparing small-scale, individual attempts to aid in the smuggling of migrants with data from UNODC's SHERLOC knowledge management portal, it appears that smuggling cases involving network-like operations are less frequent. Women most frequently assist in the smuggling of small numbers of migrants, including their own children and/or family members, although men are more likely to be involved in the first (Sanchez, 2018). In this regard, it is important to keep in mind that the Smuggling of Migrants Protocol, one of the three Protocols that supplement the United Nations Convention against Transnational Organized Crime and the main legally-binding document in this area, explicitly lists the acquisition of a financial or other material benefit, either directly or indirectly, as a component of the crime of migrant smuggling (see UNODC, 2017). The inclusion of the phrase "a financial or other material benefit" was intended to highlight that the definition would encompass the actions of organized crime groups acting for financial gain, while excluding those of individuals who supported migrants out of humanitarian concerns or strong familial ties. This is stated in the Interpretative Note to this definition. The Protocol did not intend to make it illegal for family members or support groups, like non-governmental or religious organizations, to engage in certain activities (UNODC, 2006). However, some States throughout the world have not incorporated the "financial or other material benefit" component into their national laws, and in those instances, both men and women are prosecuted for smuggling. In these situations, women may be accuseing in order to support their spouses, children, or other significant others while they are abroad or to help individualsindividuals, they have been in long-term relationships with escape violent or conflict-ridden nations.

Comparable statistical analysis to that available for human trafficking is not available for smuggling. However, the UNODC released the first Global Study on Migrant Smuggling in 2018, which includes some estimates of the total number of migrants smuggled worldwide as well as some restricted data disaggregation by age and sex. According to the study, the majority of smuggled migrants are young men. This is not to argue that women and children do not smuggle goods or services. Women make up a significant portion of smuggled migrants on some routes, most notably in parts of South-East Asia. Unaccompanied or separated children are frequently included in smuggling flows and may be especially susceptible to abuse and deceit on the part of smugglers and others. Particularly, unaccompanied or separated children have been found on the land routes leading to North America and the Mediterranean routes leading to Europe (UNODC (b), 2018).

4.5.3. Drug trafficking

"The majority of people envision a world dominated by men when they think of the illegal drug trade, including the traffickers, gangs, and kingpins. However, women are particularly affected by drugs and drug-related crimes. In their study on the effects of drug policy on women, Kasia Malinowska and Olga Rychkova state that understanding how women fit into this dynamic is crucial to getting drug policy right (2015).

The stories of well-known drug dealers and/or traffickers are frequently the main focus of discussions about drug trafficking. Yes, a few of those well-known traffickers are female. However, it's crucial to remember that the drug trafficking economy is dependent on more than just the group's leaders. In actuality, it depends heavily on physical labor—work that is frequently done by women and children. Women who have few other work options in their communities occasionally participate in the market.

The number of women who are imprisoned due to their involvement in drug trafficking is rising globally. The reasons for women getting involved in drug trafficking and staying in it are complicated, despite the fact that we frequently romanticize or glamorize women's experiences in the industry and attribute their involvement to romantic relationships with men. Not only do women typically have less access to work and educational opportunities than do men? They also tend to be among those who experience financial precarity more frequently, a phenomenon known as the "feminization of poverty" (see glossary for definition). Additionally, as we've already seen, women typically fill low-paying, high-risk roles that put them at risk of being discovered by law enforcement and, consequently, of being involved in the criminal justice system. Because of this, the percentage of women incarcerated for drug trafficking-related convictions is higher than the percentage of men in detention for drug trafficking. These trends are emphasized by the data from the UNODC 2018 World Drug Report (Figure 4.2.).

All of this is not to say that men's experiences are unimportant or that there are no risks associated with them participating in organized crime. As we have seen, men are disproportionately affected by organized crime-related violence, especially young men and teenagers from low-income backgrounds. Additionally, they frequently serve as the primary target of government initiatives like surveillance and policing.

Figure 4.2. *Men and Women in Prison for Drug-Related Offenses.*

Source. https://sherloc.unodc.org/cld/uploads/images/education/tertiary/Modules/OrganizedCrime/figure_15.2.png.

4.5.4. Wildlife Trafficking

Despite anecdotal evidence suggesting a strong gender divide in the roles played by participants in the wildlife trade, gender appears to receive very littion in research, policy, and programming related to this crime. Specifically, in conversations about how to combat the crimecrime, the gender of those who produce, trade, and consume trafficked goods is almost never brought up. One noteworthy he research done by Pamela McElwee (2012), which examined the gender aspects of wildlife crime in Vietnam and made referencereferred to social norms and/or gender-based traditions that frequently dissuade women from engaging in wildlife trafficking. McElwee claims that due to tradition or gendered roles, women are frequeed from hunting or gathering particular animals or plants, are unable to leave their homes for extended periods of time, andtime and are therefore less able to participate in the trafficking of wildlife while making room for men. McElwee further notes that some activities may be viewedmen to participate in and are thus limited to men, and that religious beliefs may forbid women from coming into contact withencountering particular types of flora or fauna. Even though these findings are important for comprehending dynamics and interactions in specific situations, they hardly fully explain the phenomenon. In fact, there are numerous instances where women have been found guilty or charged with trafficking in illegal wildlife. The "Ivory Queen" case is arguably the most famous one.

Customers are another aspect of this illegal trade that has received little research. For various reasons, men and women may buy (illegal) wildlife products. For example, men may think that certain products will boost their status and reputation in society or improve their sexual abilities (e.g., china

(Torres Cruz and McElwee, 2012) tiger bone in China. Certain products may encourage some women to purchase them because they are thought to enhance the quality and quantity of breast milk produced by nursing mothers (e.g., pangolin's scalar coat). Because of the purported medicinal benefits of illicit wildlife products, both men and women may purchase them (e.g., rheumatism, rhino horn is thought to be particularly effective), their religious significance (e.g., ivory in certain cultures) or the prestige connected to a purchase (e.g., Rhino horn is pricey, difficult to locate, and valued as a gift by some (USAID, 2017).

Attempts to combat human trafficking that fail to take gender into account when developto combat the illicit trade or to recognize the gender dimensions of the problem are likely to be unsuccessful. The majority ofMost of the reporting on wildlife trafficking concentrates on quantifying the amount of wildlife trafficked and/or its economic worth, but it ignores the underlying factors drit for the products or their cultural and social significance.

4.5.5. Cybercrime

New types of crime have emerged as a result ofbecause of technology and the spread of Internet-based services and technologies. Hearing stories of people falling victim to online scams, hackers bypassing sophisticated security measures, or minors being sexually exploited online is not unusual. The fact that a lot of smuggling and trafficking is done online worries the authorities a great deal. Adda variety of gender-based cybercrimes (e.g., sextortion and image-based sexual abuse).

Combating cybercrime presents a number ofseveral obstacles, including the fact that it encompasses a wide range of illegal activities and actors who, because they operate online, are better able to hide their identities (UNODC, 2017). We don't know a lot about the gender of those who commit cybercrime, and the findings are frequently contradictory. Cybercrime is pervasive in our daily lives, but little research has been done on it, which makes it harder for us to comprehend its scope and true nature.

Women have not been central to the majority of ethnographic and/or other types of empirical research in the field, with a few notable exceptions. These outliers typically demonstrate that men commit cybercrime at a higher rate than women (Hutchings, 2016). The media continues to imagine the world of cybercriminals despite the lack of trustworthy data. Women are typically described as stunning but socially awkward computer specialists who work alone, concealed in a world where men rule, and striving to combat the more extreme and harmful types of cybercrime (Potter, 2016; Yver, 2016; Rousseau, 2017).

A less than thrilling rationale for the constraints placed on research delving into the roles played by women in cybercrime is the global underrepresentation of women in STEM fields (science, technology, engineering, and math) (OUS/EA, 2017; Microsoft, 2018). The lack of representation of women in cybercrime may also be due to patriarchal values that are ingrained in society at large, including in science and technology, as we have seen with other crimes. It is possible that gendered stereotypes that have long prevented women from entering fields traditionally associated with men are to blame for women's lack of visibility in cybercrime, rather than just the fact that they are hidden, marginalized, or uncommon. The fact that women are frequently the targets of sexual harassment, discrimination, and hostile work environments is also related to the dearth of women i. According to Funk and Parker (2018), gender is f an impediment than an advantage to career success."

In light ofConsidering this, it should not be shocking that the majority ofmost of the res cybercrime that is currently available focuses on the experiences of men. According to Back, Soor, and La Prade (2018), hacker'shackers' motivations are as follows: they want to act destructively to vent their resentment towards other online users or organizations; they want to gain attention by showcasing their cyberspace expertise; they have political objectives; they want to achieve personal satisfaction; and they want to make money. According to Miller and Lopez (2015), men who engage in cybercrime may be able to both fulfil and perpetuate gendered social hierarchies and expectations.

4.5.6. Trafficking in Cultural Property

There is a dearth of empirical research and high-quality data in the field, despite the expansion of international treaties and the growing support for them by States, as well as reports indicating that the illicit trade in cultural property has increased rather than decreased (refer to UN General Assembly Resolution 68/186 (2013) and UN Security Council Resolutions 2199 (2015) and 2347 (2017)).

Given this, it should not be shocking that there is essentially no research on the gendered aspects of cultural property trafficking. However, some academics have found links between the protection of women's cultural remnants and violent conflicts in trafficking-prone areas (de Vido, 2015). However, the destruction and losses brought about by armed conflict are also followed by attempts to make a living made by the survivors or remaining inhabitants. According to research, there is a connection between the rise in this type of organized crime worldwide and the collapse of state-sponsored security measures. The lack of these measures encourages the emergence of actors who might try to profit monetarily or in kind from the sale of cultural property as a means of surviving (Yates and Mackenzie, 2018). However, some of the actions related to this type of trafficking do not require a connection to organized crime. Rather, a large part of the trade appears to be driven by individual decisions that are entrepreneurial in nature and motivated by necessity (Yates, Mackenzie, and Smith, 2017; Brodie, 2017).

REFERENCES

1. Acale Sánchez, M. (2019). Penal and custodial control of female criminality in Spain from a gender perspective. *Social Sciences*, *52*, 1–15.
2. Adewunmi, B. (2014). Kimberlé Crenshaw on intersectionality: "I wanted to come up with an everyday metaphor that anyone could use." *New Statesman America*.
3. Aebi, M., et al. (2021). *European Sourcebook of Crime and Criminal Justice Statistics 2021* (6th ed.). https://wp.unil.ch/europeansourcebook/printed-editions-2/6th-edition/ (accessed on 14 October 2024).
4. Aebi, M., Hashimoto, Y. Z., & Tiago, M. M. (2020). *Probation and Prisons in Europe, 2019: Key Findings of the SPACE Reports*. Council of Europe, Strasbourg.
5. Agha, S. (2009). Structural correlates of female homicide: A cross-national analysis. *Journal of Criminal Justice*, *37*, 576–585.
6. Albonetti, C. (2002). Gender and ethnicity on length of imprisonment under the federal sentencing guidelines for drug trafficking/manufacturing offenders. *Journal of Gender, Race, and Justice*, *39*, 39–60.
7. Allen, H. (1987). *Justice Unbalanced: Gender, Psychiatry and Judicial Decisions*. Open University Press.
8. Arsovska, J., & Begum, P. (2013). *From West Africa to the Balkans: Exploring Women's Roles in Transnational Organized Crime*. Springer Science+Business Media.
9. Asscher, J. J., Van der Put, C. E., & Stams, G. J. J. M. (2015). Gender differences in the impact of abuse and neglect victimization on adolescent offending behavior. *Journal of Family Violence*, *30*, 215–225.
10. Back, S., Soor, S., & LaPrade, J. (2018). Juvenile hackers: An empirical test of self-control theory and social bonding theory. *International Journal of Cybersecurity Intelligence & Cybercrime*, *1*(1), 40–55.
11. Barak, G., Leighton, P., & Flavin, J. (2010). *Class, Race, Gender and Crime: The Social Realities of Justice in America*. Rowman & Littlefield Publishers.
12. Bassichis, M. D. (2007). *'It's War in Here': A Report on the Treatment of Transgender and Intersex People in New York State Men's Prisons*. Sylvia Rivera Law Project.
13. BBC. (2015). Quién es la "Reina del Pacífico" liberada de prisión en México. *BBC Mundo*.
14. Belfrage, H., & Strand, S. (2012). Measuring the outcome of structured spousal violence risk assessments using the B-SAFER: Risk in relation

to recidivism and intervention. *Behavioral Sciences & the Law*, *30*(4), 420–430. https://doi.org/10.1002/bsl.2019.

15. Belknap, J., & Holsinger, K. (2006). The gendered nature of risk factors for delinquency. *Feminist Criminology*, *1*, 48–71.
16. Bermúdez, N. V. (2015). Entre padres y hermanos: Lazos de sangre y prácticas políticas de los allegados a muertos en contextos de violencia (Ciudad de Córdoba, Argentina). *AIBR: Revista de Antropología Iberoamericana*, *10*(3), 377–399.
17. Bernard, A. (2013). The intersectional alternative: Explaining female criminality. *Feminist Criminology*, *8*, 3–19.
18. Black, M. C., Basile, K. C., Breiding, M. J., Smith, S. G., Walters, M. L., Merrick, M. T., et al. (2011). *The National Intimate Partner and Sexual Violence Survey (NISVS): 2010 summary report*. Atlanta.
19. Blanchette, K., & Brown, S. L. (2006). *The Assessment and Treatment of Women Offenders*. Wiley.
20. Bradley, M. S., & Engen, R. L. (2016). Leaving prison: A multilevel investigation of racial, ethnic, and gender disproportionality in correctional release. *Crime & Delinquency*, *62*, 253–279.
21. Brennan, P. (2006). Sentencing female misdemeanants: An examination of the direct and indirect effects of race/ethnicity. *Justice Quarterly*, *23*, 60–95.
22. Britton, D. M. (2000). Feminism in criminology: Engendering the outlaw. *Annals of the American Academy of Political and Social Science*, *571*, 57–76.
23. Britton, D. M. (2011). *The Gender of Crime*. Rowman & Littlefield Publishers.
24. Brodie, N. (2015). The role of conservators in facilitating the theft and trafficking of cultural objects: The case of a seized Libyan statue. *Libyan Studies*, *48*, 117–123.
25. Burgess-Proctor, A. (2006). Intersections of race, class, gender and crime: Future directions for feminist criminology. *Feminist Criminology*, *1*, 27–47.
26. Burman, M. (2004). Breaking the mold: Patterns of female offending. In G. McIvor (Ed.), *Women Who Offend* (pp. 38–65). Jessica Kingsley Publishers.
27. Castiello Jones, K., Misra, J., & McCurley, K. (2013). Intersectionality in sociology. *Factsheet, Sociologists for Women in Society*.
28. Cauffman, E. (2008). Understanding the female offender. *Future of Children*, *18*, 11–42.

29. Center of American Progress & Movement Advancement Project. (2016). *UNJUST: How the Broken Criminal Justice System Fails Transgender People.* https://www.lgbtmap.org/policy-and-issue-analysis/criminal-justice-trans (accessed on 14 October 2024).
30. Chernoff, N., & Simon, R. J. (2000). Women and crime the world over. *Gender Issues*, 5–20.
31. Chesney-Lind, M. (1987). Girls and violence: An exploration of the gender gap in serious delinquent behavior. In D. H. Crowell, I. M. Evans, & C. R. O'Donnell (Eds.), *Childhood Aggression and Violence: Sources of Influence, Prevention and Control* (pp. 207–230). Plenum Press.
32. Chesney-Lind, M. (2006). Patriarchy, crime and justice: Feminist criminology in an era of backlash. *Feminist Criminology*, *1*, 6–26.
33. Chesney-Lind, M., & Shelden, R. G. (2014). *Delinquency and Juvenile Justice*. Wiley Blackwell.
34. Chu, D. C., Hebenton, B., & Toh, A. (2021). Gender equality and female offending: Evidence from international data sources. *International Journal of Offender Therapy and Comparative Criminology*, *65*, 1–24.
35. Connell, R. W. (2004). *Gender*. Polity Press.
36. Cooper, B. (2016). Intersectionality. In L. Disch & M. Hawkesworth (Eds.), *The Oxford Handbook of Feminist Theory* (pp. 385–406). Oxford University Press.
37. Cpotter. (2016). The history of women hackers. *The New School: Digital Humanities*.
38. Crew, K. B. (1991). Sex differences in criminal sentencing: Chivalry or patriarchy? *Justice Quarterly*, *8*, 59–83.
39. Cruz-Torres, M. L., & McElwee, P. (2017). Gender, livelihoods, and sustainability: Anthropological research. In S. MacGregor (Ed.), *Routledge Handbook of Gender and Environment* (pp. 133–145). Taylor and Francis.
40. Cruz, L., & Martinez Osorio, M. (2018). The place that female coca growers deserve. *DeJusticia*.
41. Dalton, K. (1961). Menstruation and crime. *British Medical Journal*, *30*, 1752–1753.
42. Daly, K. (1987). Discrimination in the criminal courts: Family, gender, and the problem of equal treatment. *Social Forces*, *66*, 152–175.
43. Daly, K. (1992). Women's pathways to felony court: Feminist theories of lawbreaking and problems of representation. *Southern California Review of Law and Women's Studies*, *2*, 11–52.
44. Damiris, I. K., McKillop, N., Christensen, L. S., Rayment-McHugh, S.,

Burton, K., & Patterson, T. (2020). Gendered judicial discourse in the sentencing of sexual offenders: A new explanatory model. *Current Issues in Criminal Justice*, 1–20.

45. De Vido, S. (2017). Mainstreaming gender in the protection of cultural heritage. In S. Pinton & L. Zagato (Eds.), *Cultural Heritage: Scenarios 2015–2017* (pp. 451–467). Sapere l'Europa.
46. Deering, R., & Mellor, D. (2009). Sentencing of male and female child sex offenders: Australian study. *Psychiatry, Psychology and Law*, *16*, 394–412.
47. Demuth, S., & Doerner, J. (2014). Gender and sentencing in the federal courts: Are women treated more leniently? *Criminal Justice Policy Review*, *25*, 242–269.
48. Denzin, N. K. (1994). Romancing the text: The qualitative researcher-writer-as-bricoleur. *Bulletin of the Council for Research in Music Education*, 15–30.
49. Derechos Humanos Integrales en Acción (DHIA). (2017). *Neither Criminals nor Illegals: Children and Adolescents in the Migrant Smuggling Market in the US-Mexico Border*. Derechos Humanos Integrales en Acción.
50. Di Meo, S. (2012). Camorra, in manette 66 affiliati alla cosca Pianese-D'Alterio. In manette anche la donna a capo del clan. *Il Sole 24 Ore*.
51. Dixon, L., & Browne, K. (2003). The heterogeneity of spouse abuse: A review. *Aggression and Violent Behavior*, *8*(1), 107–130. https://doi.org/10.1016/S1359-1789(02)00104-0.
52. Dobash, R. P., & Dobash, R. E. (2004). Women's violence to men in intimate relationships. *British Journal of Criminology*, *44*, 324–349.
53. Doerner, W. G., & Lab, S. P. (2012). *Victimology*. Elsevier.
54. EIGE. (2021). What is gender-based violence? *European Institute for Gender Equality*. https://eige.europa.eu/gender-based-violence/what-is-gender-based-violence (accessed on 14 October 2024).
55. Embry, R., & Lyons, P. M. (2012). Sex-based sentencing: Sentencing discrepancies between male and female sex offenders. *Feminist Criminology*, *7*, 146–162.
56. Enos, T. (2017). Eight things you should know about Two-Spirit people. *Indian Country Today*.
57. European Asylum Support Office (EASO). (2015). *Nigeria: Sex Trafficking of Women* (Country of Origin Information Report).
58. Franklin, C., & Fearn, N. (2008). Gender, race, and formal court decision-

making outcomes: Chivalry/paternalism conflict theory or gender conflict? *Journal of Criminal Justice*, *36*, 279–290.

59. Freiburger, T. (2010). The effects of gender, family status, and race on sentencing decisions. *Behavioral Sciences & the Law*, *28*, 378–395.
60. Freiburger, T. (2011). The impact of gender, offense type, and family role on the decision to incarcerate. *Social Justice Research*, *24*, 143–167.
61. Freiburger, T., & Hilinski, C. (2013). An examination of the interactions of race and gender on sentencing decisions using a trichotomous dependent variable. *Crime & Delinquency*, *59*, 59–86.
62. Fridel, E. (2019). Leniency for lethal ladies: Using the actor–partner interdependence model to examine gender-based sentencing disparities. *Homicide Studies*, *23*, 319–343.
63. Funk, C., & Parker, K. (2018). Women and men in STEM often at odds over workplace equity. *PEW Research Center*.
64. Gartner, R., & Jung, M. (2014). Sex, gender and homicide: Contemporary trends and patterns. In R. Gartner & B. McCarthy (Eds.), *The Oxford Handbook of Gender, Sex, and Crime* (pp. 424–447). Oxford University Press.
65. Gaub, J., & Holtfreter, K. (2015). New directions in intersections, inequality, and sentencing. *Women & Criminal Justice*, *25*, 298–312.
66. Gehring, K. S. (2018). A direct test of pathways theory. *Feminist Criminology*, *13*, 115–137.
67. Gelsthorpe, L. (2004). Female offending: A theoretical overview. In G. McIvor (Ed.), *Women Who Offend* (pp. 13–37). Jessica Kingsley Publishers.
68. Gelsthorpe, L., & Larrauri, E. (2014). Gender and crime in Europe. In S. Body-Gendrot, M. Hough, et al. (Eds.), *The Routledge Handbook of European Criminology* (pp. 188–203). Routledge.
69. Gerulaityte, E. (2018). Guna Yala: The island where women make the rules. *BBC Travel*.
70. Goethals, J., Maes, E., & Klinckhamers, P. (1997). Sex/gender-based decision-making in the criminal justice system as a possible (additional) explanation for the underrepresentation of women in official criminal statistics: A review of international literature. *International Journal of Comparative and Applied Criminal Justice*, *21*, 207–240.
71. Goldstein, D. A., Cantos, A. L., Brenner, L. H., Verborg, R. J., & Kosson, D. S. (2016). Perpetrator type moderates the relationship between severity of intimate partner violence and recidivism. *Criminal Justice and Behavior*,

43(7), 879–898. https://doi.org/10.1177/0093854815616841.

72. Goldweber, A., Broidy, L. M., & Cauffman, E. (2009). Interdisciplinary perspectives on persistent female offending: A review of theory and research. In J. Savage (Ed.), *The Development of Persistent Criminality* (pp. 205–230). Oxford University Press.
73. Goulette, N., Wooldredge, J., Frank, J., & Travis, L. III. (2015). From initial appearance to sentencing: Do female defendants experience disparate treatment? *Journal of Criminal Justice*, *43*, 406–417.
74. Gracia, E., & Merlo, J. (2016). Intimate partner violence against women and the Nordic paradox. *Social Science & Medicine*, *157*, 27–30.
75. Grant, J. M., Mottet, L. A., & Tanis, J. (2011). *Injustice at Every Turn: A Report of the National Transgender Discrimination Survey*. National Center for Transgender Equality and National Gay and Lesbian Task Force.
76. Griffin, T., & Wooldredge, J. (2006). Sex-based disparities in felony dispositions before versus after sentencing reform in Ohio. *Criminology*, *44*, 893–923.
77. Gruhl, J., Welch, S., & Spohn, C. (1984). Women as criminal defendants: A test for paternalism. *Political Research Quarterly*, *37*, 456–467.
78. Guerra, S. I. (2015). La Chota y Los Mafiosos: Mexican American casualties of the border drug war. *Latino Studies*, *13*(2), 227–244.
79. Hagan, J., & Nagel, I. (1983). Gender and crime: Offense patterns and criminal court sanctions. *University of Chicago Press Journal*, *4*, 91–144.
80. Hassett-Walker, C., Lateano, T., & di Benedetto, M. (2014). Do female sex offenders receive preferential treatment in criminal charging and sentencing? *Justice System Journal*, *35*, 62–86.
81. Hawkins Anderson, S. (2012). Girls in the juvenile justice system: The causes and correlates of girls' involvement. In S. Miller, L. D. Leve, & P. K. Kerig (Eds.), *Delinquent Girls: Contexts, Relationships and Adaptation* (pp. 41–54). Springer.
82. Hedderman, C. (2004). The 'criminogenic' needs of women offenders. In G. McIvor (Ed.), *Women Who Offend* (pp. 82–98). Jessica Kingsley Publishers.
83. Heidensohn, F. (1985). *Women and Crime*. Macmillan.
84. Heidensohn, F. (1991). Women and crime in Europe. In F. Heidensohn & M. Farrell (Eds.), *Crime in Europe* (pp. 55–71). Routledge.
85. Heidensohn, F. (2012). The future of feminist criminology. *Crime, Media, Culture*, *8*, 123–134.

86. Heidensohn, F., & Silvestri, M. (2012). Gender and crime. In M. Maguire, R. Morgan, & R. Reiner (Eds.), *The Oxford Handbook of Criminology* (pp. 336–369). Oxford University Press.
87. Heimer, K., & De Coster, S. (2011). The gendering of violent delinquency. In F. T. Cullen & R. Agnew (Eds.), *Criminological Theory: Past to Present, Essential Readings* (pp. 348–356). Oxford University Press.
88. Hilinski-Rosick, C. M. (2016). The cycle of intimate partner violence. In T. L. Freiburger & C. D. Marcum (Eds.), *Women in the Criminal Justice System: Tracking the Journey of Females and Crime* (pp. 47–66). CRC Press.
89. Hilliard, T., & Neidermeyer, P. E. (2018). The gendering of fraud: An international investigation. *Journal of Financial Crime*, *25*, 811–837.
90. Holtfreter, K. (2014). White-collar and corporate crime. In R. Gartner & B. McCarthy (Eds.), *The Oxford Handbook of Gender, Sex and Crime* (pp. 490–507). Oxford University Press.
91. Hunnicutt, G., & Broidy, L. M. (2004). Liberation and economic marginalization: A reformulation and test of (formerly?) competing models. *Journal of Research in Crime and Delinquency*, *41*, 130–155.
92. Hutchings, A., & Chua, Y. (2016). Gendering cybercrime. In T. J. Holt (Ed.), *Cybercrime Through an Interdisciplinary Lens* (pp. 167–188).
93. Ingrascì, O. (2007). *Donne D'onore, Storie Di Mafia Al Femminile*. Bruno Mondadori.
94. Innes, A., & Anderson, K. (2017). *Indigenous men and masculinities: Legacies, identities, regeneration. University of Toronto Quarterly*, *83*(3), 242–244.
95. International Organization for Migration (IOM). (2016). *Egyptian Unaccompanied Migrant Children: A Case Study on Irregular Migration*. IOM.
96. Interpeace. (2015). *Violentas Y Violentadas: Relaciones De Género En Las Maras Salvatrucha Y Barrio 18 Del Triángulo Norte De Centroamérica*.
97. Iyer, K. (2016). Here are the world's top 10 female hackers. *Techworm*.
98. Jones, D. W. (2008). *Understanding Criminal Behavior: Psychosocial Approach to Criminality*. Routledge.
99. Klein, D. (2009). Etiologija kriminaliteta žena. In Đ. Ignjatović (Ed.), *Teorije u Kriminologiji* (pp. 372–387). Pravni fakultet Univerziteta u Beogradu.
100. Koons-Witt, B. (2002). The effect of gender on the decision to incarcerate before and after the introduction of sentencing guidelines. *Criminology*, *40*, 297–327.

101. Korkmaz, S. (2021). Youth intimate partner violence. In J. Devaney et al. (Eds.), *The Routledge International Handbook of Domestic Violence and Abuse* (pp. 155–170). Routledge.
102. Kuehnle, K., & Sullivan, A. (2003). Gay and lesbian victimization: Reporting factors in domestic violence and bias incidents. *Criminal Justice and Behavior*, *30*, 85–96.
103. Lammasniemi, L. (2017). Anti-White Slavery legislation and its legacies in England. *Anti-Trafficking Review*, *9*, 64–76.
104. Leiber, M. J., & Peck, J. H. (2015). Race, gender, crime severity, and decision making in the juvenile justice system. *Crime & Delinquency*, *61*, 771–797.
105. Loinaz, I. (2014). Typologies, risk and recidivism in partner-violent men with the B-SAFER: A pilot study. *Psychology, Crime & Law*, *20*(2), 183–198. https://doi.org/10.1080/1068316X.2013.770854.
106. Lukić, N. (2019a). Nasilnički kriminalitet žena. In Đ. Ignjatović (Ed.), *Kaznena Reakcija U Srbiji, Ix Deo* (pp. 327–348). Pravni fakultet Univerziteta u Beogradu.
107. Lukić, N. (2019b). Kriminalitet maloletnica u Beogradu–Studija o identifikaciji podgrupa. *Criminology*, *3*, 257–277.
108. Lydon, J., Carrington, K., et al. (2015). *Coming Out of Concrete Closets: A Report on Black & Pink's National LGBTQ Prisoner Survey*. Black and Pink.
109. Lynch, M. J. (2016). Class, race, gender and criminology: Structured choices and the life course. In D. Milovanovic & M. D. Schwartz (Eds.), *Race, Gender and Class in Criminology* (pp. 3–28). Routledge.
110. Lysova, A. (2014). The level and dynamics of female crime in Russia. *Sociological Research*, *53*, 3–12.
111. Males, M. (2010). Have girls gone wild? In M. Chesney-Lind & N. Jones (Eds.), *Fighting for Girls: New Perspectives on Gender and Violence* (pp. 13–32). State University of New York Press.
112. Malinowska, K., & Rychkova, O. (2015). *Getting Drug Policy Right for Women and Girls*. Open Society Foundations.
113. Malloch, M., & McIvor, G. (2012). *Women, Punishment and Social Justice: Human Rights and Penal Practices*. Routledge.
114. Malterud, K. (2001). Qualitative research: Standards, challenges, and guidelines. *The Lancet*, *358*(9280), 483–488.
115. Marcus-Mendoza, S. (2016). Incarcerated women in the United States. In T. L. Freiburger & C. D. Marcum (Eds.), *Women in the Criminal Justice*

System: Tracking the Journey of Females and Crime (pp. 209–222). CRC Press.

116. Marsh, I., et al. (2006). *Theories of Crime*. Routledge.
117. McElwee, P. (2012). The gender dimensions of the illegal trade in wildlife: Local and global connections in Vietnam. In M. L. Cruz-Torres & P. McElwee (Eds.), *Gender and Sustainability: Lessons from Asia and Latin America* (pp. 71–96). University of Arizona Press.
118. McIntosh, T., & Coster, S. (2017). Indigenous insider knowledge and prison identity. *Counterfutures*, *3*, 68–98. Aotearoa.
119. Messerschmidt, J. W. (2009). Muškost i teorijska kriminologija. In Đ. Ignjatović (Ed.), *Teorije u kriminologiji* (pp. 435–438). Pravni fakultet Univerziteta u Beogradu.
120. Messerschmidt, J. W. (2011). Masculinities and crime. In F. T. Cullen & R. Agnew (Eds.), *Criminological Theory: Past to Present* (pp. 357–368). Oxford University Press.
121. Messerschmidt, J. W., & Tomsen, S. (2016). Masculinities, crime and criminal justice. *Oxford Handbooks Online*.
122. Microsoft. (2018). *Closing the STEM gap: Why STEM Classes and Careers Still Lack Girls and What We Can Do About It*. Microsoft.
123. Miller, J. (2014). Doing crime as doing gender: Masculinities, femininities and crime. In R. Gartner & B. McCarthy (Eds.), *The Oxford Handbook of Gender, Sex and Crime* (pp. 19–39). Oxford University Press.
124. Miller, J., & Carbone Lopez, K. (2015). Beyond doing gender: Incorporating race, class, place and life transitions into feminist drug research. *Substance Use & Misuse*, *50*(6), 693–707.
125. Moffitt, T. E., et al. (2004). *Sex differences in antisocial behavior: Conduct disorder, delinquency and violence in the Dunedin Longitudinal Study*. Cambridge University Press.
126. Mogul, J. L., Richie, A., & Whitlock, K. (2011). *Queer (in)justice: The Criminalization of LGBT People in the United States*. Beacon Press.
127. Naffin, N. (2016). Theorizing about female crime. In S. K. Mukherjee & J. A. Scutt (Eds.), *Women and Crime* (pp. 70–91). Routledge.
128. Nagel, I. H., & Johnson, B. L. (1994). The role of gender in a structured sentencing system: Equal treatment, policy choices, and the sentencing of female offenders under the United States sentencing guidelines. *Journal of Criminal Law and Criminology*, *85*, 181–221.
129. Nixon, J., & Humphreys, C. (2010). Marshalling the evidence: Using intersectionality in the domestic violence frame. *Social Politics*, *17*, 137–158.

130. Nowacki, J. S. (2019). Gender equality and sentencing outcomes: An examination of state courts. *Criminal Justice Policy Review*, 1–23.

131. O'Hara, C. L. (1998). Children without childhood: A feminist intervention strategy utilizing systems theory and restorative justice in treating female adolescent offenders. *Women & Therapy*, *20*, 85–101.

132. Office of the Under Secretary–Economics and Statistics Administration (OUS/EA). (2017). *Women in STEM: 2017 Update*. U.S. Secretary of Commerce.

133. Organization of American States (OAS). (2016). *Women, Drug Policies, and Incarceration: A Guide for Policy Reform in Latin America*. WOLA, IDPC, De Justicia, CIM, OAS.

134. Oskarsson, S., & Strand, S. (2021). Police perceptions of victims of intimate partner violence in same-sex relationships. In T. K. Shackelford (Ed.), *The SAGE Handbook of Domestic Violence* (pp. 352–367). SAGE.

135. Palmer, W., & Missbach, A. (2017). Trafficking within migrant smuggling operations: Are underage transporters "victims" or "perpetrators"? *Asian and Pacific Migration Journal*, *26*(3), 287–307.

136. Pattavina, A., Hirschel, D., Buzawa, E., Faggiani, D., & Bentley, H. (2007). A comparison of the police response to heterosexual versus same-sex intimate partner violence. *Violence Against Women*, *13*, 374–394.

137. Peterman, L. M., & Dixon, C. G. (2003). Domestic violence between same-sex partners: Implications for counseling. *Journal of Counseling & Development*, *81*, 40–47.

138. Petersson, J. (2020). *Identifying Risk for Recidivism Among Partner-Violent Men Reported to The Swedish Police*. Mid Sweden University.

139. Petersson, J., & Strand, S. J. M. (2020). Family-only perpetrators of intimate partner violence: A systematic review. *Trauma, Violence, & Abuse*, *21*(2), 367–381. https://doi.org/10.1177/1524838018770410.

140. Phoenix, O. (2018). Introducing a gender-sensitive approach to pre-trial assessment and probation: Evaluation of an innovation in Kenya. *Probation Journal: The Journal of Community and Criminal Justice*, *65*, 184–200.

141. Portnoy, J., et al. (2014). Biological perspectives on sex differences in crime and antisocial behavior. In R. Gartner & B. McCarthy (Eds.), *The Oxford Handbook of Gender, Sex and Crime* (pp. 260–285). Oxford University Press.

142. Prison Reform Trust. (2017). *Why Focus on Reducing Women's Imprisonment?* Publications Prison Reform Trust.

143. Putkonen, H., et al. (2011). Gender differences in homicide offenders' criminal careers, substance abuse, and mental health care: A nationwide register-based study of Finnish homicide offenders. *Criminal Behavior and Mental Health*, *21*, 51–62.
144. Reckdenwald, A., & Parker, K. F. (2008). The influence of gender inequality and marginalization on types of female offending. *Homicide Studies*, *12*, 208–226.
145. Robertson, C. B., & Burton, D. L. (2010). An exploration of differences in childhood maltreatment between violent and non-violent male delinquents. *Journal of Child & Adolescent Trauma*, *3*, 319–329.
146. Rodriguez, F., Curry, T., & Lee, G. (2006). Gender differences in criminal sentencing: Do effects vary across violent, property, and drug offenses? *Social Science Quarterly*, *87*, 318–339.
147. Romain, D. M., & Freiburger, T. L. (2016). Chivalry revisited: Gender, race/ethnicity, and offense type on domestic violence charge reduction. *Feminist Criminology*, *11*, 191–222.
148. Rope, O., & Sheahan, F. (2018). *Global Prison Trends*. Penal Reform International and Thailand Institute of Justice.
149. Rousseau, A. (2017). What being a female hacker is really like. *Teen Vogue*.
150. Russell, T., et al. (2020). A gendered-comparative exploration of women's and men's pathways to prison in Thailand. *Australian & New Zealand Journal of Criminology*, *53*, 536–562.
151. Ryan, J. (2016). Transgender issues in the criminal justice system. Retrieved from: https://www.lag.org.uk/article/202050/transgender-issues-in-the-criminal-justice-system (accessed on 14 October 2024).
152. Sanchez, G. (2016). Women's participation in the facilitation of human smuggling: The case of the U.S. Southwest. *Geopolitics*, *21*(2), 387–406.
153. Sanchez, G. (2018). Five misconceptions about migrant smuggling. *Policy Briefs*, Migration Policy Centre, European University Institute.
154. Schwartz, J. (2013). A "new" female offender or increasing social control of women's behaviour? Cross-national evidence. *Feminist Studies*, *39*, 809–810.
155. Seagrave, M., Milivojevic, S., & Pickering, S. (2012). *Sex Trafficking: International Context and Response*. Willan.
156. Shaw, M., & Skywalker, L. (2018). *Gangs, Violence, and the Role of Women and Girls: Emerging Themes and Policy and Programme Options Drawn from Interviews with Female Gang Members in Cape Town*. Global Initiative Against Transnational and Organized Crime.

157. Siegel, L. J., & Welsh, B. C. (2011). *Juvenile Delinquency, the Core.* Wadsworth, Cengage Learning.
158. Simpson, S. (1989). Feminist theory, crime, and justice. *Criminology*, *27*, 605–631.
159. Smart, C. (1995). *Law, Crime, and Sexuality: Essays in Feminism*. Sage.
160. Sokoloff, N. J., & Dupont, I. (2005). Domestic violence at the intersections of race, class, and gender. *Violence Against Women*, *11*, 38–64.
161. Spohn, C., & Beichner, D. (2000). Is preferential treatment of female offenders a thing of the past? A multisite study of gender, race, and imprisonment. *Criminal Justice Policy Review*, *11*, 149–184.
162. Steffensmeier, D., et al. (2006). Gender gap trends for violent crimes, 1980 to 2003. *Feminist Criminology*, *1*, 72–98.
163. Stone-Cadena, V., & Álvarez-Velasco, S. (2018). Historicizing mobility: Coyoterismo in the indigenous Ecuadorian migration industry. *The ANNALS of the American Academy of Political and Social Science*, *676*(1), 194–211.
164. Stubbs, J., & Tolmie, J. (2008). Battered women charged with homicide: Advancing the interests of Indigenous women. *Australian & New Zealand Journal of Criminology*, *41*(1), 138–161.
165. Sutherland, E. H., & Cressey, D. R. (1978). *Criminology*. J. B. Lippincott Company.
166. Sylvers, P., et al. (2009). Biological factors and the development of persistent criminality. In J. Savage (Ed.), *The Development of Persistent Criminality* (pp. 141–162). Oxford University Press.
167. Synowiec, O. (2018). The third gender of southern Mexico. *BBC Travel*.
168. Tasca, M., Cho, A., Spohn, C., & Rodriguez, N. (2019). The role of parental status and involvement in sentence length decisions: A comparison of men and women sentenced to prison. *Crime & Delinquency*, *65*, 1899–1924.
169. Thijssen, J., & de Ruiter, C. (2011). Identifying subtypes of spousal assaulters using the B-SAFER. *Journal of Interpersonal Violence*, *26*(7), 1307–1321.
170. Tran, T. D., Nguyen, H., & Fisher, J. (2016). Attitudes towards intimate partner violence against women among women and men in 39 low- and middle-income countries. *PLOS One*, *11*(11). https://doi.org/10.1371/journal.pone.0167438.
171. Tremblay, S. (2019). Chinese 'Queen of Ivory' jailed for 15 years in Tanzania. *CNN World*.

172. United Nations Children's Fund (UNICEF). (2017). *UNICEF Annual Report 2017*. United Nations.
173. United Nations General Assembly Resolution 68/186. (2013). Strengthening crime prevention and criminal justice responses to protect cultural property, especially with regard to its trafficking. Adopted on 18 December 2013.
174. United Nations Office of the Special Advisor on Gender Issues and the Advancement of Women (UN OSAGI). (2001). *Gender Mainstreaming: Strategy for Promoting Gender Equality*. UN Women.
175. United Nations Office on Drugs and Crime (UNODC (a)). (2018). *Global Report on Trafficking in Persons 2018*. UNODC.
176. United Nations Office on Drugs and Crime (UNODC (b)). (2018). *Global Study on Smuggling of Migrants 2018*. UNODC.
177. United Nations Office on Drugs and Crime (UNODC (c)). (2018). *World Drug Report 2018*. UNODC.
178. United Nations Office on Drugs and Crime (UNODC). (2006). *Travaux Préparatoires of The Negotiations for The Elaboration of The United Nations Convention Against Transnational Organized Crime and The Protocols Thereto*. UNODC.
179. United Nations Office on Drugs and Crime (UNODC). (2013). *Global Study on Homicide 2013*. UNODC.
180. United Nations Office on Drugs and Crime (UNODC). (2017). *Issue Paper: The Concept of "Financial or Other Material Benefit" in the Smuggling of Migrants Protocol*. UNODC.
181. United Nations Security Council. (2015). *Resolution 2199*. Adopted at the 7379th meeting on 12 February 2015.
182. United Nations Security Council. (2017). *Resolution 2347*. Adopted at the 7907th meeting on 24 March 2017.
183. United States Attorney Southern District of New York. (2006). *Sister Ping Sentenced to 35 Years in Prison for Alien Smuggling, Hostage Taking, Money Laundering, and Ransom Proceeds Conspiracy*. United States Department of Justice.
184. United States Sentencing Commission (USSC). (2017). *Quick Facts: Alien Smuggling Offenses, 2013–2017*. U.S. Sentencing Commission.
185. USAID. (2017). *What Drives Demand for Wildlife? A Situation Analysis of Consumer Demand for Wildlife Parts and Products in China, Thailand, and Vietnam Based on A Literature Review (Elephant–Pangolin–Rhino–Tiger)*. United States Agency for International Development.

186. van den Bergh, B. J., Gatherer, A., Fraser, A., & Moller, L. (2011). Imprisonment and women's health: Concerns about gender sensitivity, human rights, and public health. *Bulletin of the World Health Organization*, *89*, 689–694.

187. Walmsley, R. (2016). *World Female Imprisonment List* (4th ed.). World Prison Brief: Institute for Criminal Policy Research (ICPR).

188. Wang, T. (2021). Mismatched liberation theory: A comparative method to explain increasing female crime share in the United States. *Feminist Criminology*, 1–36.

189. Washington Office for Latin America (WOLA), IDPC, DeJusticia, CIM, Organización de Estados Americanos. (2013). *Women, Drug Policies, and Incarceration: A Guide for Policy Reform in Latin America and the Caribbean*. WOLA.

190. Williams, S. L., McKelvey, D. K., & Frieze, H. I. (2014). Intimate-partner violence. In R. Gartner & B. McCarthy (Eds.), *The Oxford Handbook of Gender, Sex, and Crime* (pp. 362–378). Oxford University Press.

191. Yates, D., & Mackenzie, S. (2018). Heritage, crisis, and community crime prevention in Nepal. *International Journal of Cultural Property*, *25*(2), 203–221.

192. Yates, D., Mackenzie, S., & Smith, E. (2017). The cultural capitalists: Notes on the ongoing reconfiguration of trafficking culture in Asia. *Crime, Media, Culture*, *13*(2), 245–254.

193. Zhang, S. X. (2012). *Looking for a Hidden Population: Trafficking of Migrant Laborers in San Diego County*. San Diego State University.

Chapter **5**

Sexual Violence and the Law

Contents

INTRODUCTION

Any harmful or unwanted sexual act or attempt to obtain a sexual act by force or violence, or any act directed against a person's sexuality without that person's consent, is considered sexual violence. This applies to anyone, regardless of relationship to the victim. This includes coerced sexual behavior, whether it be verbal, psychological, or physical, whether it is attempted or accomplished. It is one of the most painful, pervasive, and frequent human rights violations; it happens both in times of peace and in times of armed conflict. It is also widely occurring.

In addition to having significant short- and long-term effects on physical and mental health, sexual violence is a serious public health issue. These effects include an increased risk of HIV infection, suicide, and problems related to sexual and reproductive health. Another component of sexual violence is murder, which can happeofbecause of an honor killing carried out in retaliation for a sexual assault or during one. Sexual violence can affect anyone at any age and can be committed by intimate partners as well as parents, caregivers, acquaintances, and strangers, though women and girls are disproportionately affected by these aspects. It is usually an aggressive act intended to assert power and dominance over the victim rather than a crime of passion.

Because sexual assault is still highly stigmatized everywhere it occurs, different places disclose assaults at different rates. Since it is generally an underreported phenomenon, the true scope of the issue is typically underestimated in the data that are available. Furthermore, there is a dearth of research on sexual violence, which makes a deeper comprehension of the problem essential to advancing a concerted campaign against it. Sexual violence resulting from conflicts is not the same as domestic violence. People who force their spouses into sexual acts frequently think that just because they are married, their behavior is acceptable. Sexual violence during times of conflict is often an inevitable by-product of warfare caught in a never-ending cycle of impunity. Men and women are frequently raped as a means of warfare (also known as "war rape"), an attack on the enemy, and a symbol of their conquest and dehumanization as fighters, either enslaved or captured. International humanitarian law, customary law, and human rights law all strongly forbid it, but enforcement mechanisms are still shaky or non-existent in many parts of the world.

From a historical standpoint, from the time of the Ancient Greeks until the 20th century, sexual violence against women was viewed as exclusively occurring against women and as commonplace and normal in both times of peace and war. As a result, there were no warnings abourenature, scope, or tactics of this kind of violence. Sexual violence was not viewed as a minor issue until the end of the 20th century, at which point it was gradually criminalized.

As recent as the genocide in Rwanda and the Israel-Hamas conflict in 2023, sexual violence against both Israelis and Palestinians was employed in warfare.

5.1. WHAT IS SEXUAL VIOLENCE?

When someone is coerced or tricked into engaging in unwanted sexual activity against their will, it is considered sexual violencentConsent is an agreement to do something or permission for something to happen. Risk factors for non consent include age, health, disability, fear, and/or under the influence of alcohol or other drugs. Sexual violence can affect children, teenagers, adults, and senior citizens alike. Sexual abusers can be strangers, family members, close friends, or trusted individuals; the first three groups are the most prevalent.

5.1.1. Forms of Sexual Violence

Rape, incest, child sexual abuse, intimate partner violence, sexual exploitation, human trafficking, unwanted sexual contact, sexual harassment, exposure, and voyeurism are all considered forms of sexual violence under the broad definition.

Sexual violence is a social justice issue that arises from mistreatment, exploitation, and abuse of weak points. It violates human rights and has the potential to undermine someone's confidence and sense of security. Sexual assaults involve more than just sex or control. One reason for the prevalence of rape culture is power imbalances, which are frequently the result of oppression.

People of all ages, races, genders, sexual orientations, abilities, professions, income levels, and ethnicities are victims of sexual violence.

5.1.2. Impact of Sexual Violence

5.1.2.1. On Survivors

Every survivor responds differently to trauma and sexual abuse. While some might speak up straight away, others might choose to keep quiet. Many people won't talk about the assault for weeks, months, or even years. Trauma affects how victims remember things and store their memories. Recollection lapses and postponed disclosures are frequent occurrences.

5.1.2.2. On Individuals

Sexual assault can have an impact on victim's families, friends, partners, kids, spouses, and/or coworkers in addition to survivors. Supporting those close to the survivor is crucial for providing the best care possible. Anyone affected by sexual violence can receive private services from social service providers in the area.

5.1.2.3. On Communities

Fear, rage, or disbelief can be felt in workplaces, schools, neighborhoods, colleges, the military, and cultural or religious communities. Communities bear financial costs. The financial toll that a single sexual assault takes varies from $87,000 to $240,776. These expenses consist of lost contributions from the affected individuals as well as medical services, criminal justice costs, and health service fees.

5.1.3. Ways to Prevent Sexual Violence

Prevention and risk reduction are two distinct concepts. Primary prevention strategies tackle the underlying causes of sexual violence and seek to alter societal norms. They recognize that prevention is feasible. Risk-reduction strategies, like taking self-defense classes, aim to lower a person's chance of becoming a victim. Several main strategies for prevention:

1. Be a role model for respectful relationships
2. Speak up when hearing harmful comments or witnessing acts of disrespect or violence
3. Create policies at workplaces and schools
4. Talk with legislators and ask them to support prevention programs

5.1.4. Facts About Sexual Violence

1. Sexual assault victims are never at fault. When the media mentions things like the victim's attire or whether or not they were drinking, they frequently inadvertently suggest that the victim is at fault. These remarks encourage victimization.
2. Sexual assaulters typically target someone they know, and they frequently employ coercion, deception, or "charm." They might inflict harm, threaten, or use force. The lack of physical harm to the victim does not imply their consent.
3. The continuation of sexual violence is made possible by societal factors such as acceptance of sexual harassment, gender norms that are restrictive, the belief that women should be in charge of their own safety, rape jokes, violent pornography, the notion that drinking will improve sex, and the notion that some groups are superior to others (sexism, racism, heterosexism, etc.).

5.1.5. Victim Reactions and Health Impacts

1. Depression, nightmares and/or flashbacks
2. Difficulty concentrating, anxiety and/or phobias
3. Post-traumatic stress disorder (PTSD)
4. Eating disorders
5. Substance use and/or abuse

5.2. SEXUAL VIOLENCE AGAINST WOMEN: THE SCOPE OF THE PROBLEM

Sexual violence and rape are pervasive in all societies and social classes. Between 6 and 59% of women report having been sexually abused by their husbands or boyfriends at some point in their lives, according to prevalence estimates. According to two population-based studies conducted in South Africa, rape has been committed by 28% and 37% of men, respectively. It is difficult to verify the estimates of rape perpetration from high-income countries, which appear to be lower than those from low- and middle-income countries. Girls and women are far more likely to be the victims than men are the offenders, and most of the time the victim knows who the offender is. Girls are more likely to experience sexual abuse as children, especially when they are at home and in school. High rates of child sexual abuse are showing up in the research, and as our knowledge of the impact of such abuse on victimization and perpetration later on grows, so does the significance of primary prevention for sexual violence as a means of addressing early exposure to violence. Research conducted in high-income nations has historically provided the basis for much of our understanding of sexual violence. However, this is beginning to change as high-caliber research from other contexts—particularly in Africa—as well as a growing number of multi-national studies examining sexual and interpersonal violence are emerging. There is a significant research gap on sexual violence among sub-groups and populations, and most countries lack population data on the incidence of sexual violence across all categories, including children. Due to variations in definitions, research instruments, techniques, and sampling strategies, a large portion of the current literature has flaws that impair cross-study comparability. Better research is necessary. Research on the social context of sexual violence perpetration and victimization by both men and women, as well as methodological research to measure sexual violence for specific population sub-groups or violence types, such as child perpetrators or young child victims, or sexual harassment at work and school, are priorities for understanding the magnitude of sexual violence prevalence. These include assessments of the prevalence and patterns of victimization and perpetration in a range of settings, across a range of acts of sexual violence, in men and women, in adults and children.

5.2.1. Sexual Violence Against Women

Sexual violence is a serious violation of people's rights and a public health issue. It happens in both peaceful and contentious environments and transcends class and race. Males who are well-known to the victims are typically the perpetrators; they are frequently an intimate partner or, in the case of child sexual abuse, a dependable relative or neighbor. Women and children can also commit acts of sexual violenrs.

"Any sexual act,Any sexual act attempts to obtain a sexual act, or acts to traffic for sexual purposes, directed against a person using coercion, harassment, or advances made by any person regardless of their relationship to the victim, in any setting, including but not limited to home and work" is the definition of sexual violence given in the World Report on Violence and Health.

Sexual violence occurs in a wide range of contexts and situations. These include the following: rape in marriage or dating relationships; rape of non-romantic acquaintances; sexual abuse by those in positions of trust, such as clergy, medical practitioners or teachers; rape by strangers; multiple perpetrator rape; sexual contact involving trickery, deception, blackmail or of persons who are incapacitated or are too drugged, drunk or intoxicated to consent; rape during armed conflict; sexual harassment, including demanding sex in return for work, school grades or favours; unwanted sexual touching; rape of men in prisons; unwanted exposure to pornography; sexual abuse of mentally or physically disabled people; sexual abuse of boys and girls; and violent acts against sexual integrity, including female genital mutilation, inspections for virginity, forced anal examination and forced trafficking of people for the purpose of sexual exploitation. Therefore, a variety of victim-perpetrator relationships, a variety of sexual acts, a variety of coercive methods, a variety of vulnerable contexts, and a variety of settings are all included in the diversity of sexual violence.

All of these instances involve sexual acts or acts against the sexuality of men and women, and they all take place in situations where consent is either withheld or not freely given. Different countries have different laws regarding what constitutes an offense related to sexual violence. There is a great deal of variation in the range of legal definitions of "rape." For example, although marital rape is illegal in many countries and under international law, it is not illegal in 127 other countries.

5.2.2. Researching Sexual Violence: Challenges and Data Sources

One of the most significant obstacles facing victimization research is the measurement of rape or sexual assault.

There are difficulties in determining the extent of sexual violence. Sexual violence is unique among violations in that the victim is frequently unfairly held responsible for its occurrence, regardless of the context. Moreover, rape is widely considered to be defiling. Consequently, victims of sexual violence find it difficult to tell their stories because the experience is stigmatizing and shameful. Extreme social repercussions can result from sexual violence; for instance, a family may believe that the victim has brought them disgrace, and victims may be forced to wed the offender, shunned, or even killed. Another issue that stems from the stigma surrounding rape and women's internalization of deeply held, cultural beliefs about men's sexual entitlement is that they may redefine sexual violence as "not rape" after it has occurred. This prevents them from feeling as though they must take action against the offender in order to pass for "not raped." In contrast to the USA, where there is a higher rate of reporting, only about 40% of rapes are reported, it is estimated that one in every twenty five women in South Africa have ever reported their experience to the police.

According to research, when questions are framed around behaviorally specific acts—such as "being forced into sex against your will"—there is a higher likelihood of reporting sexual violence. Questions containing the highly subjective terms "rape," "violation," or "abuse" invariably yield low reporting levels. There is a great deal of discussion concerning the appropriateness of using informal constructions like "sexual intercourse" versus more formal ones like "having sex," along with the distinction between anal and vaginal penetration. The Sexual Experiences Survey (SES) was created and is widely used by researchers in the United States. The SES makes use of exact act specifications. The likelihood is that this will demonstrate cultural diversity, as demonstrated in South Africa. Men said the anatomically precise questions offended them when the SES was tested in South Africa. They said that they all understood the colloquial term "having sex" to mean engaging in vaginal sex and that they would have preferred to be questioned about it.

A variety of victim and perpetrator contexts should also be investigated, including situations in which a woman is too inebriated to give consent and multi-perpetration gang rape. For accurate determination, they must also be framed around the type of perpetrator. It is especially crucial to inquire specifically about sexual violence from close partners because, unless specifically requested, this type of abuse is frequently underreported. Depending on the operational definition, a different number of questions may be required to assess exposure to sexual violence; nonetheless, all validated measures measuring rape, attempted rape, sexual coercion, or sexual harassment employ multiple questions.

Ascertainment is also sensitive to the settings in which research is conducted, especially when in-person interviews are used, as well as to the fieldworker training and support systems. Small groups of highnd supported fieldworkersfield workers yield much higher levels of ascertainment in surveys. The use of computerized technology to complete questionnaires has also proven to be very beneficial for perpetration surveys. Our capacity to compare prevalence estimates across settings is impacted by these variations. It is important to keep these restrictions in mind when interpreting the figures presented in the literature.

Table 5.1. *Different Categories of Sexual Violence Used in the World Health Organization Multi-Country Study on Women's Health and Domestic Violence Against Women*

Category	Operational Definition
Sexual violence by an intimate partner	Physically forced to have sexual intercourse when she did not want to. Had sexual intercourse when she did not want to because she was afraid. Forced to do something sexual that she found degrading or humiliating.
Sexual violence from the age of 15 years (by non-partner)	Forced to have sex or to perform a sexual act she did not want to.
Childhood sexual abuse (before age 15 years)	Touched sexually or made to do something sexual that she did not want to.
Forced first sex	First sexual intercourse, forced or rape.

Source: https://www.sciencedirect.com/science/article/abs/pii/S1521693412001228?via%3Dihub.

The development and formalization of operational definitions for intimate partner violence by the World Health Organization (WHO) Multi-Country Study (MCS) has been extremely helpful to the field. Additionally, it offers metrics for child sexual abuse and non-partner sexual violence, but these are not gold-standard metrics due to their narrow scope. We have the instruments to compare rates of sexual violence across time and contexts thanks to the operational definitions and questionnaires. Table 5.1 presents the operational definitions used in this study for the various categories of sexual violence investigated in the WHO MCS.

The WHO MCS excluded men and concentrated on victimization. It is becoming more widely recognized that including men in our research is crucial if we are to understand the causes of sexual violence, its global reach, and the most effective ways to enhance prevention initiatives. A prevalence of perpetration measurement methodology was created for research in South Africa, utilized in the multi-country IMAGES study, and improved for the Change Project, which is managed by the Partners for Prevention of the United Nations Development Project. Over 15,000 men in seven Asian and Pacific nation-states are presently participating in research using it (Table 5.2).

Table 5.2. *A New Methodology for Measuring Prevalence of Perpetration*

Category	Operational Definition
Rape of a partner (current or previous wife or girlfriend)	Forced to have sex with you when she did not want to. Sex when he knew she didn't want it but believed she should agree because she was a wife or partner. Forced her to watch pornography when she didn't want to. Forced her to do something sexual that she did not want to do
Rape of a non-partner (a woman who was not your wife or girlfriend at the time)	Forced to have sex. Sex with a woman or girl when she was too drunk or drugged to say whether she wanted it or not.
Multiple perpetrator rape	Sex with a woman when she didn't consent to sex or was forced by 'you and other men.' Sex with a woman when she was too drunk or drugged to stop it by 'you and other men.'

Source: https://www.sciencedirect.com/science/article/abs/pii/S1521693412001228?via%3Dihub

Both country-specific studies and national surveys are good sources of information on the prevalence of sexual violence. As an illustration, the National Intimate Partner and Sexual Violence Survey (NISVS) was developed in the United States. Since its launch in 2010, the NISVS has conducted yearly interviews with adults in both Spanish and English. Reproductive health surveys and the Demographic and Health Surveys (DHS) provide data on violence against women that is specific to each country. There are restrictions on the DHS data and the Reproductive Health Survey. When compared to findings from the WHO MCS and country-based studies that specifically examine violence against women, it has been demonstrated, for instance, that DHS data consistently underreport violence against women. The DHS is working to improve its Violence Against Women module, but these efforts are not enough to address the issues with surveys that employ a large number of fieldworkers who lack sufficient training, interest in gender, or resources for dealing with vicarious trauma.

5.2.3. Sexual Violence Prevalence: What Do We Know?

Discrimination and gender inequality are the main causes of sexual violence. It happens in many contexts at an alarmingly high rate. According to the WHO MCS, between 6 and 59% of women have at some point in their lives been the victim of sexual abuse by their husbands or boyfriends (Table 5.3). According to prevalence estimates of sexual violence victimization derived from 39 different population-based studies, between 0.3 and 39% of women report having experienced intimate partner or non-intimate partner sexual violence at some point in their lives. Using data from six different Reproductive and Demographic Health Surveys, a review of violence against women in Latin American and the Caribbean revealed that between 5.8 and 13.4% of women had forced sex at some point in their lives, with up to one-third of those encounters taking place before the age of fifteen. According to studies conducted in South Africa, the prevalence of sexual violence in alescategory's ranges from 12 to 28% among women who have ever reported being raped.

Table 5.3. *Prevalence of Sexual Violence Against Women and Children*

Site	Child Sexual Abuse Before Age 15 Years (Best Estimate)	Forced First Sex	Sexual Coercion by an Intimate Partner		Non-Partner Sexual Coercion From the Age of 15 Years
	%	%	Ever%	Past 12 Months (%)	%
Bangladesh City	7.4	24.1	37.4	20.2	7.6
Bangladesh province	1.0	29.9	49.7	24.2	0.5

Brazil City	11.6	2.8	10.1	2.8	6.8
Brazil province	8.7	4.3	14.3	5.6	4.6
Ethiopia province	7.0	16.6	58.6	44.4	0.3
Japan City	13.8	0.4	6.2	1.3	3.5
Namibia City	21.3	6.0	16.5	9.1	6.4
Peru City	19.5	7.3	22.5	7.1	10.3
Peru province	18.1	23.6	46.7	22.9	11.3
Samoa	1.8	8.1	19.5	11.5	10.6
Serbia/ Montenegro City	4.2	0.7	6.3	1.1	3.9
Thailand City	8.9	3.6	29.9	17.1	6.1
Thailand province	4.9	5.3	28.9	15.6	2.6
United Republic of Tanzania City	12.2	14.3	23.0	12.8	11.5
United Republic of Tanzania province	9.5	16.6	30.7	20.2	9.4

Source: https://www.sciencedirect.com/science/article/abs/pii/S1521693412001228?via%3Dihub.

Studies conducted in affluent nations also demonstrate a comparatively elevated incidence of sexual assault. For instance, according to the US NISVS, one in seventy-one men and nearly one in five women (18.3%) reported having experienced a rape at some point in their lives. In all, 34, 28, 27, and 25% of the women in the International Violence Against Women Study's Australian, Danish, Swiss, and Swedish arms said they had ever been raped.

As was previously mentioned, when examining the prevalence of sexual violence, it is important to differentiate between the various forms of rape and the circumstances surrounding them, such as rape committed by intimate partners, rape committed by non-intimate partners, experiences of first-time forced sex, sexual abuse suffered as a child, and rape by gangs. Should this not be done, the prevalence of sexual violence is probably going to be underestimated.

5.2.3.1. Sexual Coercion by an Intimate Partner

Most victims of sexual violence are aware of the perpetrators, and most rapes take place in close relationships. Therefore, it should come as no surprise that we find higher prevalence rates when intimate partner sexual violence is distinguished from non-intimate partner sexual violence. For example, the WHO MCS dispelled the myth that most rapes happen in dark alleys committed by an unknown attacker by finding that, in all countries surveyed, sexual coercion by an intimate partner was far more common than rape by a non-intimate partner (Table 5.1). Over 50% of women in ten out of the fifteen sites under the WHO MCS reported having been coerced into having sex by a close partner. In rural Ethiopia, women in the study reported rates of up to 59% of sexual violence committed by an intimate partner.

Other types of intimate partner violence typically co-occur with sexual violence in intimate relationships. Not all cases exhibit consistency in this patterning. For instance, the WHO MCS discovered that a significant percentage of women only reported sexual violence committed by their intimate partner. In Thailand, Bangladesh, and Ethiopia, for instance, 28.9, 49.7, and 58.6% of women reported only sexual violence, while very few reported any other type of sexual violence (Table 5.3). In a similar vein, sexual violence does not necessarily outweigh physical violence. In Southwest Ethiopia, 845 ever-married women between the ages of fifteen and forty-nine participated in a community-based, cross-sectional survey that revealed a lifetime prevalence of 50.1% for sexual violence. This is significantly higher than the study's findings of 41.1% for physical violence.

Pregnancy increases the risk of intimate partner sexual assault as well. The prevalence rates of intimate partner violence against pregnant women ranged from 2.7 to 26.5%, according to a systematic review of African studies on the subject.

Intimate relationships, sexual violence is not exclusive to heterosexual couples. In South Africa, population-based study involving adult men revealed that 9.6% of men reported being victims of male-on-male sexual violence, while 3.0% reported perpetrating it; 3.3% reported having been raped by another man, and 1.2% committed male-on-male rape. Men who mate with other men (MSM) are more than four times as likely as non-MSM to report being victims of sexual violence (34.4% vs. 8.1%) and more than nine times more likely to have been raped (21.3% vs. 2.3%). In an American study, MSM found that a comparable 4% of participants reported forced sex in their close relationships. These results highlight the need for a more complex understanding of intimate relationship sexual violence in order to inform prevention initiatives and service delivery.

5.2.3.2. Non-partner Sexual Violence

Non-partner rape occurs frequently, albeit at different rates in different contexts. This group of perpetrators can include a stranger, a family member, or someone you know from sight or acquaintanceship. Comparability of estimates can be challenging at times because some only focus on completed rape while others include attempted and completed rape. The percentage of women who reported being raped by a non-intimate partner since turning 15 years old varied from less than 0.3% in Ethiopian province to 11.5% in Tanzanian province, according to the WHO MCS (Table 5.3). According to the National Intimate Partner and Sexual Violence Survey, 13.8% of female victims, or one in seven, reported having been sexually assaulted by an unknown person. According to the most recent estimates, 12.2% of adult women in Gauteng province who are part of a population-based representative sample have experienced non-partner completed rape victimization. An additional 1 in 8 respondents in this survey reported having been the victim of attempted rape. In total, 41.9% of women reported having experienced multiple rapes at the hands of an outsider. Although this is more than earlier estimates, the study's methodology was stronger, and it is consistent with the 1998 "Three Province Study" finding that 2% of women had experienced a rape in the previous year.

Once more, variations in prevalence rates are a function of the study design, the definitions applied, the setting in which the research were carried out, and actual underlying patterns of rape. When conducted correctly, with sophisticated research instruments and definitions, prevalence studies are essential for developing policies and services.

5.2.3.3. Forced First Sex

Around the world, coercion and force are often the first experiences that young girls and women have with sex. For instance, the WHO MCS study discovered that over 10% of women said their first sexual encounter was coerced in six of the 15 sites. Less than 1% of women in Bangladesh and Serbia and Montenegro reported that their first sexual experience was coerced, while the highest percentage of women in Bangladesh—between 25% and nearly 33%—reported this information (Table 5.3).

Girls are more likely than boys to experience coercion and forced sex, and adolescence is a risk period for forced first sex. In a sample of 2705 students fronethirty-nine schools in Plateau state, Nigeria, forced sexual relations was reported by 45.0% of female students and 32.0 % of male students. In Lima, Peru, a study involving young adults and adolescents revealed that 11% of males and 40% of females reported coercion during the sexual initiation process. In the Caribbean, 47.6% of female and 31.9% of male adolescents who were sexually active reported that their first sexual experience had been coerced. The overall reported prevalence of forced or coerced sex for 16-year-olds was 25.4% for male students and 28.8% for female students in a multi-country study of school-going children in 445 schools across 10 southern African countries.

Two social phenomena are largely reflected in the high prevalence of forced sex that boys reported. One is the pressure boys face to demonstrate their manliness by engaging in sexual activity when they are not ready. In addition to girlfriends, male peers are frequently the source of this pressure. The other involves pressuring boys into having sex with elderly women. In a study conducted in South Africa involving a sizable adolescent population, 3.4% of the men and 9.7% of the women admitted to being coerced into having sex. 7.8% reported unwanted physical contact, and 2.3% said they were coerced or threatened into having sex with someone who wasn't their girlfriend. The boys were in their early teens, and the women who used coercion were typically much older. The boys were obviously distressed by these acts. We must learn more about the background of forced first sex.

5.2.3.4. Multiple Perpetrator Rap

Most rapes only have one perpetrator, but in certain situations, multiple men raping one person is not uncommon. This holds true not only in some peaceful nations but also during times of war. Due to context and definitional differences, the reported prevalence of multiple perpetrator rape varies greatly amongst studies, just like it does for other types of sexual violence. While one study of adolescent research volunteers found a prevalence of 14%, studies from South Africa that have collected data on rapes involving two or more perpetrators report a multiple perpetrator rape population prevalence ranging between 7 and 9% (Table 5.4). Comparable data from Bangladesh revealed a 2% population prevalence.

In the USA, a study on "multiple person sex" (MPS) was carried out to learn more about teenagers engaging in sexual activity with three or more people. In this study, researchers defined multiple partner sex (MPS) as either consensual (i.e., "group sex" or "three-ways") or coerced (i.e., "Rape by gang"). 328 women who were attending an urban health clinic made up the study sample. In total, 7.3% of respondents said they had participated in MPS; of these, slightly more than half (52%) said they had been coerced and 43% said they had been threatened or forced.

According to reports, rapes with multiple perpetrators are generally more violent than those with just one, most gang rapists are men, and weapons are far more frequently discovered in rapes with multiple perpetrators. Reports on multiple perpetrator rape are likely to be influenced by significant under-disclosure on the part of women. This underreporting is most likely a result of the significant stigma attached to being a victim of "gang rape."

Table 5.4. *Prevalence of Multiple-Perpetrator Rape in Studies Conducted in South Africa*

Country	Study	Prevalence (%)
South Africa	Stepping Stones trial: 1400 men aged 15–26 years from rural Eastern Cape, school going volunteers in HIV prevention trial.	14
South Africa	Study of men, masculinity and rape: randomly selected general population sample of 1738 adult men from Eastern Cape and Kwa Zulu Natal.	9
South Africa	Study of GBV in Gauteng province: randomly selected general population sample of 500 men.	7

Source: https://www.sciencedirect.com/science/article/abs/pii/S1521693412001228?via%3Dihub.

5.2.4. Prevalence of Rape Perpetrati

To Like victimization, estimates of rape perpetration differ significantly among contexts. Data on the prevalence of sexual violence against partners and non-partners is lackingy ofmost countries. The only population-based data available worldwide on the incidence of rape from sizable samples of men comes from middle- and low-income nations. South Africa has taken the lead in this work (Table 5.4). High rates of rape perpetration are found in South Africa, where 28–37% of men between the ages of 18 and 49 who participated in two extensive community-based surveys admitted to having committed a full-length rape. The IMAGES15 study also discovered a high incidence of rape. For instance, compared to 9% of men in Chile and Rwanda, 24% of all men (and 36% of married men) in India said they had ever engaged in sexual violence. 10% of urban men and 15% of rural men in Bangladesh's Change Project multi-country study reported having coerced their partners into having sex at some poir toLike India, the majority of sexual assault cases that were reported in Bangladesh happened in marriages.

Based on men reporting an act that would meet legal definitions of rape or attempted rape, estimates of the percentage of adolescents who commit rapes range from 5.6% to 27% in population-based studies and studies with college men from high-income countries. A small population-based sample of US men revealed that 24.5% had committed an act that could be classified as attempted or actual rape under the law. This percentage was significantly higher than findings from a national study of US college men, where 7.7% reported engaging in conduct that could be considered rape or attempted rape, or a national study of adolescents, where 5.6% of male adolescents reported coercing a romantic partner sexually. In many high-income settings, the practice of sexually coercive behaviors that are not as severe as rape is far more prevalent than actual rape. In a study on the frequency of sexual assault among Spanish college men, for instance, 15% of the men admitted to engaging in some sexual activity with women against their will, while 5.2% ttedcommitted or attempted rape. Although there isn't enough data to confirm it at this time, prevalence estimates suggest that rape may be less common in high-income countries than in low- and middle-income ones.

5.2.5. Sexual Violence in Childhood

Child sexual abuse is a widespread issue. The lifetime prevalence rates of child abuse victimization range from 7–36% for women and 3–29% for men, according to numerous reviews and meta-analyses on the subject. According to the WHO MCS, 1% to 21% of the women surveyed said they had been sexually abused as children before the age of 15.

The culprit was typically a male relative who wasn't the father or stepfather. According to the IMAGES research, rates of child sexual abuse against boys varied widely, with figures as low as 3% in Croatia, 8% in Chile, 17% in Rwanda, and 21% in India.

Additional information on the history of child sexual abuse (including forced sexual relations and other sex acts like unwanted touch) provided by adult women was gathered from extensive national Reproductive Health surveys conducted throughout Latin America and the Caribbean. The surveys revealed prevalence rates of child sexual abuse among women in El Salvador (5.8%), Nicaragua (4.0%), Ecuador (2.9%), and Paraguay (2.6%). There are no population-based statistics on the frequency of perpetrators of child sexual abuse.

In developing nations, national surveys have revealed high prevalence of child sexual abuse. According to research from Bangladesh, a significant percentage of men surveyed (37% of urban men and 22% of rural men) said they had been sexually abused as children. Tanzania and Swaziland (for girls only) have recently hosted sizable studies on child abuse. According to the Tanzanian study, three out of every ten girls and three out of every twenty boys said they had been sexually abused. According to a Swaziland study, roughly one in three girls had been sexually abused before turning eighteen. 75% of the offenders were boys and men from the communities where the victims lived. In a survey conducted in Switzerland among over 6500 schoolchildren, 22% of girls and 8% of boys said they had at some point in their lives been the victim of sexual assault; however, only 3-5% of the respondents said they had reported the abuse. According to data from the Adverse Childhood Experiences study conducted in the United States, 24.7% of girls and 16.0% of boys reported having been sexually abused as children.

The prevalence of child sexual abuse varies widely amongst Similar toLike other forms of sexual violence, variations in definitions and methods can account for variations in prevalence. Repressed memories of the abuse may prevent disclosure or raise doubts about what "really happened." Recall bias is more likely because most research has involved asking adults about their childhood experiences.

Comparability is hampered when interviewing children due to the population's age distribution (i.e., It is impossible to determine the percentage of kids who have been abused "ever"). Similarly, it is impossible to determine the prevalence of child sexual abuse from the previous year if adults are interviewed. It is important to consider these limitations when interpreting the estimates provided by research.

5.2.6. Sexual Violence in Schools

There are many different types of sexual violence in schools, and in many nations, sexual assault and harassment are prevalent. Teachers, other school officials, and students are typically the ones who commit these crimes. Many schoolgirls are compelled to engage in transactional sexual relationships wi a result ofbecause of their poverty. In 1998, the South African Demographic and Health Survey asked participants if they had ever been raped before the age of fifteen. Of those who reported having been raped aool teachersschoolteachers accounted for 32% of the cases. In Kenya, a study involving 1206 school-age children revealed that 58% of the children surveyed had experienced sexual harassment, with peers ace majority ofmost of the offenders.

Given the covert nature of sexual violence in schools, it is challenging to determine the exact scope of the issue. It can be especially difficult for victims of rape and sexual assault to come forward in a school setting. According to research, reporting such abuses frequently elicits responses such as incredulity, denial, or the argument that since it is a common occurrence, there shouldn't be much of a fuss. Numerous nations across the globe are experiencing a lack of success in their efforts to safeguard children and offer secure educational environments.

5.3. SEXUAL VIOLENCE AGAINST WOMEN: UNDERSTANDING CROSS-CULTURAL INTERSECTIONS

Whether it is sexual or not, interpersonal violence is still a serious issue in many parts of the world. Sexual violence against women and children has long-term psychological and social repercussions. In addition to the act of sexual gratification, real or perceived power imbalances between men and women are frequently the cause of sexual violence against women. Cultural norms and values also play a significant role in this phenomenon. There are differences in gender roles and representations as well as attitudes toward sexual violence between societies that are socio-centric and egocentric. Societies categorized as feminist grant equal authority to men and women. Cultures that promote the idea that men are superior and women are inferior on a social and cultural level are likely to have higher rates of sexual violence against women. While culture plays a significant role in understanding sexual violence overall, we also need to consider the advantages and disadvantages of other cultural structures.

There is a common occurrence of interpersonal violence directed towards a real or perceived weaker partner. Regardless of a victim's gender, sexual violence is an extremely harmful and traumatic life event that has far-reaching psychological and sociological repercussions.

It frequently results in a wide range of negative emotions, humiliation, and existential questions like "Why me?" It makes the victim feel more helpless and powerless, which lowers their self-esteem and raises suspicions that they might be at risk of experiencing more violence. Women's fear of sexual violence is probably going to limit their freedom and career opportunities as well as have an impact on their long-term psychological health. Because of the associated social stigma and shame for the victim and those connected to them, as well as a combination of ignorance and inexperience in asking serious personal questions about sexual violence, sexual violence is rarely discussed in professional settings. With overtones of patriarchy, misogyny, and gender shame, it is a social and health issue.

"Any sexual act or an attempt to obtain a sexual act, unwanted sexual comments, or advances, acts to traffic or otherwise directed, against a person's sexuality using coercion, by any person regardless of their relationship to the victim in any setting, including but not limited to home and work," is how the World Health Organization (WHO) defines sexual violence. All cultures have different definitions of what constitutes sexual violence, but it still occurs.

The cross-cultural dimensions of gender-based sexual violence against women are examined in this section. While there are other types of sexual violence as well (such as male-to-male and male-transgender), in this section we will concentrate on male-to-female sexual violence.

5.3.1. Culture and Sexual Violence: The Intersections

The culture that a person is born into and grows up in greatly influences the values, attitudes, and behaviors that person possesses today. Definitions and descriptions of normalcy and psychopathology are shaped by culturular populationspopulations and societies interpret, understand, and deal with sexual acts and sexual violence is greatly influenced by their cultural background.

The use of "coercion" or force is a key component of the WHO definition of sexual violence, and it is likely that cultural norms regarding what constitutes "forced" sexual relations differ. Culturally legitimized forms of violence give rise to a continuum with transgressive coercion at one end and tolerated coercion at the other. Different cultures describe certain forms of sexual violence that are condemned and other forms that may be tolerated to a degree. For instance, under the apartheid regime in South Africa, sexual violence against black women was tolerated and only cases of rape of white women were prosecuted. In some rural parts of India, marriage and sexual relations with a girl who is not yet an adult are involved in childhood marriages. As such, it is illegal and amounts to sexual coercion. But the whole matter is legitimized by private laws defined by those who participate in these marriages, which are approved by Khap Panchayats, who select partners for marriage in some regions of North India. Similarly, young men in South Africa who think that not having sex has a negative impact on mental health regard sexual violence as acceptable.

5.3.1.1. Prevalence

From observations and literature on interpersonal violence (IPV) in the context of sexual acts, cultural aspects of sexual violence can be understood. It is expected that cultures that promote the objectification of women, making them seem inferior to men, will have higher rates of sexual violence. However, not all cases of sexual violence are reported to the appropriate authorities; in fact, due to the sensitivity of the subject, between 67 and 84% of cases may go unreported, making it challenging to obtain precise statistics and an accurate understanding of the issue. It has been suggested that certain Asian cultures, where virginity is highly prized and a woman's modesty is crucial to earning her family the much-needed respect, have higher rates of unreported sexual offenses.

There have been theories that the frequency of sexual violence may be influenced by the sex ratio. India's male-female sex ratio, or the proportion of men to women in the population, has been "historically negative," fluctuating between 930 females for every 1000 males in 1971 and 940 for every 1000 males in 2011, which is indicative of a dire state of affairs. With a sex ratio of 940 in 2011, there were roughly 37.3 million more men than women, with a male population of approximately 623.7 million and a female population of 586.4 million. Concurrently, there has been an increase in the number of cases of sexual violence; however, there may not be a direct correlation between the two. The National Crime Records Bureau reports that from 2,487 recorded rape cases in 1971 to 24,206 in 2011, there was an 873.3% increase in rape cases in India. From 2,113 cases recorded in 2001 to 7,112 cases in 2011, there has also been an almost 336% increase in child sexual abuse cases in India.

According to the framework of evolutionary psychology, competition between males for female mates arises when there is a higher male-female sex ratio (more men than women). Men who commit sexual violence may become enraged and jealous of women as a result. According to this theoretical framework, men use sexual violence as a means of assuring their female partner's sexual fidelity. Since this theory refers to fidelity, which happens in the context of a relationship, it may also imply that it is only applicable to intrarelationship sexual violence. Therefore, this theory might not be able to account for the increase in child sexual abuse incidents in situations where fidelity is unrelated. Naturally, there's a good chance that this increase would occur with more thorough and accurate reporting.

According to a paradoxical hypothesis put forth by Guttentag and Secord, having fewer women than men in a high sex ratio increases the value that men place on women, which in turn lowers the likelihood that they will use violence against their intimate partners, including sexual violence.

5.3.1.2. Meanings Attributed to Gender

The definition of a man or woman and of manhood or womanhood can change in any given socio-cultural context, with masculine identity being linked to experiences and emotions of power. The idea that men shield women from harm is fostered by paternalistic cultural models, creating the perception that women are mainly incapable of defending violence incidentsviolence include aspects of dominance, control, control, and humiliation in addition to violence. Sexual abusers use tactics like kidnapping, seclusion, coercion, manipulation, threats, and sexual abuse to gain control and power over their victims. The meaning that men attach to power may override sexual goals in such acts, even though offenders may not find the act satisfying sexually. Sexual violence against children is a prime example of this, as it is essentially an expression of power over a child's life. It is improbable that a child will resist the offender's attempts, particularly since they may not always possess the mental development necessary to recognize the wrongness of the act.

Given that men are more frequently known to commit sexual violence across cultural boundaries, it has also been suggested that gender equality may lead to an increase in male backlash and sexual violence. The current change in Indian society from a male-dominated to a gender-equal society raises the possibility that the rise in sexual violence cases in recent times is a reaction by men against the country's progress toward greater gender equality. It is also conceivable that heightened media attention could inspire some people to care deeds in order toto become somewhat famous.

5.3.1.3. Attitudes

Gender attitudes are likely to influence how male-female relationships are perceived across cultural boundaries, which in turn influences how victims and sexual offenders are perceived. Sanday examined 156 societal structures for her groundbreaking research on the cross-cultural aspects of heterosexual rape. She discovered that rape is an integral component of a socio-cultural configuration that was centered on IPV, male dominance, and a "ideology of toughness" in men and weakness in women. Following in Sanday's footsteps, Briere and Malamuth investigated whether self-reported likelihood of raping or using sexual coercion was related to sexuality variables (sexual experience, importance of sex, relationships with women, use of pornography), as well as attitudes that encouraged violence toward women. They evaluated 352 male University of Manitoba introductory psychology students and discovered that, although not exclusively based on sexuality variables, rape-supportive attitudes and a combination of attitude and sexuality variables could predict the likelihood of rape or the use of force. Therefore, it appears that personality qualities play a bigger part in the "construction" of rape.

Sexual violence may be more common in cultures with more liberal views toward sexuality, but the same attitudes may also be present in less liberal societies. Jaffee and Straus proposed a strong correlation between urbanization, poverty, the high proportion of divorced men, and the incidence of reported sexual violence, but they did not find any link between sexually liberal attitudes and sexual violence.

5.3.1.4. Stereotypes

According to Burt, rape is a psychological outgrowth of the dominant-submissive sex roles that are stereotyped in our society. Sexual violence can be predicted by socio-culturally transmitted attitudes toward women, rape, and rapists. These stereotypes are frequently absorbed from the male-dominated social environment. A culture's pervasive misogynist mindset can give rise to sexual violence. It has been mentioned that in India, cows receive better treatment than women. For instance, girls in rural India lack autonomy over their sexuality. The expectation is that they will marry and have kids, which will transfer the power over their sexuality from one man (the father) to another (the husband). As in many other cultures that may still hold onto traditional patriarchal beliefs, a man is therefore the most significant figure in a woman's life in India.

More perceived or actual power may inspire people to consider their "rights" in societies where men and their manly roles are valued more highly. Men may view a woman's refusal to engage in sexual activity as a direct threat to their masculinity, which can lead to a crisis of masculine identity and encourage the use of sexual control and violence as a coping mechanism. According to reports, victims who try to resist or flee the situation are more likely to be brutalized by the abuser, which gives the abuser an increased sense of power, as was the case with the December 2012 gang rape of Nirbhaya in New Delhi. Because patriarchal cultures tend to view any resistance from the female victim as an affront to his "manhood," it is likely that the perpetrator will turn to more violent methods of victim control in response.

There is a widely held, cliched, but false stereotype that says a man is more likely to commit sexual violence against a woman if he witnesses her being attractive, seductive, and wearing skimpy clothing when she is out alone at night. This misconception unfairly places the entire burden of the act on the victim, making her a victim of further abuse. The idea that only young, attractive, and attractively dressed women are raped is simply a myth, given the facts that even a girl child is frequently the victim of sexual violence and that acquaintance rape is more common than stranger rape. Compared to appearance or attire, the victim's perceived or actual vulnerability is a far more significant factor.

5.3.1.5. Consequences of Sexual Violence

In addition to violating the immediate victims, sexual violence can have far-reaching effects on the definition of freedom and fundamental human rights. The way that different cultures view the effects of sexual violence varies. Sexual assault victims might not disclose their trauma in socio-centric societies where shame is a common emotion, which could prevent them from reporting it. This has a detrimental impact on the victim as well as on knowledge of the actual nature of trauma and the frequency of these acts, which in turn influences policy decisions. Socio-centric cultures place a strong emphasis on interpersonal relationships, with kinship and family serving as the primary sources of individual identity. In contrast, relationships with one's "self" are central to ego-centric cultures, where "independence" is valued above "interdependence." It is claimed that emotional expressions and experiences of shame and guilt differ between socio-centric and egocentric cultures. These disparate emotional experiences result from the fundamental cultural tenet of each of these societies: Socio-centric cultures, which are more socialized, tend to produce a more socialized sense of shame that is impossible to experience in the absence of social relationships. Egocentric societies, on the other hand, tend to be more individualistic and produce a guilt that is felt more privately. As such, the victim's culture influences the victim's feelings after experiencing sexual violence.

Family members share a greater understanding of the harm caused by sexual violence in socio-centric cultures where the family's (izzat) dignity comes before that of the individual member. Conversely, the harm caused by sexual violence is centered more on the identity and dignity of the individual member in ego-centric cultures. Concepts of self thus differ as well. Hofstede has also distinguished between the cultural dimensions of masculinity and femininity in societies with distinct gender roles.

When sexual assault victims disclose their trauma, they run the risk of experiencing negative reactions, the most traumatizing of which is being held responsible for the assault. Research has demonstrated a correlation between elevated levels of gender-based discrimination and stereotyping and elevated levels of victimization. In Asian cultures, where anything that has sexual overtones is heavily stigmatized, the social stigma resulting from sexual abuse is greater.

5.3.1.6. Understanding of Socio-Sexual Processes

Sexual violence committed by men from one culture against women from another may be significantly influenced by differences in gender roles and acceptable gender behaviors between cultures. Potential partners can express their interest in or disinterest in pursuing a sexual relationship with one another through a social process called sexual bargaining. The way that gender is viewed in different cultures may have a significant impact on this process. Men from sexually conservative cultures are likely to see nonsexual activities or platonic interests of women from sexually open cultures as sexual, which could lead to acts of sexual violence. In general, a number of studies have shown that men are more prone to misunderstand and misinterpret women's platonic interests as sexual cues. This may be the consequence of men's predisposition to interpret sexual interest or their propensity to view the world in sexualized terms. Further research is necessary to determine whether men from sexually conservative cultures are more prone to make such decoding errors.

5.3.1.7. Biology Versus Culture

Like many other biological processes, sexuality is thought to be influenced by genetics. However, our cultural background also has an impact on how we perceive, comprehend, and express sexuality. Researchers have long disagreed over whether biology contributes to sexual assault. Still, more research is necessary to determine whether rape is a culturally or biologically determined act.

Although it is still debatable, the biological or evolutionary theory of sexual violence emphasizes that sexual violence is subject to evolution, just like any other aspect of life, and that it represents adaptations made over the course of evolution. It believes that men's "natural" sexual urges, which differ from women's, are the cause of sexual violence. It is believed that early evolutionary changes and adaptation for successful sexual reproduction are responsible for this variation in sexual urges. Men utilize sexual violence and other reproductive strategies to spread their sperm and fertilize as many female eggs as possible because sexual selection drives them to do so. According to this theory, engaging in sexual violence is a normal behavior that stems from a person's biological desire to procreate and has a positive overall impact on their ability to procreate. Therefore, this theory, which has been contested, acknowledges that acts of sexual violence committed by men as a result of their aggression are normal. If this theory is correct, then all men are born with a predisposition towards sexual aggression and sexual violence. Thus, this theory looks for genetic roots of sexual violence while ignoring other potential influences that may arise later in life.

Another theory contends that sexual violence is socio-culturally constructed and tries to explain it in terms of cultural explanations. Thus, it refutes the biological theory's claim that a man's sexual urges have biological roots. This theory examines additional significant variables that may be contributing to sexual violence, including moral principles, gender power dynamics, attitudes toward violence, and more. Sanday classified cultures into two groups based on these factors: those that are rape-free and those that are rape-prone. These groups are shaped by socio-cultural values; the former have low rates of rape and a more balanced gender equality, while the latter have high rates of rape and restrict women's freedom and objectification. Sanday made the observation that while rape-prone societies are common, rape-free societies are not. In a similar vein, Otterbein studied 17 different cultures and found that those with strict sexual role norms also had higher rates of sexual violence. Therefore, the socio-cultural theory explains sexual violence as a social expression of patriarchy or male power. If this theory is correct, then societies that are patriarchal will experience higher rates of sexual violence than societies that value gender equality. Thornhill and Palmer combine these two theories, contending that sexual violence is a result of the overlap of biological and cultural factors because culture is made up primarily of socially learned behaviors.

Sexual violence may also be encouraged by cultural acceptance of violence. Le Vine, for instance, noted greater incidences of rape among the Kenyan Gusii or Kisii tribe. In Gusii marriages, men are encouraged by other members of the community to inflict pain and be sexually aggressive toward their wives during sexual activity. One does this to demonstrate their power. There is a claim that the Gusii have higher rates of rape because of extramarital or premarital sexual aggression resulting from marital aggression.

Whether sexual violence is caused by biological or cultural factors, it still has a significant impact on the victim's functioning and mental health, particularly because ty reacts to the violenceviolence. Victims of negative social reactions experience higher levels of mental health problems.

5.4. RESPONSIBILITY OF SEXUAL VIOLENCE UNDER INTERNATIONAL LAW

Throughout history, there have been many conflicts where sexual assaults against women, men, and teenagers have occurred. Address the pervasive sexual abuse that takes place during wartime because it can have a negative impact on a victim's life, their family, and the community. This is why perpetrators are often not held responsible. There are fewer cases before international criminal courts, despite an increase in prosecutions. As a result, on a national level, sexual violence is typically minimal or nonexistent. But more recently, there has been a focus on investigating and prosecuting cases of sexual violence during times of war worldwide, primarily through the UK's Sexual Violence Prevention Program. However, this section examines a few little-discussed issues related to sexual violence during wartime before we can fully develop the prosecution and investigation of sexual violence in war to adequately prosecute and investigate the variety of domestic and international sexual abuse (Chinkin, 1994).

The main point of the current article, which is reproduced below, is that, on the one hand, sexual violence poses a threat to international law because it has been deliberately employed as a weapon throughout history. Because it necessitates a comprehensive understanding of two categories of responsibilities—individual criminal and state accountability—accountability, it also seriously undermines other important laws currently in effect. As was previously mentioned, the challenges that must be overcome in order to bring those responsible for the crime to justice are the main focus of this section. On the other hand, accountability is the sole means of bringing all of the criminals who ought to be held responsible for these kinds of international crimes to justice. However, international law differs from our provincial legislation in that it is answerable to the State.

Furthermore, the emphasis in the modern world is shifting from state accountabiliminal accountability, oraccountability or taking ownership of one's own actions and being accountable for them. As a result, it identifies the primary offender—the active party—as well as anyone who, in any case, planned, encouraged, supported, shielded, or helped carry out the crime. These kinds of crimes are often carried out in the midst of international or domestic conflicts, or in any other ambiguous circumstance, which begs the question of whether the active or passive executor bears personal responsibility for carrying out that international violence (MacKinnon, 2007).

5.4.1. Notion of Responsibility During

There have been wars fromsince the beginning of time. In addition, there was a great deal of discussion about whether it was possible to bring charges against someone for an international crime they had committed. The realization that individuals, not governments, are accountable for crimes took more than a millennium to come to. In the end, it was decided that criminal responsibility for international crime should belong to an individual. After a protracted period of war antiquity, it is difficult to understand why the international community found it difficult to hold the real offender accountable for the widespread atrocities they committed. This was mostly caused by views on individual criminal responsibility that were very different from those of the 20th century. To put an end to the historical atrocities carried out during times of war, ideologies and strategies were developed. Even though individual criminal accountability was formally acknowledged, no one was successfully prosecuted. The reason for this was the widespread belief that kings and other leaders should not be held accountable to other countries for crimes they committed within their own borders. This belief persisted throughout history, up until the end of World War II, among state representatives, rulers, and trustworthy military generals. The concept of national sovereignty also offered them protection, which they used as a shield from any personal criminal liability since they felt they were acting on behalf of their country. Nations and emperors felt free to utilize any atrocity to achieve their political goals (Engel Jr, 2004).

The Peace and Truce of God (Latin: Pax et treuga Dei), a historic movement that employed spiritual sanctions to reduce wartime violence, was led by the

Catholic Church in Western Europe. None of these laws, however, resulted in the prohibition of war or the establishment of individual criminal liability. When plans were made and steps were taken to bring the guilty to justice in the fifteenth century, the idea of accountability for an international crime made significant progress. However, because of state impunity or unwillingness to prosecute those responsible for international crimes, the majority failed. It was not until World War II that nations began to comprehend the horrors of the two previous world wars and the consequences of not holding those responsible accountable. To stop reprisals against victims of international crimes, a permanent international criminal court was also founded. Consequently, post-war court cases involving German and Japanese commanding officers and service officers—who were primarily responsible for international crime—set in motion the long-dormant preexisting principles. Despite a rocky start, the ICTY and the ICTR first clarified the components of responsibility. The emergence of a new corpus of law known as international criminal law was transformed by these two international criminal tribunals. But the Tokyo Tribunal applied the idea so broadly that it effectively turned into a combined criminal enterprise in the contemporary sense. The primary responsibility was not discussed by the Nuremberg International Military Court. The Yamashita case before the US Military Commission after World War II strengthened the concept of prime responsibility (Rutschmann, 2011).

5.4.2. State Responsibility

The 1648 Treatylia introduced a number ofseveral ideas, one of which was the ideology of responsibility of states, sometimes referred to as the fundamental idea or cornerstone of international law. Later on, it emerged and was made explicit by the sovereignty principle. Therefore, government commitment is one of the fundamental principles of international law that emerges from the justifications of national power, the global administrative structure, and the reasonableness of States. It implies that a country will be held acco worldwide for any damagesdamage it causes to another internationally illegal (improper) nation. The formalized work of the International Law Commission (ILC) has concentrated on the State Duty topic. This investigation has been the riskiest yet.

The ILC began work on the article outline regarding State responsibility in 1975. The ILC approved the Regulations on State Responsibility on August 9, 2001. "The General Assembly Resolu 83/56 of December 12, 20012001, noted the International Law Commission's Articles on Responsibility of states, and the United Nations States acknowledged them" (Khan, Khan, and Khan, 2022). ition to the State's customcustoms and the decisions made by the international tribunal (the pertinent case law), the ILC Articles establish the international Law of State obligation. The legal framework surrounding State accountability addresses the nature of the State's responsibility, the ensuing legal ramifications, and the manner in which that responsibility is exercised (Crawford, 2013).

5.4.3. Nature of State Responsibility

The foundation of state obligation consists of three essential elements. The first is the legal obligation for the participatinglobally adopt each other'sother's practices. The other is acting—or not acting—in a way that is against a specific government mandate. The third is that this illegal act or omission has caused harm or adverse effects. The State's obligation was established by these three fundamental pillars, which have been completed and replicated in the ILC's Articles. It claims that it violates the State's obligations to other nations and is illegal everywhere it occurs because it is an action or inaction for which the State is responsible under international law. International accountability is violated by any action that, regardless of its source or nature, conflicts with what the State is required to do under that accountability (Weiss, 2002).

Furthermore, a right genuinely results in accountability. Every universally recognized right is obligated to abide by international law. There is no distinction between contractual (conventional) and tortious obligations under international law. International obligations encompass both breach of contract and other legal duty violations. Consequently, abuse of a state's power, no matter where it comes from or what kind of abuse it commits, makes the State more accountable and necessitatesn.

As a result, in order forfor a State to waive any of its responsibilities, payment is required. In this way, the accountability of the government only grows if a state is liable for the deed or omission that establishes a violation of its legal obligations. It may have originated from the concept of "fault" or "no-fault."

It is especially important to remember that a State is accountable for wrongdoing that incites international crimes rather than the actual crimes themselves. Because there is disagreement over State responsibility, international crimes are not mentioned in the ILC Articles. The ILC draft articles acknowledged international crimes as well as international crimes. The draft Articles declared that hostility, border control, bondage, and genocide were among the other international crimes that could not be justified. These international crimes were considered offenses by the international network since they stemmed from the breach of an international agreement that was crucial to safeguarding the network's main interests (Crawford, 2002).

Thus, the International Court of Justice's ruling on Serbia's obligation to commit genocide in Bosnia is based on a summary of the situation in Bosnia-Herzegovina and the earlier case that was brought before the court. The Bosnia versus. The Republic of Bosnia-Herzegovina filed lawsuits against the Federal Republic of Yugoslavia on March 20, 1993, alleging that the latter had destroyed the Genocide Crime Convention. This led to the creation of Serbia. Two of the six states and two independent provinces were the applicant and claimant who established what was officially known as the Social Federal Republic of Yugoslavia (SFRY) until 1992. Furthermore, Serbia and the SFRY included Bosnia-Herzegovina, Montenegro, Slovenia, Croatia, Macedonia, Kosovo, and the autonomous regions of Vojvodina. Thapsed in 1991 for a number ofseveral reasons. When Bosnia and Herzegovina's parliament proclaimed its independence from the SFRY in a settlement on "sovereignty," the legal proceedings for the current lawsuit officially began in October 1991. A unique Assembly of the Serbian Nation/Assembly of the Serbian People of Bosnia – Herzegovina was declared by the Serbian Representatives in the Bosnian Parliament on October 24, 1991. On August 12, 1992, the Republika Srpska was established, signifying the formal end of the war and offering Bosnia and Herzegovina a new beginning. Bosnia and Herzegovina duly acknowledged their eligibility from the SFRY aresult of their March 1, 19921992, submission. The US, the EU, and the UN all recognized the decision on May 22, 1992 (Nollkaemper, 2003).

Additionally, Bosnia requested that the Federal Republic of Yugoslavia (FRY) or one of its replacements comply with the "Convention on the Prevention and Punishment of Genocide" by attempting to eradicate the entire thing, both nationally and ethnically, in the Republic of Bosnia and Herzegovina, but not in an imperfect manner, in a case that was brought before the International Court of Justice (ICJ). Specifically, Muslim residents have killed group members, purposely caused physical or psychological harm to group members, imposed conditions on the group that are meant to cause whole or partial bodily destruction, and suggested extra measures to prevent births within the group. The numerous killings and other offenses mentioned in the Bosnia application happened all over the states. However, the destruction of Srebrenica turned out to be a massive task for Bosnia and Herzegovina as well as the entire international community. The Yugoslav People's Army is believed to have carried out the Srebrenica massacres, ostensibly under the guidance of Serbia's capital, Belgrade. The other members of the Yugoslav armed group in Bosnia and Herzegovina, the VRS, with which Bosnian Serbs are currently affiliated, are represented in this army. Therefore, the primary inquiry to be satisfied with would be whether Serbia was responsible for the massacre. The Court was mandated to ascertain whether the FRY government, as well as the armed forces and Bosnian Serb army, were involved in the preparation, coordination, or carrying out of the Srebrenica massacre (Voigt, 2008).

The State's obligation Under Art. IX of the Genocide Convention, a State may accompany the ICJ with the responsibility to address other universal wrongdoings and widespread human rights violations that are described by bargaining and customary law, subject to the discretionary circumstances outlined in Art. 36(2) of the ICJ Statute or by the terms of a specific compromise. These problems usually stem from a larger problem, which often involves the ethics of using authority. For example, that was the situation in Nicaragua. The US is a shining example of self-preservation and jus ad bellum. Meanwhile, opportunity handles the question of whether the US is to blame for the contra's alleged violations of the law of war. Congo's most current selection. Although Uganda generally exercises control over the use of force, there are growing reports of abuses of human rights and breaches of the law of war.

This coexistence in the context of globalization is reflected in ICC Statute Article 25(2), which states. "Any provision pertaining to individual criminal responsibility in this statute shall not impair a state's obligation under international law."

One's international criminal obligations remain valid even after committing an act of state obligation. Article 58 of the ILC Articles on State Obligation for International Illegal Acts (Articles on State Accountability) declares that these articles have no bearing on any individual's independent obligations that they might have when representing a government under international law. In its commentary on the previous Article 19, the ILC said that the State is allowed to act in this way and that individual's duties "certainly does not deplete the prosecution of the State's international accountability for internationally wrongful acts" that are in these cases attributed to it by the actions of its organs. Additionally, it was stated that "an individual's criminal culpability does not eliminate the international accountability of States for acts carried out by individuals acting as state organs or officials."

5.4.4. Individual Responsibility

Due to the growing scope of international law and its branches, state accountability is gradually losing ground to individual criminal responsibility. Since handling state's concerns has been a traditional aspect of international law, the single obligation is less well-known and understood in the field. However, in recent decades, there has also been an increasing individualization of duty in IL due to the development of ICL, which establishes criminal responsibility from IHL, HRL, and domestic legislation. The International Criminal Court (ICC) is less expensive than most domestic legal systems because of the Rome Statute, which restricts criminal acts to mass killings, crimes against humanity, illegal acts of hostility, and sexual viciousness. Although individual responsibility is explicitly stated in the Convention, states cannot be held responsible for the commission of genocide. The Convention is vague when it comes to defining when a statgenocide, despite the fact thateven though Article 6 does not forbid "responsible rulers" and "public officials" from being tried and punished for the crime and that Article 1 places the burden of proof on the states to "prevent and punish" genocide (Cappelen et al., 2010).

Consequently, this subject has been the subject of countless investigations and discussions in academic literature. Paola Gaeta claims that the Convention mandated the application of federal criminal penalties in order to enforce "fundamental values of international law regardless of whether they are breached by individuals acting on behalf of a state." Therefore, since the Genocide Convention (GC)'s language requires state commitments to avoid and reject destruction as malfeasance as well as the tradition of accepting state annihilation as a legitimate goal, there is no issue with the convention's actual and plausible formulations. The Nuremberg Legacy shows that states cannot be regarded as criminal entities because crimes are committed by men, not by various levels of abstraction. Judges Shi and Koroma voiced a similar opinion in their joint statement regarding the 2007 ICJ Genocide ruling. Judge Shi and Koroma voiced concerns about the interpretation of the ruling regarding the process by which a State could be held liable for the crime of genocide in a joint statement that was appended to the decision.

5.4.5. Individual Responsibility during International Armed Conflicts (IACs)

Individual criminal responsibility for war crimes has long been acknowledged in customary international law. After being acknowledged in the Lieber Code and the Oxford Manual, this principle has been reiterated in numerous laws of war agreements. The Nuremberg and Tokyo IMT charters, the ICTFY Statute, and the ICC established criminal responsibility for war crimes committed during the international conflict. Various military manuals claim that people feel guilty about committing war crimes. Various state laws update the principle of indil responsibility with regard toregarding war crimes. This principle led to the stabbing of multiple war criminals who were accused. Both open practice and official declarations support this idea. The directive was reviewed with a variety of objectives by the UN General Assembly, UN Security Council, and UN Commission on Human Rights (UNCHR). Numerous other in organizations also looked intoinvestigated it (Kretzmer et al., 2014).

5.4.6. Individual Responsibility during Non-International Armed Conflicts

Non-International Armed Conflict (NIAC) has advanced significantly since the mid-1990s. The unique criminal obligations in relation to war crimes designated in NIAC have unquestionably been joined by three international humanitarian agreements, namely "Protocol II to the Convention on Certain Conventional Weapons, the Statute ICC, and the Second Protocol to the Hague Convention on the Protection of Cultural Property." "The Optional Protocol to the Convention on the Rights of the Child on the Participation of Children in Armed Conflict and the Ottawa Convention prohibiting the use of minefields," which stipulate that States should censure denied conduct bringing it into NIAC, are undoubtedly perceived as explicit in two other late-game schemes. The statutes of the International Criminal Tribunal for Rwanda and the Special Court for Sierra Leone make it abundantly evident that parties are criminally accountable for war crimes perpetrated during non-international armed conflicts. Many states have denounced war crimes committed in non-international armed conflicts, especially in the last ten years. There will probably be more requests made if the ICC's statute is explicitly affirmed and if the standard of complementarities is abused. National courts have prosecuted war crimes committed during non-international armed conflicts. Furthermore, there have been several official statements on national and international matters concerning the one criminal threat in NIAC since the mid-1990s (Graditzky, 1998).

In the mid-1990s, international organizations came clean and acknowledged that there had been cases of NIAC breaking the Law of War. The standards of individual criminal responsibility with regard to war crimes committed in NIAC were examined by the UNGA, UN SC, and UNCHR. Thus, in the cases of, say, "Afghanistan, Angola, Bosnia-Herzegovina, Burundi, Rwanda, Sierra Leone, Somalia, and the former Yugoslavia." Furthermore, through the Organization of African Unity, the European Union sent similar declarations to Rwanda in 1994 and Liberia in 1996. Criminal charges against those responsible for crimes committed during regional wars are guaranteed by the ICT for the former Yugoslavia and Rwanda's initial rulings. The Appeals Chamber of the ICTY found that there had only been one instance of a war crime committed during a NiAC in the Tadic case from 1995.

Both committing war crimes and attempting to commit war crimes are crimes against humanity under the law. They are also accountable for supporting, encouraging, allowing, or permitting a monstrosity to be committed. They are also responsible for organizing or supporting a committee to investigate war crimes. Combatants ought to be made financially responsible for their terrible setbacks in accordance with international law. According to a UN Secretary-

General report on how hardship is interpreted and how to build consensus and manageable improvements in Africa, the general public should be the aware target of hostility. Combative social gatherings will eventually be held responsible for their actions. The UNCHR Special Representative pointed out that individuals accused of misbehaving would likely be suspected of compensating for their misdeeds during the Gaca primers, which were established in Rwanda with the intention of eliminating suspects. Combative social gatherings need to be gradually held responsible for their actions. During the gaca aptamers set up in Rwanda to try to destroy suspects, those blamed for bad property behavior and attitude will be accused of paying remuneration for the mischief they exacerbated, according to a study on human rights in Rwanda by the UNCHR for Rwanda's Special Representative (Forsythe, 1978).

Furthermore, the Slobodan Milosevic era (1987–2000) in Serbia was marked by extraordinary international disconnection, harsh regional constraints, and violent interethnic conflict in Bosnia, Kosovo, and Croatia. The paramilitary groups and the Yugoslav national armed force (JNA), which is commanded by Serbia, legitimately participated in all three conflicts. Terrible crimes were carried out by Serbian forces against law-abiding citizens, such as the murder of 7,000 Bosnian men and boys in Srebrenica. In a well-known uprising in 2000, Milosevic lost his job because he refused to accept the consequences of the president's political decision.

Following Milosevic's overthrow, the transitional government in Serbia faced strong international pressure to bring charges against all those accountable for atrocities, including Milosevic. The transitional equity guidelines were modeled after individual trials conducted at the ICTY. From the Serbian atrocities chamber's opening in 2003, the WCC's engagement with the ICTY has served as the international community's primary assessment of Serbia's value-based initiatives. Furthermore, this capital tool judgment was authorized by the restriction agreement, which is how almost all international accolades in Serbia chose to apply for global guidance. There is no denying the Hague tribunal's exceptional historical significance in maintaining the wide range of crimes documented during the Yugoslav conflicts. The ICTY has fulfilled a vital need by compiling a body of evidence of war crimes that most likely would not have been assembled without the Hague procedures. More than 3500 spectators made their initial individual declarations known during the ICTY preliminary proceedings, giving them a platform to openly share their suffering and misfortune (UN development program, 2006). Similar to this, Serbia has experienced outstanding equity outcomes as a result of the deliberate emphasis on personal accountability (Somer, 2007). The aforementioned research indicates that the question of individual accountability for sexual violence is complicated, posing some difficult but inevitable challenges for international law. This case was similar to the one I just described in that it involved multiple crimes, such as sexual abuse, enslavement, and violence. As a result, responsibility is now separated into two categories under international law: individual responsibility and command responsibility. Every State makes sure that its soldiers are properly trained in armed conflict and are given a manual. However, because the State is unwilling to accept responsibility in such circumstances, if a soldier commits acts of sexual violence, such as rape, torture, or other physical abuse while in camp, he will be held personally accountable for those crimes.

5.4.7. Landmark Cases of Individuals Convicted Criminals

More than seventy people have been accused of crimes involving sexual violence, including assault and rape. Since the middle of 2011, almost thirty sentences have been imposed. As a resug in 1995, the ICTY looked intoinvestigated and prosecuted multiple cases of sexual assault during wartime in Bosnia and Herzegovina, which resulted in the filing of multiple indictments. Since then, over 70 people have been charged with crimes involving sexual violence, including rape and sexual assault. Since the middle of 2011, almost thirty individuals have been charged with crimes. By trying sexual assault as a war crime, a crime against humanity, and a form of genocide in several historic cases, the tribunal cleared the path for global equity in the field of sexual offenses.

Furthermore, this election of the close-by State board head of the erstwhile Bosnian Serb Democratic Party from Kozarac in northwest Bosnia-Herzegovina had a multifaceted impact on the world. The first international war crimes trials were held in Tokyo and Nuremberg. It was noteworthy in addition for the fact that the first international war crimes trial featured accusations of sexual assault. The trial demonstrated the possibility of punishing offenders as well as the possibility that the growing global criminal intent could put an end to the legalization of sexual offenses.

The Trial Chamber was informed that numerous Muslims and Croats were detained by Serbian forces in the northwest of Bosnia and Herzegovina following their capture of Prijedor's territory. One of the prisoners at the Omarska Camp was made to bite off the strategies of another prisoner by a group of men wearing formal attire, among them Duko Tadi. Tadi was found guilty by the Trial Chamber of cold-blooded treatment (a breach of the principles and norms of war) and coldhearted acts (unsity) in May 1997 as a result ofbecause of his involvement in this and other episodes.

After two years of the 1949 Geneva Exhibitions, Tadic was also found guilty of intentionally causing physical or mental suffering or actual harm to people and of being cruel to them. In its ruling, the Chamber of Appeals claimed that Duko Tadic's principle gave the men who participated in the successful ambush power and support. This situation raises serious concerns about the inmate in question as well as the various inmate's cold-bloodedness and mortification. January 2000 saw the 20-year prison sentence for Tadic.

The trial of four former Bosnian military personnel, who saw the attack as a kind of torture, established a victory for global justice and, in that sense, both an outright violation of the GC and a transgression of the rules and methods of warfare. Thus, it was alleged that three of the four accused had sexually abused native Bosnian Serbian residents who were being detained in a detention center located in Elebii, the capital of Bosnia and Herzegovina. Throughout the trial, the trial chamber discussed a number of sexual assault allegations. Camp watchman Esad Lando set up an ingesting circuit around the genitalia of two siblings in order to force them to offer themselves up for fellatio in front of other prisoners. He also wrapped a consumption wire around the genitalia of another male prisoner, forcing him to keep running between the columns. To put it another way, the ICTY considered Lando's primary responsibility for these demonstrations. Zdravko Muci, the leader of the camp, was made to answer for both of these transgressions in addition to others that his adherents had reported. The offenses were considered serious violations of wartime customs and laws (Khan et al., 2022).

In the discussion of the assault claims made by the delegate camp officer, HazimDeli, a legal benchmark has been established. The ICC categorized the assault as torture in its first decision of this type. Deli then attacked Milojka Anti and Grozdana while they were being cross-examined. In the camp, both womene judges came to the conclusionconcluded that the attacks were carried out to gather information, reject the women for not providing information, and threaten and threaten them into providing it. The cruelty inflicted on the two women was also explained by the Trial Chamber in a discriminatory manner: it was done to them just because they were female. Hazim Deli received an 18-year prison sentence, Zdravko Muci received a 9-year sentence, and Esad Lando received a 15-year prison sentence after the ICTY's Chamber of Appeals upheld the Trial Chamber's ruling. The fourth person to be charged, Zejnil Delali, was ultimately found not guilty due to insufficient evidence (Socia et al., 2020).

The main accusation made against Anto Furundzija by the ICTY was sexual assault. In the preliminary, Furundzija led cross-examinations on the various attacks claimed by a Bosnian Muslim woman. At the time, Furundzija was the leader of the Jokers, a separate unit of the "Croatian Defense Council (HVO) in Bosnia and Herzegovina." Thus, in my view, it was not Furundzija but his subordinate who attacked the woman in front of a giggling group of official's witnesses. The official of the unit, Furundija, was perceived as co-accused and complicit in the crime. Following an appeal that upheld the conviction, Furundija was given a 10-year prison sentence.

Despite the Kunarac et al final judgment characterizing rape as a weapon of war, the Radislav Krsti case established a link between rape and ethnic cleansing that was closely linked to genocide regarding Srebrenica's wrongdoings in July 1995. "Krsti founded the Drina Corps during the movement that led to the implementation of over 7,000 Bosnian Muslim young men and men from Srebrenica in July 1995. He was a General Major in the Bosnian Serb Army. In addition, as the city came under the authority of Bosnian Serb armed forces, 20 to 30,000 Muslims, primarily women, children, and the elderly, fled to the nearby village of Potoari." Between two and three thousand people were searching the UN military facility for protection. The Serbians set up the compound, hid in the throng, mingled with the people, beat, and killed. Accordingly, the troopers staged multiple acts of rape. In 2004, the Chamber of Appeals persisted in expressing strong sexual views. Krsti received a sentence of 35 years in prison.

Furthermore, research has compiled a numerical list of all the criminals implicated in various sexual violence-related crimes. As per the ICTY Statute's Art. 7(1), 32 people were found guilty as of September 2016 of committing crimes involving sexual violence. Four more people received sentences in line with Art. 7(3) of the Statute for their failure to stop or punish the criminals.

One of the Statute's raised topics is the question of criminal culpability. According to the first sentence, "Anyone who organized, encouraged, directed, carried out, or in any other way assisted and abetted in the preparation, planning, or execution of a crime covered by articles 2 to 5 of the current Statute, shall be held personally liable for the crime."

Article 7(3) states: "If a superior knew or had reasonable suspicion that a subordinate was going to commit any of the acts mentioned in articles 2 to 5 of the current Statute, or had already committed any of the acts, and the superior failed to take the necessary and reasonable measures to prevent such acts or to punish the perpetrators thereof, the superior is not relieved of criminal responsibility" (Thompson et al., 2020).

REFERENCES

1. Abbey, A., & Harnish, R. J. (1995). Perception of sexual intent: The role of gender, alcohol consumption, and rape supportive attitudes. *Sex Roles*, *32*, 297–313.
2. Abbey, A., Cozzarelli, C., McLaughlin, K., & Harnish, R. J. (1987). The effects of clothing on dyad sex composition on perceptions of sexual intent: Do women and men evaluate these cues differently? *Journal of Applied Social Psychology*, *17*, 108–126.
3. Abbey, A., McAuslan, P., Zawacki, T., et al. (2006). Cross-sectional predictors of sexual assault perpetration in a community sample of single African American and Caucasian men. *Aggressive Behavior*, *32*, 54–67.
4. Abrahams, N., Jewkes, R., Laubscher, R., et al. (2006). Intimate partner violence: Prevalence and risk factors for men in Cape Town, South Africa. *Violence and Victims*, *21*, 247–264.
5. Anderson, J. E., Abraham, M., Bruessow, M., Coleman, R. D., McCarthy, K. C., Harris-Odimgbe, T., et al. (2008). Cross-cultural perspectives on intimate partner violence. *Journal of the American Academy of Physician Assistants*, *21*, 36–44.
6. Andersson, N., Paredes-Solís, S., Milne, D., et al. (2012). Prevalence and risk factors for forced or coerced sex among school-going youth: National cross-sectional studies in 10 southern African countries in 2003 and 2007. *BMJ Open*, *2*(2), e000754.
7. Andrews, G., Cory, J., Slade, J., et al. (2004). Child sexual abuse. In *Comparative Quantification of Health Risks: Global and Regional Burden of Disease Attributable to Selected Major Risk Factors* (pp. 1851–1940). Geneva: World Health Organization.
8. Antonowicz, L. (2010). *Too Often in Silence: A Report on School-Based Violence in West and Central Africa*. UNICEF, Plan West Africa, Save the Children Sweden West Africa and Action Aid.
9. Barker, G., Contreras, J. M., Heilman, B., et al. (2011). *Evolving Men: Initial Results from the International Men and Gender Equality Survey (IMAGES)*. Washington, DC, and Rio De Janeiro: International Center for Research on Women and Instituto Promundo.
10. Baron, L., & Straus, M. A. (1989). Rape and its relation to social disorganization, pornography and inequality in the USA. *Medicine and Law*, *8*, 209–232.
11. Black, M. C., Basile, K. C., Breiding, M. J., et al. (2011). *National Intimate Partner and Sexual Violence Survey (NISVS): 2010 Summary Report*.

Atlanta, GA: National Center for Injury Prevention and Control, Centers for Disease Control and Prevention.

12. Briere, J., & Malamuth, N. M. (1983). Self-reported likelihood of sexually aggressive behavior: Attitudinal versus sexual explanations. *Journal of Research in Personality*, *17*, 315–323.
13. Butchart, A., & Phinney Harvey, A. (2006). *Preventing Child Maltreatment: A Guide to Taking Action and Generating Evidence*. Geneva: World Health Organization and International Society for Prevention of Child Abuse and Neglect.
14. Cáceres, C. F., Marín, B. V., & Hudes, E. S. (2000). Sexual coercion among youth and young adults in Lima, Peru. *Journal of Adolescent Health*, *27*, 361–367.
15. Campbell, R., Ahrens, C. E., Sefl, T., Wasco, S. M., & Barnes, H. E. (2001). Social reactions to rape victims: Healing and hurtful effects on psychological and physical health outcomes. *Violence and Victims*, *16*, 287–302.
16. Cappelen, A. W., Sørensen, E. Ø., & Tungodden, B. (2010). Responsibility for what? Fairness and individual responsibility. *European Economic Review*, *54*(3), 429–441. https://doi.org/10.1016/j.euroecorev.2009.08.005.
17. Casey, E. A., Beadnell, B., & Lindhorst, T. P. (2009). Predictors of sexually coercive behaviour in a nationally representative sample of adolescent males. *Journal of Interpersonal Violence*, *24*, 1129–1147.
18. Chinkin, C. (1994). Rape and sexual abuse of women in international law. *European Journal of International Law*, *5*(3), 326–341. https://doi.org/10.1093/oxfordjournals.ejil.a035874.
19. Cohen, M. A., & Piquero, A. R. (2009). New evidence on the monetary value of saving a high-risk youth. *Journal of Quantitative Criminology*, *25*, 25–49. https://doi.org/10.1007/s10940-008-9057-3.
20. Contreras, M., Heilman, B., Barker, G., et al. (2012). *Bridges to Adulthood: Understanding the Lifelong Influence of Men's Childhood Experiences of Violence*. Washington, DC: International Center for Research on Women (ICRW) and Rio de Janeiro: Instituto Promundo.
21. Crawford, J. (2013). *State Responsibility: The General Part* (Cambridge Studies in International and Comparative Law, Series No. 100). Cambridge University Press.
22. D'Alessio, S. J., & Stolzenberg, L. (2010). Sex ratio and male-on-female intimate partner violence. *Journal of Criminal Justice*, *38*, 555–561.
23. Daley, E. M., & Noland, V. (2001). Intimate partner violence in college

students: A cross-cultural comparison. *International Electronic Journal of Health Education*, *4*, 35–40.

24. Delisi, M., Kosloski, A., Sween, M., Hachmeister, E., Moore, M., & Drury, A. (2010). Murder by numbers: Monetary costs imposed by a sample of homicide offenders. *The Journal of Forensic Psychiatry & Psychology*, *21*, 501–513. https://doi.org/10.1080/14789940903564388.
25. Deribe, K., Beyene, B. K., Tolla, A., et al. (2012). Magnitude and correlates of intimate partner violence against women and its outcome in Southwest Ethiopia. *PLoS One*, *7*(3), e36189.
26. Dunkle, K. L., Jewkes, R. K., Brown, H. C., et al. (2004). Prevalence and patterns of gender-based violence and revictimization among women attending antenatal clinics in Soweto, South Africa. *American Journal of Epidemiology*, *160*, 230–239.
27. El-Bushra, J., & Piza Lopez, E. (1993). Gender-related violence: Its scope and relevance. *Focus on Gender*, *1*, 1–9.
28. Ellsberg, M., & Heise, L. (2005). *Researching Violence Against Women: A Practical Guide for Researchers and Activists*. Washington, DC: World Health Organization and PATH.
29. Ellsberg, M., Heise, L., Peña, R., et al. (2001). Researching domestic violence against women: Methodological and ethical considerations. *Studies in Family Planning*, *32*, 1–16.
30. Engel, C. C. (2004). Post-war syndromes: Illustrating the impact of the social psyche on notions of risk, responsibility, reason, and remedy. *The Journal of the American Academy of Psychoanalysis and Dynamic Psychiatry*, *32*(2), 321–334. https://doi.org/10.1521/jaap.32.2.321.35275.
31. Farris, C., Treat, T. A., Viken, R. J., & McFall, R. M. (2008). Sexual coercion and the misperception of sexual intent. *Clinical Psychology Review*, *28*, 48–66.
32. Finkelhor, D. (1994). The international epidemiology of child sexual abuse. *Child Abuse & Neglect*, *18*, 409–417.
33. Forsythe, D. P. (1978). Legal management of internal war: The 1977 protocol on noninternational armed conflicts. *American Journal of International Law*, *72*(2), 272–295. https://doi.org/10.2307/2199956.
34. Garcia-Moreno, C., Henrica, A. F. M., Watts, C., et al. (2005). WHO multi-country study on women's health and domestic violence against women: Initial results on prevalence, health outcomes and women's responses. Geneva: World Health Organization.
35. Gottschall, J. A., & Gottschall, T. A. (2003). Are per-incident rape-

pregnancy rates higher than per-incident consensual pregnancy rates? *Human Nature*, *14*, 1–20.

36. Graditzky, T. (1998). Individual criminal responsibility for violations of international humanitarian law committed in noninternational armed conflicts. *International Review of the Red Cross*, *38*(322), 29–56. https://doi.org/10.1017/S0020860400090756.
37. Greenfield, L. (1997). *Sex Offenses and Offenders*. Washington, DC: Bureau of Justice Statistics, U.S. Department of Justice.
38. Halcón, L. L., Beuhring, T., & Blum, R. W. (2000). A portrait of adolescent health in the Caribbean, 2000. Minnesota: WHO Collaborating Centre on Adolescent Health, Division of General Pediatrics and Adolescent Health, University of Minnesota, Minneapolis.
39. Jewkes, R. (2012). *Streamlining: Understanding Gang Rape in South Africa*. London: Forensic Psychological Services, Middlesex University.
40. Jewkes, R., & Abrahams, N. (2002). The epidemiology of rape and sexual coercion in South Africa: An overview. *Social Science & Medicine*, *55*, 1231–1244.
41. Jewkes, R., & Dartnall, E. (2007). Sexual violence. In Heggenhougen, K. & Quah, S. (Eds.), *International Encyclopaedia of Public Health* (pp. 723–731). San Diego: Academic Press.
42. Jewkes, R., Dunkle, K., Koss, M. P., et al. (2006). Rape perpetration by young, rural South African men: Prevalence, patterns and risk factors. *Social Science & Medicine*, *63*, 2949–2961.
43. Jewkes, R., Levin, J., Mbananga, N., et al. (2002). Rape of girls in South Africa. *Lancet*, *359*, 319–320.
44. Jewkes, R., Penn-Kekana, L., Levin, J., et al. (2001). Prevalence of emotional, physical and sexual abuse of women in three South African provinces. *South African Medical Journal*, *91*, 421–428.
45. Jewkes, R., Sikweyiya, Y., Morrell, R., et al. (2009). Understanding men's health and use of violence: Interface of rape and HIV in South Africa. Pretoria: Medical Research Council.
46. Jewkes, R., Sikweyiya, Y., Morrell, R., et al. (2011). Gender inequitable masculinity and sexual entitlement in rape perpetration in South Africa: Findings of a cross-sectional study. *PLoS One*, *6*, e29590.
47. Khan, A., Javed, K., Khan, A. S., & Rizwi, A. (2022). Aggression and individual criminal responsibility in the perspective of Islamic law. *Competitive Social Science Research Journal*, *3*(1), 35–48. https://cssrjournal.com/index.php/cssrjournal/article/view/47 (accessed on 14 October 2024).

48. Khan, A., Khan, A. S., & Khan, I. (2022). Responsibility of killer robots for causing civilian harm: A critique of AI application in warfare doctrine. *Pakistan Journal of International Affairs*, *5*(1), 15–33. https://doi.org/10.52337/pjia.v5i1.398.
49. Koss, M. P., Gidycz, C. A., & Wisniewski, N. (1987). The scope of rape: Incidence and prevalence of sexual aggression and victimization in a national sample of higher education students. *Journal of Consulting and Clinical Psychology*, *55*, 162–170.
50. Koukounas, E., & Letch, N. M. (2001). Psychological correlates of perception of sexual intent in women. *Journal of Social Psychology*, *141*, 443–456.
51. Kretzmer, D., Ben-Yehuda, A., & Furth, M. (2014). 'Thou shall not kill': The use of lethal force in non-international armed conflicts. *Israel Law Review*, *47*(2), 191–224. https://doi.org/10.1017/S0021223714000065.
52. Langhang, L. F., Sherr, L., & Cowan, F. M. (2010). How to improve the validity of sexual behaviour reporting: Systematic review of questionnaire delivery modes in developing countries. *Tropical Medicine and International Health*, *15*, 362–381.
53. Le Vine, R. A. (1959). Gussi sex offenses: A study in social control. *American Anthropologist*, *61*, 965–990.
54. Lenton, A. P., & Bryan, A. (2005). An affair to remember: The role of sexual scripts in perceptions of sexual intent. *Personal Relationships*, *12*, 483–498.
55. Machisa, M., Jewkes, R., Lowe-Morna, C., et al. (2011). *The War at Home*. Johannesburg, South Africa: Gender Links and Gender and Health Research Unit, South African Medical Research Council.
56. MacKinnon, C. A. (2007). The ICTR's legacy on sexual violence. *New England Journal of International and Comparative Law*, *14*, 211.
57. Martin, A. F., Vergeles, M. R., Acevedo, V. de K., et al. (2005). The involvement in sexual coercive behaviors of Spanish college men: Prevalence and risk factors. *Journal of Interpersonal Violence*, *20*, 872–891.
58. Martin, K., Vieraitis, L. M., & Britto, S. (2006). Gender equality and women's absolute status: A test of the feminist models of rape. *Violence Against Women*, *12*, 321–339.
59. Martin, S. L., & Parcesepe, A. M. (2013). Sexual assault and women's mental health. In Garcia-Moreno, C., & Riecher-Rössler, A. (Eds.), *Violence Against Women and Mental Health* (pp. 86–95). Basel: Karger.

60. McCollister, K. E., French, M. T., & Fang, H. (2010). The cost of crime to society: New crime-specific estimates for policy and program evaluation. *Drug and Alcohol Dependence*, *108*, 98–109.

61. McKibbin, W. F., Shackelford, T. K., Goetz, A. T., & Starratt, V. G. (2008). Why do men rape? An evolutionary psychological perspective. *Review of General Psychology*, *12*, 86–97.

62. Miller, T. R., Cohen, M. A., & Wiersema, B. (1996). Victim costs and consequences: A new look. https://www.ncjrs.gov/pdffiles/victcost.pdf (accessed on 14 October 2024).

63. Mouzos, J., & Makkai, T. (2004). Women's experiences of male violence: Findings from the Australian component of the International Violence Against Women Survey (IVAWS). *Research and Public Policy Series*, *56*. Canberra: Australian Institute of Criminology.

64. Naved, R. T., Huque, H., Farah, S., et al. (2011). Men's attitudes and practices regarding gender and violence against women in Bangladesh: Preliminary findings. *Special Publication No. 135*. Bangladesh: icddr.

65. Nollkaemper, A. (2003). Concurrence between individual responsibility and state responsibility in international law. *International and Comparative Law Quarterly*, *52*(3), 615–640. https://doi.org/10.1093/iclq/52.3.615.

66. Otterbein, K. (1994). A cross-cultural study of rape. In K. Otterbein (Ed.), *Feuding and Warfare* (pp. 119–132). Amsterdam: Gordon and Beach Science Publishers.

67. Ouattara, M., Sen, P., & Thomson, M. (1998). Forced marriage, forced sex: The perils of childhood for girls. *Gender and Development*, *6*, 27–33.

68. Pinheiro, P. S. (2006). Violence against children in schools and educational settings. In *World Report on Violence Against Children*. Geneva: United Nations Secretary-General's Study on Violence against Children.

69. Rennison, C. (2002). Rape and sexual assault: Reporting to police and medical attention, 1992–2000. Washington, DC: US Department of Justice, Office of Justice Programs, Bureau of Justice Statistics.

70. Reza, A., Breiding, M. J., Blanton, C., et al. (2007). Violence against children in Swaziland: Findings from a national survey on violence against children. Centers for Disease Control and Prevention and Swaziland United Nations Children's Fund.

71. Rothman, E. F., Decker, M. R., Miller, E., et al. (2012). Multi-person sex among a sample of adolescent female urban health clinic patients. *Journal of Urban Health*, *89*, 129–137.

72. Ruto, S. J. (2009). Sexual abuse of school-age children: Evidence from

Kenya. *Journal of International Cooperation in Education, 12*, 177–192.

73. Rutschmann, P. (2011). Vergangenheitsbewältigung: Historikerstreit and the notion of continued responsibility. *New German Review: A Journal of Germanic Studies, 25*(1), 5–20.
74. Schmid, C. (2012). Sexual assault on children and adolescents in Switzerland: Forms, extent and circumstances. Switzerland: UBS Optimus Foundation.
75. Shalhoub-Kevorkian, N. (1999). Towards a cultural definition of rape: Dilemmas in dealing with rape victims in Palestinian society. *Women's Studies International Forum, 22*, 157–173.
76. Shamu, S., Abrahams, N., Temmerman, M., et al. (2011). A systematic review of African studies on intimate partner violence against pregnant women: Prevalence and risk factors. *PLoS ONE, 6*, e17591.
77. Sikweyiya, Y., & Jewkes, R. (2009). Force and temptation: Contrasting South African men's accounts of coercion into sex by men and women. *Culture, Health & Sexuality, 11*, 529–541.
78. Sikweyiya, Y., Jewkes, R., & Morrell, R. (2007). Talking about rape: Men's responses to questions about rape in a research environment in South Africa. *Agenda, 74*, 48–57.
79. Slap, G. B., Lot, L., Huang, B., et al. (2003). Sexual behavior of adolescents in Nigeria: Cross-sectional survey of secondary school students. *BMJ, 4*, 15.
80. Socia, K. M., Grady, M. D., Bolder, T., Cronin, K., Hurt, C., & Vidrine, S. (2019). How background relates to perceptions of child sexual abuse prevention and policies related to individuals convicted of sex crimes. *Criminal Justice Policy Review, 31*(7), 1059–1094. https://doi.org/10.1177/0887403419873126.
81. Somer, J. (2007). Jungle justice: Passing sentence on the equality of belligerents in non-international armed conflict. *International Review of the Red Cross, 89*(867), 655–690. https://doi.org/10.1017/S1816383107001221.
82. Stephenson, R., Khosropour, C., & Sullivan, P. S. (2010). Reporting of intimate partner violence among men who have sex with men in an online survey. *West Journal of Emergency Medicine, 11*, 242–246.
83. Stoltenborgh, M., van Ijzendoorn, M. H., Euser, E. M., et al. (2011). A global perspective on child sexual abuse: Meta-analysis of prevalence around the world. *Child Maltreatment, 16*, 79–101.
84. Thompson, L., Rydberg, J., Cassidy, M., & Socia, K. M. (2019). Contextual

influences on the sentencing of individuals convicted of sexual crimes. *Sexual Abuse*, *32*(7), 778–805. https://doi.org/10.1177/1079063219852936.

85. Thompson, N. J., Potter, J. S., Sanderson, C. A., & Maibach, E. W. (1997). The relationship of sexual abuse and HIV risk behaviors among heterosexual adult female STD patients. *Child Abuse & Neglect*, *21*, 149–156.
86. Thornhill, R. (1999). The biology of human rape. *Jurimetrics Journal*, *39*, 137–147.
87. Thornhill, R., & Palmer, C. T. (2001). *A Natural History of Rape: Biological Bases of Sexual Coercion*. Massachusetts Institute of Technology Press.
88. Turquet, L., Seck, P., Azcona, G., et al. (2012). *Progress of the World's Women 2011–2012: In Pursuit of Justice*. New York: UN Women.
89. United Nations. International Law Commission, Crawford, J., & United Nations. International Law Commission. (2002). *The International Law Commission's Articles on State Responsibility: Introduction, Text and Commentaries*. Cambridge University Press.
90. Vetten, L., Jewkes, R., Sigsworth, R., et al. (2008). *Tracking Justice: The Attrition of Rape Cases Through the Criminal Justice System in Gauteng*. Johannesburg: Tshwaranang Legal Advocacy Centre.
91. Voigt, C. (2008). State responsibility for climate change damages. *Nordic Journal of International Law*, *77*(1, 2), 1–22. https://doi.org/10.1163/090273508X290672.
92. Ward, C. (1995). *Attitudes toward rape and rape victims: Survey research*. In *Attitudes Toward Rape: Feminist and Social Psychological Perspectives*. London, UK: Sage Publications.
93. Watts, C., & Zimmerman, C. (2002). Violence against women: Global scope and magnitude. *Lancet*, *359*, 1232–1237.
94. Weiss, E. B. (2002). Invoking state responsibility in the twenty-first century. *American Journal of International Law*, *96*(4), 798–816. https://doi.org/10.2307/3070679.
95. Woodhams, J., Cooke, C., Harkins, L., et al. (2012). Leadership in multiple perpetrator stranger rape. *Journal of Interpersonal Violence*, *27*, 728–752.

Chapter **6**

Reproductive Rights and Legal Frameworks

Contents

INTRODUCTION

The legal and moral freedom to choose how and when to procreate includes the availability of contraception, the ability to have an abortion, access to fertility treatments, and the right to reproductive healthcare and education. These rights stem from more general human rights concepts like equality, privacy, and bodily autonomy. Countries' legal systems pertaining to reproductive rights differ greatly from one another due to political, religious, and cultural influences. Access to abortion is still highly controversial in many areas, where legislation ranging from total legalization to total prohibition frequently reflects deep societal divisions. Even though access to contraceptives is more widely accepted, there are still social and legal barriers in some places, especially in places where religious institutions have a lot of power. Globally, agencies such as the United Nations push for universal access to reproductive health care as part of human rights and gender equality, and they implore states to protect and advance these rights. Nonetheless, resistance to reproductive rights endures because of worriese moralmoral, ethical, and demographic ramifications. The legal landscape is constantly changing, with certain nations enacting more restrictive laws while othening upopening access, underscoring the continuous fight for reproductive justice. The legal landscape is further complicated by the intersection of reproductive rights with issues of race, class, and gender, since marginalized groups frequently encounter disproportionate obstacles when attempting to exercise their rights. Legal, ethical, and social aspects of reproductive rights are continuously contested in the dynamic and contentious global discourse, which reflects larger struggles for justice, equality, and autonomy.

6.1. REPRODUCTIVE RIGHTS

Reproductive rights are freedoms and legal rights that are specific to reproduction and reproductive health and that differ between nations. The World Health Organization defines reproductive rights as follows:

1. Reproductive rights are based on the understanding that every couple and individual has the fundamental right to choose freely and responsibly how many, how often, and when to have children, as well as the right to the best possible level of sexual and reproductive health and the resources to make such decisions. They also cover everyone's right to make reproductive decisions free from violence, coercion, and discrimination.

The term "reproductive rights" can refeny or all ofall the following: the freedom to choose a free and informed reproductive path, access to high-quality reproductive healthcare, freedom from forced sterilization and contraception, the right to abortion, birth control, and freedom from coercion. Reproductive rights can also include the freedom from practices like Female Genital Mutilation (FGM), the right to menstrual health, and the right to education about STDs and other aspects of sexuality.

During the United Nations' 1968 International Conference on Human Rights, reproductive rights started to emerge as a subset of human rights. The ensuing non-binding Proclamation of Tehran, which declared that parents have a fundamental human right to freely and responsibly choose the number and spacing of their children, was the first international document to acknowledge one of these rights. The United Nations did not prioritize women's sexual, gynecological, or mental health issues until its Decade of Women (1975–1985) elevated them to a prominent position. However, states have been sluggish to include these rights in legally binding international agreements. As a result, although some of these rights have already been acknowledged by legally binding international human rights instruments, or "hard law," others have only been mentioned in non-binding recommendations and, as a result, only have the status of "soft law" in international law; still others have not been recognized by the international community and are therefore still at the advocacy stage.

6.1.1. The Reproductive Rights Composite Score

The nine component indicators of women's reproductive rights comprise the Reproductive Rights Composite Index: coverage of infertility treatments; Medicaid expansion or state Medicaid family planning eligibility expansions; the percentage of women living in counties with at least one abortion provider; waiting periods for abortions; restrictions on public funding for abortions; same-sex marriage or second-parent adoption for individuals in same-sex relationships; and mandatory sex education.

- On the composite reproductive rights index, Oregon has the highest score. It has pro-choice leaders in the Senate, House of Representatives, and Governor; it does not require parental approval, notification, or waiting periods for abortions; it offers public funding to low-income women for abortions; 78% of women live in counties with abortion providers; it has expanded Medicaid coverage under the Affordable Care Act to up to 138% of the federal poverty line; it has enacted a state Medicaid family planning eligibility expansion; it recognizes same-sex marriage; and it mandates sex education in schools. However, insurance companies are not required by law in Oregon to pay for infertility treatments. The state's top ranking represents a significant improvement over its 19th place national ranking in the 2004 Status of Women in the States report.

1. South Dakota is the state with the lowest ranking for reproductive rights. It has only 23% of women living in counties with abortion providers; it does not have a pro-choice state government; it does not require insurance companies to cover infertility treatments; it does not recognize same-sex marriage or allow second-parent adoption for same-sex couples; it requires parental consent or notification and waiting periods for abortion; it does not provide public funding to poor women for abortion; and it does not require schools to provide mandatory sex education. South Dakota was rated second to last in the 2004 Status of Women in the States report.
2. Reproductive rights are generally strongest in the West, New England, and the Mid-Atlantic region. The top ten jurisdictions, in addition to Oregon, are Connecticut, California, Hawaii, Maryland, New Jersey, New York, Vermont, and Washington.
3. Based on the composite index of reproductive rights, the Midwest and South perform the worst. Five Midwestern states—Indiana, Kansas, Michigan, Missouri, and Nebraska—are among the ten lowest-ranking states, in addition to South Dakota. This group also includes Tennessee, Louisiana, and Arkansas, three Southern states. Idaho is in the bottom ten as well.
4. The District of Columbia and seven states—Connecticut, Hawaii, Maryland, New Jersey, New York, Oregon, and Vermont—were given an A—for reproductive rights. South Dakota, Nebraska, Kansas, and Idaho were the four states with the lowest rankings, each earning an F (Table 6.1; Figure 6.1).

Table 6.1. *Best and Worst States on Women's Reproductive Rights*

State	**Rank**	**Grade**	**State**	**Rank**	**Grade**
Oregon	1	A-	**South Dakota**	**51**	**F**
Vermont	2	A-	**Nebraska**	**50**	**F**
Maryland	3	A-	**Kansas**	**49**	**F**
New Jersey	4	A-	**Idaho**	**48**	**F**
Hawaii	5	A-	**Tennessee**	**47**	**D-**

Source: https://statusofwomendata.org/explore-the-data/reproductive-rights/reproductive-rights-full-section/.

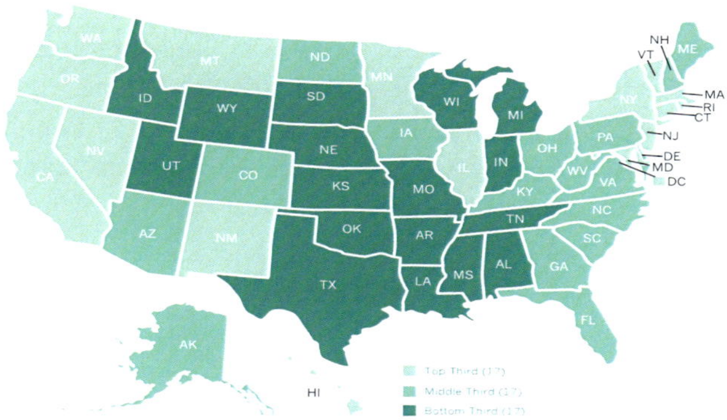

Figure 6.1. *The reproductive rights composite index.*

Source: https://statusofwomendata.org/explore-the-data/reproductive-rights/reproductive-rights-full-section/

6.1.2. Trends in Women's Reproductive Rights

States as a whole made minimal progress on two indicators between the release of the 2004 Status of Women in the States report and this one, while declining or remaining unchanged on five other indicators.

6.1.2.1. What Has Improved

1. Compared to just nine states in 2004, 12 states mandated insurance companies to cover infertility treatments as of October 2014. However, from five states in 2004 to two in 2014, the number of states requiring insurance companies to provide policyholders with at least one package covering infertility treatments decreased (IWPR, 2004; National Conference of State Legislatures, 2014).
2. In twenty-two states, the percentage of women living in counties with at least one abortion provider decreased between 2004 and, 2015; in twenty four states, it increased; and in four states and the District of Columbia, it remained unchanged.

6.1.2.2. What Has Worsened or Stayed the Same

- Compared to twenty-six states in 2004, there were thirty states in 2015 that had laws requiring waiting periods for abortions, which stipulate that a doctor cannot perform an abortion until a specific number of hours after the patient is informed of her options regarding managing a pregnancy.

- The percentage of pro-choice public officials, such as the governor (or mayor for the District of Columbia) and state legislators (or city council members for the District of Columbia), rose in fourteen states between 2004 and 2015 while falling to twenty-two states. In the District of Columbia, the other fourteen states, and IWPR (2004), the percentage of pro-choice officials remained constant (Table 6.2).
- Between 2004 and 2015, the number of jurisdictions (43) that had laws prohibiting minors from getting an abortion without parental permission or notification remained the same (Guttmacher Institute, 2004a; Table 6.2).
- Between 2004 and 2015, the number of states (17) that offer Medicaid enrolled in public funding for all or most medically necessary abortions—generally defined as those performed to preserve the woman's physical or mental health (Kaiser Family Foundation, 2014b)—remained constant (Guttmacher Institute, 2004b; Table 6.2).
- The number of jurisdictions that mandated sex education in schools (23) stayed constant between 2004 and 2015 (Guttmacher Institute, 2004c; Table 6.2).

6.1.3. Access to Abortion

America's 1973 Supreme Court case Roe v. Wade established the abortion rights legally. Despite this, state legislative and executive bodies are still engaged in a legal battle over laws pertaining to abortion access, such as those requiring waiting periods and parental consent or notification (Guttmacher Institute, 2015b). Furthermore, public funding for abortion is still a contentious topic in many states. Federal law has prohibited the use of funds for most abortions since 1977 and currently prohibits it unless the woman's life is inrdanger, or the pregnancy was the result of rape or incest (Boonstra, 2013). Although state Medicaid programs have the option to cover abortion in other situations using only state funds and not federal funds, the Affordable Care Act of 2010 reinforces these restrictions (Salganicoff et al., 2014).

Limiting access to abortion through state legislation has become a routine practice. A wide range of laws were proposed and passed in 2013 and 2014, including laws mandating ultrasounds for women prior to abortions, strict regulations aimed at abortion providers, prohibitions on women getting health insurance coverage for abortions, and laws outlawing abortions performed later in pregnancy (National Women's Law Center, 2014a, 2014b).

1. With waiting periods ranging from 18 to 72 hours, twenty six of the thirty states that as of March 2015 had laws requiring mandatory waiting periods before getting an abortion enforced these laws (Guttmacher Institute, 2015b). The legislation was not enforced in Delaware, Massachusetts, Tennessee, or Montana, but it was still included in the statutory code.
2. Parental consent or notification laws, which mandate that the parents of a minor seeking an abortion give their consent or be informed, were in placehreeforty-three states as of March 2015, and thihreeeight of those forty-three states enforced the laws. Of thighthirty-eight states, twelve required parental notice, onetwenty-one required parental approval. Oklahoma, Texas, Utah, Virginia, and Wyoming are the five states that have laws requiring parental notification and consent for minors wishing to have an abortion (Guttmacher Institute, 2015b).
3. As of March 2015, seventeen states provided funding for abortions to low-income women who met Medicaid eligibility requirements in alty ofmost medically necessary cases. Only in cases where the woman's life iangerdanger, or the pregnancy was the result of rape or incest is state funding for abortions availablseventwenty-seven states and the District of Columbia (Guttmacher Institute, 2015b). Medicaid funds can be used in five states (Indiana, Mississippi, Utah, Virginia, and Wisconsin) to pay for abortions when the woman's life is in danger, the pregnancy was the result of rape or incest, or there is a risk to the woman's physical health or a fetal abnormality. In South Dakota, abortions may only be paid for with state Medicaid funds in cases where the woman's life is in danger (Guttmacher Institute, 2015b).
4. The percentage of women aged 15 to 44 who resided in counties with access to abortion services varied across states as of 2011, the most recent year for which data are available. It was as low as 4% in Wyoming and as high as 100% in the District of Columbia and Hawaii. Less than half of the women in the bottom five states—South Dakota, West Virginia, Wyoming, Mississippi, and Arkansas—lived in counties with one or more providers. Over 90% of women resided in counties with at least one abortion provider in the top eight jurisdictions: the District of Columbia, Hawaii, California, Connecticut, Nevada, New York, New Jersey, and Massachusetts (Guttmacher Institute, 2014).
5. According to NARAL Pro-Choice America and the NARAL Pro-

Choice America Foundation (2015), as of December 2014, the governoy onetwenty-one states and the majority of state legislators supported abortion. The governor (or mayor in the case of the District of Columbia)ty ofmost legislators (the city council for the District of Columbia) were pro-choice and opposed restrictions on abortion rights in six jurisdictions: California, Connecticut, Hawaii, Oregon, Vermont, and the District of Columbia. The remaining states had a mixed system of governance.

6.1.4. The Affordable Care Act and Contraceptive Coverage

The Patient Protection and Affordable Care Act (ACA) of 2010 has increased women's access to contraceptmber ofseveral ways, including mandating that health insurance companies pay for contraceptive counseling and services as well as all FDA-approved methods of birth control at no cost to patients (U.S. Department of Human Resources, 2014). For lower-income women, who frequently struggle with the financial burden of regularly purchasing contraception, this change is especially significant (Center for Reproductive Rights, 2012). The average cost of a year's supply of birth control pills, according to the Guttmacher Institute, is eqfty onefifty-one hours of labor for a woman earning the federal minimum wage of $7.25 per hour (Sonfield, 2014). According to a nationwide study, the average annual cost of these pills for uninsured women is estimated to be $370, which represents 68% of their annual out-of-pocket medical service costs.

The only legal safeguards guaranteeing women's access to affordable contraceptives as easily as other prescription drugs existed before the Affordable Care Act (ACA) were state contraceptive equity laws (Guttmacher Institute, 2015c). According to National Women's Law Center (2012), these laws mandated that state-regulated plans that covered prescription drugs also had to cover contraceptive drugs and devices. Howevety eighttwenty-eight states mandated full or partial coverage of contraceptives; the District of Columbia and the other states lacked any legal safeguards ensuring access to reasonably priced contraception (Guttmacher Institute, 2015c). The number of women who have access to free contraception has increased dramaesult ofbecause of the Affordable Care Act (ACA). According to a study conducted on approximately 900 women with private health insurance who used prescription contraceptives, between fall 2012 (before the ACA's requirement that most women have access to contraception) and spring 2014, the percentage of women who paid nothing out of pocket for oral contraception increased from 15 to 67% (Sonfield et al., 2015). There are, however, a few significant exclusions to the ACA's contraceptive mandate. The National Women's Law Center (2015) states that some religious institutions, including churches and other houses of worship, are exempt from the mandate that birth control be covered by health insurance policies. Religiously affiliated nonprofit organizations can also request an "accommodation" if they certify their religious objections to the health insurance carrier, third party administrator, or the Department of Health and Human Services. These organizations can still obtain birth control coverage directly from the insurance company, but they are not required to cover contraceptives for their female employees (National Women's Law Center, 2015; Sobel, Salganicoff, and Kurani, 2015). Furteption ofexcept for states where there is already a contraceptive equity law requiring coverage, "grandfathered" health plans that were in place before the Affordable Care Act are temporarily released from the obligation to offer contraceptive coverage through employer-sponsored health plans. A ruling by the Supreme Court, Burwell v. Stores of Hobby Lobby, Inc. has also increased the scope of permitted exemptions to include some family-owned, "closely held" businesses that refuse to use contraception due to religious beliefs (Dreweke, 2014; National Women's Law Center, 2015). The decision means that employees of companies like Hobby Lobby, which self-insures its employees and is therefore only subject to federal law, may lose their coverage of contraceptive drugs and services, but it does not supersede state laws pertaining to contraceptive equity (Rovner, 2014). While many women now have greater access to contraception thanks to the Affordable Care Act (ACA), some are worried that the law's goal of removing barriers to all FDA-approved methods of contraception may be compromised by delays in access or denials of preferred methods due to insurance-related issues (Armstrong, 2013). Insurance companies frequently employ "medical management techniques" that can influence the course of treatment and discourage patients from using specific services, such as restricting quantity and/or supply or requiring provider authorization before providing a drug or service. Such procedures can sometimes reduce expenses and increase efficiency, but they can also obstruct or delay service delivery. Some women might not be able to access the contraceptive method that best suits them if insurers adopt policies that restrict women's options (Armstrong, 2013).

A recent study examining the insurance plan policies of twenty insurance providers in five states revealed that while most adhere to the ACA's contraceptive mandate, there are discrepancies in how the guidelines issued by the U.S. Department of Health and Human Services for contraceptive coverage are implemented. Consequently, not all insurers provide full coverage for all contraceptive methods without requiring co-payments (Sobel, Salganicoff, and Kurani, 2015). To guarantee women's access to a comprehensive selection of contraceptive methods without incurring additional costs, the state of California enacted a post-ACA law (SB 1053) on contraceptive coverage. This law restricts medical management related to contraception, surpassing federal regulations by preventing non-grandfathered and Medi-Cal plans from imposing cost-sharing requirements or introducing obstacles or delays in delivering contraceptive benefits (Sobel, Salganicoff, and Kurani, 2015).

Table 6.2. *How the States Measure Up: Women's Status on the Reproductive Rights Composite Index and Its Components*

	Composite Index			Parental Consent/ Notification	Waiting Period	Public Funding	Percent of Women Living in Counties with Providers	Pro-Choice Governor and Legislature	Medicaid Expansion or Medicaid Family Planning Expansion	Coverage of Infertility Treatments	Same-Sex Marriage or Second-Parent Adoption	Mandatory Sex Education
State	Score	Rank	Grade	Score	Score	Score	Percent	Score	Score	Score	Score	Score
Alabama	1.91	40	D+	0	0	0	41%	0.00	1	0.0	1.0[c]	0
Alaska	2.83	29	C	0	1	1	83%	0.00	0	0.0	1.0	0
Arizona	3.36	24	C+	0	0	1	86%	0.00	1	0.0	1.0	0
Arkansas	1.72	43	D	0	0	0	22%	0.00	1	1.0	0.0[c]	0
California	5.24	9	B+	0[a]	1	1	99%	1.00	1	0.5	1.0	0
Colorado	3.71	21	C+	0	1	0	88%	0.83	1	0.0	1.0	0
Connecticut	5.95	6	A–	1	1	1	95%	1.00	1	1.0	1.0	0
Delaware	3.82	20	C+	0	0[a]	0	82%	0.50	1	0.0	1.0	1
District of Columbia	5.50	8	A-	1	1	0	100%	1.00	1	0.0	1.0	1
Florida	2.79	30	C	0	1	0	79%	0.00	1	0.0	1.0	0
Georgia	2.85	28	C	0	0	0	43%	0.17	1	0.0	0.5	1
Hawaii	6.00	5	A–	1	1	1	100%	1.00	1	1.0	1.0	0
Idaho	0.81	48	F	0	0	0	31%	0.00	0	0.0	1.0	0
Illinois	4.78	13	B+	0	1	1	61%	0.67	1	1.0	1.0	0[d]
Indiana	1.89	42	D+	0	0	0	39%	0.00	1	0.0	1.0	0
Iowa	3.83	19	C+	0	1	0	50%	0.33	1	0.0	1.0	1
Kansas	0.76	49	F	0	0	0	26%	0.00	0	0.0	1.0	0
Kentucky	2.43	32	C	0	0	0	26%	0.17	1	0.0	0.0	1
Louisiana	1.62	46	D	0	0	0	37%	0.00	1	0.0	0.5	0
Maine	3.53	23	C+	1	1	0	53%	0.50	0	0.0	1.0	1
Maryland	6.14	3	A–	0	1	1	81%	0.83	1	1.0	1.0	1
Massachusetts	4.74	14	B+	0	0[a]	1	91%	0.83	1	1.0	1.0	0
Michigan	1.66	45	D	0	0	0	66%	0.00	1	0.0	0.0[c]	0
Minnesota	4.58	16	B	0	0	1	41%	0.67	1	0.0	1.0	1
Mississippi	2.09	38	C–	0	0	0	9%	0.00	1	0.0	0.0	1
Missouri	1.68	44	D	0	0	0	26%	0.17	1	0.0	0.5[c]	0
Montana	5.04	11	B+	0[a]	0[a]	1	54%	0.50	1	1.0	1.0	1
Nebraska	0.59	50	F	0	0	0	59%	0.00	0	0.0	0.0	0
Nevada	4.44	17	B	0[a]	1	0	94%	0.50	1	0.0	1.0	1
New Hampshire	3.55	22	C+	0	1	0	88%	0.67	1	0.0	1.0	0
New Jersey	6.08	4	A–	0[a]	1	1	91%	0.67	1	1.0	1.0	1
New Mexico	5.02	12	B+	0[a]	1	1	52%	0.50	1	0.0	1.0	1
New York	5.59	7	A–	1	1	1	92%	0.67	1	1.0	1.0	0
North Carolina	3.01	26	C	0	0	0	51%	0.00	1	0.0	1.0	1
North Dakota	2.27	33	C–	0	0	0	27%	0.00	1	0.0	0.0	1
Ohio	2.99	27	C	0	0	0	49%	0.00	1	1.0	0.0	1
Oklahoma	1.95	39	D+	0	0	0	45%	0.00	1	0.0	1.0	0
Oregon	6.28	1	A–	1	1	1	78%	1.00	1	0.0	1.0	1
Pennsylvania	2.53	31	C	0	0	0	53%	0.50	1	0.0	1.0	0
Rhode Island	4.63	15	B+	0	1	0	63%	0.50	1	1.0	1.0	1
South Carolina	3.07	25	C+	0	0	0	40%	0.17	1	0.0	1.0	1
South Dakota	0.23	51	F	0	0	0	23%	0.00	0	0.0	0.0	0
Tennessee	1.42	47	D–	0	0[a]	0	42%	0.00	0	0.0	0.0	1[e]
Texas	2.19	36	C–	0	0	0	69%	0.00	1[b]	0.5	0.5	0
Utah	2.16	37	C–	0	0	0	66%	0.00	0	0.0	1.0	1
Vermont	6.15	2	A–	1	1	1	65%	1.00	1	0.0	1.0	1
Virginia	2.24	34	C–	0	0	0	41%	0.33	1	0.0	1.0	0
Washington	5.20	10	B+	1	1	1	87%	0.83	1	0.0	1.0	0
West Virginia	4.35	18	B	0	0	1	18%	0.17	1	1.0	1.0	1
Wisconsin	1.90	41	D+	0	0	0	40%	0.00	1	0.0	1.0	0
Wyoming	2.21	35	C–	0	1	0	4%	0.17	1	0.0	1.0	0

Source: https://statusofwomendata.org/wp-content/uploads/2015/09/PDF-of-final-Reproductive-Rights-chapter-9-4-2015.pdf.

6.1.4.1. Emergency Contraception

Emergency contraception can prevent unintended pregnancies and give women control over the timing and size of their families. It is a form of birth control that can be taken up to several days after unprotected sex, contraceptive failure, or sexual assault. The first oral form of emergency contraception to be made available was Plan B, which was authorized for use in the US in 1999. However, other forms were later introduced (Kaiser Family Foundation, 2014c). Emergency contraception is covered by the Affordable Care Act's contraceptive provision, which mandates that all new private health plans cover all contraceptive medications and devices prescribed to patients without requiring cost-sharing (Kaiser Family Foundation, 2014c).

The topic of emergency contraception has been approached differently by state legislatures. Certain individuals have attempted to limit accessibility by denying it inclusion in state Medicaid family planning eligibility extensions or contraceptive coverage requirements, or by permitting specific pharmacists or pharmacies to decline to offer contraceptive services (Guttmacher Institute, 2015d). Others have increased access by mandating that sexual assault victims receive information about emergency contraception from emergency rooms, that these rooms provide emergency contraception to victims upon request, that women can obtain emergency contraception without a prescription, or that pharmacies or pharmacists fill all legitimate prescriptions (Guttmacher Institute, 2015d). Awareness and use of emergency contracecreased as a result ofbecause of public health and educational initiatives (Kaiser Family Foundation, 2014c). According to one study analyzing data from the National Survey of Family Growth, 11% of sexually experienced women aged 15 to 44 reported using emergency contraceptive pills at some point between 2006 and 2010, up from 4% in 2002 (Daniels, Jones, and Abma, 2013).

Women still face obstacles when trying to access emergency contraception. For instance, while the majority of women are aware that emergency contraception exists, some remain unaware of it (Kaiser Family Foundation, 2014c). Additionally, women of all ages must obtain a prescription from a doctor to access ella, the most effective form of emergency contraception for overweight or obese women, while generic and Plan B forms of emergency co available over-the-counterover the counter (Kaiser Family Foundation, 2014c). Another obstacle is that, in clinical settings, medical professionals don't always discuss emergency contraception with women, depriving some of the information they need (Kaiser Family Foundation, 2014c). According to a 2014 study conducted by the American Society for Emergency Contraception, which involved 180 pharmacies across 29 states, progestin-based EC pills are frequently kept behind the counter or not stocked on store shelves due to their high cost.

6.1.5. Native American Women and Emergency Contraception

According to research, accessing emergency contraception may be especially challenging for many Native American women. Given that Native American women experience higher rates of sexual assault than women of other races and ethnicities, this lack of access poses a serious concern for indigenous communities (Breiding et al., 2014; Kingfisher, Provost, and Asetoyer, 2012). In a study conducted by Gastozzi (2008) and Asetoyer, Luluquisen, and Millis (2009), 40 Indian Health Service (IHS) pharmacies were surveyed. Of these, n B available over-the-counterover the counter; 37.5% of the pharmacies offered an alternative form of emergency contraception.

Geographical restrictions (having to travel a great distance to find a pharmacy that provides emergency contraception) and financial barriers are two major obstacles that many Native American women who live on reservations face when trying to access emergency contraception through a commercial pharmacy outside of their reservation (Kingfisher, Asetoyer, and Provost, 2012). It is essential to enhancing women's general health and protecting their reproductive rights to increase access to emergency contraception for Native American women and other women who might not have it.

6.1.6. Medicaid Expansion and State Medicaid Family Planning Eligibility Expansions

The Affordable Care Act has improved women's access to contraception by increasing the number of people who have health insurance dition to requiring the majority ofmost health insurers to cover contraceptive counseling and services and all FDA-approved methods of contraception. By allowing adult children to remain on their parent's healte plans until the age of twenty sixtwenty-six, the Affordable Care Act (ACA) has significantly decreased the rates of uninsurance among women between the ages of 18 and 24. From 2008 to 2014, the percentage of uninsured women in this age group fell from 24.9 to 15.9%.

Throughout this time frame, the percentage of uninsured women across all age groups decreased by roughly 18%, going from 13% in 2008 to 106.6% in the first nine months of 2014 (Martinez and Cohen, 2009, 2015). There is currently a lack of complete data indicating how women's health insurance has changed since the ACA.

Through modifications to Medicaid, a public health insurance program for those with low incomes, the ACA has also increased the number of people who have health insurance. The ACA aims to expand Medibility to all people under sixty fivesixty-five who are not eligible for Medicare and have incomes up to 138% of the federal poverty line in order to assist those who may have previously struggled to afford insurance. Previously, eligibility was limited to those who met certain income requirements in addition to being prearent of a dependent child, sixty fivesixty-five years of age or older, or disabled (National Conference of State Legislatures, 2011). Along with other health care services, this change expands the pool of women eligible to receive family planning services; states have the option to refuse this Medicaid expansion. According to the Kaiser Family Foundation (2015), as of April 2015, five states were debating whether to implement the Medicaid expansion, while 29 states and the District of Columbia had already made the decision.

The Affordable Care Act (ACA) gives states a new way to modify their state Medicaid program in order to increase eligibility for family planning coverage in addition to the general Medicaid expansion. Prior to the ACA, states had the ability to extend their programs by requesting from the Centers for Medicare and Medicaid Services a waiver of federal policy (Guttmacher Institute, 2015e). States that wish to expand family planning through Medicaid now have two options: they can expedite the process by requesting a waiver from the federal government, which is a temporary solution, or they can modify their Medicaid program permanently by enacting a State Plan Amendment (Guttmach, 2015e).

1. pril 2015, twenty eighttwenty-eight states—states, including Texas, which had an expansion funded entirely by the state—had either waived or amended their state plans to allow family planning services to those who would not otherwise be eligible. The income ceiling for states that have extended their programs varied, with Virginia having the lowest income ceiling at 105% of the federal poverty line (which includes postpartum coverage loss) and Wisconsin having the highest income ceil of the federal poverty line.
2. Twenty fiveTwenty-five states offered family planning benefits to people based on their income, with the majority of these states having an income ceiling at or close to federal povere. Out of the twenty eighttwenty-eight statesstates, that increased eligibility for family planning services through Medicaid. Rhode Island and Wyoming only offered these benefits if a woman lost coverage after giving birth, while one state—Florida—offered them to women who lost Medicaid coverage for any reason, regardless of income.
3. Younger than 19-year-olds are among the eligible population, as defined by twenty states, for Medicaid coverage of family planning services. Individuals who are 18 years old were included in three states (Georgia, Missouri, and Pennsylvania), but those who are younger than 18 were excluded (Guttmacher Institute, 20

4. According to the Guttmacher Institute 2015e2015 and the Kaiser Family Foundation (2015), sixteen states had both expanded Medicaid eligibility for family planning and Medicaid overall as of April 2015. Thirteen states had passed family planning legislation but had not embraced the Medicaid expansion, while fourteen states and the Districtad expanded Medicaid overall but not in the area ofin family planning eligibility. Eight states (Table 6.2) had not implemented a state family planning expansion or expanded Medicaid overall. These states are Alaska, Idaho, Kansas, Maine, Nebraska, South Dakota, Tennessee, and Utah.

6.1.7. Other Family Planning Policies and Resources

6.1.7.1. Access to Fertility Treatments

Men and women may have more options when it comes to reproduction thanks to infertility treatments, but they are frequently unaffordable, particularly if insurance does not cover them. By June 2014, laws mandating insurance companies to pay for infertility treatments had been passed by the legislatures of 12 states: Arkansas, Connecticut, Hawaii, Illinois, Maryland, Massachusetts, Montana, New Jersey, New York, Ohio, Rhode Island, and West Virginia. Insurance companies were also required to provide infertility coverage to policyholders in Texas and California (National Conference of State Legislatures, 2015).

6.1.7.2. Mandatory Sex Education in Schools

According to research, sex education is essential for providing young men and women with the knowledge they need to make responsible sexual decisions and prevent disease and unintended pregnancy (Douglas 2007). Sex education is mandated in 22 states and the District of Columbia's schools. One of these states, Tennessee, mandates that sex education be taught in schools if the pregnancy rate among 15- to 17-year-olds is 19 per 1,000 or greater. All 23 jurisdictions that have enacted legislation mandating sex education alsodeficiency Virus (HIV) education, with the exception ofexcept for two states: Mississippi and North Dakota. Information about contraception must be included in the curriculum in 18 states and the District of Columbia, and information about abstinence must be included in 37 states (Guttmacher Institute 2015f).

6.1.7.3. Same-Sex Marriage and Second-Parent Adoption

The laws governing same-sex couple's ability to create the families they desire have undergone significant modifications in recent years. State courts have a great deal of authority to define what legally qualifies as a lesbian and gay family because there is no federal legislation that guarantees same-sex couples the same parenthood rights as married couples of different sexes. They have previously used this authority in a variety of ways, such as preventing lesbian and gay people from lawfully adopting their partner's children or giving them this ability through second-parent adoption, which gives second parents in same-sex relationships the same legal rights as biological parents. These rights encompass, among other things, the authority to make decisions about the child's health care and custodial rights in the event of a divorce or death.

When the 2004 Status of Women in the States report by IWPR was released, the only way for many lesbian and gay people to be able to legally co-parent their children was through second-parent adoption. From then on, new options have become available to same as marriage has been recognized for them in thirty seventhirty-seven states and the District of Columbia, either through legislation or as a result of a state or federal court ruling (National Center for Lesbian Rights, 2015). Married same-sex couples now share the same parental rights as married heterosexual couples when they have a child together. Furthermore, many individuals in sax couples who marry after one or both partners have a childchild, or children now have the possibility of adopting a child through stepparent adoption, a legal process available to married couples where the nonbiological parent adopts the child or children of their spouse. This is because the recognition of same-sex marriage p this option.

Same-sex couples could marry in thirty seventhirty-seven states and the District of Columbia as of April, 2015; in four more states, they could adopt a stepparent or second parent through certain counties that had either approved gay marriage or permitted second-parent adoption, though no state legislation or appellate court ruling specifically permitting it was in place. Same-sex marriage or second-parent adoption is prohibited in nine states. Nebraska and Ohio, two states that forbid same-sex unions, have laws that expressly forbid second-parent adoption for any couple. According to the National Center for Lesbian Rights (2014), one state that forbids same-sex marriage is Mississippi, which also forbids second-parent adoption for same-sex couples but permits it for different-sex couples.

6.1.8. LGBT Reproductive Rights

The topic of who should be a parent has a long and complex history in the United States, and LGBT people have frequently been at the center of this discussi though the traditional definition of the family is changingchanging, and LGBT people's reproductive rights are becoming more widely acknowledged, many

LGBT people still encounter obstacles when trying to become parents. Finding a culturally competent healthcare provider is just one of these difficulties; others include overt discrimination or legal restrictions on adopting, foster parenting, surrogating, or using donor insemination (Cooper and Cates, 2006; Lambda Legal, 2015).

1. In the US, there are an estimated 122,000 same-sex couples raising children under the age of eighteen. Compared to single same-sex couples, married same-sex couples are significantly more likely to be parents (27% versus 15%; Gates, 2015).
2. Even though same-sex couples are less likely than different-sex couples to be parents, they are almost three times more likely to be foster or adoptive parents (4.0% compared with 1.4%; Gates, 2015). However, compared to 90% of children of different-sex couples, only 61% of children of same-sex couples are biologically related to one of their parents.
3. Compared to 24% of white women in same-sex couples, more than one-third (35%) of women of color are raising a child under the age of eighteen (Gates, 2015). In terms of same-sex relationships, 71% of married couples and 81% of single couples with children under the age of eighteen are made up of women.
4. There is a ban on discrimination against LGBT parents who wish to foster a child in six states: California, Massachusetts, New Jersey, Oregon, Rhode Island, and Wisconsin. LGBT parents are not allowed to foster children e, Nebraska. There is silence on the matter from forty threeforty-three states as well as the District of Colment Advancement Project, 2015).
5. LGBT paree tocan petition for statewide joint adoption in thirty fivethirty-five states as well as the District of Columbia. When requesting a joint adoption, same-sex couples must comply with certain legal requirements in three states: Mississippi, Michigan, and Louisiana. The state of same-sex couple's joint adoption is unclear in 12 states (Movement Advancement Project, 2015).

6.1.9. Fertility, Natality, and Infant Health

6.1.9.1. Women's Fertility

Women's propensity to marry and have children later in life has contributed to the recent decline in the fertility rate for women in the United States. The median age of women in 2013 was 26.6 years when they got married for the first time, compared to 20.3% in 1960 (U.S. Census Bureau, 2013; Cohn et al., 2011). In 2013, the mean age for women at the time of their first birth was 26.0 years, compared with 21.4 years in 1970 (Martin et al., 2015a; Mathews and Brady, 2009).

The United States had a fertility rate of 62.5 live births per 1,000 women aged 15 to 44 in 2013. Since 1960, when there were 118.0 births per 1,000 people, the fertility rate has significantly decreased (Martin et al., 2015a). The fertility rate for women aged 15 to 44 fell from 66.1 to 62.5 births per 1,000 women in the ten years between 2003 and 2013 (Martin et al., 2015a).

1. At 50.8 live births per 1,000 women aged 15 to 44, New Hampshire has the lowest fertility rate in the country. Vermont and Rhode Island have the next lowest rates, at 51.4 and 51.6 live births per 1,000 respectively. Together with these three states, Connecticut, Maine, Massachusetts, New York, and Pennsylvania are the other five Northeastern states that rank in the top ten states with the lowest fertility rates. Among the ten jurisdictions with the lowest fertility rates are the District of Columbia and Oregon (Martin et al., 2015a).
2. Utah has the highest fertility rate in the nation at 80.9 live births per 1,000, with South Dakota (78.1 per 1,000) and Alaska (77.8 per 1,000) close behind. Hawaii, Idaho, Kansas, Nebraska, North Dakota, Oklahoma, and Texas are also among the ten states with the highest fertility rates (Martin et al., 2015a).

6.1.9.2. Prenatal Care

Pregnant women who receive care throughout their pregna higher chance of giving birth to healthy children. Similar toLike 2001, when 83% of all mothers received prenatal care this early in their pregnancy, 84% of American women started receiving prenatal care in the first trimtheir pregnancy in 2011. Native American women saw a 12% point12%-point increase in the percentage of women starting prenatal care in the first trimester of pregnancy between 2001 and 2011 (from 69 to 81%). The percentage of Hispanic and Black women has increased by seven points, respectively, from 76 to 83% and from 74 to 81%. While the percentage of white women receiving early prenatal care decreased from 89 to 86%, the percentage of Asian/Pacific Islander women starting prenatal care in the first trimester has remained constant at 84% (IWPR 2004; Table 6.3).

Compared to white women, pregnant women of color are more likely to start prenatal care later in their pregnancy or not at all. In contrast to 5.4% of Asian/Pacific Islander women, 7.6% of Hispanic women, 10.0% of black women, and 11.3% of Native American women, only 4.4% of white women nationwide received late or no prenata07 and 2013 (Child Trends, 2014). This study analyzed natalityanalyzed data from the Centers for Disease Control and Prevention.

6.1.9.3. Low Birth Weight

In many US states, low birth weight is a health concern. According to Martin et al 2015b., 8% of babies born in the US in 2013 were underweight (weighing less than five pounds, eight ounces). Non-Hispanic black women were the most likely of the major racial and ethnic groups to give birth to babies with low birth weights (13%). Asian/Pacific Islander women (8.3%), Native American women (7.5%), Hispanic women (7.1%), and white women (7.0%) Martin et al., 2015a.

The percentage of low-birth-weight babies nationwide grew marginally betwee rising from 77.7% to 80.0%. The percentage of low birth weig-birth-weight babies among Blacks remained constant at 13 pointpoints 1% in both years, while it slightly increased among Whites and Native Americans, going from 6.8 to 7.0% for Whiteo 7.5% for Native Americans. The percentage of low birth weightlow-birth-weight babies rose more significantly among Asian/Pacific Islanders and Hispanics (6.5 to 7.1% for Asian/Pacific Islanders, and 7.5 to 8.3% for Hispanics; IWPR 2004 and Table 6.3).

States differ in their proportions of babies born with low birth weight.

1. At 5.8%, Alaska has the lowest percentage of babies born with low birth weights, followed by 6.3% in each of Oregon and South Dakota. The top 11 states also include California, Iowa, Minnesota, Nebraska, New Hampshire, North Dakota, Vermont, and Washington (New Hampshire and California are tied for 10th .5%, Mississippi has the highest percentage of low birth weightlow-birth-weight babies—roughly twice as higith the highest ranking, Alaska. The number of low birth weightlow-birth-weight babies born in the South is generally higher in these states: West Virginia, Alabama, Arkansas, Georgia, Louisiana, North Carolina, South Carolina, Tennessee, and the District of Columbia all rank in the bottom twelve. This group also includes New Mexico and Colorado, which is tied for 40th place with North Carolina, Arkansas, and North Carolina.

6.1.9.4. ***Infant Mortality***

The overall infant mortality rate in the United States is 6.0 per 1,000 live births. Black women and Native American women have the highest rates of infant mortality (11.2 and 8.4 per 1,000 live births, respectively), while Asian/Pacific

Islander women (4.1 per 1,000 live births), white women (5.0 per 1,000 live births), and Hispanic women (5.1 per 1,000 live births) have the lowest rates among women of the largest racial and ethnic groups.

Table 6.3. *Prenatal Care, Infant Mortality, and Low Birth Weight by Race and Ethnicity, United States*

Percent of Mothers Beginning Prenatal Care in the First Trimester of Pregnancy[a]	
All Women	83.6%
White	85.7%
Hispanic	82.6%
Black	80.9%
Asian/Pacific Islander	83.9%
Native American	81.0%
Infant Mortality Rate (deaths of infants under age one per 1,000 live births)[b]	
All Women	6.0
White	5.0
Hispanic	5.1
Black	11.2
Asian/Pacific Islander	4.1
Native American	8.4
Percent of Low Birth-Weight Babies (less than 5 lbs., 8 oz.)[c]	
All Women	8.0%
White	7.0%
Hispanic	7.1%
Black	13.1%
Asian/Pacific Islander	8.3%
Native American	7.5%

Source: https://statusofwomendata.org/wp-content/uploads/2015/09/PDF-of-final-Reproductive-Rights-chapter-9-4-2015.pdf.

The decline in infant mortality rates was evident among Caucasian women, dropping from 5.7 to 5.0 per 1,000 births. For African American women, the rate decreased from 13.5 to 11.2 within the same timeframe. Native American women experienced a reduction from 9.7 to 8.4 deaths per 1,000 live births, while the rate for Hispanic women lowered from 5.4 to 5.1. Among Asian and Pacific Islander women, the infant mortality rate dropped from 4.7 to 4.1 per 1,000 births (IWPR 2004; Table 6.3).

Infant mortality rates vary across states.

1. With 4.2 infant mortality per 1,000, New Hampshire and Massachusetts have the lowest rates in the country; Vermont is next with 4.3 infant mortality per 1,000. Geographically distributed are the other eleven states in the top eleven: Nevada, California,

Colorado, Hawaii, Nebraska, New Jersey, New York, and Utah (where rates are 5 points per 1,000 in both Hawaii and New York).

2. At 9.0 infant deaths per 1,000 lis, Alabama has the highest infant mortality rate in the country—country, more than the states with the lowest rates. The South has a large number ofmany the lowest rankings: Alabama, Louisiana, Mississippi, North Carolina, and South Carolina are among the bottom ten states. This group also includes the District of Columbia, Delaware, Ohio, Oklahoma, and South Dakota.

6.2. IMPACT OF REPRODUCTIVE HEALTH AND REPRODUCTIVE RIGHTS ON ECONOMIC DEVELOPMENT

Development cannot occur without good health, and health itself is a sign of development since it represents advancements in the social, environmental, economic, and security spheres of human endeavor. A population that is free from illness and disability and lives to a ripe old age is considered to be in perfect health. To improve the state of maternal health and women's reproductive health, reproductive rights and health are essential. The improvement of women's reproductive rights and health is essential to both advancing economic development and reducing poverty. For any development endeavor to be sustainable, it is imperative that women, above all, are included. Encouraging women's reproductive health and rights will not only empower them but also fight poverty and illness while boosting the economy. Among the promises made at Johannesburg are the advancement of women's equal access to and participation in decision-making, the mainstreaming of gender perspectives in all policies and strategies, and the improvement of women's status, health, and economic welfare through full and equal access to economic opportunities and health care services.

Development is the ability of all people to reach their full potential, live dignified, productive, and creative lives that satisfy their needs and desires while carrying out their responsibilities and exercising their rights. The opportunities available to women in both public and private life are restricted when their reproductive rights are neglected. (IFRC 2010) Human rights that are inalienable and inextricably linked to other fundamental rights are reproductive rights. The reproductive health rights of women are crucial to achieving gender equality and female empowerment. The foundation of sustainable development is the rights to health and the well-being of individuals. Programs for reproductive health are crucial for preserving both men's and women's dignity. A twenty-year plan has been adopted to guarantee that everyone's rights to reproductive and sexual health are protected, and governments have submitted programs of action to guarantee that everyone has access to reproductive health care by the year 2015.

6.3. PROMOTING REPRODUCTIVE RIGHTS THROUGH HUMAN RIGHTS-BASED APPROACH TO DEVELOPMENT

A conceptual and analytical framework that incorporates human rights norms, standards, and principles into all development work is known as a Human Rights-Based Approach, or HRBA. The following are included in the UN Statement of Common Understanding of Human Rights-Based Approach to Development Cooperation and Programming.

- Human rights as outlined in the Universal Declaration of Human Rights and other international human rights instruments should be promoted by all development cooperation programs, policies, and technical assistance.
- Every aspect of development cooperation and programming, across all industries and phases of the programming process, is guided by human rights standards found in and principles derived from the Universal Declaration of Human Rights and other international human rights instruments.
- The ability of "right-holders" to assert their rights and of "duty-bearers" to fulfill their commitments are both strengthened by development cooperation.

Furthermore, UNFPA incorporates gender responsiveness and cultural sensitivity as essential components of an HRBA into its programming. Every development effort in an HRBA to programming aims to achieve a desired result via a legal process. Human rights principles guarantee the legitimacy of the process and human rights standards define the desired result in an HRBA to development. In this regard, an HRBA provides objective standards for determining the goals and strategies of development initiatives.

HRBA is based on a list of basic human rights principles developed by the United Nations that are of consequence for development initiatives. The principles that form the fundamental basis of a HRBA are:

- Universality, inalienability, and indivisibility of human rights;
- Interdependence and inter-relatedness;

- Equality and non-discrimination;
- Participation and inclusion; and
- Accountability and rule of law.

Every stage of the program cycle is anchored in a system of rights and related obligations set forth by international law under a HRBA. While there is no universal recipe for a HRBA, a HRBA can add important dimensions to development practice such as:

1. A Human Rights-Based Approach (HRBA) strengthens the foundation for political advocacy and social mobilization by basing programming goals on widely accepted principles and nationalational legal frameworks that emphasize duty bearer's accountability.
2. In order toTo implement more comprehensive policy and programming responses, HRBA offers an analytical lens through which to view the complexity of development problems, including the identification of underlying and root causes of issues. For example, in the field of sexual and reproductive health, an HRBA can support more comprehensive multisectoral responses that go beyond a health sector approach and vertical programming interventions, like those in the areas of family planning or maternal health.
3. HRBA increases focus on the most marginalized and excluded in society as their human rights are the most widely denied.
4. HRBA raises awareness of human rights issues and encourages the most disadvantaged people to participate in development processes. A HRBA lowers the possibility of setbacks in the development agenda and produces more sustainable results by enabling people to exercise their rights.
5. HRBA promotes the rule of law thereby reducing impunity, creating avenues for accountability and increasing access to justice.
6. The risk of elites gaining control over development resources is decreased and the ability to confront the underlying mechanisms that give rise to inequality is strengthened when the human rights principles of participation, accountability, equality, and non-discrimination are incorporated into the process of development.
7. HRBA helps to reduce the risk of violence by detecting growing conflicts and providing a legitimate framework of entitlements and obligations to address them.

In the 1990s, HRBA was initially created and put into practcies as part of development programs. Since then, an increasing number of organizations—

organizations, including NGOs, multilateral organizations, and cooperation agencies—have been progressively integrating an HRBA into their practices and policies. As a result of member state's 2005 World Summit Outcome commitment to include human rights into development policies, more states are implementing HRBAs in other areas of government work, such as budgeting and planning. National Organizations for Human Rights. (NHRIs), non-governmental organizations (NGOs), and other human rights and development stakeholders play a crucial role in assisting the government in implementing an HRBA and incorporating an HRBA into their own internal policies and procedures.

6.3.1. Universality, Inalienability, Indivisibility, and Interdependence of Human Rights

Human rights are inalienable, which means they cannot be taken away by force or voluntarily ceded, and universal, which means they apply to all people everywhere. Therefore, care should be taken to ensure that no group is overlooked when overseeing the state's work on reproductive rights and offering guidance to the government and parliament. Examples of such groups include adolescents, low-income women, rural and indigenous communities, LGBT people, sex workers, people with disabilities, migrants, and children. A needs assessment can help an NHRI decide which groups to focus on creating its own programs, it should make sure to take into account all groups. Similar toLike this, a government may reasonably choose to start serving the most alized groups due to resource limitations.

Furthermore, human rights are inseparable. All ofAll these aspects—civil, cultural, economic, political, and social—are fundamental to each and every human being's dignity. As a result, they are all equal in status as rights and cannot be arranged in a hierarchy from the outset. A National Health and Rehabilitation Institute (NHRI) ought to guarantee the preservation, observance, and advancement of every facet of reproductive rights.

Finally, human rights are linked and dependent upon one another. The fulfillment of one right frequently necessitates the fulfillment of another. Lack of access to reproductive health care can impact one's right to life, and women's rarticipation can be linked to the efficacy of reproductive rights (women who have the ability tocould choose whether and when to have children, for example, have a better chance of participating in political debates). This idea pushes NHRIs to examine reproductive rights from a broad perspective. Additionally, it exhorts NHRIs to be open-minded in their selection of partners for the adncement of reproductive rights.

6.3.2. Equality and Non-Discrimination

Every person is equal asto a human being, according to the Universal Declaration of Human Rights. All people are entitled to treatment without discrimination of any kind because of the inherent dignity of every human being. This includes consideration for factors such as gender, age, race, color, religion, property, disability, language, national or social origin,opinion, place of birth, or other statuses like marital status and sexual orientation.

In order toTo achieve true equality of treatment, nondiscrimination is associated with both equality and giving vulnerable groups extra consideration. Discrimination is wrong regardless of whether it is deliberate or not, and states are responsible for it even if a private party is the source of the discrimination due to their duty to protect cimple, a private employer is prohibited from discriminating against a woman at work on the basis ofbased on her marital status and her reproductive age. The state is required to step in if that occurs. The state may be held liable for violating the right to be free from discrimination if it does not takp this kind of discrimination.

It is illegal to deny someone access to health care on the basis ofbased on their membership in a specific group, nationality, gender, age, HIV status, or any other factor. This makes discrimination by private actors particularly pertinent to health issues, including reproductive health issues. For instance, discrimination under state jurisdiction may be established if medical personnel refuse to provide young single women with access to contraceptives due to their marital status. The state must enact anti-discrimination laws, make sure that appropriate contractual clauses are included, and launch educational programs to guarantee that such incidents do not occur.

Because they are women, it is illegal to deny them access to healthcare, including reproductive healthcare. This is taken to mean that the state cannot refuse access to health services that are necessary only for women, like post-abortion care and services pertaining to pregnancy and its complications. Discriminating against women based on their marital status or any other reason, including HIV status or pregnancy, is prohibited as well. States have obligations to prevent discrimination beyond interfering with an individual's right. States have a duty to guarantee that health information and services are accessible to all individuals, including marginalized and excluded groups, arising from their obligations to combat discrimination. States must also act to guaranteethey pass and the policies they implement not only do not discriminate against any particular groupgroup becure equal treatment. For laws to ensure equality, de facto differences must be taken into accountconsidered. States also need to take action to provide women the freedom to make decisions about their sexual and reproductive health without fear of violence, coercion, or discrimination. The state is responsible for making sure that girls and women can make these choices without facing discrimination. If women and girls do not already have this right, the state must ensure that they do by implementing affirmative action policies, among other things. In accordance with the non-discrimination principle, the state must guarantee equal access to (reproductive) health care for all groups, regardless of factors such as sex, age, ethnicity, place of residence, disability, etc. Among other things, this means ensuring that even the most impoverished individuals who live far from urban centers have access to reproductive health care.

Anti-discrimination and equality policies need to be carefully considered throughout the entire state machinery. For example, if a law discriminates against women or other groups in practice, it is not enough to say that it is gender neutral. State-approved laws and policies must support de facto equality, which means that each person will truly experience the same benefits and consequences from these laws and policies. Violence against women is considered a form of discrimination against women by the Committee on the Elimination of All Forms of Discrimination Against Women. States need to take action to address violence against women and guarantee that victims of gender-based violence, such as rape and incest, have access to sensitive counseling services. Women's reproductive rights and sexual health are directly impacted by violence against them, as previously stated.

States should also make sure that teenagers are not subjected to discrimination and have access to resources on family planning, contraception, the risks associated with getting pregnant too young, how to prevent HIV/AIDS and other STDs, and appropriate services related to sexual and reproductive health. Due to their youth, adolescents should not be subjected to discrimination; rather, they should be at the center of laws and policies pertaining to reproductive issues. One of an NHRI's primary responsibilities is to ensure that a state protects reproductive rights without discrimination and to offer pertinent ae state formulates and executes reproductive policy.

6.3.3. Participation and Inclusion

A human rightHuman rights are protected by numerous human rights instruments is participation. Every individual and every group has the right to actively, freely, and meaningfully contribute to, and enjoy the fruits of development that enables the realization of fundamental freedoms and human rights. This is known as participation and inclusion. This makes sure that everyone takes responsibility for the procedures and the end products. Empowerment and participation are linked. In addition to consultation, participation involves giving people the power to actively participate in decisions that directly impact them. Throughout any programming process, it is imperative to establish dedicated channels for participation, with a particular emphasis on the most marginalized and vulnerable groups. Women, particularly teenage girls, need to be the center of attention when it comes to reproductive rights. Adolescent boys and young men must also be included, especially when it comes to the use of contraceptives and efforts to change perceptions of gender roles. Women must be empowered to make decisions about their bodies freely, and men must be made aware of the importance of gender equality.

Moreover, empowerment calls for accountability and inclusiveness. As a result, when choosing strategies and objectives related to reproductive rights, beneficiaries, stakeholders, and partners must be involved, and service providers must always be held responsible. Concerns about empowerment should extend beyond the final product ont to include the means of achieving it and the institutions responsible for carrying it out. In order toTo achieve universal access to reproductive rights, participation should be seen as both a goal and a tool since it indicates that the affected individuals have made their own decisions. Since participation and ownership are closely related, it is crucial to implement reproductive rights.

The right to information is closely related to empowerment and participation because these concepts cannot exist without accurate information. Regarding reproductive rights, there should be widespread access ation on family planning, HIV/AIDS and other STIs, contraception, cervical cancer, and pre- and postnatalpost-natal care. In a similar vein, meaningful participation in all phases of policymaking, implementation, monitoring, and evaluation requires access to information, including information on public expenditures, budgetary allotments, and government policies. Because of this, the public needs to have easy access to local, regional, and federal organizations that deal with sexual and reproductive health and rights. Reproductive rights information should be readily available, transparent, timely, and in a language and format that is understandable to the most vulnerable people, such as the illiterate.

An NHRI should take action to guarantee that all parties, including marginalized groups, are included in its own programs. When working with reproductive rights, an NHRI should prioritize issues such as the state's program design, which should guarantee the appropriate participation and empowerment of the affected individuals and gro***6.3.4. Accountability and Rule of Law***

Human rights instrual norms and standards that StatesStates, and other duty-bearers are required to abide by. In the event thatIf duty-bearers fail to comply, rights-holders should have the option to hold them accountable for their failure to comply by initiating proceedings for appropriate redress before a competent court, an NHRI, an administrative body, or something similar in line with the guidelines and procedures set forth by law. Government policies should be transparently planned, designed, and implemented to provide right holders with a genuine opportunity to hold duty bearers accountable at every stage.

To achieve this, it is necessary to have transparent decision-making procedures and standards, well-defined roles and responsibilities, information accessibility, and strong accountability mechanisms. To guarantee that the rights-holders (individuals and groups) can utilize the resources available to them, it is imperative to enhance their capacity in addition to guaranteeing that the processes are transparent at all levels and that recourse opportunities exist.

Accountability is crucial within the duty-bearer community as well as between duty-bearers and rights-holders. Internal accountability between health workers and the health systems they work for is linked to accountability between health workers and the users they serve in the health system, particularly when it comes to reproductive health. The central government of Ceará, Brazil, actively fostered relationships between the government, communities, and health professionals in order to foster this kind of synergy. A program would only be launched by the central government in response to community demands for local government co-sponsorship. After it got underway, the program hired medical professionals through open, transparent procedures that told the local population about the goals of the program, the credentials needed for medical professionals, and what kind of services to expect. Health workers received support through technical training, supervision, and public relations campaigns aimed at boosting morale, in addition to community support and monitoring. Finally, the central government avoided negative interference from both local party representatives and supervising nurses by ensuring that all stakeholders had something to gain from supporting the program. By carrying out its protective mandate, which includes accepting complaints about alleged violations of human rights and closely observing how the state complies with rulings and recommendations, an NHRI can contribute to the establishment of accountability and the rule of law. It can also assist by giving government advice on how to create open, transparent procedures. Campaigns to raise awareness among right holders should enable them to hold duty bearers accountable.

6.3.5. Availability, Accessibility, Acceptability, and Quality

The right to health is closely linked to the right to reproduction. Women have the right to "reproductive health care services, goods, and facilities that are" readily available, easily accessible, socially acceptable, and of high quality. By ensuring that development outcomes and interventions are in line with the recommendations given by the 3AQ framework, HRBA implements the normative content of the right to health. Public policies that seek to provide universal access to sexual and reproductive health, for example, ought to incorporate specific interventions and program deliverables that guarantee health services fulfill a minimal standard of quality and are acceptable to the target population's culture.

The 3AQ framework in relation to reproductive rights is further developed below:

a) **Availability**: Facilities, products, services, and programs related to sexual and reproductive health and healthcare should be widely accessible throughout the nation. The WHO Action Programme on Essential Drugs defines essential drugs (including antiretroviral therapy) as those that are provided by hospitals, clinics, and other health-related facilities with trained medical and professional personnel. It also includes other services related to sexual and reproductive health, such as informational materials and contraception. Fundamental elementhealth, like access to clean, potable water and proper sanitary facilities, are typically also taken into accountconsidered.

b) **Accessibility**: Access to facilities, products, and services related to sexual and reproductive health must be universal throughout the nation, free from discrimination. Accessibility has four overlapping dimensions:

- **Non-discrimination:** Facilities, products, and services related to sexual and reproductive health must be available to everyone, including the most marginalized groups in society, both legally and practically. This means that no one should be denied access based on any of the banned categories, including race, religion, age, sex, health, disability, or any other status like marital status or sexual orientation.
- **Physical accessibility:** All segments of the population, particularly marginalized groups like women, the impoverished, adolescents, and young adults; women who have survived violence and abuse; people living with HIV; sex workers; people of color and indigenous people; people with disabilities; refugees and internally displaced people; and elderly people, must have safe physical access to sexual and reproductive health facilities, goods, and services. In addition, accessibility denotes that, even in remote locations, medical services and fundamental health determinants like clean, drinkable water and sufficient sanitary facilities are

physically reachable. In addition, accessibility involves providing people with disabilities with appropriate access to buildings. Information materials need to be available to the blind, illiterate, and speakers of all languages.

- **Economic accessibility (affordability):** All people must be able to afford sexual and reproductive health facilities, products, and services. Paymentelated to the underlying determinants of health and sexual and reproductive health care must be made on the basis ofbased on equality, guaranteeing that all individuals, including those from socially disadvantaged backgrounds, can affese services, whether they are provided privately or publicly. It is imperative for equality that health costs not beare not borne disproportionately by impoverished households relative to wealthier households.
- **Information accessibility:** The freedom to look for, accept, and share ideas and information about matters of sexual and reproductive health is a component of accessibility. However, the right to the confidentiality of one's personal health information should not be compromised by information accessibility.

c) **Acceptability**: All resources related to sexual and reproductive health must respect medical ethics and be appropriate for the local culture, that is sensitive to gender and life-cycle requirements, considerate of the cultures of individuals, minorities, peoples, and communities, as well as intended to maintain confidentiality and enhance the health of those involved.

d) **Quality**: Facilities, products, and services related to sexual and reproductive health must be of high quality and suitable from a medical and scientific standpoint. For example, this calls for qualified medical professionals, medications that have been approved by science and are not expired, hospital supplies and contraception, safe and drinkable water, and proper sanitation.

6.4. LEGAL AND INSTITUTIONAL FRAMEWORK ON REPRODUCTIVE HEALTH IN NIGERIA

a) The 1999 Constitution of the Federal Republic of Nigeria

Everyone in Nigeria has the right to life and the respect for human dignity guaranteed by the constitution. The Constitution states that every citizen has an obligation to live in peace, harmony, and the spirit of common brotherhood while also respecting the rights and legitimate interests of other citizens. The right to a private and family life is also protected by the Constitution, and women are granted the freedom from discrimination based on their gender, nationality, or religion. The principles of justice, equality, and freedom form the basis of the Constitution's social goal. The constitution promises to uphold and advance human dignity and acknowledges the sanctity of the human person. The Nigerian State promises to focus her policies on making sure that everyone who works has their health, safety, and welfare protected and not abused, as well as that everyone has access to quality medical care.

b) African Charter on Human and People's Rights

All people have the right to be treated with respect for their inherent dignity and to have their legal status recognized by the African Charter on Human and People's Rights. Every person has the additional right to the best possible state of physical and mental well-being, and State parties are obligated to take all reasonable steps to safeguard the health and availability of medical care for their citizens. The abolition of all forms of discrimination against women and the defense of their rights, as well as the rights of children, are also urged upon the states. Under the African Human and People's Rights (Ratification and Enforcement) Act, Nigeria ratified the aforementioned African Charter on Human and People's Rights.

c) The Nigerian Health Policy

Within the limits of the government's resources, the Nigerian health policy seeks to provide comprehensive primary healthcare that is preventive, restorative, rehabilitative, and protective. The Policy aims to promote a participatory approach to health development, thereby increasing women's involvement in health decision-making; to provide easily accessible, reasonably priced, and well-equipped health facilities; to legislate and enforce suitable protective measures for women workers; to eliminate harmful traditional practices that have a negative impact on women's and girl's health; and more. In order to achieve the goal of health for all citizens to a level of health that permits all citizens to lead socially and economically productive lives at the highest possible level by the year 2000 and beyond, the policy commits the federal, state, and local governments of Nigeria, as well as all the people, to intensive action. The national health policy, which takes gender equality into consideration, aims to improve the quality, affordability, and accessibility of health services provided by the national health system, thereby improving the health of Nigerians and contributing to the attainment of the Millennium Development Goals.

d) Convention for the Elimination of All Forms of Discrimination against Women (CEDAW)

The aforementioned convention upholds belief in the equality of men and women, as well as in the fundamental human rights, worth, and dignity of the human person. According to the Convention, everyone is entitled to all the freedoms and rights outlined in it, without exception, and that all people are created free, equal, and endowed with inherent dignity and rights. It is discriminatory for a State party to refuse to lawfully allow the performance of specific reproductive health services for women, as stated in the Convention.

e) The Criminal and Penal Codes

The major statutes listed above, known as the codes, define offenses and specify the penalties for committing crimes like sexual assault and rape as well as other serious offenses that seriously violate women's reproductive rights. Despite the difficulties in obtaining corroboration in cases of sexual offenses, these Codes prohibit a person charged with a sexual offense from being found guilty based solely on the uncorroborated testimony of one witness.

f) The Criminal Procedure Act

The Criminal Procedure Act recognized women's right to procreate by requiring that, prior to imposing a death sentence on a woman found guilty of a capital crime, her pregnancy status be ascertained. A pregnant woman cannot receive a death sentence. Rather, she receives a life sentence in prison.

6.4.1. Sustainable Framework on Women Reproductive Health

A society's prenatal care and attention practices reveal a great deal about it. The government bears the responsibility of guaranteeing that women's reproductive health and rights to health are not only upheld but also encouraged. Advancement, protection, and promotion of reproductive health and rights are the responsibilities of the government. This is a global mandate.

6.4.1.1. The Place of Law in Reproductive Health

Important markers of the government's commitment to advancing and defending women's reproductive rights are laws and policies. A society's affairs can only be regulated by the government through the use of laws. The State can give its reproductive health policies the desired effect by means of legislation. Women's social environments are shaped by law, which also offers a means of conceptualizing, advancing, and defending women's reproductive rights. Laws and policies establish the framework that allows the government to influence people's behavior. To guarantee unrestricted access to reproductive health care services, legislation must be implemented. Nigeria requires health laws to fortify the healthcare system and to inspire the government to address injustices against women. While laws that prevent women from fully exercising their reproductive rights should be changed, gender-sensitive laws, policies, and enforceable legislation that support women's full enjoyment of their rights should be strengthened.

6.4.1.2. Participation

Women and society both benefit when they are given the freedom to choose how they want to conceive. A society cannot be considered healthy unless women's rights to equality and full participation are guaranteed. To have a healthy society in Nigeria, health programs in that country must accept this fact. Disregarding women's autonomy to make decisions that impact them has detrimental effects on their personal freedom. Reproductive health problems can be solved with the help of active participation in reproductive health issues.

6.4.1.3. Awareness Creation

The fact that adults have concerns related to their sexual and reproductive health that are rarely brought up or readily addressed was emphasized in Cairo (1994). Similarly, teenagers are especially open to having their reproductive rights violated because they do not have access to adequate information or services. Boys and girls should be made more conscious of sex education in order to make them more aware of the negative effects of reckless sexual behavior. Adopting social education that teaches respect for physical integrity is advised, as was done in Mexico in 1975.

6.4.1.4. Right Based Approach to Reproductie

Productive health from a health-based perspective is a worthwhile goal in and of itself. Women's human rights include the freedomfreedom to control and make responsible decisions about their sexual orientation and reproductive health without being subjected to coercion, discrimination, or violence. Adopting a client-based, right-based approach that takes gender equity and equality, reproductive rights, and healthcare for women into account is important. A right-based approach like this should establish a strong connection between human rights and health in order to advocate for the health of women and youth.

6.4.1.5. Information

Power comes from knowledge. One of the things that affects the health of any population is the availability of information and medical care. States are required by the Beijing Platform of Action of 1995 to take all reasonable steps to provide access to information, education, and means to exercise the rights of men and women to control reproduction. As a result, states have an obligation to address issues related to women's reproductive health, according to Cook (1992). Enhancing thrian health system and providing the required information and healthcare services that address women's sexual and reproductive healthhealth, and all human rights are critical components of a framework. This will facilitate universal access to the knowledge required to safeguard their sexual and reproductive health services.

6.4.1.6. Integration of Reproductive Health into National Health Policies and Programmes

The maintenance of people's health is influenced by the health system. The emphasis of the Nigerian health system should be on the necessity of providing universal access to reproductive health care. Reproductive health for women should be included in national health strategies and initiatives. This will guarantee the advancement of gender equality and women's reproductive health. To improve the performance of health systems, it is impacknowledge the importance of disease programs, health systems, and research. The Nigerian health system needs to be improved in order toto provide fair, universal coverage. This can be achieved by increasing health financing, recruiting, and training. It is important to prioritize funding for reproductive health care. Donors and financial institutions should be persuaded to support the endeavors of mainstreaming women's reproductive health into their budgets in this way. To ensure that everyone has access to comprehensive healthcare, health infrastructures should be reinforced.

REFERENCES

1. American Society for Emergency Contraception. (2014). *EC on the Shelf: Real-World Access in the OTC Era*.
2. Bjorklund, A. (2006). Does family policy affect fertility? Lessons from Sweden. *Journal of Population Economics*, *19*, 3–24.
3. Bongaarts, J. (1994). The impact of population policies: Comment. *Population and Development Review*, *20*, 616–620.
4. Buckles, K. (2008). Understanding the returns to delayed childbearing for working women. *The American Economic Review*, *98*(2), 403–407.
5. Burke, A., & Simmons, A. (2014). *Increased Coverage of Preventive Services with Zero Cost Sharing Under the Affordable Care Act*. Washington, DC: U.S. Department of Health and Human Services, Office of the Assistant Secretary for Planning and Evaluation.
6. Center for Mississippi Health Policy. (2012). *Medicaid Expansion: An Overview of Potential Impacts in Mississippi*.
7. Child Trends Databank. (2014). *Late or No Prenatal Care: Indicators on Children and Youth*. Bethesda, MD: Child Trends.
8. Cooper, L., & Cates, P. (2006). *Too High a Price: The Case Against Restricting Gay Parenting*. New York, NY: American Civil Liberties Union.
9. Farley, J. U., & Samuel, S. J. (1981). Potential impact on birth rates of reforms in laws governing contraceptive marketing. *Policy Science*, *13*, 439–458.
10. Foster, A., & Roy, N. (1997). The dynamics of education and fertility: Evidence from a family planning experiment.
11. Gates, G. (2015). *Demographics of Married and Unmarried Same-Sex Couples: Analyses of the 2013 American Community Survey*. Los Angeles, CA: The Williams Institute at UCLA School of Law.
12. Gattozzi, E. (2008). *Indigenous Women's Reproductive Justice: A Survey of the Availability of Plan B® and Emergency Contraceptives within Indian Health Service*. Lake Andes, SD: Native American Women's Health Education Resource Center.
13. Guttmacher Institute. (2004a). *Parental Involvement in Minors' Abortions*. Washington, DC: Guttmacher Institute.
14. Guttmacher Institute. (2004b). *State Funding of Abortion Under Medicaid*. Washington, DC: Guttmacher Institute.

15. Guttmacher Institute. (2004c). *State Sex and STD/HIV Education Policy*. Washington, DC: Guttmacher Institute.
16. Guttmacher Institute. (2015d). *Emergency Contraception*. Washington, DC: Guttmacher Institute.
17. Guttmacher Institute. (2015e). *Medicaid Family Planning Eligibility Expansions*. Washington, DC: Guttmacher Institute.
18. Hamilton, B. E., Martin, J. A., Osterman, M. J. K., Curtin, S. C., & Mathews, T. J. (2014). Births: Preliminary data for 2013. *National Vital Statistics Reports*, *63*(2). Hyattsville, MD: Centers for Disease Control and Prevention, National Center for Health Statistics.
19. Hock, H. (2007). *The Pill and the College Attainment of American Women and Men*. Tallahassee, FL: Florida State University.
20. International Federation of Red Cross and Red Crescent Societies. (2010). *Strategy 2020: Saving Lives, Changing Minds*. Geneva. Available at: www.ifrc.org.Global/Publications/general/strategy-2020.pdf (accessed on 14 October 2024).
21. Kaiser Family Foundation. (2015). *Status of State Action on the Medicaid Expansion Decision*.
22. Kellogg, E. H., Kline, D. K., & Stepan, J. (1975). *The World's Laws and Practices on Population and Sexuality Education*. Medford, MA: Law and Population Programme, Fletcher School of Law and Diplomacy, Tufts University.
23. Kirby, D. (2007). *Emerging Answers 2007: Research Findings on Programs to Reduce Teen Pregnancy and Sexually Transmitted Diseases*. Washington, DC: The National Campaign to Prevent Teen and Unplanned Pregnancy.
24. Klerman, J. A. (1999). U.S. abortion policy and fertility. *The American Economic Review*, *89*, 261–264.
25. Martinez, M. E., & Cohen, R. A. (2015). *Health Insurance Coverage: Early Release of Estimates from the National Health Interview Survey, January–September 2014*. Hyattsville, MD: Centers for Disease Control and Prevention, National Center for Health Statistics.
26. Miller, A. R. (2011). The effects of motherhood timing on career path. *Journal of Population Economics*, *24*(3), 1071–1100.
27. National Women's Law Center. (2012). *Contraceptive Equity Laws in Your State: Know Your Rights–Use Your Rights, A Consumer Guide*. Washington, DC: National Women's Law Center.

28. Rahman, A., Katzive, L., & Henshaw, S. K. (1998). A global review of laws on induced abortion, 1985–1997. *International Family Planning Perspectives*, *24*, 56–64.
29. Ross, J., Stover, J., & Adelaja, D. (2007). Family planning programs in 2004: New assessments in a changing environment. *International Family Planning Perspectives*, *33*, 22–30.
30. Sonfield, A. (2014). Contraceptive coverage at the U.S. Supreme Court: Countering rhetoric with evidence. *Guttmacher Institute Policy Review*, *17*(1).
31. Stepan, J., & Kellogg, E. H. (1974). *The World's Laws on Contraceptives*. Law and Population Monograph Series, *17*.

Chapter 7

Gender, Family Law, and Custody Issues

Contents

INTRODUCTION

The body of laws governing family relationships, such as marriage and divorce, childcare, and associated financial issues, is known as family law.

Family law was historically closely related to the law of property and succession. Based on the records that are currently available, it is likely that the primary source of family law originated from the property and economic issues that arose when a woman was transferred from her father's family to her husband's authority and guardianship. Legal notions like guardianship, custody, and legitimacy were linked to family power dynamics and financial interests, even in relation to the parent-child relationship. In addition, family law has historically dealt with questions of personal status, such as whether someone should be regarded as married or single, legitimate or illegitimate. However, the circumstances and significance of these distinctions frequently stem from the law of property.

Criminal law and other areas of law, including family law, havesinterest in similar social issues. The very difficult problem of violence within the family, for instance, has drawn a lot of attention since the late 20th century. This violence can take the form of physical abuse or violence committed by an adult against another adult or against a child, or it can take another form. In extreme circumstances, the only practical course of action might be to end cohabitation or place an abused child in foster or public care. The process of ending a marriage or other marital union is called a divorce, sometimes referred to as dissolution of marriage. Under the laws of the specific nation or state, divorce typically involves the cancellation or reorganization of the legal obligations and responsibilities of marriage, thereby severing the matrimonial ties between a married couple. It can be defined as the official dissolution of a marriage by a judge or other authority figure. It's the formal procedure for dissolving a marriage. While divorce laws vary greatly between nations, most require approval from a court or other authority through a legal process that may include property distribution, child custody, alimony (spousal support), child visitation/access, parenting time, child support, and debt division. Since monogamy is mandated by law infmost countries, divorce permits each former partner to remarry.

With legal separation or *de jure* separation (a legal process by which a married couple may formalize a de facto separation while remaining legally married) or with de facto separation (a process where the spouses informally stop cohabiting), divorce differs from annulment, which declares the marriage null and void. Divorce can occur for a variety of reasons, such as infidelity or a personality conflict with one or both spouses, incompatibility sexually or a lack of independence.

7.1. FAMILY FROM A GENDER PERSPECTIVE: EVOLUTION AND THE CURRENT SITUATION

The way in which laws, like family law, govern families and family relations is greatly influenced by the structure of the family and the relationships that exist within it. The evolution of the concept of family from a traditionally grounded, male-dominated (by husband or father) model to a gender-equality-based model is an important consideration in the study of gender perspectives on family law. The discussion will center on the evolution of gender equality in family law and policies, along with the ways in which these advancements can be enhanced to promote greater gender equality in families in modern societies.

The rise of an urban, industrial, and highly mobile society over time has altered the traditional nuclear family structure, which consists of a man and a woman with children living together. This has also resulted in the nuclear family becoming more isolated and inggrowing non-traditional forms of companionship. The division of work and home responsibilities is one of the structural changes linked to industrialization.

The oppression of children by parents and the dominance of men over women are justified by a traditional family model. Based on this conception of the family, discriminatory family laws serve as a justification for the patriarchal male dominance and the oppression of parents by appearing to be legal. Nonetheless, throughout history, laws and policies have changed in various ways depending etysociety. In order to take inionconsideration, the multiplicity and diversity of ways that human relations and the family institution are shaped in modern societies, more egalitarian family laws have been developed.

Since the end of World War II, the role of the family has changed more quickly in contemporary industrialized societies. It is argued that the most important factors in the evolution of family structure have been the rise in women's earning power and capital investment, as well as their increased participation in the labor market. This argument is supported by changes in the family formation process in several modern industrialized countries.

In the final decades of the 20th century, various interpretations of whnesdefined a family have supplanted the traditional family. This is caused by several things, such as the rise in divorce rates, the increase in the number of women working for pay, and the rise in the number of homes headed by women. The evolution of gender relations and the dismantling of essentialist gender roles in society have changed the structure of families throughout the course of the last century in many European countries.

These days, a marriage contract is not always the first step towards starting a family in many societies. The role of men in the family has gradually diminished, and in many European nations—including Andorra, Austria, Croatia, Cyprus, Greece, Denmark, Sweden, Finland, Iceland, Norway, Ireland, Italy, Spain, Slovenia, Switzerland, Portugal, the Netherlands, Malta, Liechtenstein, Luxembourg, Germany, and France—the cohabitation and marriage of same-sex couples are accepted by law. Same-sex social and legal visibility is said to have entered the family structures in these nations. Compared to other European nations, the Nordic countries were at the forefront of recognizing same-sex marriage and parenthood legally.

Today's family model is different from the patriarchal one in that it allows both mothers and fathers to equally exercise their rights and responsibilities over their children, whether within the context of a formal marriage or a de facto union. We also come across single-parent households, same-sex families, etc. The demands of feminist movements and LGBTQIA+ groups, as well as the acceptance of the principle of equality and non-discrimination on the basis of sex, sexual orientation, or gender identity in international and national legal texts, have all played a significant role in the gradual process leading to the emergence of new family models.

Since the structure of traditional/mainstream family law is based on a gender binary system that values and privileges men, gender competent family law and policies are the primary means of promoting gender equality in many countries.

Changes in gender and gender relations lead to gender equality. Gender equality policies governing women's lives in the home and public sphere began to emerge in the Nordic countries in the 1880s. The reform of marriage law, which called for the removal of a husband's authority in a marriage and the awarding of economic independence to women, was at the center of the women's movements in all of the Nordic countries in 1905. Thus, in 1909, the Nordic nations came together to form the Scandinavian law committee, which sought to improve gender equality in the region by harmonizing marriage laws. Reforms pertaining to the liberal formation and dissolution of marriage in 1913 and the gender equality legal effects of marriage in 1918 were implemented as a result of the committee's findings.

The marriage law reform in the Nordic countries introduced a dual-breadwinner family model. According to this model, women's domestic labor is acknowledged legally as a means of supporting the family. Eugenic ideologies were also used in the Nordic countries at the time to impose marriage restrictions on the elderly, the mentally challenged, immigrants, people with deaf-muteness, and those with large families. The relationship between the gendered division of labor, unpaid work, and gender equality in the labor market—which promotes women's employment and values care giving—is highlighted by family policy in the Nordic countries. The Nordic model combines work and family responsibilities with free, high-quality childcare, acknowledging individualism while highlighting the shared responsibility for family care. This strategy is known as defamilization.

As a component of the Nordic model of gender equality, the Swedish welfare state places a strong emphasis on equality for all through universal benefits. In Sweden, the nuclear family gave way to the individual family member in the 1960s as women's roles as mothers and workers entered the family policy conversation.

When it comes to family policy, Sweden has adopted a more progressive stance than many other nations worldwide. For instance, in 1974, women were granted the right to divorce their partners for any reason, and in 1975, they were granted the right to an abortion up until the 18th week of pregnancy without having to give a reason. However, Sweden and other Nordic nations still have a long way to go in terms of LGBTQIA+ issues. In Sweden, for instance, assisted reproduction using donated sperm has been permitted for single individuals since 2016 as well as for same-sex couples since 2005. But in Sweden, egg donation is only permitted for couples of the opposite sex, meaning that gay men are not eligible to receive egg donations. Prior to 2013 transgender individuals were not only unable to preserve their gem cells for use in gender affirming treatments, but they were also required to undergo sterilization in order to undergo legal gender transition in Sweden.

In Europe, granting LGBTQIA+ individuals family rights has been a contentious issue since the year 2000. As a result, many European nations consider same-sex partnerships and civil unions to be legal. However, most of Europe does not yet have legal same-sex marriage. For instance, Switzerland recently approved same-sex marriage legislation through a 2021 referendum. Parenthood rights still have limited legal recognition in a few European nations, including Serbia, Italy, and Spain. Furthermore, very few nations have given transgender and queer couples equal parenting rights. For instance, Norway replaced its 1993-enacted Registered Partnership Law with a gender-neutral Marriage Law in 2009. Lesbian, gay, and straight couples now have equal rights to marriage and parenthood under the new law, but trans parenthood is not recognized. It wasn't until 2019 that transgender people could be included on their children's documentation in Sweden thanks to the legal recognition of transparenthood. In addition, trans women are acknowledged as mothers and trans men as fathers when they become parents.

Application of intersectional analysis and conceptualization of multiple inequality grounds are beneficial to legal change and the development of gender equal family policies. When addressing gender equality family policies, consideration must be given to social divisions of sexuality as well as discrimination based on "race," class, ethnicity, age, disability, and religion. "The material scope of EU directives on gender equality encompasses everything from parental leave, pregnancy protection, equal pay, and equal treatment in employment and self-employment to access to services and social rights."

7.2. GENDER AND MARRIAGE PERSPECTIVES

Husbands and wives engage in shared experiences and interactions during marriages, which may give rise to varying perceptions of the quality of the partnershipdly, few little arch havehas examined whether gender differences exist in the structure of marital quality, and even fewer have assessed whether genetic and environmental factors that impact marital quality are gender-specific.

7.2.1. Discrimination against Married Women: Evolution to the Present Situation

The traditional family model, shaped by European religious, cultural, political, and philosophical traditions, has traditionally been the marriage-based family. As the only person with parental authority, the husband was the head of the household and could make decisions about everything pertaining to the marriage, as well as the upbringing and education of young children. This was a patriarchal household. The husband had the authority to control his wife for the sake of good family governance, including the ability to forbid her from taking part in any extramarital activities that were deemed to be in conflict with her responsibilities to the family.

In this sense, the codifications regarded the husband as the head of the household and thus the person to make decisions regarding family matters. In a division of labor based on the concepts of inequality and submission, charge ofoversaw taking care of the family members and running the home. This led to a marriage in which the woman faced prejudice against he result ofbecause of her status as a wife. Married women were subservient to their husbands and owed them obedience, hence they lacked capacity and autonomy. Before marriage, women were legally under the guardianship of their fathers; after that, the husband assumed legal guardianship of his wife. Due to the significant limitations placed on women's abilities, married women were viewed as having a lower status than their husbands. The woman gained the right to adopt her husband's name and—more importantly—achieve his family status through marriage. Marital authority applied to married women as well in the property's vicinity. The fact that the husband had legal guardianship over the wife suggests that she was practically in his "possession." Thus, prerogatives granted to the husband, his spouse, and regarding his property represented marital authority (Collier, 2010).

As we can see, the law governing marriage mirrored the gender norms attached to married people. In this way, married women faced especially severe discrimination because of their status in marriage. When the single woman chose to get married, she discovered that her circumstances had gotten worse due to the influence of her family. Rather than affording her additional freedoms or rights recognition, her new marital status put her in a position of extreme discrimination and inequality. More significantly number ofmany the aforementioned limitations continued long into the twentieth century in the legal frameworks of Western European nations.

It's interesting to note that feminists have attacked marriage on the grounds that it wasn't a legal contract ever since William Thompson published his critique of the "white slave code" of marriage in 1825. Marriage is specifically criticized for being referred to as a contract when, in reality, it is much more of an institution in which oe husband—parties has exercised the authority of a slave owner over his wife.

Marriage in Europe changed during the period of the two World Wars, moving from a customary model that prioritized the husband to one that was based on the equality of the spouse's respective rights and responsibilities. On the other hand, the change was implemented in 1920 in certain countries (like Sweden) and from 1981 onwards in other countries (like Spain).

As a result, the wife's submission to the marital authority to determine where to live, obtain citizenship, or have her husband's last name imposed vanished. The equality of the spouses with regard to their relationship with their children was demonstrated by designating the husband and wife as equal legal guardians of their joint children.

The husband's authority over the management and distribution of assets vanished as well. The suppression of the wife's unilateral responsibilities was brought about by the normative shift towards marital equality, which was accompanied by reciprocal rights and duties of respect and protection between the spouses. A fundamental tenet of European law was the notion of marriage as a cooperative endeavor, founded on equality, to which each spouse contributed in accordance with their ability. It is now difficult to defend any restriction of an individual's rights based solely on their marital status because the dignity and moral and legal equality of spouses have been accepted as a fundamental pillar of the system since the various reforms that have altered family law.

7.2.2. The Right to Marry and Form a Family

To begin, it should be noted that marriage is a voluntary legal union between two individuals who may or may not be of the same sex and who typically, but not always, reside together. This depends on whether same-sex marriage is permitted by national laws.

According to Article 8 of the Convention for the Protection of Human Rights and Fundamental Freedoms (also known as "the Convention"), which upholds the right to a private and family life, formal or de jure family relationships are typical circumstances.

In this context, the European Court of Human Rights has stressed that "the relationship that results from a lawful and genuine marriage must, at any rate, be included in the word family, whatever else it may mean." "Men and women of marriageable age have the right to marry and to find a family, subject to the national laws governing the exercise of this right," reads Article 12 of the that ArticleArticle 12 of the Convention does not provide an unrestricted right because it includes the phrase "according to the national laws governing the exercise of this right." "A certain amount of leeway has been granted to the national legislature to regulate the legal ramifications of marriage and establish provisions regarding the resulting family ties, subjecting the right laid down in Article 12 to certain conditions." The restrictions resulting from national law cannot limit or diminish the right to marry in a way that compromises the fundamental nature of the right.

Two rights are independently protected by Article 12 the right to marry and the right to start a family. In essence, the former is "the right to acquire a status, to form a legal relationship." Conceived in the context of Article 12, the right to start a family requires marriage (couples who cohabit outside of marriage, however, are entitled to protection under Article 8).

Even in situations where there is no desire or chance of having children, a person's right to marry is protected. The right to start a family includes a married couple's ability to procreate and bear children, but it does not require an in actually bebe able to become pregnant. Therefore, it is believed that a couple's incapacity to conceive or raise a child does not automatically deny them the right to get married.

The right to marry and the right to remarry are treated equally under Article 12. As a result, in situations where the contracting state acknowledges the possibility of severing the marital bond through a divorce, the right to remarry is guaranteed to divorced individuals (Melby et al., 2006).

The primary result of marriage is the establishment of a marital status, which sparks the e a number ofseveral responsibilities and relationships within the context of a community. A legal relationship is formed through marriage, and this relationship is reflected in each spouse's personal life and property.

7.2.3. Personal Aspects (Equal Rights and Duties of the Spouses)

Ag to rulingsthe rulings from the European Court of Human Rights, cohabitation is not the same as marriage, which is distinguished from it by a number of rights and responsibilities. All of these responsibilities and rights that result from marriage are governed by the equality principle. The law outlines the responsibilities and rights of spouses in an equit into accountconsidering their gender. One of the great democratic triumphs that has become an indelible part of our legal culture is the acknowledgment of equality and equal rights between spouses. The Universal Declaration of Human Right's Article 16, which states that spouses "are entitled to equal rights as to marriage, during marriage and at its dissolution," is the model for Article 12. In 1984, Protocol No. 7 to the Convention for the Protection of Human Rights and Fundamental Freedoms included a the equalityequality of spouses. It should be mentioned that a married woman is not violating any marital obligations when she decides on her own to end her pregnancy.

7.2.4. Patrimonial Aspects (Management of Marital Property)

If it was previously stated that the property sphere demonstrated the husband's initiative and the wife's submission to his authority, then the property sphere demonstrated the same principle. After getting married, the woman was no longer able to make decisions about her property or enter into agreements without her husband's approval. The husband gains this authority of dominance from the father. The wife's ability to act was limited by her husband's dominance over her property. In addition to representing the wife and allowing her to conduct business, the husband oversaw the marital assets. According to traditional law, a wife could only carry out specific acts with her husband's consent. Married women were also prohibited from trading without a marriage license. One illustration of the wife's secondary role was the dowry, which was meant to make up for the husband's obligation to provide for her.

The marginalization of married women with regard to managing and dividing marital assets has been eradie majority ofMost countries' laws now properly divide the management of matrimonial property between the two spouses, rather than attributing it to the husband. However, a sizable portion of women still perform household duties, either solely or in addition to outside employment.

The legal system must provide an answer to a number of questions regarding the life partnership that begins with marriage, which have an impact on the financial relationships between the spouses as well as those with other parties. Many questions need to have legal answers given to them, including how to share in the responsibilities of a marriage, how management powers are divided between the spouses, how their assets are arranged, and how their assets' liability to third parties is related. The normative answer to each of these queries is based on the idea of equality between spouses. As a result, one spouse is no longer required to represent the other in court, and since marriage does not limit a person's ability to use their legal rights, spouses can continue to interact financially with one another and with third parties.

Concerning the particular property regimes that apply to the spouses (usually community or separation of property), community property regimes—wherein both spouses have a common property—form an equthe event thatif there is an unequal distribution of income between the two spouses, as was the case when the woman got married and focused solely on taking care of the house. Separate property regimes are the most appropriate way to ensure the equality and full capacity ofas a result ofbecause of women entering the workforce and changes in gender roles. Separation of property systems may be unjust to the spouse; historically, the woman has contributed to the growth and development of the other spouse's assets despite having little or no initial as.***5. Non BinaryNon-Binary Marriage***

Marriage is traditionally understood to be a union of individuals who are not of the same biological sex. The belief that a marriage can only be between a man and a woman has been disproved by the changes that social evolution has brought about in the institution of marriage. The desire to uphold the distinction between sexual roles that forms the basis of traditional marriage is inevitably reflected in the opposition to samage of ArticleArticle 12 of the Convention appears to indicate that two people of different sexes are the ones who possess the right to marry. However, Article 9 CFR makes no explicit reference to the gender of the spouses and does not discuss their sexual orientation.

The European Court of Human Rights initially denied transgender people the ability to marry members of their own biological sex. The Convention's Article 12 established the conventional understanding of marriage as a union between a man and a woman, which served as the foundation for the discussion. Nonetheless, marriages between transsexuals and individuals of the same biological sex were legal in a few European states. In the case of *Goodwin v. The UK*, July 11, 2002, a new phase in the recognition of transsexuals' right to marriage was initiated when it was acknowledged that being asexual is not inherently a barrier to marriage and that, as a result, transsexuals had the right to marry. It should be noted that the Yogyakarta Principles plus 10 (2017) state that "no status, such as marriage, may be invoked as such to prevent the legal recognition of a person's gender identity."

Regarding individuals who identify as homosexual, while cultural advancements have significantly altered the institution of marriage since the Convention's adoption, opinions on same-sex marriage are divided throughout Europe. The European Court of Human Rights has ruled that the Convention does not require the Contracting States to allow same-sex couples to marry since it is commonly believed that marriage bestows unique rights and a specific status on its participants. According to the European Court of Human Rights, protecting marriage is, in theory, a basic and acceptable justification that can be used to support treating married and single couples differently. Therefore, states are allowed to treat married and single couples differently, especially when it comes to issues pertaining to social and fiscal policy like social security, pensions, and taxes. These findingseven in light ofconsidering the gradual shift that States have made in this regard. More and more nations are permitting same-sex marriages, and others are providing stable same-sex relationships outside of the formal marriage institution with legal protections (civil partnerships).

7.3. GENDER PERSPECTIVE AND DIVORCE/SEPARATION

The grounds for divorce differ greatly between nations. One may view marriage as a status symbol, a contract, or any combination of these. If viewed as a contspouse's incapacityinability or refusal to carry out the terms of the agreement could give rise to the other spouse's right to file for divorce. On the other hand, divorce is simply blameless in certain nations. This implies that the reasons why a party or parties wish to separate are irrelevant. They don't needame for the divorcedivorce in order to separate of their own free will. Both at-fault and no-fault divorce options are available in many jurisdictions.

7.3.1. The Impact of Gender on the Temporary or Final Break-Up of the Marital Relationship

One area where gender studies have made a more noticeable and substantial contribution to legal studies is the temporary or fiution of a marriagemarriage. The reason is twofold: first, there is a direct correlation between the effects of divorce on the personal and patrimonial circumstances of the divorcing parties and the roles that culture and society traditionally assigns to each gender; second, there is a relationship between the way that divorce and marriage are viewed and the characteristics that are intrinsic to each gender, whether it be transgender, female, or male. While the legal systems of the various countries in which we have Western legal traditions have different approaches to separation and divorce, we can argue that their common goal is to treat spouses equally, both in terms of formal and substantive treatment.

The main goal of such a regime is to correct the imbalances that the establishment, regulation, suspension, and interruption of the marriage have caused between the partners. These imbalances can be attributed to a variety of factors, including their shared attitudes toward negotiation and litigation, their respective levels of commitment to family life, their likelihood of starting a family in the future, and their methods for juggling the needs of the family with their personal and professional goals.

7.3.2. Gender Equality and the Grounds for Separation/Divorce

Along with the evolution of societal perceptions of gender, the legislative and judicial strategies employed to achieve this goal have undergone profound transformations over time. Giving each spouse the freedom to file for separation and divorce on equal terms and without the other's permission has been the first, and simplest, ality.

The majority ofMost legal systems have gradually transitioned from a fault-based divorce and separation process to a non-fault model, wherein each spouse may obtain a divorce and separation based only on the claim that there has been a "irretrievable breakdown" of the marriage. This approach, which is mirrored in the acquis commun, is what the Principles of European Family Law have chosen. Certain laws still include the common grounds for divorce, to which the gender shift of one of the spouses was compelled by scientific advancements; however, these grounds merely supplement the "irretrievable breakdown" claim, not replace it. Furthermore, fault still plays a significant role in most legal systems, but it has different consequences depending on the situation, including the existence and amount of maintenance, welfare-linked rights, and the rights of separated or divorced spouses to inherit property. However, courts have evolved their interpretation of fault itself. Case law now holds that one spouse's adultery does not automatically imply guilt; rather, fault arises only when the other spouse's behavior was such that it infringes upon their dignity.

7.3.3. Gender Equality and the Consequences of Separation/ Divorce: The Distribution of Marital Property

The second strategy focuses on the outcomes of separation or divorce rather than the reasons for it, with the goal of encouraging formal equality between the partners in addressing the challenges of the marriage. Stated differently, the attainment of gender equality necessitates a precise evaluation and administration of the regulations governing the distribution of marital property and assets among the partners, as well as the distribution of monetary resources, commonly referred to as maintenance.

In terms of how marital property was divided during a period when women were viker sex, the majority ofmost laws tried to address the inequality by making the community of goods the default rule. To put it briefly, the goal of this kind of regime is to prevent one spouse—typically, the husband—from being the only one with ownership of marital property simply because he is the only one with the right to work and, thus, the only one with the means to acquire assets.

In actuality, the community regime stipulates that even if only one spouse purchases any goods during the marriage, the other spouse is entitled to an ideal half of those goods, such as earned qualifying periods for pensions. This indicates that marital property will be split equally between the parties in the event of a divorce, on the one hand, and that ownership of such property cannot be transferred without the agreement of both spouses.

Not all systems used the community of goods to address the issue of gender equality. In certain of them, there is no set default system inever, courts are able tocan divide marital property between ex-spouses in a way that best addresses the financial or economic disparities brought on by the divorce, even if this division proves to be unfair and includes the spouse's personal belongings.

A cursory examination of picates that, in light ofconsidering the evolution of women's roles in society, particularly with regard to their ability to work, couples are increasingly choosing to adopt other conventional regimes, such as the separation of goods, in which each spouse maintains ownership of the goods that they personally purchased, rather than sticking with the default one.

7.3.4. Gender Equality and the Consequences of Separation/ Divorce: Maintenance

In terms of the financial fallout from a divorce or separation, after-separation or post-divorce maintenance regulate implemented in order toto achieve gendhin this particular fieldfield, legislation and predominantly judicial precedents are consistently undergoing changes. Initially, the tendency was to grant a periodic se who would have sufferedsuffered financially post-divorce. The decision to grant the alimony and the determination of its amount were primarily influenced by three factors: the compensatory perspective, the retributive perspective, and the considerations of hardship.

Challenging the spouse who gave up his or her career or personal goals to take care of the family and the family home was known as punishment; providing the weaker spouse with enough resources to live on was known as hardship; and compensating the spouse who gave up his or her career or personal goals for the family and the family home was known as compensation.

The definition of that "live by" concept's threshold has always been one of the most conteInitially, the majority ofmost systems tended to maintain that the spouse should receive a periodic allowance that would allow them to maintain the same standard of living that they—and, for the most part, she—had while they were married.

Related to this, the length of the periodic allowance typically matched the life expectancy of the weaker spouse. However, this strategy makes sense only if the weaker spouse is unable to take other steps to equalize its status, like going it alone and finding employment.

In the absence of this, the strategy runs the risk of discriminating against the stronger gender. In fact, the weaker spouse may be incentivized to act opportunistically because they will always receive maintenance, even if they don't try to become financially independent. On the other hand, the length of the periodic obligation to pay the allowance fosters a further bond of economic dependence between the spouses, making it impossible for them to begin a new life together.

For these reasons, the so-called "clean break philosophy," which has been interpreted differently by the legal systems, haslly shifted in the court'scourts and legislator's approaches. In certain cases, it referred to the residual nature of maintenance and the predominance of alternative remedies, such as mechanisms for pension sharing or property adjustment; in other cases, it referred to the payment of maintenance in one lump sum as opposed to a periodic allowance or the restriction of maintenance duration.

The fundamental idea is that the less wealthy spouse ought to be supported in achieving financial independence as quickly as possible and severing their connections with the other spouse—as well as with the court, since all remedies that do not entail a continuing duty are immune to judicial review.

Gender-based objections and concerns have been raised by these novel approaches, particularly among family law experts and attorneys. First, it has been noted that women are still paid less than men, so achieving financial independence after a divorce, or shortly afterward, does not lead to gender equality or a rebalancing of the roles held by the two spouses. Second, the "clean-break philosophy" frequently ignores the fact that women who have chosen to put their family's needs ahead of their own careers may find it difficult to reenter the workforce and find employment that will pay them a sufficient salary according to the compensating criterion.

The aforementioned risks necessitate a thorough analysis of the situation using a case-by-case methodology and a reasonable application of general guidelines. The Scottish legislation provides an effective and fairly equitable model based on those considerations.

The courts have gradually abandoned the "standard of living" criterion in favor of a hybrid of the readjustment principle and a compensating criterion since the introduction of the "clean-break philosophy." According to this perspective, maintenance orders nowadays ought to be intended to provide enough money to the spouse who has given up on personal or professional goals so that the family can adapt to the new circumstances and find employment that is consistent with the path that was formally pursued before being interrupted by marriage.

The latter strategy's gender neutrality is one of its advantages. Courts are able to move past the binary male-female antithesis and concentrate on the unique characteristics that underlie the genders because of the practical evaluation of the case's circumstances and the effective level of commitment made by the spouses to their marriage. This adaptable strategy might be especially useful in separation and divorce cases involving same-sex partners or transgender individuals.

7.3.5. From Gender Equality to Party Autonomy: The Recognition of Divorce Agreements

The legal recognition and enforcement of prenuptial or postnuptial agreements governing the terms of separation and divorce has been another development in the evolution of the relationship between gender and the dissolution of marriage. The underlying tenet is that autonomy should follow equality because a married couple has an equal opportunity for personal development and growth, and as such, decisions about how to shape their cohabitation as well as their breakup should be made with them in mind.

This assumes that during the agreement-making process, the spouses were genuinely on equal footing. Courts typically exercise extra caution when applying contract law doctrines that protect weaker parties, like moral duress, fraud, and unconscionability from a common law perspective, in order to provide such substantive equality.

Using skilled mediators or negotiators with specialized knowledge of the various negotiation strategies typical to each gender would surely be a crucial upstream tool for achieving such substantive equality between the parties.

7.4. GENDER PERSPECTIVE AND ESTABLISHMENT/ CONTESTATION OF PARENTHOOD

7.4.1. Filiation Rights

As we've already mentioned, the patriarchal family gave the father special treatment because he was the family's head. The preference for assigning the paternal surname over the maternal surname when establishing a son or daughter's filiation legally was one manifestation of this hegemonic position. The father's surname was given, even if the individual's maternal and paternal filiation had been established; if both surnames could be given, the paternal surname was given precedence.shment of an egalitarian familyegalitarian model entails acknowledging that mothers and fathers have equal rights and obligations with regard to their children, it would be against this egalitarian model for national legislation to continue to favor the paternal surname. The Italian legislation that mandates the paternal surname be assigned to children and prevents parents from freely and consensually choosing between the paternal and maternal surnames is in violation of Article 14 (prohibition of discrimination) in relation to Article 8 (right to respect for private and family life) of the European Convention on Human Rights, according to the European Court of Human Right's (ECtHR) ruling in the *Cusan and Fazzo vs Italy* case.

7.4.2. Adoption

According to Principle 24 of the Yogyakarta Principles, states must take all reasonable steps to protect a person's right to find a family, including granting access to adom discrimination on the basis ofbased on gender identity or sexual orientation. It also entails taking the required steps to guarantee that the child's best interests will always come first in all decisions involving children made by courts and other institutions, and that no family member's or other individual's gender identity or sexual orientation will be deemed to be incompatible with the child's best interests.

However, the European Court of Human Rights has not confirmed that there is a right to adopt. Nonetheless, it has confirmed that prejudices or discriminatory considerations based on the sexual orientation of those submitting adoption applications should not have an impact on the selection procedures or the assessment of potential adoptive parent's suitability. The ECtHR made a ruling in this regard in the *Case Fretté vs. France* that the applicant's sexual orientation was not a factor in any discrimination during the selection process. Nonetheless, there are a few opposing views to this ruling that contend the applicant's homosexuality was a factor in the adoption's denial.

The European Court of Human Rights (ECtHR) ruled in the E.*B. vs France* case that there was discrimination based on the applicant's sexual orientation during the selection process. Nonetheless, there are a few dissenting opinions to this ruling, arguing that the applicant's partner's lack of participation in the adoption process meant the decision was made with the child's welfare in mind.

7.4.3. Paternity Investigation and Filiation Proceedings

Conversely, paternity claims emerge as a child's entitlement in situations where the father has renounced his duty to keep the mother from being the only one required to shoulder the child's upbringing. But, a man who wishes to take on full responsibility for the upbringing and care of his child may also assert paternity claims.Fartherould be remembered that a number ofseveral rights are at stake in these claims, including the father's right to family, the mother's right to privacy, and the child's right to privacy.

7.4.4. Filiation and Transgender

Many legal questions arise in relation to the paternity or maternity of transgender persons, for example, does a trans-woman have to stay the father? Can sh mother of the child? And vice-versavice versa. The answers to these queries will vary depending on whether the parentage determination was made before or after the gender change, as well as whether it was corrected in the registry.

7.4.5. Assisted Procreation

In terms of medically assisted reproduction, which encompasses assisted reproductive technology, the advancements in this field have contributed to the emergence of new family models, to the extent that they enable same-sex couples and single individuals to become parents.

Specifically, anonymous sperm donor assisted reproduction enables a woman to become a single mother with no obligation to the biological father. Female couples who want to become mothers also use this procedure. Both women's motherhood is acknowledged by law in some cases.

In others, on the other hand, this procedure only recognizes the woman's legal motherhood after she gives birth to the child. In the latter case, the woman who has acted as a mother but has no legal connection to the child faces some legal issues, particularly when the couple separates.

However, surrogacy makes it possible for men who want to parent alone, as well as male couples and couples where one partner is unable to gestate, to become ough assisted procreation. In order toTo become pregnant (using her genetic material, the intended parent's genetic material, or the genetic material of a donor) and give birth to a child who will be given to the intended parents, one or more people (the intended parents) enter into a contract with a woman (the surrogate mother). Surrogacy is prohibited in the majority of nations, including Germany, Sweden, and Spain. There are many who areof and opposed to surrogacy regulationregulations.

The arguments in favor of this procedure are numerous and include the claim that if it were legalized, males who desire to be single fathers and male couples instead of single women and female or heterosexual couples would not be able to become biological parents through assisted reproduction. Additionally, this industry contends that a law protecting the surrogate mother's rights would not violate them but rather serve as a choice she makes in exercising her reproductive autonomy. Some of those in favor of it contend that it ought to be provided without charge in order to prevent the commodification of women. Conversely, some contend that the surrogate mother ought to be paid, just like in other assisted reproductive procedures like egg and sperm donation.

The anti-surrogacy movement claims, among other things, that surrogacy violates women's rights and contributes to their commodification—turning women's bodies into objects, as is the case, for example, in prostitutiploitation, given that the majority ofmost surrogate mothers are typically low-income women who reside in nations with higher levels of income inequality. Additionally, they contend that, in its altruistic form, it devalues pregnancy and childbirth, just as other traditionally feminine roles—like housework and childrearing—have done.

Several rulings on surrogacy have been made by the ECtHR. In each of these rulings, the European Court of Human Rights has addressed the issue of foreign-born children whose filiation is meant to be registered in the intended parent's home country, where this practice is forbidden. The ECtHR has left it ue's discretion to decide whether or notwhether to legalize this practice, though, in these rulings.

Lastly, women whsisted reproduction have the ability tocan postpone becoming mothers through techniques like egg cryopreservation. There are voices in favor of and against this reality. On the one hand, women can choose to postpone motherhood in order to concentrate on their professional careers, exercising their right to reproductive autonomy. Instead of establishing policies that allow women to balance work and family life and create an egalitarian model where childrearing is part of men's work and family life, defending the benefits of these procedures and technology for women in the labor market implies imposing on them the parameters of a typically male work model where pregnancy, childbirth, and childrearing are not contemplated.

In summary, assisted reproduction has facilitated the emergence of new family structures but has also raised contentious issues that remain unresolved or give rise to opposing viewpoints. Surrogacy is one of the most troublesome topics. Some contend that a law protecting surrogate mothers is compliant with women's right to reproductive autonomy. Conversely, some contend that surrogacy infringes upon women's rights and advances the commodification of women.

7.5. GENDER PERSPECTIVE AND PARENTAL RESPONSIBILITY, CHILD CUSTODY, AND CHILD SUPPORT

The creation of an androcentric society was made feasible by the adoption of a particular family structure as the fundamental unit of social organization. A family was a social unit made up of various individuals, possessions, and assets that was ruled by the father in his capacity as the head of the household. As a result, the *pater familias* in ancient Rome had authority over his spouse, kids, slaves, and possessions. Over the ages, this patriarchal family structure has persisted. Though there were some changes, the fundamental idea stayed the same: the father made decisions for the family, including those involving his children, as the male's hegemonic role in the public sphere was transferred to the family. Women continued to live in the home and fulfill their roles as mothers and wives at the discretion of their husbands or fathers.

The distinction between private and public domains—feminine and masculine—grew more pronounced during the nineteenth-century industrial revolution. A family abandons a rural way of life in which all members of the family worked as laborers from a very young age and the family produced its own resources. As a result of industrialization, which moved production outside the home and into factories, the fathed to find outside employment in order toto support the family.

Some women began working in factories and entering the labor market, despite the fact that the majority of them stayed at home to take care of their families and children. In addition, children's rights started to take shape. Following the lead of child protection, women came to be seen as the most qualified caregivers for young children, and children were no longer viewed as labor forces. The man was in charge of providing the family's financial support in his roles as husband and father. Without assuming the father's doin the family, the woman was in charge ofoversaw the children's upbringing and the household. The nineteenth-century codification movement adopted and legitimized this patriarchal model, providing it with legal suppeven though the mother actually performedperformed the tasks of childrearing, caring for, and educating the children, the father was given authority and decision-making power over the children in the nineteenth-century civil codes, with the mother occupying a secondary or subsidiary role. To the mother's detriment, the father continued to have parental authority over the kids following the divorce. Even after her husband passed away, the widow continued to hold this subordinate role, giving another male family member—the grandfather, an older brother, or the woman's new husband—the authority to make decisions regarding the children.

Parental authority, as defined by the Spanish Civil Code, has been stripped of its previous meaning as the father's hegemonic power and is now understood as a responsibility that both married and single parents, as well as people of different sexes, exercise on an equal basis and for the benefit of their children. Further instances of joint parental responsibility are delineated in Italian Civil Code Article 316.

In international law, this co-responsibility principle is also present. Accordingly, States Parties shall take all necessary steps to ensure "the recognition of the common responsibility of men and women in the upbringing and development of their children, it being understood that the interest of the children is the primordial consideration in all cases," as stated in Article 5b of the Convention on the Elimination of All Forms of Discrimination Against Women (CEDAW), which was adopted on December 18, 1979. Furthermore, according to Article 16.1(d) and (f) of the CEDAW, States Parties are required to guarantee, based on gender equality, the same rights and obligations as parents in matters pertaining to their children, regardless of their marital status. In addition, when it comes to guardianship, wardship, trusteeship, and adoption of children, the interests of the children must always come first. Furthermore, States Parties shall make every effort to ensure that the principle that both parents share responsibility for the child's upbringing and development is recognized, according to Article 18.1 of the United Nations Convention on the Rights of the Child, which was adopted on November 20, 1988. The child's upbringing and development are primarily the responsibility of the parent or, in some cases, legal guardian. Their primary concern will be the child's best interests. It is feasible to maintain the Convention on the Rights of the Child's relationship with the welfare of children by incorporating the concept of co-responsibility into it. The latter, though, is what has to direct the performance of this joint duty. Furthermore, it is important to remember that the best interests of the child must always come first in all decisions involving them, as stated in Article 3.1 of the Convention on the Rights of the Child. However, as we will see below, since the child's interest is a vague concept, it can also be exploited to maintain gender inequality. Accordingly, the General Comment No. Paragraph 34 of Committee on the Rights of the Children's Report No. 14 (2013) emphasizes that the concept of the child's best interests is flexible enough to adapt to the unique circumstances of each child and to change as knowledge about child development does.

Gradually, a patriarchal family structure gave way to one in which the mother and father carry out their parental duties equally. This change has surely been largely influenced by the demands of feminist movements. The concept of equality and non-discrimination based on sex has progressively been addressed by both national and international legal texts; as a result, the regulation of parental responsibility must also take this into account. Similarly, other family models are being considered as a result of the outlawing of discrimination based on sexual orientation or gender identity and the progressive recognition of the rights of LGTBQIA+ groups with regard to marriage, adoption, and access to assisted reproductive technologies.

Gender roles and stereotypes, however, continue to have a significant impact on children's upbringing, care, and education despite the official recognition of equality in the exercise of parental responsibility. This leads to siterial inequality. It occurs as a result ofbecause of men entering the domestic sphere either later, incompletely, and unequally than women, who have entered the labor market and public sphere. Because of this, women continue to be the ones who take time off work for maternity leave, leaves of absence, and reduced work hours in order to care for their families. Women continue to be perceived as having a harder time juggling work and family obligations since they are typically the ones responsible for taking care of the home. It has thus been argued that, in actuality, the patriarchal roles and aspects of the current family model coexist with egalitarian systemic characteristics. It demonstrates that material equality is still a long way off. In order to overcome these barriers, constructive and inclusive actions are needed, but they must avoid becoming paternalistic in the sense that the policies implemented serve to reinforce gender stereotypes and other forms of inequality rather than to advance equality. Furthermore, implementing policies that are narrowly focused on a single topic or area is no longer sufficient to implement a gender perspective. Rather, cross-sectional actions that eliminate gender stereotypes and inequalities are needed, involving various domains (legal, social, educational, etc.). in a cohesive manner.

However, in cases of divorce or when parents are not living together, there is a clear disparity in the care and responsibility of their children. The implications of the cohabitation break-up in parental responsibilities are conditioned by the way the family is conceived and the roles that its members play within it. As a result, upon the divorce or cohabitation breakup, the father was initially awarded custody of the children due to his preferential role in making decisions regarding the children during the marriage cohabitation. The mother who was separated or divorced did not live together, she did not take part in decision-making, and she might even lose the ability to see her kids.

As we have seen above, the idea that it is in the child's best interests to remain in the mother's care is gaining traction under the influence of child protection measures, and as a result, the balance of custody has gradually shifted towards the mother. The father has visiting rights and is in charge of paying maintenance. In these cases of the parent's breakup from cohabitation, the father's role as provider and the mother's role as caregiver remain, along with the dissociation between public and privatarrangement is upheld, despite the fact thateven though the legal texts govern custody in an equitable manner that favors the parent who is best suited to care for the child over the father or mother. The rationale behind this is that in this challenging decision, judges select the parent who had been raising and taking care of the children up until the separation—primarily the mother—in accordance with the principle of the child's welfare. Because of the sole custody arrangement, the mother is really still responsible for the majority of the children's upbringing and education. This situation gets worse when the father disregards his parental duties, such as by not making child support payments. However, fathers contended that this custody model forbids them from having an open relationship with their children and even from taking part in decisions that are crucial to their education or health when the custody figure also entails these parental responsibilities and places an undue financial burden on them (moving out of the family home, paying alimony). At this point the debate on joint or shared custody arises.

Following the breakdown of the parent's cohabitation, joint custody seems to be an egalitarian promotes shared responsibility. In order toTo promote the children's wellbeing, joint custody would allow parents to share parenting responsibilities and encourage a flexible relationship between the kids and both parents following the end of cohabitation.

However, this type of custody is subject to criticism. A critical voice claims that the inclusion of this regime in legal texts preserves the disparities between mothers and fathers in childrearing, rather than the detriment of women. In particular, thisThis viewpoint contends that women still bear the majority of the childrearing burden despite significant changes in the family structure and the growing involvement of men in childcare. Shared custody would not make up for this imbalance if the father had not been involved in childrearing prior to the separation. Because of this, this critical voice believes that shared custody should neither be mandated by the courts nor regulated in legal texts as a preferential system. This opinion statconsideration should be given to the parent'sparents' level of dedication during their cohabitation before choosing this regime; that is, shared custody should be awarded when both parents have contributed similarly to the upbringing of their children. This critical viewpoint also takes into account the possibility that this custody arrangement would be workable in societies (like Sweden, for example) where structural changes have been implemented to remove the barriers preventing the consolidation of an egalitarian family model (free childcare from birth, work schedules that are rationalized to prioritize family life balance, parental leave for both parents under equal circumstances, and so on). But not in communities where the prerequisites aren't met and the family model isn't nearly as equal as it should be. The most vocal opponents of shared custody contend that it is a patriarchal and sexist request. They contend that there is no real interest in sharing in the up of children and that the majority of father'sfathers' rights movements that call for it are only attempting to escape their financial obligations and hold onto the dominant position they once held within the patriarchal family.

Cohabitation and caregiving under physical joint custody promote co-responsib. However, this arrangement won't always work—work, for instance, if the parents live far away from one another—in which case alternate models that emphasize shared responsibility should be selected. As a result, one parent may be granted physical custody, while the non-residential parent may have frequent visitation rights. This establishes both parent's obligations to provide for the child's financial needs as well as their joint legal custody, parental responsibility, or parental authority, depending on the terminology used in each legal system. This means that one parent may be able to influence decisions regarding the child's health, education, or other significant matters.

The children's welfare must be considered in cases of shared custody or other co-responsibility models involving the children. Furthermore, the Convention on the Rights of the Child stipulates in Article 3.1 that the child's best interests must come first, preceding those of the parents. However, in any case, the child's interests cannot be used as a justification for maintaining unequal circumstances. Stated differently, it is imperative to prevent the adoption of a system of sole or shared custody in the name of the child's welfare, not because the circumstances warrant it, but rather because of the perpetuation of gender-based stereotypes or beliefs (e.g., parent's sexual orientation, fathers are unfit to care for small children, labor women make bad mothers, boys should be cared for by fathers and girls by mothers, among others). As previoned, this necessitates looking into a number ofseveral things, including the parent's relationship with the child and each other prior to the breakup of their cohabitation. Thus, in situations where there has been violence directed towards the child or where one parent has used violence against the other, joint custody would not be possible.

In conclusion, legal texts now depict a family model in which parents have equal rights and responsibilities over their children, gradually replacing the patriarchal family. This state of equal rights and responsibilities must be upheldbest interests of the child even after parent'sthe parent's cohabitation ends. In te system of shared custody develops as a way toto encourage joint parenting following a divorce. But even with the official acknowledgement of equality, gender norms and stereotypes still hold significant sway in families, meaning that mothers are often the primary caregivers for their children. As a result, it is necessary to dispel stereotypes by taking steps that support an equalitarian family structure where both parents share parental responsibilities for their children. y event, the needs of the child must come firstfirst, and gender norms cannot be enforced through this approach.

7.6. DOMESTIC VIOLENCE

Abuse or violence thlace in a domestic environment, like a marriagemarriage or cohabitation, is referred to as domestic violence. Intimate partner violence, which can occur in relationships or between ex-spouses or partners, is commonly referred to as domestic violence. It is when one of the parties in an intimate relationship abuses the other. Domestic violence, in its widest definition, also includes abuse of parents, children, or the elderly. It can take many different forms, such as verbal, emotional, physical, financial, religious, reproductive, or a combination of these. It includes the use of technology to harass, control, monitor, stalk, or hack people. It can take many different forms, from subtle, coercive forms to marital rape and other violent physical abuse, such as choking, beatings, female genital mutilation, and acid throwing that can cause disfigurement or death. Stoning, bride burning, honor killing, and dowry death are examples of domestic murder; these crimes occasionally involve family members (Woodlock, 2017).

The majority ofMost victims of domestic abuse worldwide are women, and the types of violence that women face are typically more severe. According to estimates from the World Health Organization (WHO), one in three women will experience domestic abuse at some point in their lives. Certain nations may view domestic violence as legitimate or lawful, especially when there is evidence of real or suspected adultery on the side of the woman. Studies have demonstrated a clear and substantial relationship between the prevalence of domestic violence and a nation's degree of gender inequality, with higher rates of domestic violence occurring in nations with lower levels of gender equality. One of the most underreported crimes in the world, for both men and women, is domestic violence.

Domestic violence frequently happens when the perpetrator feels entitled to it, or when they think it's reasonable, justifiable, or unlikely to be caught on camera. Children and other family members may feel that such violence is acceptable or condoned, which could start an intergenerational cycle of violence. Many people may view their experiences as out-of-control family conflicts, leading them to fail to identify as either abusers or victims. There are significant differences between nations when it comes to domestic violence awareness, perception, definition, and documentation. In addition, forced or child marriages are frequently the setting for domestic violence (Halket et al., 2013).

There may be a cycle of abuse in abusive relationships, wherein hostilities flare up and an act of violence is committed, followed by a time of calm and reconciliation. Domestic violence victims can find themselves in such situations due to a variety of factors, including fear, shame, lack of financial resources, traumatic bonding to the abuser, power and control, isolation, and the need to protect their children. Victims of abuse may suffer from physical impairments, dysregulated aggression, mental illness, chronic health issues, financial hardship, and a poor capacity for forming positive relationships. Serious psychological conditions like Post-Traumatic Stress Disorder (PTSD) may be experienced by victims. Youngsters raised in violent homes frequently exhibit psychological issues such as hyper-vigilance to threats, avoidance, and dysregulated aggression, all of which can lead to vicarious traumatization (Schechter et al., 2007).

7.6.1. Forms

Not all cases of domestic abuse are the same. There are notable variations in the frequency, severity, goal, and result. Domestic violence can take many different forms, such as sexual abuse, controlling or domineering behavior, intimidation, stalking, passive/covert abuse (such as neglect), physical aggression or assault (such as hitting, kicking, biting, shoving, restraining, slapping, throwing objects, beating up, etc.), or threats thereof. It can also refer to trespassing, harassment, kidnapping, illegal imprisonment, endangerment, riminal coercion.

7.6.1.1. Physical

Contact meantmeans to inflict fear, pain, injury, other physical suffering, or bodily harm is referred to as physical abuse. Physical abuse is one method of coercive control where the victim is kept under control. Physical abuse in a relationship can have complicated dynamics. Other abusive behaviors, such as threats, intimidation, and limiting victim autonomy through manipulation, detainment, and other forms of personal restriction, may culminate in phl violence. Physical abuse can also take the formsform of sleep deprivation, forcedcohol use, and denial of medical care. In order toTo inflict emotional harm on the victim, it can also involve physically harming other targets, like children or pets.

In the context of domestic violence, strangulation has drawn a lot of attention. Despite being one of the deadliest types of domestic abuse, strangulation has frequently gone unreported due to a lack of external injuries, a lack of social awareness, and a lack of medical knowledge. Because of this, numerous US states have passed legislation prohibiting strangulation in recent years (Sorenson et al., 2014).

Domestic violence-related homicides account for a higher percentage of female homicides than male homicides. Intimate partners, either past or present, are responsible for over half of the killings of women in the United States. Intimate partners were responsible for 37% of women's murders in the UK, compared to 6% for men. Intimate partners killed between 40 and 70% of women who were murdered in the US, Israel, South Africa, Australia, and Canada. According to the World Health Organization, approximately 38% of female homicides worldwide are carried out by close companions.

A woman is more vulnerable to abuse during pregnancy, and even long-term abuse may worsen, endangering the health of both the mother and the unborn child. When an abuser decides not to harm the unborn child, pregnancy can also result in a halt to domestic violence. After giving birth, women who have been pregnant are most vulnerable to domestic violence.

When acid is thrown at victims—typically their faces—it can cause severe injuries, such as permanent scarring and long-term blindness. Acid attacks are an extreme kind of violence. These are commonly a form of revenge against a woman for rejecting a marriage proposal or sexual advance.

Planned domestic homicides, also known as honor killings, are committed in the Middle East and other parts of the world because the killers think their victim has brought shame to the family or community. Human Rights Watch claims that women are typically the targets of honor killings when they refuse to get married in an arranged marriage, when they are sexually assaulted, when they file for divorce, or when they are suspected of adultery. If a bride's absence of blood on her wedding night is used as evidence that she is not a virgin, she may face severe violence, even an honor killing, in certain parts of the world where there is a strong social expectation for a woman to be a virgin before marriage.

In a case of domestic violence known as "bride burning" or "dowry killing," a recently married woman is murdered at home by her husband or his family because they are unhappy with the dowry her family gave her. Demands for an increased or extended dowry after marriage frequently lead to the act. The majority of Dowry violence occurs in South Asia, particularly in India. Unofficial estimates place the number of dowry deaths in India at least three times higher than the 8,618 cases the National Crime Records Bureau reported in 2011.

7.6.1.2. Sexual

According to the WHO, sexual abuse includes any attempt to obtain a sexual act, unwanted sexual remarks or advances, and acts that are directed against a person's sexuality through coercion or trafficking. It also entails mandatory examinations for female genital mutilation and virginity. Sexual abuse happens when someone is verbally coerced into consenting, is incapable of comprehending the nature or circumstances of the act, is unable to refuse participation, or is unable to express their unwillingness to engage in a sexual act. These scenarios are in addition to the act being initiated physically. This may be the result of coercion or intimidation, underage immaturity, disease, disability, or the influence of alcohol or other drugs.

Rape victims often face severe familial violence, including honor killings, because they are perceived as having brought shame or dishonor to their families in many cultures. This is particularly true in the event that the victim gets pregnant.

The World Health Organization defines female genital mutilation as any procedure that involves the removal of all or part of the external female genitalia or any other harm to the female genital organs for purposes other than medical ones. Over 125 million females alive today have undergone this surgery, which is mostly concentrated in 29 Middle Eastern and African nations.

One instance of familial sexual violence is incest, which is defined as sexual contact between an adult relative and a child. Certain cultures have ritualized forms of child sexual abuse wherein the child is coerced into having sex with an adult, possibly in exchange for cash or goods, and this occurs with the family's knowledge and consent. For example, in Malawi, as a kind of initiation, some parents set up sex between their daughters and an older man known as a hyena. The first international agreement to address child sexual abuse that takes place in the family or at home was the Council of Europe Convention on the Protection of Children against Sexual Exploitation and Sexual Abuse.

Coerced reproduction, also known as reproductive coercion, refers to a range of behaviors aimed at pressuring or forcing a partner to become pregnant or terminate a pregnancy. These behaviors can also be threats or acts of violence against a partner's reproductive rights, health, or decision-making. Forced sexual relations, fear of or incapacity to chootraceptive method, fear of violence following a sexualsexual refusal, and abusive partner interference with healthcare access are all linked to reproductive coercion.

In certain societies, women are socially obligated to procreate upon marriage. For instance, paying a bride price in northern Ghana denotes a woman's obligation to procreate, and birth control users risk violence and other negative consequences. The World Health Organization defines sexual violence as including forced marriage, cohabitation, and pregnancy, including wife inheritance. Levirate marriage, also known as wife inheritance, is a sort of marriage in which the widow's brother must wed her deceased husband, and the brother of the deceased man must wed the widow.

Non-consensual penetration committed against a spouse is known as marital rape. In many countries, it is legal and underreported, partly because of the perception that marriage constitutes an irreversible consent for a woman to have sex with her husband whenever he pleases. In Lebanon, for instance, while discussing a proposed law that would criminalize marital rape, Sheik Ahmad Al-Kurdi, a judge in the Sunni religious court, said that the law "could lead to the imprisonment of the man where in reality he is exercising the least of his marital rights." Since the 1960s, feminists have systematically worked to make marital rape a crime worldwide. According to a 2006 UN study, at least 104 countries had laws that made marital rape a crime. Marital rape was once widely accepted or disregarded by the law and society, but it is now increasingly illegalized and rejected by international agreements. The provisions of the Istanbul Convention, the first legally binding agreement in Europe addressing violence against women, bind the nations that have ratified it to the obligation of making non-consensual sexual acts against a spouse or partner unlawful. The agreement became operative in August 2014.

7.6.1.3. Emotional

An ongoing pattern of behavior that dehumanizes, threatens, intimidates, or consistently undermines one's own worth is known as emotional or psychological abuse. As per the Istanbul Convention, psychological violence refers to the deliberate act of significantly compromising an individual's psychological integrity by means of coercion or threats.

Minimizing, threatening, isolating, humiliating in public, relentless criticism, continuous devaluation of the self, coercive control, persistent stonewalling, and gaslighting are examples of emotional abuse. One prevalent psychological intimidation tactic is stalking, which is typically carried out by intimate partners, past or present. The power dynamic in a relationship is significantly impacted by victim's perceptions that their partner has almost complete control over them, which empowers the offender and de-empowers the victim. Depression is a common condition among victims, which increases their risk of eating disorders, drug and alcohol abuse, and suicide.

Coercive control refers to the use of manipulation, isolation, and deprivation of autonomy in order to subjugate an individual and make them dependent on the controller. Verbal abuse, punishment, humiliation, threats, and intimidation are some of the behaviors involved. Physical abuse or other forms of physical harm or terror can be used as a form of coercive control. The deprivation of the victht to liberty and diminished capacity for free will maywill constitute an infringement on their human rights. Abusers frequently dehumanize, threaten, deny basic necessities and personal access, isolate, and use spyware to monitor their victim's daily routine. Typically, victims experience intense feelings of fear and anxiety that negatively impact their personal, financsical, and psychological well-being.

7.6.1.4. EconomicEconomics

A type of abuse known as economic abuse, also known as financial abuse, occurs when one intimate partner controls the other's access to financial resources. Marital property is utilized as a tool for dominance. Economic abuse can take many forms, such as keeping a spouse from acquiring resources, restricting what the victim can use, or taking advantage of the victim's financial resources in other ways. Economic abuse reduces the victim's ability to support themselves and increases their reliance on the abuser. It also limits the victim's access to resources such as assets, career advancement, work, and education. Economic abuse includes pressuring or forcing a family member to sign papers, sell items, or alter a will.

An allowance may be given to the victim, enabling strict oversight of their expenditures and preventing spending without the offender's approval, which could otherwise result in debt accumulation or the deplevictim's savings. Conflicts over financial expendituresexpenditure may lead to additional physical, sexual, or psychological abuse as payback. Economic abuse can have very serious repercussions in regions of the world where women must rely on their husband's income to survive (because there are few opportunities for female employment and little government assistance). There is a correlation between malnourishment in mothers and children and abusive relationships. For instance, depriving someone of food is a recognized form of abuse within the family in India.

7.6.2. Contributing Factors

A major contributing factor to domestic violence is the perception that verbal or physical abuse is okay. Substance abuse, illiteracy, mental health issues, inadequate coping mechanisms, maltreatment during childhood, and an overwhelming reliance on the abuser are additional risk factors.

Establishing and sustaining relationships based on power and control over victims is a primary motivation behind acts of domestic and interpersonal violence in relationships.

The morality of batterers is not in line with the law or societal norms. According to research, the main problem with abusers is that they intentionally choose to offend in order to satisfy their own desires.

Men who commit violent crimes tend to have three traits in common: they are narcissistic, deliberately lack empathy, and prioritize their needs over those of others. Instead of the abuser's self-serving desire for power and control over their victim, perpetrators psychologically manipulate the victim into believing that their inadequacy as a wife, lover, or human being is the reason behind their abuse and violence.

7.6.2.1. Cycle of abuse theory

Four phases make up the model of an abuse cycle that Lenore E. Walker presented. When tensions increase, there is first a build-up of abuse until there is an incident of domestic violence. There is a calm phase after the abuser exhibits kindness and love during the reconciliation stage. When things are quiet, the victim of abuse might have hope that things will get better. Tensions then start to rise, and the cycle repeats itself.

7.6.2.2. Intergenerational violence

One feature that abusers have in common is that they experienced abuse as children. They were a part of a series of domestic violence intergenerational cycles. Converseloes not imply that a child who experiences or witnesseswitnesses' violence will grow up to commit abuse themselves. Reducing violence may involve more than just managing the abuseabuse; it may also involve understanding and breaking the patterns of intergenerational abuse.

Children-focused responses imply that life events shape a person's likelihood of participating in family violence (as a victim or as an offender). Scholars endorsing this theory propose that it is helpful to consider three origins of domestic violence: socialization in childhood, prior experiences in adolescent couple relationships, and strain levels in an individual's current life. Individuals who witness their parents mistreating one another or who experienced abuse themselves may adopt abusive behaviors in adult relationships.

According to research, children who experience physical punishment on a regular basis are more likely to act violently toward family members, including intiners, as adults. Individuals who receive more spankingsspanking as kids are more likely to support hitting a partner as adults. They also report higher levels of marital discord and generalized feelings of rage. Even after adjusting for other variables, several studies have shown that physical punishment is linked to increased levels of hostility toward parents, siblings, peers, and spouses. Numerous longitudinal studies indicate that the experience of physical punishment does have a direct causal effect on subsequent aggressive behaviors, even though these associations do not prove a causal relationship. According to this research, physically abusing children (smacking, slapping, or spanking them) is associated with more antisocial behavior, including dating violence, and a weaker internalization of values like empathy, altruism, and resistance to temptation.

Around the world, a young bride moves in with her husband's family in some patrilineal societies. As a new girl in the home, she starts as having the lowest (or among the lowest) position in the family, is often subjected to violence and abuse, and is, in particular, strongly controlled by the parents-in-law: with the arrival of the daughter-in-law in the family, the mother-in-law's status is elevated and she now has (often for the first time in her life) substantial power over someone else, and "this family system itself tends to produce a cycle of violence in which the formerly abused bride becomes the abusing mother-in-law to her new daughter-in-law." Amnesty International writes that, in Tajikistan, "it is almost an initiation ritual for the mother-in-law to put her daughter-in-law through the same torments she went through herself as a young wife."

7.6.2.3. Biological and Psychological Theories

Neuroscience studies these factors, which include brain dysfunction and heredity. Psychological theories concentrate on the offender's mental health and personality traits. Sudden outbursts of anger, a lack of impulse control, and low self-esteem are examples of personality traitumerous theories contend that psychopathology plays a rolerole, and that childhood abuse makes some people more violent adults. There is a connection between adult domestic violence and juvenile delinquency.

Domestic abusers have a high rate of psychopathology, according to studies. For example, research indicates that in these studies of domestic violence, about 80% of the men who were referred by the court or who self-referred had diagnosable psychopathology, usually personality disorders. In the general population, personality disorders are thought to affect 15-20% of people. The chance of psychopathology in these men approaches 100% as the violence in the relationship gets more severe and persistent.

Dutton contends that men who abuse their wives have borderline personalities that are formed early in life, offering a psychological profile of such men. These psychological theories are, however, controversial. Gelles contends that psychological theories are narrow and cites findings from other researchers showing that only 10% or fewer of people match this psychological profile. He contends that psychopathy, mental illness, and personality traits are less significant factors than social factors.

Domestic violence can be explained evolutionary psychologically as an attempt by men to maintain sexual exclusivity and control female reproduction. Certain parts of the world view violence related to extramarital relations as justified. In Diyarbakir, Turkey, for example, a survey conducted asked respondents if they thought a woman who had committed adultery should be executed, and 21% thought her ears or nose should be amputated.

According to a 1997 study, domestic abusers engage in more mate retention behaviors than the typical person, which are an attempt to keep the relationship going with their partner. According to the report, men were more likely than women to use intrasexual threats, submission and debasement, and resource display as a means of retaining their partners.

7.6.2.4. Social theories

7.6.2.4.1. General

Social theories, which include rational choice theories, examine outside elements in the environment of the offender, such as family dynamics, stress, and social learning.

According to social learning theory, people pick up new skills by watching and imitating the actions of others. When a behavior is reinforced positively, it persists. One is more likely to imitate violent behavior if they witness it. If therevorable outcomes (e.g., the victim submits to the violenceviolence), the behavior is probably going to continue.

William Goode proposed resource theory in 1971. Women who are the primary carers for their children and who rely heavily on their spouse for financial support (such as homemakers or housewives, women with disabilities, or women without jobs) worry about having to shoulder more debt should they decide to end their marriage. Because of their dependency, they have less resources and fewer options to deal with or influence their spouse's behavior.

Eqng couples are less likely to argue and, in the event thatif they do, are less likely to use violence. One partner may abuse the other if they want to be in charge and have power in the marriage. This can involve using children (threatening to take them away), acting like the "master of the castle," utilizing coercion and threats, intimidation, emotional abuse, economic abuse, isolation, and making light of the situation.

According to another report, when it comes to mistreating their partner, domestic abusers may be so overcome with rage that they mistakenly believe they are the victim. Psychologically, the abusers present themselves as the victim because they feel they have been wronged, primarily because of negative emotions and coation problems between partners.

7.6.2.4.2. Social stressStress

Living in a family setting can put more strain on an individual and increase stress. Tensions may be exacerbated by social pressures brought on by insufficient money or other issues within the family.

Stress does not always lead to violence, but it can be one of the reactions that certain people have to it. Because poverty often results in stress and arguments over money and other issues, families and couples may be more prone to domestic violence. Some theorize that poverty may make it more difficult for a man to fulfill his vision of what it means to be a successful man, so he fears losing respect and honor. A theory suggests that he may resort to misogyny, drug abuse, and crime as ways to express his masculinity when he is unable to provide for his wife and keep control.

Similar social pressures may be experienced by same-sex couples. Furthermore, internalized homophobia has been connected to violence in same-sex relationships. This has resulted in low self-esteem and anger in both the victim and the offender. Another thing that seems to be preventing victims from getting help is internalized homophobia. In the LGBT community, heterosexism can also be a major contributing factor to domestic abuse.

Heterosexism is a social ideology that perpetuates the idea that heterosexuality is morally superior, better than homosexuality, and normative. As such, it can impede services and cause sexual minorities to have negative self-images. Biases, discrimination, and insensitivity to sexual orientation are examples of heterosexism in the legal and medical sectors. For instance, as of 2006, seven states specifically prohibited LGBT people from requesting protective orders, which contributed to the spread of ideas about LGBT subjugation and feelings of helplessness and rage.

7.6.2.4.3. Power and control

Abusers utilize physical, sexual, and other forms of abuse as a means of gaining power and control in their relationships.

According to a causalist perspective, domestic violence is a tactic used to seize or hold onto power and control over the victim. This perspective is consistent with Bancroft's cost-benefit theory, which holds that abusers benefit from their actions in ways other than or in addition to gaining control over their victim(s). He backs up his claim with evidence, saying that most abusers are perfectly capable of controlling themselves but opt not to for a variety of reasons.

Occasionally, one partner tries to exert total control and power over the other through a variety of means, including physical abuse. The offender tries to dictate to the victim what she or he should do on a social, personal, professional, and financial level.

The extensively used Duluth Domestic Abuse Intervention Project is deeply entwined with issues of power and control. To demonstrate this, they created the Power and Control Wheel, which has power and control at its core and spokes that stand in for various techniques. Coercion and threats, intimidation, emotional abuse, isolation, minimization, blaming and denyihildren, economic abuse, and privilege are among the spoke'sthe titles.

This model's detractors claim it ignores studies that connect drug abuse and psychological issues with domestic violence. The usefulness of treating domestic violence with ideas like male privilege is called into question because some recent research on patterns in domestic violence has revealed that women are more likely to physically abuse their partner in relationships where only one partner is violent. Participation in reciprocal domestic violence appears to be the strongest predictor of injury caused by domestic violence, according to some recent research on the subject.

7.6.2.5. Non-subordination theory

Within feminist legal theory, non-subordination theory—also known as dominance theory—focuses on the disparity in power betwn. According to non-subordination theory, men in particular inin society exploit the gender differences between men and women to maintain this power disparity. Non-subordination theory, in contrast to other areas of feminist legal theory, concentrates particularly on specific sexual behaviors, such as control over women's sexuality, sexual harassment, pornography, and violence against women in general. Non-subordination theory, according to Catharine MacKinnon, is the most appropriate approach to handle these specific problems since they primarily impact women. In contrast to other theories such as difference theory, formal equality, and substantive equality, MacKinnon supports non-subordination theory, arguing that sexual violence and other forms of violence against women are better understood as more central inequalities for women rather than as a matter of sameness and difference. Non-subordination theory is a foundation for understanding domestic violence and the reasons behind it, even though it has been extensively explored in the evaluation of different types of sexual violence against women. Because the majority of victims of domestic violence are women, non-subordination theory approaches the problem as a subset of the larger issue of violence against women.

The non-subordination theory's proponents offer various explanations for why they believe it best explains domestic violence. First, there are some recurrent patterns in domestic violence that suggest it is a form of subordination rather than an outburst of rage or arguments. This is partially demonstrated by the fact that victims of domestic abuse are frequently mistreated in a range of contexts and with a range of tools. For instance, victims are occasionally beaten after they have fallen asleep or after being taken away from the abuser, and in addition to physical abuse, abuse frequently takes the form of financial or psychological abuse.

These instances are used by proponents of non-subordination theory to refute the myth that violent outbursts or heated arguments are invariably the cause of battering. Additionally, when abusing their victims, batterers frequently use devious and calculated strategies. These might include looking for and destroying a treasured item of hers or striking her in places where she would be ashamed to display her bruises, like her scalp. When the batterer and the victim have children together, these behaviors can be even more helpful to the batterer because the batterer typically has financial control over the family, which deters the victim from leaving even if doing so would endanger the children.

Professor Martha Mahoney of the University of Miami School of Law provides more proof that domestic violence is used to subjugate victims to their batterers by citing the phenomenon of separation assault, in which a batterer assaults a victim again while they are trying or have tried to leave an abusive relationship. The idea that violence is being used to coerce the victim into continuing to obey the batterer's wishes is supported by the batterer's refusal to let the victim end the relationship. Though anger may be a byproduct of these behaviors, non-subordination theorists contend that all of these actions—the range of abusive behaviors and settings, taking advantage of the victim's children, and assault upon separation—indicate a deeper issue than simply an incapacity to control one's anger. Non-subordination theory states that the goal of these behaviors is to maintain the victim's and occasionally the family's subordination to the batterer.

Second, the frequency of domestic violence outweighs the theory that it is only the product of a batterer's rage, which is why non-subordination theory is used to explain it. According to Professor Mahoney, people find it hard to understand how common domestic violence is in society because of the sensationalism that is created in media coverage of particularly horrifying cases. Nonetheless, up to 50% of Americans regularly experience domestic abuse, with women making up the vast majority of victims. The overwhelming number of Americans who become victims of domestic abuse indicates that controlling one's anger is not the only cause of this problem. According to the non-subordination theory, the reason why domestic violence occurs so frequently is not because of the batterer's uncontrollable anger but rather his desire to subjugate the victim. Some feminist legal theories, according to proponents of non-subordination theory, fail to explain the prevalence or the phenomenon of domestic violence in general.

Non-subordination theory detractors claim that the issues it raises are unaddressed by the theory. Non-subordination theory proponents, for instance, disagree with some of the ways that the legal system has dealt with domestic abuse, such as mandatory arrest or prosecution guidelines. By requiring police to detain suspected domestic abusers and prosecutors to pursue those cases, these policies strip law enforcement of their discretion. The subject of required arrests is one that is frequently discussed. Critics contend that it diminishes the agency of victims, dissuades women from achieving self-determination by undervaluing alternative resources, and increases the vulnerability of victims to domestic violence. It has been demonstrated that states with mandatory arrest le 60% greater homicide rates, which is consistent with the drop indrop-in reporting rates. Proponents of these laws argue that knowing one will be arrested will deter future domestic violence, and that in certain cases, the criminal justice system is the only avenue to assist victims of domestic abuse. Supporters of the non-subordination theory contend that by making women follow certain procedures, these policies only work to furtthem and exacerbate the trauma they already endured as a result ofbecause of the abuse. Some academics contend that alternative forms of feminist legal theory are more suited to address issues of domestic and sexual violence, but non-subordination theory by itself does not provide any better or more appropriate solutions.

7.6.2.6. Substance Abuse

Abuse of alcohol usually coexists with domestic violence. Of victims of domestic abuse, two thirds have reported drinking alcohol. Intimate violence is more common among moderate drinkers than among light and abstainers; nonetheless, heavy or binge drinkers typically commit the most persistent and severe forms of aggression. Alcohol use is positively correlated with the likelihood, frequency, and severity of physical attacks. Following behavioral treatment for marital alcoholism, violence consequently declines.

7.6.3. Social Influences

.7.6.3.1. *Cultural View*

Though opinions on domestic violence differ from person to person and between cultures, the idea is generally misunderstood outside of the West. The idea is either outright banned or widely accepted in some nations.the fact that the majority of these nations view the husband and wifehusband-and-wife relationship as one in which the wife is required to submit to her husband rather than as one of equality. Some nations have codified this in their laws; in Yemen, for instance, marriage laws mandate that a wife obey her husband and not leave the house without his consent.

Violence against Women in Families and Relationships states that most people around the world believe that wife-beating is acceptable in certain situations, most notably when there is real or suspected infidelity among wives or when they are acting in a "disobedient" manner toward a husband or partner.

Many times, society (men and women alike) views these violent acts against a wife as the product of the wife's behavior, which is viewed as her fault, rather than as abuse. Extreme behaviors, like honor killings, are frequently accepted by a powerful segment of the populace. According to a survey, 33.4% of teenagers in Amman, the capital of Jordan, supported honor killings.

This survey was carried in the capital of Jordan, which is much more liberal than other parts of the country; the researchers said that "we would expect that in the more rural and traditional parts of Jordan, support for honor killings would be even higher."

In a 2012 news story, The Washington Post reported, "The Reuters Trust Law group named India one of the worst countries in the world for women this year, partly because [domestic violence] there is often seen as deserved. A 2012 report by UNICEF found that 57% of Indian boys and 53% of girls between the ages of 15 and 19 think wife-beating is justified."

Most people in society view such violent responses as appropriate in conservative cultures, where a wife who dresses too modestly may face serious violence from her husband or family. In an Afghan survey, 62% of women stated that a husband has the right to beat his wife if she wears inappropriate clothing. One of the challenges in addressing domestic violence legally, according to Antonia Parvanova, is that men in many societies where men predominate do not realize that it is illegal for them to use violence against their wives. She said, referring to a case that occurred in Bulgaria, "A husband was tried for severely beating his wife and when the judge a him if he understood what he did and if he's sorry, the husband saidsaid, 'But she's my wife.' He doesn't even understand that he has no right to beat her." The UN Population Fund writes that: "In some developing countries, practices that subjugate and harm women – such as wife-beating, killings in the name of honor, female genital mutilation/cutting and dowry deaths – are condoned as being part of the natural order of things."

Another reason for legal impunity is strong public opinion in some societies that reconciliation is preferable to punishment in cases of domestic violence. According to a study, 64% of Colombian public officials stated that they would press for a reconciliation be involved in an intimate partner abuse case if they were in charge ofoversaw handling it.

Victim blaming is also prevalent in many societies, including in Western countries: a 2010 Eurobarometer poll found that 52% of respondents agreed with the assertion that the "provocative behavior of women" was a cause of violence against women; with respondents in Cyprus, Denmark, Estonia, Finland, Latvia, Lithuania, Malta and Slovenia being most likely to agree with the assertion (more than 70% in each of these countries).

7.6.3.2. Religion

Regarding the impact of religion on domestic violence, there is disagreement. Religions such as Judaism, Christianity, and Islam have historically encouraged households headed by men, and violence against women has long been accepted in society.

Divergent opinions exist regarding Islam's impact on domestic violence. Some authors contend that Islam is linked to violence against women, particularly in the form of honor killings. However, others, like Tahira Shahid Khan, a professor at Aga Khan University in Pakistan who specializes in women's issues, contend that these acts are the result of women's subordination and men's dominance in society rather than the religion itself. In many Western nations, the relationship between Islam, immigration, and violence against women is a contentious topic of public (such as media) and political discourse.

Attending church regularly among Christians leads to a decrease in the likelihood of men and women committing domestic violence against their partners. This decrease is not attributed to an increased sense of support and community integration, which, while present, have minimon the commission of domestic violence. Even after taking into accountconsidering variations in psychological issues like depressive symptoms, low self-esteem, and alcoholism, the protective effect of frequent church attendance remains. It is worth noting that theologically conservative people do not have a higher tendency towards domestic violence. However, highly conservative men are significantly more prone to committing domestic violence when their partners hold strongly liberal views.

Women now fear ending abusive marriages due to Catholic teaching on divorce. Catholic bishops, however, make it clear that no one is required to stay in an abusive marriage.

Regarding wife beating, medieval Jewish authorities held differing opinions. While the majority of rabbis in Islamic countries accepted it as a means of discipline, those in Christian France and Germany typically saw it as grounds for an instantaneous divorce.

7.6.3.3. Custom and Tradition

Certain types of domestic violence are often perpetuated by regional customs and traditions. These customs and traditions include female genital mutilation (FGM), strict dress codes for women that may be enforced through violence by family members, strong requirements of female virginity before the wedding and violence related to non-conforming women and girls, child and forced marriages, dowries, and son preference—a desire of a family to have a boy and not a girl—which can lead to abuse and neglect of girls by disappointed family members.

In 2018, a study found that 38% of women in sub-Saharan Africa and 29% in Europe and South Asia, respectively, justified abuse, with the highest percentage of 47%. These high rates may be the result of women being more afraid to defy tradition and societal norms in less economically developed nations because they fear retaliation, whereas in more economically developed nations, women have greater access to education and will not submit to customs that violate their fundamental human rights.

Human Rights Watch reported in 2003 that traditions like the "bride price," which is a payment a man makes to the family of a woman he wants to marry, effectiverchase his wife's reproductive rights and sexual favors, highlight men'smen socially sanctioned right to control the terms of sex and to use force to do so. With laws passed in a number of nations, there has been progress in recent years in addressing traditional practices that put women in danger. An

NGO called the Inter-African Committee on Traditional Practices Affecting the Health of Women and Children works to alter social norms, increase awareness, and pass legislation prohibiting harmful customs that have an adverse effect on the health of women and children in Africa. The Istaention was ratified by the Council of Europe and mandates that ratifyingratify states enact laws outlawing acts of violence that were previously excused by tradition, culture, or the pursu, or they must rectify behavior that is deemed unacceptable. In order toTo provide guidelines for addressing and managing violence through the creation of effective laws, law enforcement policies and practices, and community activities to break down societal norms that condone violence, criminalize it, and create effective support systems for survivors of violence, the UN created the Handbook on Effective Police Responses to Violence against Women.

Women who have experienced domestic abuse are frequently reluctant to seek official assistance because they live in societies where the police and legal system are perceived as corrupt and abusive.

7.6.4. Effects

7.6.4.1. Physical

A domestic violence incident can result in acute injuries such as bruises, broken bones, head trauma, lacerations, and internal bleeding that need to be treated medically and admitted to the hospital. Chronic illnesses like arthritis, irritable bowel syndrome, chronic pain, pelvic pain, ulcers, and migraines have all been connected to victims of domestic abuse. Pregnant victims of domestic abuse are more likely to miscarry, go into premature labor, and risk harming or killing the unborn child.

Recent studies show a strong correlation between higher rates of numerous chronic conditions and exposure to all forms of domestic violence and abuse. The most compelling data comes from the Adverse Childhood Experiences Study, which links exposure to abuse or neglect to increased rates of chronic illnesses, high-risk health behaviors, and shortened life spans in adulthood. Since the early 1990s, there has been a growing body of evidence linking physical health and violence against women.

7.6.4.2. HIV/AIDS

According to the WHO, women who are in abusive relationships have a markedly increased risk of HIV/AIDS. According to the WHO, women in abusive relationships frequently feel pressured to engage in sexual activity, struggle to negotiate safer sex with their partners, and struggle to get the testing they need when they suspect they may be HIV positive. Over ten years of cross-sectional studies conducted in Rwanda, Tanzania, South Africa, and India have consistently shown that women who have been victims of intimate partner violence have a higher risk of HIV infection. The WHO stated that:

There is strong evidence to support ending intimate partner violence on its own and lowering the risk of HIV/AIDS among women and girls. There are both direct and indirect mechanisms through which HIV/AIDS and violence against women interact, according to the evidence.

Similar effects of the HIV/AIDS status on domestic violence also extend to same-sex relationships. According to Heintz and Melendez's research, same-sex people may find it difficult to broach the subject of safe sex due to factors like a diminished sense of control over their relationship, a fear of violence, and unequal power dynamics. About 50% of the study participants who reported violent incidents said they had been forced into sexual encounters; of them, only 50% said they had used safe sex practices. Fear of abuse and deceit in safe-sex practices were barriers to safer sex. In the end, Heintz and Melendez's research found that because it reduces the number of safe sex encounters, sexual assault and abuse in same-sex relationships pose a serious risk for HIV/AIDS infection. These incidents also increase the stigma and fear associated with having safe-sex conversations and disclosing one's STD status.

7.6.4.3. Psychological

Victims who continue to live with their abusers frequently report experiencing elevated levels of stress, fear, and anxiety. Because victims are frequently subjected to harsh criticism and made to feel guilty for "provoking" the abuse, depression is also common. According to reports, 60% of victims have a significantly elevated risk of suicide and satisfy the diagnostic criteria for depression, either during or after the relationship ends. Individuals who experience emotional or physical abuse frequently experience depression due to a sense of unworthiness. Because of the increased risk of suicide and other traumatic symptoms, it is suggested that many people who experience these feelings seek therapy. These feelings frequently last for a long time.

Domestic abuse victims frequently experience long-term anxiety and panic in addition to depression, and they also fit the diagnostic criteria for both panic disorder and generalized anxiety disorder. The psychological impact of domestic violence that is most frequently discussed is Post-Traumatic Stress Disorder (PTSD), which is typified by intrusive images, nightmares, an exaggerated startle response, flashbacks, and avoidance of triggers that e abuse. Research has demonstrated the significance of taking into accountconsidering the impact of domestic violence and its psychophysiologic aftereffects on women who are mothers ofdren and infants. Despite a traumatized mother's best efforts, a number ofseveral studies have demonstrated that PTSD related to maternal interpersonal violence can affect how their child responds to domestic violence and other traumatic events.

7.6.4.4. Financial

According to a 2024 study published in the Quarterly Journal of Economics, women who start relationships with (ultimately) physically abusive men experience large and significant wage losses, and their employment immediately declines when they move in together. The study used Finnish administrative data with unique identifiers for both victims and perpetrators of domestic violence. This increases the victim's financial reliance on the abuser, which makes it more difficult for them to leave the relationship.

The extent to which the abuse has robbed victims of their autonomy can come as a shock when they finally leave theirhe victim typically has very little money of their own and few people theypeople can rely on when they need help because of economic abuse and isolation. It has been demonstrated that this is one of the biggest barriers that victims of domestic abuse must overcome and the main thing that can deter them from fleeing their abusers.

Domestic abuse victims frequently lack the specialized skills, education, and training needed to find gainful employment in addition to lacking financial resources. They may also have multiple children to support. Thirty-six major US cities cited domestic violence as one of the main causes of homelessness in their areas in 2003. Furthermore, according to reports, one in three women are homeless as a result of leaving a relationship involving domestic violence. If a victim is successful in finding rental housing, her apartment building probably has zero tolerance policies for crime; even if they are the victims of violence rather than the offenders, these policies may result in their eviction. Even though there are a lot more women's shelters and community resources available to victims of domestic abuse now, many victims still do not receive the help they require because these organizations frequently have a small staff in comparison to the hundreds of victims who seek help.

Domestic abuse victims are often denied access to desired occupations, resulting in a form of occupational apartheid. This is especially true for women and children. Abusive partners may restrict career options and foster a work environment devoid of purpose, which bolsters low self-esteem and low self-efficacy in one's capacity to carry out daily duties in a satisfactory manner. Functional losses, an inability to maintain the skills required for employment, and an inability to function in the workplace also have an impact on work. Another way the abuser maintains control over the victims is by making them feel very alone in their lives, with few or no friends.

7.6.5. Management

Law enforcement, counseling, medical services, and other preventive and intervention measures can all be used to manage domestic violence. Individuals involved in domestic abuse might need to see an ER doctor, family doctor, or other primary care provider for medical attention.

Another strategy for managing the effects of domestic violence is counseling. Counseling for the abused person may involve determining the extent, kind, and presence of abuse. A lethality assessment is a tool help identify the most effective course of treatment for a client and alsoand assist the client in identifying more subtly abusive behaviors in their relationship. Because many victims of domestic violence downplay the severity of their circumstances, only roughly half of the participants in a study of victims of ated to domestic abuse acknowledged that their abuser was capable of killingcould kill them. Safety planning, which enables victims to prepare for potentially hazardous circumstances and is useful whether or not they choose to stay with their offender, is another crucial element.

Offenders may use counseling to reduce the likelihood of domestic violence in the future or to end the violence and mend the damage it has caused. Currently, the majority of convicted or self-referred offenders participate in programs designed for those who have abused their intimate partners. These are given in a group setting for one or two hours each week for a predetermined amount of time. Program facilitators lead participants through a curriculum of modules designed for adult education that incorporate a range of therapeutic modalities, primarily psycho education and cognitive behavioral therapy. The usefulness of these programs is still up for debate. There seems to be a risk of doing harm, even though some partners and ex-partners of offenders have seen improvements in their circumstances. In addition to group work, other strategies include one-on-one and conjoint talks to help end the violence and reestablish the victim's safety and dignity.

Providing safe shelter, crisis intervention, advocacy, education, and prevention programs are some of the strategies used in prevention and intervention to stop domestic abuse. In situations involving animal abuse, emergency rooms, mental health facilities, and legal systems, community screening for domestic violence can be conducted more methodically. Mobile apps are among the tools that are being developed to make screening for domestic violence easier. The Duluth Model, also known as the Domestic Abuse Intervention Project, is a multidisciplinary program that was created to address the problem of domestic violence by coordinating the efforts of various agencies that deal with domestic conflict. Its goal is to reduce domestic violence against women.

REFERENCES

1. Collier, R. (2010). Fatherhood, law and father's rights: Rethinking the relationship between gender and welfare. In J. Wallbank, S. Choudhry, & J. Herring (Eds.), *Rights, Gender and Family Law* (pp. 119–143). Routledge.
2. Halket, M. M., Gormley, K., Mello, N., Rosenthal, L., & Mirkin, M. P. (2013). Stay with or leave the abuser? The effects of domestic violence victim's decision on attributions made by young adults. *Journal of Family Violence, 29*, 35–49.
3. Kantola, J., & Nousiainen, K. (2009). Institutionalizing intersectionality in Europe: Introducing the theme. *International Feminist Journal of Politics, 11*, 459–477.
4. Karlsson Sjögren, Å. (2011). Matrimony, property and power: Marriage settlements in Sweden 1870–1920. *Scandinavian Journal of History, 36*, 443–461.
5. Melby, K., Pylkkänen, A., Rosenbeck, B., & Wetterberg, C. C. (2006). The Nordic model of marriage. *Women's History Review, 15*, 651–661.
6. Mol, C. (2016). Reasons for regulating informal relationships: A comparison of nine European jurisdictions. *Utrecht Law Review, 12*, 98–113.
7. Schechter, D. S., Zygmunt, A., Coates, S. W., Davies, M., Trabka, K. A., McCaw, J., Kolodji, A., & Robinson, J. L. (2007). Caregiver traumatization adversely impacts young children's mental representations on the MacArthur Story Stem Battery. *Attachment & Human Development, 9*(3), 187–205.
8. Schuler, S. R., Hashemi, S. M., Riley, A. P., & Akhter, S. (1996). Credit programs, patriarchy and men's violence against women in rural Bangladesh. *Social Science & Medicine, 12*, 1729–1742.
9. Schumm, R., & Abbotts, C. (2017). Spousal maintenance and gender inequality. *Family Law*, 1116–1118.
10. Song, J., & Lai, W. (2020). Cohabitation and gender equality. *China Review, 20*, 53–80.
11. Sorenson, S. B., Joshi, M., & Sivitz, E. (2014). A systematic review of the epidemiology of nonfatal strangulation, a human rights and health concern. *American Journal of Public Health, 104*(11), e54–e61.
12. Wallbank, J. (2010). (En)gendering the fusion of rights and responsibilities in the law of contact. In J. Wallbank, S. Choudhry, & J. Herring (Eds.), *Rights, Gender and Family Law* (pp. 93–118). Routledge.
13. Woodlock, D. (2017). The abuse of technology in domestic violence and stalking. *Violence Against Women, 23*(5), 584–602.

Chapter **8**

Women in the Criminal Justice System

Contents

INTRODUCTION

A fair, effective, and efficient criminal justice system depends on having a thorough understanding of the various ways that different groups of people experience crime, both as victims and as offenders. Gender is one of the ways that society divides people. Numerous studies have demonstrated that men and women interact with the criminal justice system and are affected by crime in different ways. The majority of people accused, found guilty, and imprisoned for violent crimes are still men, but women are more likely than men to be victims of violent crimes. Research indicates that there is a high prevalence of victimization among people who identify as gender non-conforming, despite the paucity of data on this population. Particularly gendered crimes include sexual assault, intimate partner violence, and domestic homicide, where men comm ofmost of the crimes and women make up the majority of the victims and survivors.

When it comes to crime, women are less likely to be imprisoned, are accused and found guilty of less serious crimes, and get involved for different reasons than men do. However, because women make up a comparatively small percentage of those incarcerated, many correctional programs are based on research done with men. It is necessary to evaluate how women get involved in crime and how best to meet their needs while they are in custo toto target interventions to prevent crime and develop policies aimed at the fair and rehabilitative treatment of offenders. This is especially crucial because the proportion of women serving time in Canadian jails and prisons is rising.

8.1. WOMEN'S RISK FACTORS

A lot of women and girls commit crimes for a variety of reasons: things that are more common among women than among men (like child sexual abuse and other forms of sexual victimization), things that happen in intimate relationships between women (like emotional, physical, and financial coercion), and things that are unusual for men (like sex work and retaliation against abusive family members or partners). While males are usually the ones linked to these types of crimes, women can also be financially abused or feel pressured to use drugs or commit crimes by relatives or other close relatives. Men are not exempt from childhood abuse and other forms of interpersonal victimization; however, women are more likely to face mental health issues, substance use disorders, and intimate partner violence as a result of these risk factors, which can all lead to their involvement in the criminal justice system.

Women and men commit crimes in different ways, with women often committing crimes for different reasons and in different amounts. Women encounter unique obstacles related to parenting, health, and finances, which impact their incarceration experience and their chances of success upon release. In addition, women's coping mechanisms for violence and trauma are different from men's, as is the frequency and severity of their mental health symptoms.

8.1.1. Child Abuse and Adversity

Women's paths to incarceration are significantly influenced by maltreatment as children. Over 90% of women who are involved in the criminal justice system had some type of childhood trauma, which could include being the victim of physical or sexual abuse, bullying, gang violence, violence in relationships, or witnessing extreme violence, including murder. The evidence that is currently at of maleabout male incarceration experiencing physical abuse during childhood at a rate equal to or higher than that of female incarceration is conflicting, but females consistently report higher rates of sexual abuse during childhood. Despite the lack of national data, between half and three-quarters of women in prison samples report having been sexually assaulted. Furthermore, many women report that their experiences of abuse escalate enter intoenter intimate partner relationships later in life, whereas men in prison report that their experiences of violent victimization by peers and caregivers decline throughout adolescence and into adulthood.

Research on non-incarcerated individuals reveals a strong correlation between various forms of childhood maltreatment and adve number ofseveral unfavorable adult outcomes, such as chronic illness and overdose death (Greene et al., 2014). Among women involved in the justice system, these correlations are stronger. Compared to men and women involved in the justice system in the community, women involved in the justice system report more Adverse Childhood Experiences (ACEs), which include childhood abuse and neglect, family instability factors, and witnessing violence in the home. Higher rates of arrest are linked to increased ACEs, particularly for women with mental health disorders. For instance, 84% of the women in prison reported a history of ACEs, compared to 69% of the women in the community, in a study that included 500 women incarcerated in California and about 4,700 women enrolled in a health maintenance organization (Messina & Grella, 2006). The likelihood that a woman had suffered four or more ACEs was 11.7 times higher among incarcerated women than among community women (32% compared to 19%).

Adversity and maltreatment as children are also closely linked to women's use of violence in relationships. Each additional type oldhood abuseabuses a woman experienced was linked to a 17% increase in her use of threats and intimidation and a 13% increase in her use of severe physical violence (physically restraint, kicking, punching, or stabbing) in her intimate relationships, according to a study of about 1,100 women incarcerated in California (Saxena & Messina, 2021).

8.1.2. Intimate Partner Violence

Intimate partner violence is a major risk factor for women involved in the criminal justice system, and romantic relationships are frequently a major entry point for criminal activity and drug abuse. Over 70% of women serving time in jails or prisons report having been victims of intimate partner violence in the past, which can take many different forms, from threats and intimidation to physical or sexual assault (Daly, 1992). In a study involving 115 women incarcerated, for instance, 77% of the women reported having experienced intimate partner violence; of these, 93% reported physical abuse, 32% reported partner rape, and 63% reported that a weapon was used during the incident. According to research, these estimates might be underestimated because some women may not recognize certain behaviors as intimate partner violence, such as coercive sex, hitting, kicking, and other fear tactics, or prolonged experiences of violence across multiple relationships (from parents and caregivers to intimate partners (Evans et al., 2016).

According to research, people in positions of authority over women involved in the justice system, such as judges and law enforcement officials, seldom comprehend the influence of abuse and violence on the criminal behavior of women. For instance, some women claim they were threatened or coerced into committing crimes or hiding them, while others assert that they confessed to a more significant role in a crime during their arrest and sentencing in order to shield an abusive intimate partner from punishment or to avoid a longer prison sentence for the partner. For many, these strategn an effort toto stop abuse in the future. Other women might use force to protect themselves. Stakeholders in the system often lack understanding of these behaviors, which leads to stigmatization, particularly for women who suffer from mental health or drug use disorders.

Intimate partner abuse is rarely discussed in criminal court proceedings of entry intoentering the system or as a factor in women's decision to use violence as a form of self-defense or to defend their children or other loved ones. At least 30% of those serving time for murder or manslaughter—many of whom are serving life sentences—were defending themselves or a loved one during the crime that resulted in their conviction, according to an analysis based on more than 600 survey responses from women incarcerated.

Accordingh, a number ofseveral negative outcomes, such as re-victimization, criminal behavior, engaging in sex work, and homelessness, are frequently preceded by problematic interpersonal relationships for many women involved in the justice system (Cov8). A number ofSeveral factors, such as the coercive actions of abusers and system stakeholder's ignorance of the dynamics of interpersonal violence, can be blamed for the transformation of "victims" into "offenders." Many women who are victims of intimate partner violence experience poverty and unstable housing as a result of these forces, which raises the risk of substance abuse and crimes related to survival for the women and their children.

8.1.3. Traumatic Brain Injury

Any type of brain injury that changes how the brain functions, such as a blunt object impact or other types of pressure or injury, is referred to as a Traumatic Brain Injury (TBI). Depending on the extent of the injury, traumatic brain injury (TBI) can have a wide range of effects on brain function. Symptoms can include altered consciousness and behavior, headaches, exhaustion, sleeplessness, dizziness, seizures, and deficits in motor, sensory, and cognitive functions. TBI frequently causes mental health issues like mood disorders and difficulty controlling anger. People may also become more irritable and struggle to control their emotions. These adjustments may strain relationships and interfere with day-to-day activities. Approximately 25% of TBIs are caused by interpersonal violence, many of which have mild symptoms.

Research on Traumatic Brain Injury (TBI) and its effects is well established, although it primarily focuses on males. Men are more likely than women to sustain a Traumatic Brain Injury (TBI) in community and military samples; in incarcerated samples, women are marginally more likely to suffer a TBI than men. The last ten years have seen a significant increase in research on TBIs brought on by intimate partner violence (Costello & Greenwald, 2022). According to estimates, women suffer 11–12 times as many Traumatic Brain Injury (TBIs) from intimate partner violence than do athletes and members of the armed forces put together. Due to difficulties with measurement and sampling, estimates of the prevalence of TBI among women who suffer from intimate partner violence range widely (from 50% to 92%).

TBIs associated with violence against intimate partners can result from being pushed or thrown to the ground, being violently shaken, being strangled, or receiving a blow to the head (with a fist or heavy object). In a study of 900 Black women aged 18 to 55 in Maryland and the U.S. Virgin Islands, half of the 540 women who self-reported intimate partner violence had sustained a TBI (Campbell et al., 2018). 36% had been strangled, and 56% had suffered serious facial injuries, with 4% of the females suffering a broken or dislocated jaw. In 2017, a narrative review of prior research revealed that intimate partner violence and Traumatic Brain Injury (TBI) frequently act as risk factors for one another, creating a dangerous cycle. If left untreated, a Traumatic Brain Injury (TBI) from abuse can lead to cognitive impairment, memory loss, and mood swings, all of which raise the victim's risk of recurrent abuse and further brain injuries.

8.1.4. Mental Health and Substance Use Disorders

Whether mental health disorders are measured as a general condition or as a specific diagnostic category, women consistently report higher rates of mental health disorders than men in samples of incarcerated individuals. In the most recent year for which national data were available, 2011–2012, for instance, 66% of women and 68% of men in prison or jail had a diagnosis of a mental health illness, compared to 35% of men and 41% of men in jail or prison. Women also reported significantly higher rates of post-traumatic stress disorder (PTSD; 21% of women versus 6% of men) than their male counterparts in prison. Additionally, women were more likely than men to meet the threshold for serious psychological distress (20% of women in prison and 32% of women in jail, compared to 14% of men in prison and 26% of men in jail) (Baranyi et al., 2018).

Women who are involved in the justice system are also more likely than men to have been diagnosed with a substance abuse problem and to have been under the influence of alcohol when they committed their offense. For instance, 69–72% of women, compared to 57% of men, fit the criteria for a substance use disorder. Women were significantly more likely than men (10%) to have used methamphetamines in the month prior to incarceration (15–17%), and nearly half (46–49%) of women in prison used drugs at the time of their offense, compared to 36%–41% of men (Bronson et al., 2017).

In the general population, the prevalence of co-occurring mental health and drug use disorders is approximately 3%, but among those incarcerated in jails, it is estimated to be as high as 10% for men and 22% for women. Childhood abuse and intimate partner violence are associated with a higher risk of substance misuse and substance use disorders. Many women reported using substances to cope with the symptoms of untreated mental health conditions and the aftereffects of trauma.

*8.1.5. Failure-t*ile

A large number ofmany women come into contact with the criminal justice system as a result of their direct involvement in criminal activity, some are charged with crimes simply for observing their children being abused and "failing to protect" them—even though they did not commit the abuse themselves. Failing to report child abuse can result in nalties in forty sevenforty-seven states due to failure-to-protect laws. While such laws are commonplace across the U.S., the potential consequences imposed by these laws vary. Children identified as victims in these situations may be taken from their homes and placed under the care of the child welfare system in certain states, while the non-offending parent—typically a woman—may face criminal charges in other states. In seven states (Oklahoma, Missouri, Nebraska, Nevada, South Carolina, West Virginia, and Texas), parents who did not commit the crime but were either witnesses to it or were suspected of knowing about it could receive life sentences or sentences of 99 years.

Despite being designed to shield children from abuse, laws that fail to protect women who are also victims of abuse at home have a disproportionately negative effect on them. These laws apply to anyone who knows or suspects that a child is being abused and does not report the abuse; this applies even to those who have been the victims of abuse themselves and choose not to report because of coercion, fear of reprisals, or other reasons related to their experience with domestic abuse or intimate partner violence. Allowing children to witness one parent abusing the other can also result in failure-to-protect charges in many states.

8.1.6. Sex Work

Young women and transgender persons are disproportionately affected by the crimiex work. The majority ofMost sex trafficking victims are young women, and arrests tend to target women and transgender persons even in cases where men are involved as clients or traffickers. Approximately 20,000 people were arrested for prostitution in 2019, the most recent year for which statistics were available, and 63% of those arrested were female. However, a focus on sex work undervalues the frequency with which women trade sex for cash or drugs.

Women's involvement in sex work is explained from two main points of view. The empowerment paradigm contends that some women choose sex work to satisfy their immediate financial needs in the setting of scarce employment opportunities, while the oppression paradigm emphasizes how drug use, homelessness, poverty, and abuse during childhood force some women into the profession.

8.1.7. Juvenile Justice System Involvement

Although the Commission focuses on women joining the adult criminal justice system, it is crucial to comprehend the trends among young girls involved in the juvenile justice system. The number of girls involved in the juvenile justice system who subsequently enter or remain in contact with the adult criminal justice system is not officially recorded. However, according to information from the 2016 Survey of Prison Inmates, 45% of women who were incarcerated admitted to having been arrested before turning 18 at least once. Numerous risk factors that contribute to women's involvem the system also affect girl'sgirls' involvement in the juvenile justice system; these factors include housing and economic instability, experiences of abuse and domestic violence, and difficulties with mental and physical health.

8.1.7.1. Juvenile Arrests and Sentencing

Since the mid-1990s, the overall rate of juvenile arrests has decreased significantly (Council on Criminal Justice, 2023). Boy's arrest rates increased between 1980 and 1996, reaching a high of 5,704 per 100,000 male youth residents, after which they started a general decline. The arrest rate decreased by 78% between 1996 and 2019 and by 37% between 2019 and 2020 as a result of measures taken in response to the COVID-19 pandemic. The boys arrest rate was 809 in 2020, the most recent year for which data were available, indicating a decline of 86% from the peak. In 1997, the number of girls arrested per 100,000 female youth residents reached a peak of 1,802. After that, the rate dropped gradually until 2012, at which point it dropped more quickly. The arrest rate for girls decreased by 68% between 1997 and 2019. Responses to the COVID-19 pandemic caused a 41% decrease in girl's arrest rates from 2019 to 2020, which corresponded to an 81% decline from peak to 2020. Over time, the proportion of juvenile arrests that involve girls has increased gradually and steadily. In 1980, girls made up 15% of all juvenile arrests; by 2020, that number had increased to 23%.

Over time, there have also been changes in the offenses that resulted in girls being arrested. For instance, from 1980 to 2020, the percentage of girls arrested for violent crimes nearly doubled, from 10% to 19% of all arrests. In a similar vein, the percentage of girls arrested for property crimes rose from 18% in 1980 to 38% in 2010, when it fell to 29% in 2020. Compared to arrests for violent and property crimes, the percentage of girls who were arrested for drug offenses has fluctuated more. Approximately 15% of all drug-related arrests during the early 1980s were made of girls. In the mid-1990s, this share reached a low of 11% before gradually increasing once more. In 2020, 25% of all drug offense arrests involved girls.

The National Incident-Based Reporting System (NIBRS) provided the Federal Bureau of Investigation (FBI) with information regarding approximately 366,000 juvenile arrests for serious violent and property crimes in 2022, along with the individual's racial and ethnic background. About 115,000, or slightly less than one-third, or 32%, of these arrests involved young girls. 14% were Black, 17% were Hispanic, 3% were American Indian/Alaska Native, 1% were Asian, and less than 1% were Native Hawaiian or other Pacific Islanders. Of the girls who were arrested, nearly half (45%) were White. The number of girls who self-identified as multiracial or whose race and ethnicity were unknown was not disclosed.

Since higher numbers of arrests are typically associated with larger racial and ethnic groups, the raw number of arrests within a race or ethnic group may mask significant information regarding racial disproportionality (and vice versa). It is not possible to extract arrest rates from the available NIBRS data. Data on the juvenile arrest rate for all juvenile arrests in 2020 wver they were not gender-specificgender specific. Compared to White youth (1,080 per 100,000), Black youth (2,481 per 100,000) and American Indian/Alaska Native (1,815 per 100,000) had substantially higher rates. Research indicates that Black girls are more than twice as likely as White girls to be charged as adults and be transferred to the adult criminal justice system, even though the number of girls prosecuted as adults is smaller than that of boys (194 girls compared to 2,537 boys in 2020) [Office of Juvenile Justice and Delinquency Prevention. (2024)].

8.1.7.2. Girls in Residential Custody

There were roughly 3,500 girls in residential custody in 2021 compared to 14,500 in 1999, a 75% decrease. Over the same period, the number of boys decreased by 76%, from about 93,000 to 21,000. Approximately 14% of all children in detention were girls on average. Of the approximately 3,550 girls in residential custody in 2021, 44% had convictions for violent crimes, 18% for property crimes, 6% for drug offenses, and 9% for public order offenses. 8% were being held for status offenses, and about 16% were being held for a technical violation of their supervision. 13% of all youth detained for violent offenses were girls, 14% for property crimes, and 22% for drug offenses. Girls made up 37% of all youth detained for status offenses, comprising 30% of truant youth, 37% of running away youth, and 39% of youth detained for "incorrigibility."

Compared to Asian, Hispanic, and White girls, Black and Native American girls are significantly more likely to be in residential custody. The overall placement rate for girls17 in 2020 was 35 per 100,000, but100,000 but compared to their White peers (24 per 100,000), Native American girls (112 per 100,000) were four times more likely to be in custody, and Black girls (77 per 100,000) were more than three times more likely. Asian girls had an 83% lower rate of residential placements (4 per 100,000), while the rate for Hispanic girls (27 per 100,000) was about the same as that of White girls.

8.1.7.3. Girls in Residential Custody by Race, 2020

In ared to youth in the general publicpublic (7–9%), girls who identify as lesbian, gay, or bisexual are disproportionately represented in juvenile residential custody (40%). LGBTQ+ youth have a higher chance of experiencing homelessness, rejection from family, and bullying and abuse from peers or family members, which increases their likelihood of coming into contact with the juvenile justice system. Girls reported five or more ACEs at a rate of 45%, which is nearly twice as high as the rate reported by boys (27%) in a sample of youth involved in the juvenile justice system. Compared to 7% of boys, nearly a third (31%) of girls reported experiencing sexual abuse (Baglivio et al., 2014). Girls mak larger percentage of young peoplepeople who are incarcerated for low-level offenses than boys do. 34% of all minors detained in 2019 for status offenses (e.g., truancy, and breaking curfew) were female. Girls made up more than half of the young people in residential placements for running away. Girl's school-based discipline and subsequent involvement in the juvenile justice system have been linked to early abuse.

Effective preventative and intervention straes to stop girls from engaging within the adult criminal justice system are still elusive, despite the fact that much is known about how girls interact with the juvenile justice system. Furthermore, little is known about how youth's interactions with the criminal justice system have been impacted by rising social media use and disruptions to school and social life brought on by the pandemic. In addition to determining the connections between these factors and drug abuse, intimate partner violence, criminal activity, arrests, and incarceration, more research is requiredamine how these factors impact girl'sa girl's mental and physical health, relationships with family and peers, and acaduccess. Improving knowledge of girl'sgirls' paths can aid in the creation and evaluation of focused initiatives to meet the changing needs and risks of girls and keep them out of adult criminal justice systems.

8.2. INCARCERATION OF WOMEN

Globally, the number of women incarcerated in correctional facilities has increased to approximately 741,000, representing a 17% increase since 2010.

8.2.1. Prison Population

Men make up the great majority of those behind bars worldwide. Criminal justice systems worldwide have handled incarcerated women differently from the beginning to the end of the process, from arrest to sentencing to the use of punitive measures. This discrepancy is mostly caused by real demographic differences in the seriousness of crimes committed by the prison populations of men and women, as well as the enduring belief in society at large that female offenders are more rehabilitable than their male counterparts.

Despite making up a smaller percentage of all prisoners worldwide, the number of women behind bars is increasing at a rate double that of men. The majority of the world's incarcerated population, including women, is found in China, Russia, and the United States (Byrne et al., 2015). Policies pertaining to the sentencing and parole of female inmates are subject to change, which may account for some trends observed in the global increase in the prison population of women. The global trend of gender-blind sentencing in criminal justice systems has led to a marked rise in the imprisonment rate of women. Women's incarceration rates are further increased by high rates of re-entry and re-offending, which are also caused by the concurrent elimination of parole and harshening of penalties for parole violations in many parts of the world.

8.2.2. Social and Political Conditions Leading to Incarceration

Global advancements in the political response to social issues, particularly th drug epidemic, have sparked a number ofseveral shifts in the demographics of prison populations and, as a result, the conditions under which inmates are housed. The high number of female low-level offenders, who are typically imprisoned for drug use or possession, has been attributed to the War on Drugs. The so-called "War on Drugs" has been widely promoted by Western nations, especially the United States (Reynolds and Marylee, 2008).

Although the kinds of crimes for which female prisoners are incarcerated are not uniformly represented across the globe, it is commonly known that a number of underlying social injustices give impacted women a disproportionately high likelihood of committing crimes and ending up behind bars. The most notable of these circumstances is poverty, along with the factors that contribute to it. Around the world, women in low-income households typically put in a disproportionate amount of work to take care of the home, provide food for the family, and educate the kids. This coexists with disparities in education, income, pregnancy, and the prevalence of domestic and physical abuse. Another injustice that is partly to blame for the high ie of impoverished women in particular isis the lack of access to mental health care. Many women who are incarcerated have mental health disorders, and the lack of treatment for these conditions can be directly linked to their incarceration.

8.2.3. Prison Conditions

Early facilities were regarded as cruel and cared for people's health and safety very little. The strong preyed on the weak in a large room housing both men and women. In most of the Western world, female prison guards were no longer the only gender in place as of 1964. As of that year, women and men were employed in American women's prisons as guards. Nonetheless, laws in certain states mandate the appointment of a female superintendent along with female officers. Some facilities are deemed "unisex" and house both male and in separate areas, although the majority ofmost states only have one or two institutions specifically for women.

The quality of living in prisons varies greatly between those located in different parts of the world and even within the same nation. There is a lack of consistency in prison living conditions due to differences in national wealth, how national budgets are distributed, and the various approaches taken to criminal rehabilitation. Variability in the environmental quality of women's prisons is also caused by other phenomena, such as the privatization of prisons in many nations with sizable prison populations, like the United States. When a corporation takes over the management of a prison and its finances, the ruling government has less control over the upkeep of prison regulations and the welfare of inmates. The question of whether private prisons should remain open is a topic of much ongoing political discussion.

Women are among the prison population with specific health needs that are frequently ignored. For instance, a study published in the journal Health and Social Care in the Community discovered that women's unique mental and physical health needs are understudied and inadequately met in England and Wales, the two countries with the highest rates of incarceration in Europe. Of the prisoners, 40% reported long-term health issues, compared to 33% of male inmates.

8.2.4. By Jurisdiction

8.2.4.1. Great Britain

After a new law was passed in Great Britain in 1996, women serving prison terms are no longer required to be restrained while giving birth. No one should be subjected to cruel or inhumane punishment, according to the British services for human rights and the United Nations standard minimum rules for the treatment of prisoners. Some prisoners feel so humiliated by their restraints that they won't attend funerals or childcare events. Although British women fought for the freedom to give birth to their children without being restrained, they still have to be restrained when being transported to and from the hospital. In Britain, more women than men attempt to evade the legal system. Nearly half of the women who manage to get away do so while getting care at a hospital.

8.2.4.2. Hong Kong

In 2017, the World Prisons Brief reported that women comprised approximately 20.8% of Hong Kong's prison population. As of around 2017, Hong Kong has the highest percentage of women under correctional supervision of any sovereign state or dependency, with the exception of extremely small nations or microstates. If the 279 women on remand were taken into account, the number of women under correctional supervision at Hong Kong Correctional Services in August 2017 was 1,764 instead of 1,486. Bauhinia House, Tai Lam Centre for Women, Chi Lan Rehabilitation Centre, Lai King Correctional Institution, Lo Wu Correctional Institution, Wai Lan Rehabilitation Centre, and Nei Kwu Correctional Institution are just a few of the women-only facilities in Hong Kong.

8.2.4.3. Mainland China

It has generally been found to be challenging to compare statistical data regarding China's female incarceration rate to that of other nations. Notwithstanding, certain academics contended in 2003 that roughly 25% of the total US female population would be comparable to the entire Chinese female prison population (Hartney and Christopher, 2006). As of August 2014, the International Centre for Prison Studies reports that, with 84,600 female prisoners, or 5.1% of the total Chinese prison population, China has the second-largest women's prison population in the world (after the United States).

In China, the percentage of women behind bars has risen by 46% in the past ten years. The proportion of women incarcerated nationwide is a mere 6% of the total population. China is on track tothan the United States, despite the fact thateven though the statistic regarding the total number of women incarcerated is difficult to accurately evaluate due to the underreporting of these cases.

8.2.4.4. New Zealand

There are three prisons in New Zealand that are dedicated to housing women. These consist of the following: Christchurch Women's Prison, Arohata Women's Prison, and Auckland Region Women's Corrections Facility (ARWCF). While incarcerated, women are provided with a range of prisoner support programs at these facilities. These include breastfeeding and bonding areas, mental and physical disability support, baby unit spaces for new moms, cultural activities, and special food accommodations for dietary restrictions. Although many of these programs require permission and are assessed on a case-by-case basis, these prisons have recently begun to provide these choices to women who are incarcerated.

Between 1996 and 2005, the total number of women convicted in New Zealand increased by 111%. In 1963, women accounted for 7:7% of those found guilty in New Zealand's legal system; offenses against property were the primary reason for arrests, while other offenses included assault and/or crime against persons. Then, in lower court systems, the percentage of women incarcerated rose to 11% in 1972. With essentially the same two central convictions once more. In most first-world natioincluding New Zealand, prosecuted females had,had on average, fewer prior convictions than prosecuted males as of 1996. In New Zealand, the number of women serving prison sentences reached a peak in 2010 and has subsequently declined (Jeffries, Samantha, and Greg Newbold, 2016). The percentage of women who are convicted is up to 23% as of 2014. At 33% of all convictions for women, crimes against property account for a larger percentage than the overall 23%. Greg Newbold reports that a 1991 Department of Justice study found that men were twice as likely as women to commit a more serious crime.

While there are far more men than women in New Zealand's correctional facilities, the number of women behind bars is increasing at a rate that is noticeably faster than that of men. Not only in New Zealand, but globally as well, the incarceration rate for women has been rising. The most recent theory put forth to explain the increase holds that the criminal justice system is evolving rather than women's crime rates rising. Due to this shift, minor offenses—which women are statistically more likely to commit—are receiving more attention. Professor of Criminology at the University of Stirling Gill McIvor provides evidence to support this theory in a 2010 study that shows a correlation between the rise in female incarceration rates in New Zealand and the severity of crimes committed by women. In addition, McIvor asserts that New Zealand women are underrepresented in more serious crimes like violent crimes and overrepresented in less serious crimes like fraud and theft.

The number of female inmates in each of these facilities has slightly increased, according to data from 2014. Even though women only make up 7:4% of all incarcerated people in New Zealand, according to the Department of Corrections, the population increases are specifically linked to four major crime categories. Theft and related offenses, robbery, extortion, and related offenses, illicit drug offenses, and fraud offenses are among them. The lowest category, illicit drug offenses, had the smallest increase, at 40%, compared to three of these four categories, which saw increases of 60%.

8.2.4.5. Russia

About 60,500 women were housed in the Russian Criminal Justice system as of March 1, 2012, accounting for 8.1% of the nation's total prison population.

Russia has been sluggish to enact laws protecting the rights of those who are behind bars, particularly women. There are some criminal laws in Russia that regulate how women are treated and treated in the criminal justice system; however, these laws are mainly restricted to the status of incarcerated women who are child bearers and appear to place more emphasis on the rights and status of children incarcerated with their mothers, with the exception of a law prohibiting women from receiving the death penalty. For example, a woman's sentence may be reduced, canceled, or postponed if she is pregnant or has a child under the age of fourteen. Furthermore, women who are incarcerated and have children are entitled to "more rations and clothing, better living conditions, and specialized medical services." Inadequate medical care and crowded living conditions are faced by women who are childless. In addition, women are frequently transported from transit prisons to their ultimate destination—regardless of where that destination is—over a two-month journey.

8.2.4.6. United States

In the 1870s, American authorities started keeping women and men apart in correctional facilities. Mount Pleasant Female Prison in Ossining, New York was the first female correctional facility in the United States with dedicated buildings and staff; however, the facility relied somewhat on the adjacent men's prison, Sing Sing, for its operations (Banks, 2011). 34 women's prisons were constructed in the, 1930s; by 1990, the nation had 71 such facilities; however, five years later, there were 150.

According to Nicole Hahn Rafter's historical account in Partial Justice: Women in State Prisons, state prisons for women in the US developed in three waves as opposed to prisons intended for men. First, female inmates suffered daily degrading treatment and sexual assaults while housed with male inmates in the "general population." After being segregated from the general population and given less resources than male n prisons suffered from neglect in an attempt toto partially address these problems. The third stage of development saw women imprisoned in totally separate, fortress-like facilities with the aim of brainwashing them into conforming to traditional gender roles (Rafter, 1985).

The Prisoners in 2014 report by the Bureau of Justice Statistics determined that Black women make up 23% of incarcerated women in the United States. Black women comprise about 14% of the U.S. female population and because corrections agencies do not separate prisoner data by race and gender

There are presently 23 states without legislation prohibiting the shackling of pregnant inmates. The United Nations Guidelines for the Treatment of Female Prisoners and Non-custodial Measures for Female Offenders, which specifically prohibit the use of restraint devices on women during labor, childbirth, or the immediate postpartum period, are broken by this. "Shackling during pregnancy, delivery, and the postpartum period are different. Some states, like Maryland and New York, forbade all forms of restraints both before and after childbirth, while others forbade shackling during active delivery but allowed it both before and after. Rhode Island is currently the only state that allows women who are unlawfully shackled to pursue a private right of action.

The prison guards, not the medical staff, are in complete control of the restraints when pregnant women are shackled. These shackling techniques have drawn a lot of criticism due to the harm they do to the fetus and the mother. As per a 2016 study, there are specific safety risks associated with shackles, which include "the possibility of falls causing injury or placental abruption, labor progressing slowly due to limited mobility, and emergency care being delayed when correctional officers have to take off shackles for assessment or intervention." Furthermore, shackling can result in trauma, amplify pre-existing trauma, or worsen symptoms associated with post-traumatic experiences. Medical professionals have verified that there is a very low risk of impending harm or escape when safer measures, like de-escalation tactics, are employed, even though shackles are justified as being required to prevent flight risk or the potential to harm others.

Medical professionals and prisoners have complained that shackling during pregnancy and the postpartum period persists, despite calls for legislation to outlaw this practice and the legislative restrictions that are currently in place. The federal government does not require the gathering of information about female prisoner's pregnancies and deliveries. As a result, it is unclear how frequently and how these practices still happen.

8.2.5. Rape and Sexual Assault in Prison

For a very long time, rape has been a regular occurrence in female prisons in both the US and the UK. According to a report, staff members in England and Wales are forcing female prisoners into having sex in exchange for various favors like alcohol and cigarettes. Given that it is difficult to know the whole truth about what happens behind prison walls and that inmates frequently lack legal recourse to seek justice for abuse and rape, rape may even be more common than reports suggest. The Alabama prison scandal at the Julia Tutwiler Prison for Women exposed egregious sexual misconduct, including rape, committed by male staff members against female inmates in the United States (Chuck, 2014). There were few and insignificant penalties for sexual offenders, but humiliation and solitary confinement would be meted out for reporting these abuses.

Karen White, a transgender prisoner in the United Kingdom, was given a life sentence in 2018 after she admitted to sexually assaulting two other women prisoners at HM Prison New Hall near Wakefield, West Yorkshire, and raping them. The prosecution, however, claimed that White used a "transgender persona" despite being born a man. In September 2017, she was detained there under remand. The judge called White, who began transitioning while incarcerated, a "predator" and a threat to women and children (Parveen, 2018).

8.2.6. Drug Offenders

The percentage of female drug offenders who were imprisoned between 2010 and 2011 was 5.77%, down from 6% in 2010. The U.S. has also closely examined the care given to female drug offenders. Within the U.S. Women have been found to report higher rates of childhood trauma, abuse, addiction, PTSD, interpersonal violence, adolescent conduct disorder, homelessness, and chronic physical and mental health issues than male prisoners. As a result, women are more likely to engage in criminal activity or suffer from severe addictions. A challenge faced by female offenders is that, although they require more specialized tbstance abuse due to their gender, the majority ofmost programs that address this issue are male-oriented, such as Therapeutic Community (TC) models (Messina et al., 2009). As substance abuse treatment is not fairly granted in prisons across the U.S., recidivism is likely to go up within 2011, with the most serious offense for 59.4% of women incarcerated in federal prisons being drug violations.

8.2.7. Children of Incarcerated Parents

A 2007 report published by the Bureau of Justice Statistics (BJS) states that during the 17 years from 1990 to 2007, the number of children whose mothers were incarcerated doubled. During that time, 11.7 million children had parents incarcerated; these children were primarily Black and Hispanic. Children whose mothers are incarcerated often have behavioral issues and sleep disorders. Furthermore, a study conducted by Child Welfare Services (CWS) finds that children whose parents are incarcerated are more likely than other CWS-treated children to be in a vulnerable situation.

In the 2000s, the constitutional rights of pregnant prisoners in US jails were expanded and codified. According to data from 2010, the United States' rates of incarceration for women are rising at a faster rate than those for men. Among women incarcerated, one in four are pregnant. There are less than half of US prisons with formal policies regarding medical care for pregnant inmates. Prenatal services are available in approximately 48% of jails. Just 15% of these 48% of prisons have programs in place to assist new mothers in finding suitable jobs after giving birth. Furthermore, only 15% of prisons have rules requiring pregnant inmates to work little or nothing at all. Pregnant inmates face harsh treatment from prison staff across the country due to the widespread belief that they are not "worthy enough to have children." Psychological stressors can arise for pregnant inmates both during their pregnancy and the childbirth process.ce, women can be tethered to their beds in thirty fivethirty-five states during labor and delivery. Many lawsuits allege that shackling was used during childbirth in states where the practice is prohibited.

8.3. WOMEN AS PROFESSIONALS

A small but increasing proportion of police officers are women. Sworn female police officers now make up roughly 13% of the country on average, compared to just 3% in the 1970s. Fortunately, organizations and law enforcement associations around the nation are beginning to acknowledge the advantages of hiring, developing, and elevating more female officers. An increasing number of people are realizing the distinct and important professional attributes that women frequently bring to law enforcement, which is contributing to the positive trend toward building a more balanced public safety force. These attributes are thought to improve law enforcement organization's capacity to positively influence the communities they serve.

8.3.1. Primary Benefits of Recruiting More Women to Work in Law Enforcement

Although hiring a diverse workforce is a need recognized by most departments and law enforcement agencies, diversity initiatives tend to prioritize ethnicity over gender. That is a problem because nearly half of the population has been shut out of a career in which they could make a big, positive difference, as women make up such a small minority of sworn law enforcement officers. This is true despite overwhelming evidence that women are significantly changing the culture of policing. It is very beneficial that they bring their unique set of skills to a traditionally male-dominated culture. Women are adept at defusing potentially explosive situations through communication, a skill that is becoming more and more valued in many sheriff's and police departments. Departments that have hired women understand how important they are in defusing tense situations. These four examples show how women are improving the ways law enforcement operates.

1. **Officers who are female are less likely to use excessive force.** Women officers are less likely to pull their weapon or use excessive force, which is one of the most widely recognized advantages of encouraging more women into criminal justice careers. They are far less frequently sued than men, which saves cities millions of dollars in legal bills. The 2019 National Institute of Justice Special Report:

Women in Policing, Breaking Barriers and Blazing a Path references a Journal of Criminal Justice Study that supports this assertion. The use of force by female officers is less common than that of male officers, and police misconduct is substantially more common among male officers than it is among women, according to meta-analyses.

These elements are particularly crucial when police use of force is being scrutinized more closely, which frequently results in higher levels of hostility between the police and the communities they serve. First off, de-escalation techniques are more frequently used by female law enforcement officers in tense situations due to their potential effectiveness as well as the fact that women are sometimes at a physical disadvantage when interacting with suspects. This raises the question, why are women less likely to use force? We do have to rely on those other skills and abilities because female officers are generally smaller and less physically strong than their male counterparts.

2. Women officers are adept at handling sex crimes and violence against women. Addressing violence against women and sex crimes is a crucial area in which women in law enforcement can make a difference. According to a University of Zurich study, "violent crimes against women, especially domestic violence, are reported to the police at significantly higher rates as female representation among officers increases in that area." This study also discovered a significant decrease in the rates of intimate partner homicide and recurring domestic abuse as the proportion of female officers rises. Studies on reports of rape and sexual assault cases revealed similar results: higher reporting rates of rape incidents and higher clearance rates for rape cases are correlated with a larger proportion of women in the policing workforce.

3. **Enhancing police-community relations can be facilitated by female officers.** Research has repeatedly shown that women have a variety of qualities that make them reliable partners in their communities, which eventually contributes to better relations between the police and the community. Women are better at interpersonal communication than men, which contributes to more productive work practices. Compared to male officers, female officers are less likely to use excessive force, be named in a lawsuit, or use force.

4. **Consequently, these elements have made it possible for women to**

enhance police-community relations more successfully. Female cops can contribute to the creation of safe, livable communities because historically, women have raised the majority of the children, and what more do we want for our children than a safe place to grow up? Women may view law enforcement from quite different angles when they approach the matter in that manner.

5. **Women are better at solving problems than men are.** Research demonstrates that diverse workforces are more resilient, creative, and effective than homogenous workforces, and that broad-minded teams perform better when making decisions and resolving issues. These findings go beyond the gender binary. Furthermore, it has been demonstrated that women are better at solving problems—a crucial skill for those working in law enforcement. Women are already known to solve cases of violence against women more effectively, to use less force, and to solve problems more adeptly than men. Additionally, combining the strengths of men and women in the workforce improves both the workplace environment and the quality of services provided to our communities.

8.3.2. Encouraging More Women to Pursue Careers in Law Enforcement

There are a number of reasons why there aren't more women working in law enforcement agencies today, despite the fact that women have such a positive impact on the field: stereotypes, male-focused recruitment campaigns, and physical ability tests that favor upper body strength in men. There is a growing recognition of the positive impact that women can have in law enforcement, but more needs to be done to encourage more women into this field. One example of a recruiting effort aimed at women comes from the U.S. Border Patrol and a hiring push focused exclusively on women.

8.3.2.1. The 30×30 Initiative

The 30×30 Initiative was started in response to a 2018 National Institute of Justice report. Its goals include having 30% more women in police recruit classes by 2030 and making sure that police culture and policies purposefully foster the professional success of qualified female officers. The 30×30 Initiative, driven by thorough research and analysis, has discovered that law enforcement agencies and communities benefit from women officers because they:

- Use less force and less excessive force
- Are named in fewer complaints and lawsuits

- Are perceived by communities as being more honest and compassionate
- See better outcomes for crime victims, especially in sexual assault cases
- Make fewer discretionary arrests, especially of non-white residents

Currently, the 30×30 Initiative is being advanced by a coalition of professional organizations, researchers, and police leaders. They are gradually but firmly increasing public awareness of the value of female representation in law enforcement through their advocacy. As of right now, 115 law enforcement organizations nationwide have committed to taking the lead in promoting women in law enforcement. These organizations are required by the 30x30 Pledge to:

- Take measures to increase the representation of women in all ranks of law enforcement;
- Ensure that policies and procedures are free of all bias;
- Promote equitable hiring, retention and promotion of women officers; and
- Ensure their culture is inclusive, respectful and supportive of women in all ranks and roles of law enforcement.

8.3.3. The Importance of Education for Female Law Enforcement Leaders

Though it was once disputed, law enforcement leaders of all genders now agree that education is crucial and should be a top priority. At all levels of law enforcement, there is a positive correlation between education and job performance, according to recent research. A national dialogue regarding increasing the educational requirements for police officers has been initiated by the calls for police reform that have been made recently, as well as the growing body of evidence that shows the many benefits that an educated police force can have. Advanced education in specialized areas of the field, like leadership, conflict resolution, and routine day-to-day tasks, is especially beneficial for female law enforcement officers. It can make one's resume stand out and help one get ready for interviews and promotional exams.

Therefore, even though an advanced degree was not previously required for law enforcement professionals, times are quickly changing. It can be argued that law enforcement nowadays requires a diverse leadership team with 21st century competencies beyond the scope of undergraduate or traditional police academy training.

REFERENCES

1. Baglivio, M. T., Epps, N., Swartz, K., Huq, M. S., Sheer, A., & Hardt, N. S. (2014). The prevalence of adverse childhood experiences (ACE) in the lives of juvenile offenders. *Journal of Juvenile Justice, 3*(2). Retrieved from: https://static1.squarespace.com/static/63814a32e86ac444e02b316e/t/6387fa3ce873f17c5522616f/1669855806114/Prevalence_of_ACE.pdf (accessed on 14 October 2024).
2. Banks, C. (2003). *Women in Prison: A Reference Handbook.* ABC-CLIO. p. 5.
3. Baranyi, G., Cassidy, M., Fazel, S., Priebe, S., & Mundt, A. P. (2018). Prevalence of posttraumatic stress disorder in prisoners. *Epidemiologic Reviews, 40*(1), 134–145. https://www.ncbi.nlm.nih.gov/pmc/articles/PMC5982805/ (accessed on 14 October 2024).
4. Bronson, J., Stroop, J., Zimmer, S., & Berzofsky, M. (2017). Drug use, dependence, and abuse among state prisoners and jail inmates, 2007–2009 (NCJ 250546). Bureau of Justice Statistics. https://bjs.ojp.gov/content/pub/pdf/dudaspji0709.pdf (accessed on 14 October 2024).
5. Byrne, J. M., Pattavina, A., & Taxman, F. S. (2015). International trends in prison upsizing and downsizing: In search of evidence of a global rehabilitation revolution. *Victims & Offenders, 10*(4), 420–451. https://doi.org/10.1080/15564886.2015.1078186.
6. Campbell, J. C., Anderson, J. C., McFadgion, A., Gill, J., Zink, E., Patch, M., & Campbell, D. (2018). The effects of intimate partner violence and probable traumatic brain injury on central nervous system symptoms. *Journal of Women's Health, 27*(6), 761–767. https://doi.org/10.1089/jwh.2016.6311.
7. Chuck, E. (2014). "Frequent and severe" sexual violence alleged at women's prison in Alabama. *US News*.
8. Costello, K., & Greenwald, B. D. (2022). Update on domestic violence and traumatic brain injury: A narrative review. *Brain Sciences, 12*(1), 122. https://www.ncbi.nlm.nih.gov/pmc/articles/PMC8773525/#B11-brainsci-12-00122 (accessed on 14 October 2024).
9. Council on Criminal Justice. (2023). The footprint: Tracking the size of America's criminal justice system. https://counciloncj.foleon.com/the-footprint-trends-in-crime-arrests-and-the-total-correctional-population/the-footprint/ (accessed on 14 October 2024).
10. Covington, S. (1998). The relational theory of women's psychological development: Implications for the criminal justice system. Presented

at the 50th Annual Meeting of the American Society of Criminology. https://www.centerforgenderandjustice.org/site/assets/files/1545/relationaltheory.pdf (accessed on 14 October 2024).

11. Daly, K. (1992). Women's pathways to felony court: Feminist theories of lawbreaking and problems of representation. *Southern California Review of Law & Women's Studies, 2*, 11. https://heinonline.org/HOL/LandingPage?handle=hein.journals/scws2&div=8&id=&page= (accessed on 14 October 2024).
12. Evans, M., Gregory, A., Feder, G., Howarth, E., & Hegarty, K. (2016). "Even 'daily' is not enough": How well do we measure domestic violence and abuse? —A think-aloud study of a commonly used self-report scale. *Violence & Victims, 31*(1), 3–26. https://doi.org/10.1891/0886-6708.VV-D-15-00024.
13. Greene, C. A., Ford, J. D., Wakefield, D. B., & Barry, L. C. (2014). Posttraumatic stress mediates the relationship between childhood victimization and current mental health burden in newly incarcerated adults. *Child Abuse & Neglect, 38*(10), 1569–1580. http://dx.doi.org/10.1016/j.chiabu.2014.07.006.
14. Hartney, C. (2006). US rates of incarceration: A global perspective. Research from the National Council on Crime and Delinquency.
15. Jeffries, S., & Newbold, G. (2016). Analysing trends in the imprisonment of women in Australia and New Zealand. *Psychiatry, Psychology, and Law, 23*(2), 184–206. https://doi.org/10.1080/13218719.2015.1035619.
16. Messina, N., & Grella, C. (2006). Childhood trauma and women's health outcomes in a California prison population. *American Journal of Public Health, 96*(10), 1842–1848. https://www.ncbi.nlm.nih.gov/pmc/articles/PMC1586137/ (accessed on 14 October 2024).
17. Messina, N., Grella, C. E., Cartier, J., & Torres, S. (2009). A randomized experimental study of gender-responsive substance abuse treatment for women in prison. *Journal of Substance Abuse Treatment, 38*(2), 97–107. https://doi.org/10.1016/j.jsat.2009.09.004.
18. Office of Juvenile Justice and Delinquency Prevention. (2024). Youth in the adult criminal justice system. Literature review: A product of the model programs guide. https://ojjdp.ojp.gov/model-programs-guide/literature-reviews/youth-in-the-adult-criminal-justice-system (accessed on 14 October 2024).
19. Parveen, N. (2018). Transgender prisoner who sexually assaulted inmates jailed for life. *The Guardian*.

20. Rafter, N. H. (1985). *Partial Justice: Women in State Prisons, 1800–1935*. Northeastern University Press. ISBN 978-0930350635.
21. Reynolds, M. (2008). The war on drugs, prison building, and globalization: Catalysts for the global incarceration of women. *NWSA Journal, 20*(1).
22. Saxena, P., & Messina, N. (2021). Trajectories of victimization to violence among incarcerated women. *Health & Justice, 9*, 1–12. https://link.springer.com/article/10.1186/s40352-021-00144-8.

Chapter 9

LGBTQ+ Rights and Legal Challenges

Contents

INTRODUCTION

LGBT is an acronym for Lesbian, gay, bisexual, and transgender. Rather than being limited to lesbian, gay, bisexual, or transgender individuals, it can also apply to anyone who identifies as non-heterosexual, non-heteroromantic, or non-cisgender. While LGBTQ+ adds a plus sign for members of the community for whom LGBTQ does not fully capture or reflect their identity, the LGBTQ variant adds a Q for those who identify as queer (which can be synonymous with LGBT) or who are unsure of their sexual or gender identity. There are many more variations of the acronym that exist, like 2SLGBTQ+ (adding two-spirit for a term specific to Indigenous North Americans), LGBTQIA+ (adding intersex, asexual, aromantic, and agender), and LGBT+ (simplified to encompass the Q concept within the plus sign). Not everyone agrees that the LGBT label encompasses everything that it is meant to. The acronym's letters are rearranged in the GLBT and GLBTQ variants. The initialism, along with a few of its popular variations, has served as a catch-all term for marginalized gender identities and sexualities since its introduction in the late 1980s. Some people favor the umbrella term queer. In the late 1980s, the term gay (or gay and lesbian) started to be replaced with the earlier initialism LGB to refer to the larger community. The abbreviated LGB is still in use when transgender persons are not included.

9.1. CONCEPT OF LGBT

Lesbian, gay, bisexual, and transgender/transsexual individuals make up the LGBT community. It is acknowledged, nevertheless, that not everyone whose gender identity is not predicated on a conventional gender binary or whose sexuality is not heterosexual is necessarily included in those four letters. The symbol '+' is utilized to encompass individuals whose identities defy conventional binary concepts of male and female, or who choose to identify themselves with alternative categories that reflect their gender identity or personal sexuality. This will encompass those who identify as pansexual—individuals drawn to all sexes and genders—questioning—individuals who investigate their sexual orientation or/and gender identity—or queer—a general term designating people who do not fit into established norms. But keep in mind that some people might not want to associate themselvear categorycategory.

In addition, the term "LGBTQ community" is frequently used to describe any LGBTQ person, regardless of gender identity, culture, or location, as well as groups of LGBTQ people who engage in or support LGBTQ activism. LGBTQ is frequently expanded in corresponding ways, as in LGBTQIA, or is rendered more simply as LGBTQ+. LGBTQ communities have been understood to encompass a variety of sexual orientations and identities beyond those directly referred to in the acronym LGBTQ since the early 21st century, among them, for example, "questioning," "intersex," and "agender."

9.1.1. Sexual Orientations and Gender Identities

The definition of sexual orientation and its relationship to gender identity are frequently unclear. Patterns of emotional, romantic, and sexual attraction to other people are referred to as sexual orientation. There are three sexual orientations that exist traditionally:

- heterosexual (attraction to people of the opposite sex),
- bisexual (attraction to people of both sexes) and
- homosexual (attraction to people of the same sex).

There are many more labels that can be used to characterize the range of sexual identities besides these three. There is a wide range of options between heterosexual and homosexual on the sexual orientation continuum. Moreover, some individuals might choose not to associate themselves with a specific sexual orientation. Some individuals do not identify as homosexual, even though they have relationships with other men or women. They may have sex with individuals of the other sex while doing so, but they do not wish to be labeled as bisexual. There is no consensus on the factors that determine sexual orientation; current research considers both environmental factors and biological factors, such as genes, brain structure, or hormones. Sexual orientation cannot be changed on a whim and is not something that can be chosen or preferred. Other labels for sexual orientation include plurisexual (referring to people who are attracted to people of multiple genders) and monosexual (referring to people who feel attracted to people of one gender).

People who identify as LGBT+ may choose to come out as gay or lesbian. "Coming out" or "coming out of the closet" refers to this process. Usually, friends, acquaintances, and family are the first to get involved. But coming out is not required, and it should always be a matter of person each individualeveryone as to whether or not to tell others. Nobody should feel compelled or under pressure to come out. Acknowledging and accepting one's own sexual orientation and/or gender identity is typically the first step towards coming out. LGBT+ persons frequently reside in communities that are intolerant of those who don't fit the mold. As a result, coming out can be a very difficult process that is frequently fraught with danger and anxiety about being rejected, laughed at, harassed, or even physically attacked. It can be extremely stressful and frustrating to hide one's gender identity and/or sexual orientation and to be unable to communicate one's own needs for an extended period of time. Coming out helps people get over these bad emotions and, for many, can result in a sense of relief, particularly when they receive an encouraging and accepting response. It might also be linked to a genuine risk of violence or rejection, though.

The coming out process is associated with controversy. Certain LGBT+ movements highlight the affirmative and positive impact that coming out can have. They contend that public disclosure, particularly from well-known figures, increases societal acceptance of LGBT+ individuals. However, a lot of queer theorists think that this is the same as self-labelling, where a person labels themselves as part of an oppressive system where sexual orientations other than heterosexual are linked to negative traits and connotations. This serves as more evidence that the choice to come out or not should be made privately and after careful thought. Individuals experience coming out in different ways, and it may take some time for them to feel confident and at ease enough to discuss it with others. In order to assist young people in their process of coming out, youth work is crucial. When a young person chooses to come out to a youth worker who is close to them, the youth worker needs to be ready to listen, show compassion and understanding, and maintain an open mind. The young person is sharing a very significant and intimate item. A youth worker should direct a young person seeking assistance to organizations that offer specialized support and counseling to LGBT+ individuals if they are unsure of how to respond to them or believe they require more guidance.

9.1.2. LGBT+ Movements

The emergence of an urban gay and lesbian culture in the 1920s and 1930s is credited with giving rise to the organized LGBT+ movements. The development of homosexual organizations started only after World War II. In 1946, a group of gay men and later lesbian women met in the Netherlands under the moniker "The Shakespeare Club," which they later renamed C. O. C. This was an abbreviation for the "Centre for Culture and Leisure," which was first used following the organization's founding. C. O. C. is regarded as the world's oldest organization for lesbian, gay, bisexual, and transgender people.

The first lesbian and gay organizations in the United States were founded in 1950 in Los Angeles by a small group of men who founded the Mattachine Society. The Daughters of Bilitis, a San Francisco-based lesbian organization with a predominantly male membership, joined the Society in 1955. The inception of the homosexual political movement is commonly linked to the events of June 27, 1969, when the New York City police raided The Stonewall Inn, a gay bar located in Greenwich Village. Contrary to predictions, the bar's patrons retaliated, sparking three nights of rioting and the painting of "gay power" slogans on nearby buildings. A broad grassroots movement for gay liberation emerged almost immediately. Due in large part to the radicmen, African-AmericansAfrican Americans, and anti-war demonstrators in the 1960s, homosexuals contested all forms of discrimination and punishment that society had imposed on them. By making the decision to "come out of the closet" and reveal their identities in public, they significantly accelerated a larger movement for social change.

Lesbian and gay communities in Western Europe have evolved from being an underground subculture to a well-organized community, especially in larger cities. These developments are generally observed in these countries. This frequently entails bringing people together through gay-friendly businesses, political clubs, social service organizations, community centers, and places of worship. Openly gay candior office in a number ofseveral places. Gay men and lesbian women realized during these battles that they did not and would not fit into the socially accepted gender norms. In addition to questioning the heterosexual norm, homosexuals also questioned stereotypes of what men and women ought to look like, act like, and play in society. These challenges to oppressive social norms have been met with dramatic methods that have raised awareness of the struggles, like lesbian women "kissing in" on a German town square. They have also frequently employed conventional political strategies like advocacy and lobbying. The inclusion of LGBT issues in discussions on equal opportunities, human rights, and general social policy has been greatly aided by the presence of openly gay and lesbian politicians as well as groups like the International Lesbian and Gay Association (ILGA) and the International Gay, Lesbian, Bisexual and Transgender Youth and Students Organization (IGLYO).

June was declared LGBT Pride month in response to the Stonewall riots, and since then, numerous LGBT Pride festivals and marches have been planned worldwide (though in some areas, they also happen at other times). In addition to encouraging equality, dignity, and self-affirmation, these festivals and marches have grown in importance as a means of mainstreaming the LGBT+ movement and raising awareness of its members.

9.1.3. Gender-based violence towards LGBT+ people

When gender-based violence is brought up, violence against LGBT+ individuals is frequently disregarded. For instance, it is not uncommon for those who injure LGBT+ persons to "justify" their acts by expressing distaste for homosexual masculinities or gay sexuality. In addition to being a result of insufficient institutional and legal protections for LGBT+ individuals in many European and other countries, gender-based violence against LGBT+ people is also a result of ignorance of this type of violence. Terms like "homophobia," "biphobia," and "transphobia" refer to feelings of fear, distaste, or animosity toward lesbian, gay, bisexual, and transgender individuals. Such animosity is typically fueled by deeply held preconceptions and stereotypes as well as a negative social and political environment that marginalizes LGBT+ people. It can appear in a variety of ways, such as:

- Utilizing taunts, insulting jokes, or language that disparages LGBT+ individuals. Even when these statements are made with good intentions, LGBT+ persons may suffer as a result.
- School bullying can take many different forms, including exclusion, violent crimes against young LGBT+ people, and threats. Young people who experience such behavior frequently feel scared, hurt, or excluded. Additionally, some schools may have a very hostile environment toward individuals who don't fit into traditional gender roles, which could unintentionally or purposely encourage homophobia, biphobia, or transphobia.
- Hate crimes and hate speech: Hate crimes, particularly online, are a common occurrence for young LGBT+ people. This might not always be the result of personal t+ individuals as a whole maymay still be impacted by general targeting. Young LGBTuffer greatly as a result ofbecause of such behavior; it undermines their sense of self-worth and confidence, obstructs their coming-out process, and makes them feel alone. Suicidal thoughts have been sparked by hate speech directed towards LGBT+ individuals. Hate crimes are acts of violence against another person that are driven by prejudice and intolerance against that person due to that person's real or perceived race, ethnicity, national origin, sexual orientation, gender identity, religion, or disability, among other reasons. A few examples of hate crimes are assault, harassment, insults, rape, torture, property damage, and murder.
- Discrimination includes things like preventing young LGBT+ people from attending school or finding employment, not having gender-neutral restrooms for those who don't identify as assigned sex or a particular gender, having limited or no access to medical care, and having insufficient laws allowing non-heterosexual couples to form legally recognized partnerships or unions.
- Other forms of violence include coercing gays and lesbians into therapy that changes their sexual orientation; these practices are currently prohibited in many nations. In certain nations, having a sexual orientation other than heterosexual is illegal and punishable by law, including the death penalty.

9.1.3.1. Domestic violence in LGBT relationships

Because few people haveg with the particular aspectsaspects of domestic violence in same-sex relationships and because "mainstream" services for domestic violence do not always recognize it, it is more difficult for victims and the services providing support to identify domestic violence in LGBT+ relationships. Nonetheless, data indicates that the incidence of violence in relationships involving heterosexuals, homosexuals, and lesbians is roughly equal (one in four). The main points of similarity and difference between domestic violence against people of the same gender and people of the opposite gender are outlined below. Similarities include the type of abuse, the victim's potential for isolation, the perpetrator's control over them, and the workings of the "cycle of violence."

Differences include:

a) **Isolation.** Being LGBT+ in a homophobic society can exacerbate the isolation that comes with domestic abuse. Within the LGBT+ community, silence about domestic abuse further isolates the victim and increases the abuser's power. The issue of a small community space within LGBT+ networks is another one. Maintaining privacy and ending a relationship may be more challenging in these situations.

b) **Heterosexist manipulation.** Threats to "speak out about" a victim's gender identity or sexual orientation to friends, family, coworkers, or a landlord are common among abusers. Furthermore, it's possible that someone receiving current support services will be forced to "come out" against their will.

c) **Fear of further oppression.** The LGBT+ community, being a marginalized and misrepresented group, is frequently reluctant to confront matters that they believe will further tarnish their reputation.

d) **Gender myths.** People assume that two men in a fight must be equals. Similarly, gay, bi- sexual and transgendered (GBT) men often reject the idea that they can be victims. Given social assumptions about 'deviance,' it might also be assumed that the violence is part of a sadomasochistic relationship.

e) **The context of historical oppression.** LGBT+ individuals should proceed with extreme caution when contacting shelters, social service organizations, domestic violence services, law enforcement, and courts. LGBT+ victims may worry about becoming victims again as a result of homophobia, incredulity, rejection, and dehumanization from organizations with a track record of marginalizing, hostile, and violently attacking the LGBT community.

9.1.4. The LGBT Community

A broad coalition of groups that are diverse in terms of gender, sexual orientation, race/ethnicity, and socioeconomic status is referred to as the "lesbian, gay, bisexual, and transgender community" (or "LGBT community"). The committee therefore wants to emphasize how important it is to understand that the various populations represented by the letters "L," "G," "B," and "T" are distinct groups, each with its own unique health-related concerns and needs, even though this report focuses on the community contained within the acronym LGBT. Because these groups are frequently treated as a single population under umbrella terms like LGBT in popular media and some modern scientific discourse, the committee feels it is imperative to highlight these differences at the outset of this report. In addition, these groups share a number of experiences, chief among them being the experience of stigmatization, as will be covered in more detail below.

Sexual orientation, which is commonly understood in terms of sexual attraction, behavior, identity, or some combination of these dimensions, defines lesbians, gay men, and bisexual men and women. They both acknowledge that they are not exclusively heterosexual in terms of sexual orientation. However, this category of "nonheterosexuals" encompasses both genders; homosexual and bisexual people; those who identify as gay, lesbian, or bisexual, among other terms; and those who do not identify as such but nevertheless feel attracted to or participate in same-sex relationships. Each group's health is significantly impacted by these differences, as the report explains throughout.

Unlike lesbians, gay men, and bisexual men and women, transgender individuals are identified by their gender presentation and identity. This group includes people whose gender expression deviates markedly from what is customarily associated with or typical for that sex, or whose gender identity is different from the sex originally assigned to them at birth (i.e., individuals who defy or reject conventional cultural conceptions of gender in terms of the male-female dichotomy, as well as those who identify as male at birth but later identify as female and those who identify as female at birth but later identify as male. The gender identity, expression, and sexual orientation of transgender people vary widely. While some transgender people have had medical procedures to change their sexual anatomy and physiology, others do not want to have such operations done in the future. It is possible for transgender individuals to identify as heterosexual, homosexual, or bisexual. While most gay men, bisexuals, and lesbians are not transgender, some are. Transgender individuals who identify as male to female are referred to as MtF, transgender females, or transwomen, and those who identify as female to male are referred to as FtM, transgender males, or transmen. Not all transgender individuals fall into one of these binary classifications. Health disparities exist between transgender individuals and nontransgender individuals, as well as between transgender males and females, as one might anticipate.

While the term "LGBT" is a useful and appropriate way to describe the collective populations of lesbian, gay, bisexual, and transgender individuals, it can also mask the multitude of distinctions that exist between these groups of people who identify as sexual and gender minorities. For example, putting gay men and lesbians under the same umbrella obscures the differences in gender experiences among homosexuals. Similarly, combining the experiences of men and women who identify as bisexual tends to mask gender differences. Furthermore, "LGB" leaves out individuals whose experience includes same-sex attractions or behaviors but who do not adopt a nonheterosexual identity, to the extent that lesbian, gay, and bisexual are understood as identity labels. Furthermore, the needs and concerns of the transgender population—which is made up of many different groups—are different from those of lesbians, bisexual women and men, and gay men. As previously mentioned, there are significant similarities among the populations that comprise the LGBT community in addition to their numerous differences.

9.1.4.1. Commonalities among LGBT Populations

The committee believes that the main commonality among lesbians, gay men, bisexual women and men, and transgender people is their historically marginalized social status relative to society's cultural norm of the exclusively heterosexual individual who complies with traditional gender roles and expectations. This makes lesbians, gay men, bisexual women and men, and transgender people an appropriate focus for this report as a combined population. Stated differently, these groups are considered "other" due to the fact that their members defy heterosexuality and gender norms. Because of their "otherness," they are the target of stigma, which breeds prejudice, discrimination, and violence. These factors also contribute to the general disregard for their health needs by society and many of the health disparities covered in this report. For some, additional aspects of inequality like race, ethnicity, and socioeconomic status may exacerbate this "otherness," leading to stigma on several levels.

Picture a society in which gender nonconformity, same-sex attraction, and same-sex sexual behavior are widely acas normal aspects of the human experience in order toto gain a better understanding of the relationship between health and sexuality- and gender-related stigma. There would be no discrimination, no social stigma, and no embarrassment or personal shame associated with belonging to any of the groups that make up LGBT in this world. LGBTQ people's health would be threatened by a wide range of issues in this world, including major chronic illnesses like cancer and heart disease, infectious diseases, mental health disorders, environmental hazards, the threat of violence and terrorism, and many other factors that compromise human "physical, mental, and social well-being." Overall though, these problems would be the same as those that face the majority of people. Particularly for LGBT people, only a few characteristics would stand out. If the Institute of Medicine (IOM) released a report on LGBT health issues, there would be minimal justification for it.

But the idealized world this thought experiment describes is not the one we live in. Lesbians, gay men, bisexuals, and transgender people have not historically been understood or accepted as belonging to the normal range of human experience. Rather, they have been stigmatized as abnormal people. Ithe full range of health risks that the general publicpublic faces, LGBT individuals also face a significant and poorly understood set of additional health risks, primarily as a result of social stigma. Although the experience of stigma varies amongst sexual and gender minorities, stigmatization has a significant impact on all of these group's lives and consequently has an impact on their health. Unlike members of many other marginalized groups, LGBT people are often invisible to researchers and healthcare professionals. If we are to eradicate the health disparities covered in this report, one of the most important goals is to overcome this invisibleness in health care services and research settings.

It's crucial to remember that LGBT people have not been the helpless targets of prejudice and discrimination, despite the stigma that members of sexual and gender minority groups frequently experience. LGBT people have made significant progress in the last few decades in creating a community infrastructure that meets their health needs and in getting government and scientific bodies to acknowledge their health concerns. These accomplishments attest to their dedication to fighting stigma and actively pursuing equal treatment in all spheres of their lives, including having access to quality healthcare and closing gaps in health care. In fact, some of the research includeport shows how remarkably resilient these population'spopulations' psychological makeup can be, even when faced with significant stress. As this report explains, stigma against sexual and gender minorities in modern-day America poses a number of difficulties for researchers and medical professionals. For example, many lesbian, gay, bisexual, and transgender people choose not to disclose their gender identity or sexual orientation to researchers or medical professionals out of fear of discrimination and prejudice. Furthermore, researchers who choose to study LGBT issues run the risk of being marginalized or discredited regardless of their own sexual orientation or gender identity (Kempner, 2008), and healthcare professionals rarely receive training in particular issues related to the care of LGBT patients.

9.1.4.2. ***Differences within LGBT Populations***

In addition to being distinct populations in and of themselves, lesbians, gay men, bisexual women and men, and transgender people are also diverse groups whose members differ greatly in terms of age, race and ethnicity, location, social background, religiositraphic traits. This report specifically takes into accountconsiders a few significant subgroups of the LGBT population because many of these variables are closely linked to health status, health concerns, and access to care. These subgroups include:

- **Age cohort**—Age has an impact on needs and experiences. Compared to older lesbians who can't find appropriate grief counseling services or gay adult men without health insurance, bisexual adolescents who are struggling with coming out in an unsupportive environment have different health needs. Furthermore, no two people develop in the same way at any given age. A self-identified "queer" youth who comes out during her adolescent years may not go through the developmental process in the s an older adult who comes out as gay in his 50s. Similar toLike this, experiences throughout life vary depending on the era in which people are born, as will be covered in more detail below. An adolescent coming out in 2010 would, for instance, encounter a different milieu than one coming out in the 1960s. Furthermore, some people see changes in their relationships and sexual attraction throughout their lives. For instance, some transgender individuals are clearly nonconforming of gender roles when they are young and come out at a young age, while others are able to conform and might wait until much later in life to come out.
- **Race and ethnicity**—An LGBT person's experiences are shaped by ideas of community, traditional roles, religiosity, and cultural influences related to race and ethnicity. The degree to which an individual identifies with the LGBT community, the process of coming out, the availability of support, the affirmation of gender-variant expression, and other factors that ultimately impact health outcomes are all influenced by the racial and ethnic communities to which they belong. LGBT non-Hispanic white people may have very different experiences than members of racial and ethnic minority groups.

- **Educational level and socioeconomic status**—The social standing and educational attainment of an LGBT person influence how they interact with society. Since income levels are typically correlated with educational attainment, community members with higher education levels may reside in better neighborhoods with better access to healthcare and be able to lead healthier lives thanks to things like grocery stores that carry fresh produce and safe walking areas. Conversely, LGBT individuals who drop out of school or reside in underprivileged areas might face greater obstacles to receiving care, which could lead to worse health outcomes.
- **Geographic location**—For LGBT people, geographic location has a big impact on their physical and mental health outcomes. Rural or less LGBT-populated areas may make someone feel less at ease coming out, provide less family and friend support, and make it harder for them to connect with the LGBT community. It's possible that LGBT people living in rural areas have less access to medical professionals who are at ease or knowledgeable about treating LGBT patients. On the other hand, LGBT persons residing in places with greater LGBT populations might have greater access to support services and medical professionals who specialize in treating LGBT patients.

Although these areas represent critical dimensions of the experiences of LGBT individuals, the relationships of these variables to health care disparities and health status have not been extensively studied.

9.2. LGBT RIGHTS

People all over the world suffer from injustice, brutality, and occasionally even execution due to their identity, appearance, or the people they love. Gender identity and sexual orientation are essential parts of who we are and should never be the source of abuse or discrimination. Human Rights Watch advocates for the rights of LGBT+ individuals, with its activists representing a wide range of identities and concerns. We gather information about and reveal global abuses related to sexual orientation and gender identity, such as torture, executions, killings, arrests under false pretenses, unfair treatment, censorship, medical mistreatment, discrimination in employment and housing, domestic abuse, abuses of children, and denial of family rights and recognition. We support legislation and regulations that uphold the dignity of every individual. Our goal is for everyone to be able to fully enjoy their rights in the world. Lesbian, homosexual, bisexual, transgender, and other individuals who do not fit into conventional gender or sexuality categories are all entitled to human rights known as LGBT+ rights. However, in reality, these rights are frequently not as well-protected heterosexual and cisgender individuals. LGBT+ rights include, butinclude but are not limited to: social rights (e.g., changing legal gender, engaging in intimate relationships, getting married, adopting children from the same sex, and not facing discrimination at work); economic rights (e.g., not being discriminated against at work); political rights (e.g., being able to publicly advocate for themselves and their communities). LGBT+ people are able to live fulfilling lives because these rights are protected.

9.2.1. Gay Rights Prior to the 20th Century

Religious proscriptions against same-sex relationships—especiallnd women—long stigmatized this kind of behavior, but the majority ofmost European legal codes said nothing about homosexuality or bisexuality. Many predominantly Muslim nation's legal systems applied Islamic law (Sharīah) in a variety of ways, criminalizing and punishing many sexual or quasi-sexual acts—including same-sex intimacy—with harsh consequences that could even include death.

Lawmakers in England started classifying male-to-male sex relationships as criminal rather than merely immoral in the 16th century. During Henry VIII's reign in the 1530s, England passed the Buggery Act, making male-to-male sex a crime with a death sentence. Up until 1861, sodomy in England and Great Britain was still a capital offense, carrying a hanging sentence. Two decades later, in 1885, an amendment sponsored by Henry Du Pré Labouchere was passed by Parliament, making any form of sexual behavior between men punishable by law (lesbian sexual relations, on the other hand, were exempt from prosecution because they were unthinkable to male legislators). Similarly, in the early 1870s, when Germany was combining the civil codes of several independent kingdoms, Paragraph 175 of the German penal code was added. This provision outlawed same-sex male relationships and imposed penalties such as detention and loss of civil rights.

9.2.1.1. The Beginning of the Gay Rights Movement

Gay rights "movements" were very rare before the end of the 19th century. In fact, Oscar Wilde's lover, Lord Alfred ("Bosie") Douglas, wrote, "I [homosexuality] am the love that dare not speak its name" in his poem "Two Loves" (1894). The establishment of the Scientific-Humanitarian Committee (Wissenschaftlich-humanitäres Komitee; WhK) in Berlin in 1897 gave voice to homosexual and bisexual men and women. They started by circulating a petition to have the Imperial Penal Code's Paragraph 175 repealed. By 1922, the committee had established about 25 local chapters and had published emancipation literature, organized rallies, and pushed for legislative reform throughout Germany, the Netherlands, and Austria. Magnus Hirschfeld, one of the founders of WhK, established the Institute for Sexual Science (Institut für Sexualwissenschaft) in 1919. Decades later, other scientific institutions with a focus on sex research, like the Kinsey Institute for Research in Sex, Gender, and Reproduction in the United States, were anticipated by this establishment. In 1928, at a conference held in Copenhagen, he also contributed to the establishment of the World League of Sexual Reform as a sponsor.

Gay and bisexual men and women enjoyed some degree of freedom in Germany, especially during the Weimar period, which was the time between the end of World War I and the Nazi takeover, despite Paragraph 175 and the WhK's failure to get its repeal. Gay nightlife was accepted in many larger German cities, and there were more gay publications available. In fact, some historians claim that in Berlin in the 1920s, there were more gay bars and publications than in New York City sixty years later. This comparatively liberal era came to an end with the rise of Adolf Hitler to power. He gave the order to enforce Paragraph 175 more strictly, and on May 6, 1933, German student athletes set fire to the institute's materials in a public square and ransacked Hirschfeld's archives. Other organizations were established outside of Germany as well. For instance, Edward Carpenter and Havelock Ellis established the British Society for the Study of Sex Psychology in 1914 with the dual goals of promotion and education, and German immigrant Henry Gerber established the Illinois-chartered Society for Human Right

Even with the establishment of these groups, homosexuals and bisexual'sbisexuals' political activity was typically very covert. It's true that police frequently harassed gays wherever they gathered. The Second World War and its aftermath started to alter that. The war increased the number of young people moving to cities and raised awareness of the LGBT community. The government and the police in particular reacted negatively to this increased visibility in the United States: they frequently fired gay civil servants, the military tried to expel gay soldiers from their ranks (a practice that dates back to World War II), and police vice squads regularly raided gay bars and detained their patrons. Gays did, however, also engage in more political activity, primarily focused on decriminalizing sodomy.

9.2.1.2. The Gay Rights Movement Since the Mid-20th Century

Gay organizations started to spring up in greater numbers starting in the middle of the 20th century. In Amsterdam, the Cultuur en Ontspannings Centrum, also known as the "Culture and Recreation Center," was established in 1946. The Mattachine Society was the first significant male organization in the United

States, founded in 1950–1951 by Harry Hay in Los Angeles. The name of the organization is said to have originated from a medieval French society of masked players, the Société Mattachine, to symbolize the public "masking" of homosexuality. Meanwhile, the Daughters of Bilitis, named after Pierre Louÿs' Sapphic love poems, Chansons de Bilitis, were a prominent women's organization, founded in 1955 by Phyllis Lyon and Del Martin in San Francisco. Additionally, a national gay periodical called One was published in the US and won a U.S. S. decision by the Supreme Court allowing it to be mailed through the U. S. Postal Service. A decade later, Parliament enacted the recommendation in the form of the Sexual Offenses Act, which removed private homosexual liaisons between consenting adults from the purview of criminal law. The groundbreaking report, known as the Wolfenden Report, was released in 1957 by a commission headed by Sir John Wolfenden.

Though the gay rights movement was starting to succeed in enacting laws, especially in western Europe, the United States may have been the single country where gay activism truly took off. The Stonewall Inn, a gay bar in Greenwich Village, New York City, was raided by the police early on June 28, 1969. A 45-minute riot that drew nearly 400 participants continued the following nights. Gay Pride celebrations are held in June each year to honor "Stonewall," not just in the U.S. S. cities as well as a number of other nations (some countries also host Gay Pride events at other times of the year). Gay political organizations grew rapidly in the 1970s and 1980s, especially in the US and Europe, and expanded to other regions of the world, though there were wide variations in their success, size, and level of acceptance by the government. Organizations advocating for legal and social reforms included the Human Rights Campaign, the National Gay and Lesbian Task Force, ACT UP (AIDS Coalition to Unleash Power) in the United States, Stonewall and Outrage! In the United Kingdom, and several dozen other similar groups in continental Europe and beyond. Furthermore, in Coventry, England, the transnational International Lesbian and Gay Association was established in 1978. Having changed its name to the International Lesbian, Gay, Bisexual, Trans and Intersex Association (ILGA World) and moved its headquarters to Geneva, the organization is now a major player in coordinating global initiatives to advance human rights and combat prejudice against LGBTQ and intersex people.

When the Democratic Party included a plank regarding sexual orientation in its nondiscrimination clause, gay activists in the US gained support from the party in 1980. This encouragement, combined with campaigns by gay activists pushing gay men and women to "come out of the closet" (in fact, National Coming Out Day was created in the late 1980s and is observed on October 11 in most countries today), pushed gay men and women to run for office. Ann Arbor,

Michigan residents Jerry DeGrieck and Nancy Wechsler were the country's first openly gay public servants. In 1972, both DeGrieck and Wechsler were elected to the city council and came out. Wechsler was replaced on the council in 1974 by Kathy Kozachenko, who became the first openly gay person to win office after coming out by running as a lesbian. Harvey Milk, a gay rights activist, was elected to the San Francisco Board of Supervisors in 1977. The following year, he was assassinated. 1983 saw Gerry Studds, a U.S. S. a representative from Massachusetts, made history by being the first elected official to come out as gay. Barney Frank, an additional U.S. S. While serving in Congress in the 1980s, the Massachusetts House of Representatives also came out. Into the twenty-first century, he remained a significant figure in the Democratic Party and that body. Tammy Baldwin, a politician from Wisconsin, made history by being the first to be elected to both the U.S. S. 1998's House and the U.S. S. Senate in 2012. When Annise Parker was elected mayor of Houston in 2009, the city became the fourth largest in the United States. S. the largest to choose an openly gay politician as mayor at that point. Furthermore, Pete Buttigieg became the first openly gay cabinet member in American history two years after Lori Lightfoot was elected as the first openly gay mayor of Chicago in 2019.

Securing marriage rights for same-sex couples (see same-sex marriage) and fighting the HIV/AIDS epidemic, as well as advocating for funding for research and nondiscriminatory policies in housing, employment, and other spheres of civil society, are other major issues that have been central to the gay rights movement since the 1970s. Additionally, the ban on gay and lesbian individuals serving in the military must be lifted. In 2010 Democratic Pres. Acts signed by Barack Obama invalidated the U.S. s. gays and lesbians to serve in the military provided they kept their sexual orientation a secret and abstained from engaging in homosexual behavior. This policy, known as "Don't Ask, Don't Tell," was repealed in 2011, thereby ending the military's prohibition on homosexuals. Same-sex couple's ability to get married was acknowledged by the Supreme Court in 2013 (Obergefell v. Hodges) and in 2020 the Court held that it was unlawful to fire a worker for being gay or transgender in accordance with Title VII of the Civil Rights Act (1964), which forbids discrimination based on sexual orientation (Bostock v. Clayton County, Georgia.

9.2.2. Lesbian Rights

Lesbian rights are those social and legal protections that guarantee lesbian people receive equal treatment and respect in all spheres of life. These rights, which are a subset of LGBTQ+ rights, are concentrated on the particular difficulties and prejudice that lesbian women encounter because of their sexual orientation. Lesbians have faced discrimination and marginalization throughout history, including violence, legal repercussions, and social exclusion. The struggle for equal treatment in areas like marriage, adoption, employment, healthcare, and protection from hate crimes is a part of the lesbian rights movement. Lesbians have gained significant legal rights around the world, including the ability to marry, adopt children, and receive spousal benefits. The scope of these rights, however, differs greatly amongst nations, as some continue to outlaw same-sex unions or refuse to recognize lesbian partnerships as legitimate. Given that lesbians experience discrimination based on both their sexual orientation and gender, lesbian rights are frequently recognized in conjunction with more general women's rights issues.

Many lesbians have played important roles in activism and advocacy for the LGBTQ+ rights movement, which has been closely linked to the lesbian rights movement. Lesbian rights and the feminist movement are intertwined, especially when it comes to promoting reproductive rights, shielding victims of domestic abuse, and dispelling gender stereotypes. Lesbian women continue to face particular difficulties despite advancements in many areas, such as the dual discrimination of sexism and homophobia, which can lead to exclusion from both the LGBTQ+ and feminist communities. Lesbian rights pertain to the social acceptance and integration of lesbian identities in media representation, public life, and cultural narratives. This entails combating damaging stereotypes and elevating lesbian relationships and individual's visibility. Lesbian rights also require a strong push for inclusive education, where sexual orientation is accepted and valued. Lesbian rights are essentially about making sure that lesbian people have the same opportunities, rights, and protections as everyone else, and can live freely and authentically without worrying about prejudice or injury. In order to ensure that lesbian women's voices are heard and their rights are upheld in all spheres of life, the ongoing fight for these rights emphasizes the significance of intersectional approaches.

9.2.3. Transgender Rights

The term "transgender rights" refers to the legal, social, and human rights that are intended to guarantee that transgender people receive equal treatment, equality, and dignity in all spheres of life. Individuals who identify as transgender are those whose gender identity is different from the sex they were assigned at birth. They are fighting for their rights against discriminatory practices, legal frameworks, and deeply ingrained social norms that frequently marginalize them. These rights include the freedom to live a life that is consistent with one's gender identity without encountering prejudice, violence, or discrimination.

Legal recognition of gender identity is one of the central tenets of transgender rights. This includes the freedom to modify one's name and gender marker on official records, such as passports, driver's licenses, and birth certificates, without encountering unjustified obstacles. For transgender people to travel, access services, and engage fully in society without having their identity questioned or invalidated, legal recognition is essential. However, there are significant regional differences in how simple it is for transgender individuals to exercise these rights, with some nations making it difficult or impossible for them to legally change their gender. Another important area where transgender rights are frequently contested is healthcare. In healthcare settings, transgender people frequently experience discrimination. This includes being refused access to essential medical treatments like hormone therapy or gender-affirming surgery. One of the most important aspects of transgender rights is the ability to obtain professional, courteous, and reasonably priced healthcare that caters to the unique needs of transgender individuals. This includes protection from practices like conversion therapy, which aims to alter a person's gender identity, and mental health support. Transgender rights must also include rights to housing and employment. Comparatively speaking to the general population, transgender people experience greater rates of unemployment, homelessness, and poverty because they frequnter high levels of discrimination in the job and when looking for housing. In order toTo guarantee transgender people can live in dignity and security, anti-discrimination laws that shield them from being fired, turned down for employment, or refused housing due to their gender identity are crucial. Another essential component of transgender rights is protection from hate crimes and acts of violence. Transgender people are disproportionately the targets of violence, including physical assaults, harassment, and even murder. This is especially true for transgender women of color. One of the main objectives of the transgender rights movement is to guarantee that laws protecting transgender victims are sensitive and respectful, and that transgender people are protected from hate crimes. In the struggle for transgender rights, acceptance in society and education are also important factors. Advocates strive to guarantee that transgender students are treated with respect, safe, and supportive environments in schools. This includes providing them with facilities that correspond to their gender identity and addressing them using the names and pronouns of their choice. Campaigns for public education and increased visibility are intended to dispel stigma, dispel preconceptions, and advance knowledge of transgender identities.

9.2.4. Global Recognition of Human Rights for Lesbian, Gay, Bisexual, and Transgender People

It is commonly acknowledged that human rights and health are interdependent. All people are entitled to unalienable, indivisible human rights. The Universal

Declaration of Human Rights (UDHR) covers the following topics: equality; freedom from discrimination; life, liberty, and personal security; freedom from torture and degrading treatment; equality before the law; marriage and family rights; and recognition as a person. Articles 1, 2, 3, 5, 6, 7, and 16 of the UDHR address these topics, in that order. Certain groups of people—Lesbian, Gay, Bisexual, and Transgender (LGBT) people in particular—are frequently and everywhere denied their right to the full range of human rights. This is the ultimate human rights violation, putting LGBT people in many countries at risk of abuse, discrimination, ill health, and even death.

Any group of people whose human rights are denied are being denied their humanity, and this has a serious negative influence on their health. LGBT people may face discrimination at work and housing, which can make it difficult for them to afford food, shelter, and medical care; lack of benefits, which can make it difficult to pay for medical care and financial security); stress and harassment, which can harm mental health and/or lead to substance abuse, smoking, overeating, or suicide; isolation, which can cause depression; taking sexual risks, which can expose oneself and loved ones to risks related to sexual health, including HIV; physical abuse and injuries; and/or torture and death. Health care organizations may reduce fear of discrimination and discrimination itself, as well as improve health outcomes, if they adopt a rights-based approach to providing health care for LGBT people by formally acknowledging their existence and focusing health interventions on their needs.

LGBT (lesbian, gay, bisexual, and transgender) persons face prejudice, mistreatment, torture, and occasionally state-sponsored execution in many societies. Many human rights abuses are covered by laws that nations use to punish those who commit them. Human rights violations are not considered to have occurred when abuses against LGBT people are committed in most countries. Certain nations, like Saudi Arabia and Iran, have laws mandating the death penalty for "practicing homosexuals." Same-sex behavior is illegal in at least 40 countries for men and women combined, and illegal in at least 35 more for men alone. The nations that have been in the news lately in this regard are Saudi Arabia, India, Uzbekistan, and Nigeria. Both civil law and sharia, the regulations governing Islamic practice, make homosexual behavior illegal in many Muslim nations. LGBT persons are frequently and widely abused by police in many countries, including the United States. Notable abuse cases have recently surfaced in Cameroon, Uganda, Zimbabwe, India, Nepal, Guatemala, Ecuador, Honduras, Colombia, Peru, and Taiwan. In many nations, discrimination in employment and housing is acceptable and even legal. Laws that grant benefits to citizens, such as those in the United States, do not accord LGBT couples the same benefits. For instance, a United States Government

Accountability Office (GAO) report listed over 1,000 benefits, rights, and privileges—such as taxation and Social Security survivor benefits—that the federal government grants to married couples of different sexes but not to same-sex couples. Legal protections are likewise deficient. The District of Columbia, along with 34 of the 50 US states, do not have laws against discrimination based on sexual orientation. Twenty states lack "hate-crime" legislation that lists sexual orientation as one of the protected classes. Even less protection is afforded to transgender identity.

Couples who get married legally gain a lot of extra advantages and protections. Only a small number of countries—currently, Belgium, the Netherlands, Spain, and Canada—recognize the right of LGBT people to get married and start families. By the end of 2006, it is anticipated that South Africa, which was the first nation to include sexual orientation as a status exempt from discrimination in its Constitution in 1996, will permit same-sex marriages. Inheritance rights are granted to same-sex couples in Brazil, where state and federal laws forbid discrimination based on sexual orientation. Same-sex couples enjoy certain benefits in a number of European nations (Denmark, Sweden, Norway, Finland, the UK, France, Germany, Switzerland, Portugal, Slovenia, Croatia, and Iceland), but not as many as heterosexual couples do in Israel and New Zealand. Only one state in the US, Massachusetts, as of May 2004, allowed same-sex couples to get civil marriage rights; however, these rights were limited to state provisions and did not include the more than 1,000 federal benefits previously mentioned. In order to give unmarried couples certain benefits (again, not equal to marriage rights), the following states have passed laws: California, Connecticut, the District of Columbia, Hawaii, Maine, New Jersey, and Vermont.

Major international human rights organizations have only recently made the commitment to include the rights of LGBT people in the field of human rights. Human rights groups that focus on LGBT human rights violations include Human Rights Watch and Amnesty International. Specialized human rights organizations for LGBT people have existed for a lot longer. For instance, the International Gay and Lesbian Human Rights Commission (IGLHRC) was established sixteen years ago with the goal of ensuring that LGBT individuals and communities who are subjected to discrimination or abuse on the basis of their sexual orientation, gender identity, or HIV status can fully enjoy their human rights. Similarly, the International Lesbian and Gay Association (ILGA) has been fighting for LGBT people's equal rights for the past 28 years.

The UN has shown some support for LGBT people's human rights. "The United Nations cannot condone any persecution of, or discrimination against, people on any grounds," declared UN Secretary-General Kofi Annan in August

2003, expressing his support for LGBT nondiscrimination. According to the UN Human Rights Committee, which oversees adherence to the International Covenant on Civil and Political Rights, discrimination based on sexual orientation is forbidden by Articles 2 and 26 of the Covenant and that laws penalizing adult consensual homosexual acts violate the Covenant's guarantees of nondiscrimination and privacy. However, because of the threat of resistance from a number of sources, including the Vatican, nations in the Organization of Islamic Cooperation (OIC), and, more recently, the US, advocates are still hesitant to use UN fora to assert the human rights of LGBT populations.

LGBT activists were denied access to the UN Economic and Social Council (ECOSOC) this year after the Council rejected the Danish Association of Gays and Lesbians and the International Lesbian and Gay Alliance's application for observer status. For the first time in its history, the Council denied a nongovernmental organization's (NGO's) application without providing the customary hearings to applicants, at the request of Iran, Sudan, and the US. Given that the US had voted in favor of ILGA observer status in 2002, the action represented a policy reversal. In a coordinated letter to US Secretary of State Condoleeza Rice, forty-one human rights organizations denounced the US action. A Brazilian draft resolution to the UN Commission on Human Rights that would have outlawed discrimination based on sexual orientation was rejected by the US in 2003 and 2004 due to ideological differences with the resolution. The US Department of State's increased documentation of LGBT human rights abuses worldwide is rendered laughable by the recent US action at the UN. Both the reported quantity of human rights violations and the reported number of nations where such violations have taken place have increased in the Department of State's annual report to Congress, entitled Country Reportsman Rights Practices.

Human rights violations against LGBT individuals persist. The type of abusesabuse and their effects are demonstrated by two recent instances. FannyAnn Eddy, a lesbian activist, was brutally murdered in the Sierra Leone Lesbian and Gay Association's office a few months after she passionately addressed the UN Commission on Human Rights in 2004. Her speech about the risks LGBT people face in Sierra Leone and throughout Africa is paraphrased in the following quotes. Using "culture, tradition, religion, and societal norms to deny our existence," she began, sending the message that "discrimination, violence, and overall indignity are tolerated." She went on to discuss the ongoing fear that LGBT people face, saying, "Fear of the police and officials who have the authority to arrest and detain us simply because of our sexual orientation; Fear that our families will disown us; Fear that we will be forced out of [our] family homes; Fear that we will be left homeless, without food, and forced to turn to sex work in order to survive; Fear within our communities, where we face constant harassment and violence from neighbors and others [while the]... homophobic attacks go unpunished by authorities."

Next, Eddy discussed the link between the risk of HIV transmission and the denial of the existence of the LGBT community. 90% of men who have sex with other men also have sex with women, either as their wives or girlfriends, according to a recent study conducted in December 2003 by the Sierra Leone Lesbian and Gay Association in partnership with Health Way Sierra Leone. 85% of that group claimed not to use condoms. Clearly, these men in Sierra Leone are not receiving the message about sexual education and HIV transmission. It is evident that many men marry because it is socially required of them rather than because they have an innate desire to do so. This is because they live in a culture that makes them fear for their lives or their freedom due to their sexual orientation. Their wives and girlfriends are in danger as well as themselves because of the silence surrounding them and the unwillingness to recognize their existence or take care of their medical needs. "Respect for human rights can transform society," she said in closing. It may help people realize that, at the end of the day, we are all just human and deserving of respect and dignity. Vulnerabilities ce. Human rights breaches motivated by sexual orientation or gender identity occur on a daily basisdaily in Africa and across the world. You can assist us in overcoming these injustices and obtaining our complete set of liberties and rights in every society, including my dear Sierra Leone. "Another deadly attack occurred in February 2006, this time in South Africa. A mob stoned and killed Zoliswa Nkonyana, a lesbian, as she was strolling down a street in a township in the Cape Flats with her partner. Despite South Africa's constitution's prohibition on discrimination, this took place. Regardless of culture or social conventions, every human being is entitled to certain fundamental rights. In addition to ensuring that LGBT people have access to health services, advocating for the recognition of LGBT human rights entails understanding LGBT issues, speaking out against discrimination, and being aware of the various ways that LGBT people's human rights are violated. For LGBT people to be granted human rights, principles muned in international and national laws and policies. Prejudices must also be confronted in order forfor others to view LGBT people as fellow human beings deserving of all human rights.

9.2.5. Discrimination

LGBT people have long been the targets of prejudice. They have endured hate crimes, been classified as mentally ill, had their identities forcibly changed, and been barred from homes, workplaces, and public areas. Studies on surveys reveal that LGBT people frequently experience personal discrimination. This covers offensive language, sexual harassment, and physical aggression. A National Public Radio survey indicates that one in five LGBTQ Americans have encountered discrimination in public due to their identity. This covers employment, housing, education, and law enforcement. In addition, the study shows that LGBTQ individuals of color are twice as likely as LGBTQ individuals of white to encounter discrimination, particularly in the form of job applications and encounters with law enforcement. A third of Americans who identify as LGBTQ think that laws and government policies are the main source of the issue, while the remaining individuals attribute it to personal prejudice. Many LGBTQ Americans try to avoid situations or places out of fear of discrimination, such as bathrooms, medical care, or calling the police, as a result of their experiences with discrimination in public.

According to a CAP survey, discrimination against LGBT individuals is experienced by 25.2% of the population and has a negative impact on their living conditions and general well-being. This discrimination is based on the individual's sexual orientation or gender identity. Many LGBT people alter their lives out of fear of discrimination; they may hide their relationships, put off getting medical care, avoid social situations, etc. According to survey data published in a study by UCLA School of Law, 298.8% of LGBT employees reported facing discrimination at work, including being fired or passed over for employment. Compared to white LGBT employees, LGBT employees of color were significantly more likely to report that their gender identity or sexual orientation prevented them from being hired. Compared to cisgender LGB employees, transgender employees were more likely to experience discrimination because of their LGBT identity. Only 27.8% of cisgender LGB employees reported experiencing discrimination because of their identity, compared to nearly half (48.8%) of transgender employees. Furthermore, more than half (57.0%) of LGBT employees who experienced discrimination claimed that their employer or fellow employees had suggested that the unfair treatment was related to their religious convictions. Within the U. S. laws allowing child welfare agencies to refuse services to LGBT people of their moral or religious convictions have been passed in a few states. Comparably, on the basis ofbased on moral or religious convictions, some states permit medical professionals to refuse specific treatments or drugs to members of the LGBT community. Furthermore, some states allow companies to refuse to work with LGBT individuals or same-sex couples, especially when it comes to wedding-related services, on the grounds of moral or religious convictions.

Cochran and psychologist Vickie M. Mays of the University of California investigated whether persistent discrimination among LGB people exacerbates anxiety, depression, and other stress-related mental health issues in a 2001 study that looked at potential underlying causes of mental disorders in LGB people. Strong evidence of a connection between the two was discovered by the writers. The researchers compared the assessments of perceived discrimination, as well as lifetime and everyday experiences with discrimination, including being turned down for a job or bank loan, made by 2,844 heterosexual respondents and 74 LGB respondents. The team discovered that in every category linked to discrimination, LGB respondents reported higher rates of perceived discrimination than heterosexuals.

Instead, the review points out that the results of earlier research indicated. Psychosocial stressors such as gender nonconformity, early awareness of being gay, victimization, lack of support, school dropout, family issues, friend's suicide attempts, homelessness, substance abuse, and other psychiatric disorders were found to be significantly linked to the number of suicide attempts. While some of these stressors are also experienced by heterosexual teenagers, research indicates that gay adolescents are more likely to experience them. Even with the recent advancements in LGBT rights, gay men still face high rates of depression and loneliness following their coming out.

9.2.6. Intersections of Race

LGBT people of color frequently face prejudice, stereotyping, and discrimination due to their race in addition to their sexual orientation and gender identity, as opposed to white LGBT people. Nadal and associates talk about the experience of LGBTQ individuals of color with intersectional microaggressions, which are directed towards different facets of their social identities. These unfavorable encounters and microaggressions may originate from heterosexual and cisgender white people, heterosexual and cisgender people of their own race, or the predominantly white LGBT community itself. In LGBT settings, some LGBT people of color do not feel welcome or adequately represented. A thorough and methodical analysis of the literature on the experiences of LGBT people of color that has been published to date reveals a recurring theme of exclusion in LGBT communities that are predominately white. These spaces are often dominated by White LGBT people, they espouse Western and White values, and they frequently make LGBT people of color feel as though they have to choose between their gender and sexual orientation community and their racial community. Generally speaking, white LGBT people are viewed as the epitome of LGBT culture and values in Western society, where they are subtly coded as such.

In popular discourse, the subject of coming out, or disclosing ontation and gender identity to the public, is linked to white expectations and values.

One particular studystudy found that LGBT participants of color viewed their family's silence about their identity as supportive and accepting, despite the fact that white Western culture places value on the ability to speak openly about one's identity with family. For instance, coming out is seen as a family affair rather than an individual one in collectivist cultures. In addition, the annual National Coming Out Day is centered around white viewpoints as a way to support LGBT people in feeling free and at ease with their identity. Nonetheless, National Coming Out Day is seen negatively by some LGBT people of color. Coming out publicly can have negative effects on people of color's sense of personal safety as well as their relationships with their families and the community. It's possible that White LGBT individuals will further isolate their LGBT siblings of Color as a result of their collective rejection of these disparities in coming out perspectives.

9.3. ESSENCE OF GAY AND LESBIAN RIGHTS

Although the term "gay" was once slang, it has become widely accepted in recent years and is preferred over the more formal and older term "homosexual" by many people who are attracted to people of the same sex. The fight for social and legal equality is just one facet of a larger gay and lesbian movement that has been working to improve gay men's and lesbian's self-image, create institutions for the gay community, and alter attitudes toward homosexuality since the late 1960s. Even though there are records of homosexuality in every historical era and culture, the gay and lesbian rights movement didn't begin until a self-aware, gay-identified subculture emerged that was prepared to publicly voice its demands for equality. Until the 1960s, almost all gay men and lesbians kept their sexual orientation a secret and often agreed with the prevailing social view that homosexuality was sinful, sick, or both. Men and women who identify as gay but conceal their sexual orientation are referred to as being in the closet. The Daughters of Bilitis (1956) and the Mattachine Society (1951) were the first national gay organizations in the United States. Gay and lesbian organizations were given a boost by the 1960s civil rights movement, and the late 1960s women's movement clarified the connection between political participation and individual identity.

When the patrons of the Stonewall Inn, a gay bar in New York City's Greenwich Village, violently resisted being taken into custody by city police officers who had raided the establishment in 1969, it was a turning point for gay men and lesbians. Younger gay men and lesbians who rejected prejudice and harmful stereotypes came to view Stonewall as a symbol of a new way of thinking. When gay men and lesbians made the decision to come out of the closet and became more outspoken, U.S. S. It prompted society to reconsider preconceived notions about homosexuality. National organizations like the Human Rights Campaign, the Lambda Defense and Education Fund, and the National Gay Task Force have been instrumental in combating discriminatory treatment, even though the majority of gay and lesbian rights activism is still local. For instance, the American Psychiatric Association was persuaded to remove homosexuality from its list of mental disorders in 1974 by the National Gay Task Force's successful lobbying efforts. Legislative action as well as court challenges have contributed to the recognition of gay and lesbian rights. More empathetic legislative hearings have resulted from gay and lesbian organization's capacity to contribute large sums of money to political candidates.

9.3.1. Criminal Prexual Activity

Because homosexual behavior has historically been illegal in the United States, the majority ofmost gay men and lesbians stayed hidden until the contemporary movement for equality. S. the past. Oral and anal sex—both of which have been called sodomy—are considered forms of homosexual activity. During the colonial era, when a conviction for a crime against nature could result in the death penalty, there were laws prohibiting sodomy. While very few, if any, people have ever been put to death for sodomy, the crime has always carried severe penalties; as of 2003, sodomy is still considered a felony in states with sodomy laws (Arkansas, however, classified sodomy as a Class A misdemeanor).

The repeal of sodomy statutes has become a topproponents of gay and lesbian rights. Twenty-seven states have eliminated these laws, typically as a result ofbecause of a broader overhaul of the criminal code and an acknowledgment that both heterosexual and homosexual people participate in oral and anal sex. The Court dismissed the claim that a right to privacy covering homosexual activity had been established by earlier rulings, such as those on abortion and contraception. The Court also dismissed the claim that the Fifth and Fourteenth Amendment's due process clauses grant a basic right to practice homosexuality. Justice Bryon R. Dot White, writing for the majority, responded to the claim that homosexual activity should be protected when it takes place in a private home by pointing out that otherwise illegal conduct is not always immune whenever it occurs in a home. For instance, since it takes place at home, possession of drugs or stolen property is not protected.

The gay and lesbian rights movement suffered because of Hardwick, which gave opponents a platform to argue that it was ludicrous to give people who commit crimes civil rights. The Supreme Court decided to reevaluate whether sodomy laws were constitutional in December 2002. 14 states still had in effect sodomy laws as of 2003. Only homosexual behavior is covered by these sodomy laws in four of these states, including Texas.

Tyron Garner and John Lawrence were found guilty of sodomy in 1998 under Tex. Pen. Code § 21.06. Officers entered an apartment after receiving a false report that the two men were in possession of illegal weapons. Inside, they discovered the men having sex. After their sodomy conviction, they were each hit with a $200 fine. After they challenged their convictions, a Texas appellate court determined that the sodomy statute did not contravene the U.S. S. or the constitutions of Texas. Lawrence v. Texas, S.W 41. 3d 349. A request for discretionary review was turned down by the Texas Court of Criminal Appeals, but the U. S. Certiorari was granted by the top court. The ruling of the lower court was overturned by the court in June 2003. The majority opinion was written by Justice Kennedy, who said that the petitioners had a right to privacy. By criminalizing their private sexual activity, the State is unable to diminish their existence or dictate their future. They have complete freedom to act as they please without interference from the government thanks to the Due Process Clause.

9.3.2. Antidiscrimination Laws

Legislation that forbids discrimination based on sexual orientation in public service, employment, housing, or other public accommodations has been pushed for by supporters of gay and lesbian rights. Numerous U. S. To achieve these goals, cities have passed gay rights ordinances. Wisconsin was the first state to enact legislation supporting gay rights in 1982. In the 1980s and 1990s, gay men and lesbians battled for the right to serve in the armed forces on a national level through legal battles. A number of legal actions were taken in an attempt to overturn military policy that required discharge for revealing one's homosexual orientation. The Navy's policy against homosexual behavior was upheld by the Ninth Circuit Court of Appeals because it was founded on the professional judgment of the Navy, which determined that homosexual behavior gravely jeopardizes the accomplishment of the military mission. The court of appeals, however, decided that Meinhold's admission of his sexual orientation was not a reason for his dismissal. The court believed that Meinhold had not shown a clear, expressed desire to engage in homosexual activity. The armed services must therefore concentrate on individuals who are likely to engage in prohibited conduct as well as prohibited conduct itself.

After President Bill Clinton was elected in November 1992, the matter entered the political sphere. Clinton pledged during the campaign to use his power as the head of state to end the military's prohibition on homosexuality. That being said, the Joint Chiefs of Staff, led by General Colin L. Powell and numerous other high-ranking Pentagon officials vehemently opposed Clinton's proposal, arguing that lifting the ban would disrupt military discipline, order, and morale. Congress, led by Senator Sam Nunn (D-GA), the influential Armed Services Committee chairman, insisted on having a chance to offer feedback on the plan. Early in his presidency, Clinton gave in to mounting pressure and consented to a six-month postponement of the ban's lifting. In addition to ordering the military to stop questioning incoming recruits about their sexual orientation and to halt investigations to find gays in uniform, he also agreed to establish a temporary policy created by Nunn and suspended ongoing cases aimed at discharging gays, provided that the allegations were based solely on the individual's status as a gay person and not on improper behavior. Don't ask, don't tell became a permanent policy in September 1993 when it was enacted by Congress. This policy instructed gay men and lesbians who wished to serve in the military to conceal their sexual orientation.

Laws that would occasionally classify homosexuals as a protected class have also been considered by Congress. These laws have, however, encountered fierce opposition. For example, the Hate Crimes Prevention Act of 1999 was reintroduced by a bipartisan congressional group in 1999, and it would have granted federal authorities the authority to look into and prosecute crimes based on sexual orientation in addition to other types of hate crimes. The measure failed to pass Congress even though it had 192 sponsors. As of right now, hate crimes can only be prosecuted in cases where the victim is singled out for participating in federally protected activities, like voting, serving on a jury, or going to public school.

9.3.3. Legal Recognition of Gay and Lesbian Relationships

Gay and lesbian activists have worked to have homosexual relationships recognized legally. A gay couple is currently treated differently from a married heterosexual couple under the law. Thus, same-sex couples are denied the benefits of tax law and probate. For instance, unless the deceased specified in a will that the surviving partner would receive such an entitlement, the surviving partner in a same-sex relationship would not be entitled to any of the deceased's property upon death. Health benefits became especially important to gay couples with the emergence of Acquired Immune Deficiency Syndrome (AIDS). A same-sex partner of an employee who is not employed by the organization is not eligible to enroll in the employee's health plan unless the employer or government agency specifically provides for same-sex couples. Gay and lesbian activists first turned their attention to domestic partnership laws, which would have allowed unmarried couples to register their relationship with a municipality, in response to these disparities. A number of cities have attempted to implement domestic partnership, but only New York City, Madison, Wisconsin, Takoma Park, Maryland, Berkeley, San Francisco, Santa Cruz, and West Hollywood,

California have passed ordinances of this kind.

Gay and lesbian couples in Hawaii attempted a more radical redefining of the family and domestic relationships by filing a lawsuit after being denied a marriage license. In the case of Baehr v., the Hawaii Supreme Court heard arguments on same-sex marriage. Lewin, 74 Haw. 530, 852 P. 2d 44 (1993). The court determined that Hawaii's constitution's ban on sex discrimination was violated by f same-sex couples from getting married. In order to ascertain whether the state had a compelling interest to forbidin forbidding the issuance of licenses, the court remanded the case. The trial court in Hawaii determined that there was no justification, much less a compelling one as outlined by the Supreme Court, for forbidding same-sex marriages. The court also decided that these couples ought to be permitted to wed. The voters in Hawaii passed a referendum to amend the state constitution, allowing the state Legislature to limit marriage to men and women exclusively, while the case was pending before the Hawaii Supreme Court. Hawaii's couples lawsuit was dropped as a result, and the state limited marriage to be between men and women.

Because states customarily grant marriages performed in other states full faith and credit (full legal recognition), same-sex marriage is a topic of national interest. Several state legislatures passed laws prohibiting recognition of gay and lesbian unions after realizing that such unions might be legally recognized in their home states only after traveling to Hawaii to get married. In response, Congress passed the Defense of Marriage Act (1 U.S.C.A. § 7). The act defines marriage as a legal union between a man and a woman, depriving same-sex spouses of certain federal benefits and entitlements. Additionally, it gives states the authority to outlaw same-sex unions within their boundaries and to reject unions formed in another state. While the country has focused on issues like same-sex marriage, local gay and lesbian organizations have devoted their time to defending gay fathers and lesbian mothers who have lost their children in custody disputes. In one case, the mother was given custody back after the Virginia Court of Appeals overturned the ruling on the grounds that it was an abuse of the court's discretion. This case highlights the difficulties gay men and lesbians face in the legal system. According to estimates from the National Center for Lesbian Rights, between 1985 and 1994, the courts granted parental rights to only about one hundred homosexuals.

9.3.4. Legislative and Judicial Responses after Romer v. Evans

Local and's reactions to Romer were not all the same. Gays and lesbians now have more legal rights thanks to a large number ofmany governmental entities. Ten states, the District of Columbia, 27 cou 150 cities had enacted legislation shielding gays and lesbians from discrimination by the year 2000. The majority ofMost laws only forbade discrimination against homosexuals in the workplace. A few laws, however, went further and prohibited discrimination against gays by landlords, credit institutions, healthcare providers, and public accommodations. On the other hand, other municipal and state governments passed laws restricting the civil rights of homosexuals. These laws, in contrast to Colorado's Amendment 2, did not aim to fully bar gays and lesbians from pursuing legal action against discrimination. Rather, some local and state governments attempted to prohibit lesbians and gays from exercising specific legal rights that have historically only been available to heterosexuals. The two most common targets of these anti-gay laws remain to be the right to marry and the right to adopt children.

9.3.5. Same-Sex Marriage: A Civil Right or a Moral Wrong?

From the United States' founding. S. Since the late 1960s, members of the gay and lesbian rights movement have worked to secure the civil rights already accorded to racial and ethnic minorities. While some progress has been made in these attempts to amend the law, same-sex marriage—a fundamental issue for gay and lesbian couples—has encountered strong opposition, even from proponents of gay rights. In addition to requiring a change in the law, same-sex marriage is divisive because it raises many questions about what constitutes a family and a marriage. The topic is rife with social and cultural symbols and beliefs that compel participants in the discussion to reevaluate their fundamental presumptions about the structure of social life. Some gays and lesbians question the wisdom of same-sex marriage, even though heterosexuals make up the vast majority of those opposed. Many same-sex couples believe they are married for all intents and purposes, according to proponents of same-sex marriage. The state government in this instance needs to formally acknowledge the exisof these marriages. That's all that's missing. The loss of legal rights and benefits that heterosexual marriages enjoysenjoy is a consequence of the denial of legal recognition, which is considered sexual discrimination. Therefore, in a same-sex relationship, a surviving partner does not have a legal claim to any part of the deceased's probate estate unless that partner's surviving spouse is named in the deceased partner's will; in a heterosexual marriage, however, a surviving spouse is entitled to such assets. Furthermore, same-sex couples are not eligible for the same health benefits as married heterosexual couples.

The constitutional ideas of due process and equal protection serve as the foundation for the legal justifications for same-sex unions. The case established that prohibiting marriages based solely on race is a denial of due process, and that the establishment of such classifications denied couples equal protection under the law because they served no purpose other than to engage in racial discrimination that was clearly justified. The definition-of-marriage argument, the moral tradition argument, and the pragmatic argument are the three main points of contention raised by those who oppose same-sex unions. The debate over the definition of marriage is based on fundamental social and cultural presumptions. Some who oppose marriage argue that it is exclusive to heterosexual couples and does not allow for the union of same-sex couples. Therefore, even if a statute does not specifically refer to husband and wife, it could still have only taken heterosexual couples into consideration when describing marriage. Using this justification, the Kentucky Court of Appeals declared that same-sex marriages are illegal, citing the long-standing belief that marriage is between a man and a woman and the lack of evidence to the contrary. Same-sex marriage proponents contend that because historians have disregs, courts have not been shown evidence to the contrary. Several historians and legal experts have come to the conclusionconcluded that same-sex relationships are accepted in both Western and non-Western cultures as a result of extensive research on the history and anthropology of homosexuality. In European history, the end of the Middle Ages and the emergence of nation-states marked the beginning of the stigmatization and closeting of gays and lesbians. Therefore, the colonization of North America occurred at a time when same-sex relationships were no longer protected by law or culture.

The claim that heterosexual marriage is motivated by the need for procreation—something that same-sex couples are unable to accomplish—is another defense of moral tradition that is frequently made. Same-sex marriage proponents point out that heterosexual couples who are unable to conceive are not refused a marriage license. Infertile, elderly, and disabled people may decide to get married for purposes other than having children. Furthermore, in order to get around physical restrictions on reproduction, heterosexual and homosexual couples have benefited from technological advancements like artificial insemination and in vitro fertilization. The moral tradition argument's detractors claim that it is founded on erroneous interpretations of history and the Bible. They point out that many religious authorities are in favor of same-sex unions and that many same-sex couples formally sanctify their union through a religious ceremony officiated by a clergyman or rabbi. People who advocate for gay and lesbian rights in general but not for same-sex marriage specifically tend to make the pragmatic argument against same-sex marriage. They argue that the demand for marriage will spark opposition to the gay and lesbian rights movement as a whole. Furthermore, allowing same-sex unions would be seen as endorsing homosexuality. The practical stance is that homosexuals and lesbians ought to be protected and tolerated; it does not, however, extend to advocating for the acceptance of an alternative way of life or the extension of the conventional definition of marriage. These arguments are put forth by homosexual opponents, and some gays and lesbians are not overly excited about the idea of same-sex marriage. This group holds that because heterosexual marriage has historically created a hierarchical relationship that has resulted in women's subordination, it is not a good role model for gays and lesbians. The institution of marriage has contributed to other types of social dysfunction, such as economic disempowerment and domestic abuse. The claim that same-sex marriage will absorb gays and lesbians into the mainstream and sap the radicalism inherent in their lifestyle is another argument against it. Gay and lesbian leaders will present couples who most closely resemble their mainstream, heterosexual counterparts when advocating for same-sex marriage. Skeptics have viewed this argument as romanticizing the movement. Not all gays and lesbians fall into the radical category, and many should anticipate benefiting from the legal protection that same-sex marriage provides. Reaction has been forceful and prompt when the discussion has veered into the legal sphere. Advocates of same-sex unions achieved success in the 1990s when state bans on the unions were overturned by courts in Hawaii in 1993 and in both states that followed. Voters in Hawaii approved a state constitutional amendment that gives legislators the power to define marriusively a partnership between a man and a woman. Similarly, a similar amendment was approved by a 2–1 vote in Alaska, andAlaska and plans to put judicial nominees through a legislative screening process that would weed out candidates who supported same-sex marriages were also put forth. Politicians react to this kind of public opinion. Same-sex marriage has faced strong opposition from Congress and state legislatures; by the late 1990s, several state legislaturesederal lawmakers had passed outright bans. The Defense of Marriage Act (DOMA), enacted by Congress in 1996, grants statesstates the authority to reject same-sex unions consummated in another state. By establishing the first clear federal definitions of marriage and spouse in exclusively heterosexual terms, DOMA delivered a sharp critique to its supporters, even though the law's very name suggested that the institution of marriage required defense against them.

Although there hasn't been much of a national push for same-sex marriage acceptance, gays and lesbians have benefited from certain legal advancements in the early 2000s. Many cities have expanded insurance and health benefits to domestic partners, including New York City. In 2000, lawmakers in Vermont enacted a landmark civil union law, granting homosexual and lesbian couples a status akin to matrimony. While not fully legalizing same-sex unions, the civil union law made it possible for partners to obtain benefits that are available throughout the state. Due to the important issues involved, the discussion of same-sex marriage inevitably becomes contentious. Proponents believe that because marriage is socially constructed, it can change to reflect societal preferences. Less flexibility is seen by opponents, who point to morality, tradition, and family integrity as justifications.

REFERENCES

1. Barber, M. E., Drescher, J., & Rosario, V. (2012). The GAP online LGBT mental health curriculum. *Journal of Gay & Lesbian Mental Health, 16*(1), 41–48.
2. Blechner, M. J. (2005). The gay Harry Stack Sullivan: Interactions between his life, clinical work, and theory. *Contemporary Psychoanalysis, 45*(1), 1–19.
3. Drescher, J. (2008). A history of homosexuality and organized psychoanalysis. *Journal of the American Academy of Psychoanalysis & Dynamic Psychiatry, 36*(3), 443–460.
4. Drescher, J. (2010). Queer diagnoses: Parallels and contrasts in the history of homosexuality, gender variance, and the Diagnostic and Statistical Manual (DSM). *Archives of Sexual Behavior, 39*, 427–460.
5. Drescher, J. (2015). Out of DSM: Depathologizing homosexuality. *Behavioral Sciences, 5*, 565–575.
6. Drescher, J., & Byne, W. (2017). Gender identity, gender variance, and gender dysphoria. In B. J. Sadock, V. A. Sadock, & P. Ruiz (Eds.), *Kaplan and Sadock's Comprehensive Textbook of Psychiatry* (10th ed., pp. 2023–2039). Philadelphia, PA: Wolters Kluwer.
7. Drescher, J., & Byne, W. (2017). Homosexuality, gay and lesbian identities, and homosexual behavior. In B. J. Sadock, V. A. Sadock, & P. Ruiz (Eds.), *Kaplan and Sadock's Comprehensive Textbook of Psychiatry* (10th ed., pp. 1982–2013). Philadelphia, PA: Wolters Kluwer.
8. Drescher, J., & Merlino, J. P. (2007). *American Psychiatry and Homosexuality: An Oral History*. New York: Harrington Park Press.
9. Institute of Medicine. (2011). *The Health of Lesbian, Gay, Bisexual, and Transgender People: Building A Foundation for Better Understanding*. Washington, DC: The National Academies Press.
10. Kameny, F. (2009). How it all started. *Journal of Gay & Lesbian Mental Health, 13*(2), 76–81.
11. Silverstein, C. (2011). Events in New York City leading to the deletion of homosexuality as a mental disorder by the American Psychiatric Association. *Division 44 Newsletter, 27*(1), 13–15.
12. Wake, N. (2011). *Private Practices: Harry Stack Sullivan, the Science of Homosexuality, and American Liberalism*. New Brunswick, NJ: Rutgers University Press.

13. Zucker, K. J., & Spitzer, R. L. (2005). Was the gender identity disorder of Childhood diagnosis introduced into DSM-III as a backdoor maneuver to replace homosexuality? A historical note. *Journal of Sex & Marital Therapy, 31*, 31–42.

Chapter **10**

Race, Gender, and the Law

Contents

INTRODUCTION

The complex and dynamic landscape where legal doctrines and societal norms intersect and profoundly impact the experiences of individuals and groups is revealed by the intersection of race, gender, and the law. Laws have historically perpetuated gender and racial inequality in many nations, ingraining systematic prejudices into legal frameworks that have disadvantaged particular groups of people. For instance, Jim Crow laws and other policies that maintained racial hierarchy and denied Black Americans the right to vote once made racial segregation and discrimination in the US legally acceptable. Similarly, legal theories that restricted women's rights in domains like work, education, and family law helped to institutionalize gender discrimination.

Legal reforms in the last few decades have attempted to rectify these disparities. The Voting Rights Act of 1965 and the Civil Rights Act of 1964 played a crucial role in advancing racial equality and destroying institutional racism. In the historic Brown v. Board of Education (1954) overturned the separate but equal principle established by Plessy v. to declare racial segregation in public schools unconstitutional. Ferguson, 1896. Similarly, the feminist movement of the 1960s and 1970s brought about important legislative changes, including the Equal Pay Act of 1963 and Title IX of the Education Amendments of 1972, which aimed to end discrimination against women in the workplace and in schools.

Notwithstanding these developments, racial and gender inequalities remain complex issues in legal frameworks. Kimberlé Crenshaw popularized the term "intersectionality," which refers to the ways in which people's experiences of discrimination vary based on the ways in which multiple identity factors—such as gender and race—interact. For instance, laws aimed only at combating gender or racial discrimination may not adequately addresissuesissues Black women may face. Courts and legislators have frequently found it difficult to incorporate intersectional perspectives into legal doctrines and protections, leading to an uneven response from the legal system to these challenges.

Movements for racial justice and LGBTQ+ rights have added complexity and richness to the legal field in recent years. The ruling made by the Supreme Court in Obergefell v. In 2015, Hodges made same-sex marriage legal, indicating a wider acceptance of LGBTQ+ rights. Concurrently, the Black Lives Matter movement has prompted calls for legal changes to address systemic racism and brought racial disparities in criminal justice and policing back into the public eye. The dynamic field of the intersection of race, gender, and the law reflects the ongoing struggles and achievements of society. Legal systems need to address these intersections more thoroughly as they drder toto advance equality and justice for all people.

10.1. EXAMINE THE INTERSECTION OF RACE AND GENDER IN LEGAL CONTEXTS

In legal contexts, the intersection of race and gender draws attention to the complex interactions between systemic injustices that influence the lives and consequences of those who encounter various forms of discrimination. This intersectional analysis highlights how laws and legal institutions frequently fall short in addressicultiesdifficulties faced by people who are at the intersection of racial and gender identities. It is based on the groundbreaking work of Kimberlé Crenshaw.

Gender and race have historically been the main targets of legal discrimination. For example, during the American period of racial segregation, laws like the Jim Crow laws specifically enforced racial segregation and denied Black citizens the right to vote, while legislative frameworks did little to address the unique needs of Black women. Similarly, legal theories that limited women's rights to property, work, and legal counsel were firmly rooted in gender discrimination. Gender equality took a major step forward when *Reed v. Reed* (1971) challenged the systemic bias ingrained in laws that favored men over women in matters of inheritance and other legal rights.

But the intersection of gender and race frequently shows that legal changes meant to address either problem separately are insufficient. For instance, the legal struggles for gender equality and racial equality usually function in isolation from one another, ignoring the compounding discrimination that women of color face. Black women's experiences in employment law differ from those of Black men or White women, frequently involving harassment and discrimination based on both race and gender. In *DeGraffenreid v. General Motors* (1976), the court found it difficult to handle the intertwining nature of allegations of racial and gender discrimination, leading to a ruling that did not adequately r difficultiesdifficulties Black women confront in the workplace.

The limited ability of the legal system to handle intersectional issues often reflects institutional biases and broader societal attitudes. Laws that address racial or gender discrimination in isolation may overlook important facets of the lived experiences of marginalized groups because intersectionality emphasizes that the effects of discrimination are multiplicative rather than additive. For instance, the Violence Against Women Act (VAWA), although a significant step in combating gender-based violence, has come under criticism for failing to adequately attend to the needs of women of color who experience both racial and gender-based violence, leaving them without access to resources and customized support. The goal of recent social and legal movements has been to close these gaps. The *McCleskey v. Kemp* (1987) ruling on racial bias in sentencing provides an example of the challenges courts face in resolving systemic problems involving intersections with other forms of discrimination. However, instances such as *Grutter v. Bollinger* (2003) and the discussions on affirmative action that followed show that efforts are still being made to update legal standards to reflect a more complex understanding of gender and race.

Furthermore, the advocacy of critical race theory and intersectional feminism continues to drive the need for more comprehensive legal frameworks that acknowledge and address the complex nature of discrimination. Legal reforms can more accurately represent the complex realities of people who experience multiple forms of marginalization by incorporating knowledge from these fields.

In legal contexts, the intersection of gender and race exposes the shortcomings of singular anti-discrimination strategies and emphasizes the need for more comprehensive and adaptabctics. In order toTo effectively address these intersections, it is necessary to gain a deeper understanding of how various forms of discrimination interact, affecting the lives of those who are marginalized and the fight for justice and equality.

10.1.1. Gender in Legal Contexts

Reflecting larger cultural shifts towards gender equality and the recognition of various gender identities, the place of gender in legal contexts has been a central topic of discussion in both ongoing legal reform and reform legislation. Throughout history, laws and practices that systematically disadvantaged women and marginalized individuals who identify as gender non-conforming have served to entrench gender inequalities within the legal system. For example, women's rights in areas like employment, family law, and property ownership were restricted by legal doctrines and statutes for a large portion of the 19th and early 20th centuries. An affecting example of this kind of institutional discrimination is the legal doctrine of coverture, which merged a married woman's legal identity with her husband's identity. In the middle of the 20th century, the feminist movement sparked important legislative changes aimed at eliminating these disparities. The Equal Pay Act of 1963 was a landmark piece of legislation that required equalwork in an effort toto address wage disparities between men and women. Similarly, Title VII of the Civil Rights Act of 1964 made it illegal to discriminate in the workplace on the basis of sex or any other attribute, which was a significant step toward achieving gender equality in the workplace. Women's participation in sports and higher education has significantly improved since Title IX of the Education Amendments of 1972 was passed, outlawing sex-based discrimination in educational programs and activities, further advancing gender equity (Figure 10.1).

Figure 10.1. *The role of gender in legal contexts.*

https://theamikusqriae.com/wp-content/uploads/2021/11/libra-justice-law-1452535.jpg.

Despite these developments, discrimination based on genxists in a number ofseveral forms. For instance, women are still impacted by wage disparities, especially women of color who frequently face exacerbated inequalities. The glass ceiling theory serves as an example of how institutional impediments can prevent women from advancing in their careers even in the face of equal performance and qualifications. Legal challenges in this field have brought attention to the need for more proactive and nuanced approaches to combat discrimination, both overt and covert.

Additionally, gender expression and identity have come under intense legal scrutiny. The legal system has made progress in recognizing and safeguarding transgender and non-binary people, even though there are still issues. The Supreme Court's famous ruling in Bostock v. The 2020 Clayton County case was a landmark decision that confation on the basis ofbased on gender identity or sexual orientation is classified as sex discrimination under Title VII. This decision established a precedent for additional legal protections for people who identify as gender non-conforming and highlighted the legal system's growing recognition of LGBTQ+ rights.

Furthermore, there have been advancements as well as setbacks in the legal responses to harassment and violence against women. Enacted in 1994, the Violence Against Women Act (VAWA) represented a revolutionary attempt to combat gender-based violence by providing federal funding for services and legal safeguards. Critics counter that poor execution and support for underprivileged groups, such as transgender people and women of color, have undermined its efficacy.

The study of gendered justice law looks at how legal systems deal with the complex issues of race and gender, both of which they frequently fail to address. This idea highlights the necessity of having a legal system that actively addresses the ways that racial and gender inequalitynd not just acknowledgesacknowledge their effects. Understanding that race and gender are not distinct categories but rather entwined aspects of identity that affect people's experiences in the legal system is necessary for gendered justice. It demands changes that take into consideration how these intersections give rise to particular kinds of disadvantage and discrimination.

10.1.2. Historical Context and Legal Foundations

In theem has frequently servedfrequently served to uphold disparities in gender and race. One example of gender-based legal discrimination in the US is the doctrine of coverture, which merged a married woman's legal identity under her husband's. Women's rights to employment, property, and legal counsel were restricted. Simultaneously, racial segregation laws such as the Jim Crow laws enforced racial hierarchies and deprived Black people of their rights; this included Black women whose struggles were exacerbated by their gender.

Significant legal reforms were sparked by the 20th-century feminist and civil rights movements. Racial and gender discrimination were the targets of the Equal Pay Act of 1963 and the Civil Rights Act of 1964, respectively. These laws, which recognized the need for legal safeguards against discriminatory practices based on both race and gender, represented a significant step toward gendered justice. In a similar vein, the famous Supreme Court decision in Brown v. Racial segregation in schools was abolished by the Board of Education in 1954, and Reed v. Women's rights have come a long way since Reed (1971) opposed inheritance laws that discriminate against women.

10.1.2.1. Intersectionality and Gendered Justice

The understanding of gendered justice revolves around the concept of intersectionality, which was first introduced by Kimberlé Crenshaw. Intersectionality emphasizes that people's experiences of discrimination are shaped by the interaction of multiple facets of their identity, such as race and gender, rather than occurring in discrete categories. This implies that for women of color, the experiences of discrimination they encounter are not simply cumulative, but rather intersect in distinct ways that are frequently disregarded by established legal frameworks.

For instance, the wage gap is a racial as well as a gender issue. When compared to white women and men, women of color frequently experience larger wage disparities. Historically, the legal response to wage discrimination has primarily addressed gender issues, failing to adequately address the compounding effects of discrimination based on both race and gender. Wage discrimination can be legally addressed through the Equal Pay Act and Title VII of the Civil Rights Act, but women of color often face additional obstacles that these laws do not fully address.

10.1.3. Challenges in Legal Protections

Legal safeguards have made progress in combating discrimination based on race and gender, but there are still gaps in providing for the needs of those who experience discrimination that overlaps with other forms of discrimination. For example, Title VII of the Civil Rights Act forbids discrimination in the workplace on the basis of race and gender, but women of color frequently experience intersectional discrimination, which calls for more complex legal recognition. Situations like DeGraffenreid v. The challenges courts encounter when handling allegations of intersectional discrimination are exemplified by General Motors (1976). The DeGraffenreid court overlooked how Black women's experiences were distinct due to the combined effects of gender and racial discrimination, which limited the efficacy of legal remedies.

Comparably, legal responses to violence against women have gotten better over time, but there are still particular issues that women of color face that aren't always sufficiently addressed. Essential protections have been offered by the Violence Against Women Act (VAWA), but systemic racism may still present additional obstacles for women of color, whose needs are not always fully met. Women of color who experience both racial and gender-based violence may not receive enough support and protection if the intersectional nature of violence is not taken into account.

10.1.3.1. Policing and Incarceration

In matters pertaining to law enforcement and incarceration, the intersection of race and gender is especially noticeable. When racial and gender biases combine, women of color experience disproportionately harsh treatment within the criminal justice system. Women of color are disproportionately targeted by police tactics like racial profiling, which increases the likelihood of arrests and associated legal repercussions. These differences are made worse by gender-specific forms of discrimination, such as the criminalization of survival sex work. The intersectional effects of gender and race are also reflected in sentencing differences. When it comes to similar offenses, women of color frequently receive harsher sentences than their white counterparts. Women of color have been disproportionately impacted by the war on drugs and mandatory minimum sentencing laws, which has led to higher incarceration rates and harsher, there are particular difficultiesdifficulties in the reentry process for women of color who have served time in prison. These women experience discrimination based on their race and gender, which makes it harder for them to find work, find housing, and access social services. The stigma attached to having a criminal record and the additional challenges that women of color face make it imperative that specialized support services be provided to address these interrelated problems.

10.1.4. Gender and Race in Law and Political Economy

This multidisciplinary event aims to investigate the relationship between gender and race and political economy and law in comparative transnational contexts, with a focus on European perspectives and legacies. From a range of interdisciplinary perspectives, speakers will discuss this overarching theme in relation to three important overlapping legal notions that structure the economy: value, labor, and property.

Particularly in continental Europe, the concepts of "race" and "gender" are frequently eliminated or marginalized in the mainstream legal discourse surrounding the economy. However, feminists, critical race theorists, and other critical scholars have shown for decades that meaningful engagements with concepts of gender and race are necessary for any meaningful understanding of how the economy functions.

Materialist feminists demonstrated that analyses of capitalism and neoliberalism need to place racialized conceptions of gender front and center. They also have a long history of making the connection between the current el crisis and their economic analysesanalysis. These insights have been incorporated by some legal scholars to demonstrate the interplay between gender relations and law in the economic structuring process. They demonstrated, for instance, how economic law creates gendered "workers" and molds concepts of sexuality and the family. They questioned the distinctions between the welfare state, the family, and economic law as well as the private and public spheres. In continental Europe, this kind of scholarship continues to be largely marginalized despite its rich contributions. Comparably, critical scholars disproved the notion that markets are "race-blind," demonstrating how capitalist economies and the ways in which they are governed are inextricably linked to and perpetuate racial hierarchies and colonial legacies. These observations have had a significant impact on international public law, and a portion of the research has by this point become well-established and indispensable. Still very much a blind spot, however, are ideas like "racial capitalism," "post-colonialism," or "decolonial thought" in other academic disciplines like European or transnational legal studies. This is especially true when studying domestic law, both private and public. Put another way, academics and educators in continental Europe continue to primarily funcr the premise that family, corporatecorporation, property, and contract law are all racialized. The workshop aims to further explore what they mean in relation to law, European perspectives and legacies, and is situated in the intellectual spaces opened up by feminist and other critical schethodological insights.

10.2 .WOMEN2. WOMEN OF COLOR FACE UNIQUE CHALLENGES IN THE LEGAL SYSTEM

Given the intersections of race, gender, and socioeconomic status, women of color encounter unique challenges within the legal system. Their experiences in different legal contexts, such as employment and education, criminal justice and family law, are influenced by these barriers that are specific to them and frequently lead to compounded forms of discrimination. Due to the complexity of these issues, legal reform and social justice require an intersectional approach.

10.2.1. Employment and Economic Inequality

When it comes to the workplace, women of color face a great deal of discrimination when it comes to white women. Wage disparities continue despite improvements in anti-discrimination legislation, such as Title VII of the Civil Rights Act of 1964 and the Equal Pay Act of 1963. In comparison to white women and men, women of color—especially Black and Latina women—face an even more pronounced wage gap. For example, in the US, for every dollar earned by white men, Black women make about 63 cents and Latina women make about 55 cents. Occupational segregation, which places a disproportionate number of women of color in lower-paying jobs with fewer opportunities for advancement, exacerbates this disparity.

Furthermore, prejudices against women of color in the workplace frequently collide with preconceptions about both their gender and race, creating unique kinds of harassment and exclusion. Research indicates that women of color face a higher likelihood of encountering racial stereotyping, microaggressions, and obstacles to their professional growth. The way the legal system has handled these problems has been inconsistent. Since *DeGraffenreid v. General Motors* (1976) brought attention to the shortcomings of conventional anti-discrimination laws in addressing intersectional discrimination, legal interpretations have frequently found it difficult to adequately address the complex forms of bias that women of color experience.

10.2.2. Education and Institutional Barriers

Women of color encounter obstacles in education that affect their performance in the classroom and in the workplace. Systemic problems continue even in the face of laws like Title IX, which attempts to stop sex-based discrimination in the classroom. Women of color frequently attend underfunded institutions with fewer resources, which may have an impact on their ability to complete their education and get into higher education. Students of color are disproportionately affected by the school-to-prison pipeline because of policies that lead to higher rates of suspension and expulsion for Black and Latina students than for their White counterparts. Institutions of higher learning provide opportunities, but they also pose difficulties for women of color.

They are underrepresented in faculty positions and frequently experience gender- and race-based microaggressions, which may limit their access to mentorship and support. Affirmative action laws have been part of the legal system's attempts to address these disparities; however, these laws are usually contested and differ greatly from jurisdiction to jurisdiction. Cases from the Supreme Court such as Grutter v. (2003) Bollinger and Fisher v. Affirmative action in higher education has been discussed by University of Texas (2016), but discussions about how well these policies serve the needs of women of color remain.

10.2.3. Criminal Justice System and Mass Incarceration

There is also the crwhich presents particular difficultiesdifficulties for women of color. Differences in the effects of policing, sentencing, and incarceration arise from the intersection of race and gender. Harsh sentencing policies, such as mandatory minimums and the war on drugs, which have disproportionately targeted communities of color, are more likely to affect women of color. Due to systemic racial and gender biases, Black and Latina women are frequently incarcerated at higher rates than White women for comparable offenses.

Women of color are also more likely to experience higher rates of abuse and violence, which may have an impact on how they interact with the criminal justice system. Women of color who have experienced domestic abuse, for instance, may be charged with crimes connected to their victimization, such as self-defense against violent partners. Over time, the legal protections for victims of sexual assault and domestic abuse have grown; however, because of institutional racism and gender biases in the legal system, women of color frequently face obstaclesining these protections.

10.2.4.Family4. Family Law and Reproductive Justice

Women of color are disproportionately affected by family law issues. Women of color may experience prejudices that influence the results of legal proceedings in cases involving child custody, child support, and domestic abuse. Stereotypes regarding parenting skills and financial status, for example, can affect custody decisions and disadvantage women of color. Furthermore, the way the legal system handles child welfare can be biased; investigations into allegations of child abuse and neglect tend to focus more on families of color, which frequently results in the separation of children from their parents in an environment of structural injustice.

Another crucial area where women of color encounter particular difficulties is reproductive justice. The relationship between gender and race affects who can access reproductive health care, such as abortion and contraception. Access to comprehensive reproductive health care may be hampered for women of color, especially those from low-income backgrounds, by financial hardships, insurance issues, or discriminatory practices. Compounding these difficulties are historical and systemic factors, such as forced sterilizations and insufficient access to healthcare.

10.2.5. Intersectional Advocacy and Legal Reform

Legal reform must take an intersectional, nuanced approach in order to address the particular difficulties faced by women of color. Kimberlé Crenshaw popularized the term "intersectionality," which highlights the significance of understanding how different types of discrimination interact to affect people's experiences. When developing policies and putting reforms into place, legal advocates and legislators need to take these intersecting identities into account.

Advocating for more inclusive anti-discrimination laws, specialized support programs, and legislative changes meant to lessen inequalities in employment, education, and criminal justice have all been attempts to address these issues. Systemic biases, for example, can be addressed by efforts to improve workplace equity, such as diversity and inclusion programs. To address inequities in the criminal justice system, legislative changes that are directed toward decreasing mass imprisonment and changing sentencing guidelines are essential. Advocating for policies that address the unique needs of women of color, such as greater access to childcare, healthcare, and legal support, can help lessen some of the disparities these people experience in the areas of family law and reproductive justice.

A more equitable legal system must also promote social and legal support networks that are sensitive to the needs of diverse communities and culturally competent. The legal system presents distinct challenges for women of color because of the interplay between race, gender, and socioeconomic status. These difficulties show up in a number of areas, such as family law,ustice, work, and education.

In order toTo address these problems, legal reform must take a comprehensive and intersectional approach that acknowledges and addresses the complex forms of discrimination that women of color experience. Policymakers and advocates can endeavor to create a more equitable legal system that promotes justice and equality for all people, regardless of their race, gender, or socioeconomic backgrounnd addressing these particular challengeschallenges.

10.2.6. Integrated Approaches to Challenges facing the Criminal Justice System

Globally, criminal justice systems encounter numerous obstacles. To effectively address them, coordinated and integrated approaches are necessary, and the UN is crucial in this regard. The need to address emerging forms of criminality and improve responses to long-standing criminal behaviors that permeate societies, such as corruption and violence against women and children, are among the challenges posed by the persistently high rates of crime and violence.

Numerous criminal justice systems worldwide are beset by an excessive number of cases and inadequate financan resources. This results in a number ofseveral problems with the justice system, such as high rates of impunity, long delays in the administration of justice, excessive use of pretrial detention, inadequate use of alternative sentencing options, overcrowded prisons unable to perform their rehabilitative role, and high recidivism rates.

Criminal justice systems frequently experience compartmentalization, a lack of integration among the various elements of the criminal justice chain, and a lack of coordination and collaboration with other sectors—such as the social welfare, health, and education sectors—that are crucial to ensuring integrated responses to crime and violence.

To address these issues, the United Nations standards and norms in criminal justice and crime prevention are a trustworthy source. With minimum standard rules or basic principles on a wide range of criminal justice issues, they help Member States achieve a fair, efficient, aonate criminal justice system. In order toTo help Member States meet their unique needs and circumstances, the UN Office on Drugs and Crime (UNODC) supports them in using these standards and norms, which stand for the best practices that States can adopt.

10.2.6.1. Violence against women

The second goal under Sustainable Development Goal 5 on gender equality is to eradicate all forms of violence against all women and girls in both public and private domains. The prevalence of violence against women is startlingly high worldwide, and it happens in all contexts of development. It takes on physical, sexual, and psychological forms through various criminal activities, including trafficking in persons for sexual exploitation, female genital mutilation, child marriage, and violence against intimate partners.

Globally, one in three women has been the victim of physical or sexual abuse, primarily at the hands of a close companion. One in two female homicide victims is murdered by a spouse or other family member. Violence against women and children is not considered a serious crime in many societies, and as a result, it is not reported to the police or dealt with by the legal system.

This is true even though they have negative and enduring effects on women's and girl's safety, health, and well-being as well as those of their families and communities. In order to guarantee that victims receive the protection and assistance they need, coordination between the police, social services, health, and justice sectors is essential. One of the main obstacles in addressing violence against women is that victim-centered processes are often absent, and another is that gender-sensitive approaches are not well-known. These elements may cause victims to lose faith in criminal justice systems, and in certain nations, there may be a high level of impunity for offenders.

The United Nations system takes an integrated approach to addressing violence against women. UN Women, the UN Development Programme (UNDP), the UN Population Fund (UNFPA), UNODC and the World Health Organization run the UN Joint Global Programme to support Member States in effectively tackling violence against women and providing services for women and girls. The initiative is running pilots in 10 countries: Cambodia, Egypt, Guatemala, Kiribati, Mozambique, Pakistan, Peru, Solomon Islands, Tunisia and Viet Nam, with a view to a global roll-out.

10.2.6.2. Violence against children

Violence is a serious threat to sustainable development and affects millions of children worldwide, regardless of their culture, class, education, income level, or ethnic origin. Although it is not officially recognized, the majority of violent crimes against children are tacitly accepted in society. It frequently goes unreported, unpunished, and unprosecuted.

Children have a right to be shielded psychological harm and abuse. In the event thatIf minors are harmed, states must take all necessary steps to support their social reintegration, physical and mental healing, and recovery. The protection of minors in conflict with the law from torture and other cruel, inhuman, or degrading treatment or punishment, the use of detention as a last resort, the avoidance of placing them in adult prisons, and the promotion of their reintegration into society are other important safeguards that states should guarantee.

Children who experience abuse may not be able to assert their legal rights because they may not have access to legal representation, education about the legal system, or medical care. The Global Programme to End Violence Against Children of the United Nations Development Committee assists its member nations in fortifying their legal frameworks in order to effectively deter and address child abuse.

One of the most serious forms of violence against children is the recruitment and exploitation of kids by violent extremist and terrorist organizations. In-depth advice and training on preventing child involvement with violent extremist and terrorist groups, facilitating the rehabilitation and reintegration of children connected to these groups, and guaranteeing that the proper care when they come into contact withencounter the legal system have been given by UNODC to Member States.

More than 30 countries have benefited from aid in this area over the past four years. Thanks to technical support from several UN agencies, including UNODC, over 100 children in Niger who had been imprisoned due to their affiliation with Boko Haram were freed from detention and given to the child protection system to begin the process of reintegrating into their communities.

10.2.6.3. Support and protection for victims

In criminal justice systems, victims of crime are frequently the ones who are most neglected. In order to stop secondary victimization and revictimization and to increase incident reporting, it is essential to provide more support and protection for victims.

Another action that can improve support and protection for crime victims is access to legal aid. For female offenders, who usually originate from underprivileged and marginalized backgrounds, this is especially crucial. In contrast to traditional criminal justice systems, restorative justice offers individuals impacted by crime a voice and a chance to take part in the case's resolution.

It can be a practical method for gi. In order to ensure offenders rehabilitation andoffenders' rehabilitation, social reintegration and lower reoffending rates, criminal justice systems must carefully balance the needs of victims for justice and reparations, communities and societies needs for safety and protection, and the need to hold offenders accountable.

10.2.7. Women's Participation in Law

The legal field is still resolutely dominated by men, and women attorneys frequently experience abuse, discrimination, and disempowerment. If it is to fairly serve all citizens for whom it seeks to provide justice, it urgently needs reform, spearheaded by women. The International Bar Association reports that although women make up 51% of the legal profession, they only hold 32% of senior positions. Women hold 26% of senior positions in the judiciary and comprise 43% of all judges. The representation of women lawyers is not uniform, and racial and ethnic differences in representation among women are intensified. According to a McKinsey and Company study conducted in North America, women's representation sharply declines from the post-associate level to the partner and management committee levels, with women of color being significantly underrepresented across the board. Furthermore, according to an American Bar Association survey, women of color face discrimination due to a larger pay gap (including when compared to white women) and fewer promotions. They are also more likely to have their competencies questioned and to be mistaken for administrative, custodial, or court staff members.

In general, women attorneys are more likely to have their conversations cut off, even when serving as judges, to have non-legal office chores assigned to them, and to see a decline in their careers after having children. Violence and harassment are frequent ways that discrimination against members of the legal profession manifests itself. The results of the International Bar Association's largest-ever survey on sexual harassment and bullying in the legal industry indicate that these issues are widespread in the industry and disproportionately impact women. Even though they hold a high position in the industry, female judges are nevertheless subject to harassment and violence in the workplace. Acts such as sextortion, sexual harassment, sex discrimination, gender bias, unequal gender representation, gender stereotyping, and other forms of inappropriate sexual conduct have been identified as gender-related judicial integrity issues by the Global Judiciary Integrity Network, which was established by the United Nations Office on Drugs and Crime (Figure 10.2.).

Figure 10.2. *Women's Participation in Law.*

https://sdg-action.org/wp-content/uploads/2023/03/Upreti_main-1024x546.jpg.

10.2.7.1. Root

The main reasons why many women are not succeedingfailing in the legal profession are discriminatory practices, gender-blind policies, and structural gaps that deny women lawyers the resources they need to succeed. There is no clear correlation between their glaringly low representation in higher positions, high concentration in lower-level employment, lack of advancement, and higher attrition rate and their incompetence as attorneys.

Rather these trends persist due to a combination of factors, including:

- the pervasive attitudes of superiors and peers that embody sexist and harmful gender stereotypes
- violence and harassment in the world of work
- women's disproportionate burden of caring responsibilities
- Women lawyers operate in a male-dominated world and a profession that is primarily designed for male success. Harmful gender stereotypes, internalized by most to some degree, make many discriminatory behaviors and expectations seem natural, for example:
- the notion that men should be paid more for work of equal value because they are the breadwinners
- once women have children, their place is in the home as their primary role is of a caregiver

Similarly, violence and harassment in the workplace are expressions of unequal power relations and misogynistic attitudes that are all too often accepted as the norm – as is victim-blaming premised on the idea that women somehow provoke these behaviors.

10.2.7.1.1. Why is this a problem?

It may seem ironic given that the victims in question are women trained in the use of the law, who are presumably less easily victimized than those in precarious jobs and capable of defending their rights, but the current state of the legal profession reveals a troubling picture of abuse and female disempowerment. It denotes unfairness, needless suffering, and a loss of opportunity for women despite their potential.

The right to participate equally in the legal profession has already been earned by those who complete their legal education. It also raises doubts about the ability of a justice system beset by violence and inequality to administer justice. The absence of accountability calls into question the efficacy and very purpose of an essentially unjust legal system, which is incompatible with the idea of the rule of law.

It also calls into question the integrity of the profession and the few) women who hold leadership roles at the momentnow. Who will spearhead the necessary reforms to change the legan is a contentious question, especially in light ofconsidering the notable absence of those members of the profession who are most negatively impacted by the current structural barriers and discriminatory practices, and how their absence benefits the status quo that benefits the powerful.

10.2.7.1.2. UN goals and initiatives

The legal profession can undergo significant transformation by implementing a number of the Sustainable Development Goals (SDGs) in a comprehensive and well-rounded manner. Ensuring women's full and effective participation and equal opportunities for leadership at all levels of decision-making in political, economic, and public life is a specific target of SDG 5 on gender equality (Target 5.5). The percentage of women in managerial roles (Indicator 5.5.2) will be used to gauge this. SDG 5 also asks for the abolition of all forms of violence and discrimination against women, as well as the acknowledgment and appreciation of unpaid caregiving and household labor through the provision of public services, infrastructure, social protection laws, and shared responsibility initiatives.

SDG 8 on labor is especially important because it protects worker's rights and promotes safe and secure working conditions for all (Target 8.8), which will increase the number of women in the legal profession. It suggests adhering to several instruments of the International Labour Organization (ILO) (Indicator 8.8.2) which might be broadened to cover the recommendations 206 and 190 of the ILO regarding harassment and violence.

The representation of people on all grounds in the judiciary and public service, including sex, is covered by SDG 16 on peaceful and just institutions (Indicator 16.7.1). Additionally, it demands an end to bribery and corruption in all its manifestations (Target 16.5), which may be extended to the offense of "sextortion" as defined by the International Association of Women Judges.

10.2.7.1.3. Recommendations

Women lawyers must actively participate in multifaceted structural reform of the legal profession due to the compounded disadvantages and risks they face in the field. Employers, the government, and other social actors must acknowledge the systematic problem of women's underrepresentation in the legal field. They have to put into practice transformative, rights-based solutions that start with the most affected individuals. Investing in solutions that tackle the underlying structural causes of the barriers is more important than just funding bandaids created from a management (i.e., human resources) standpoint. Beyond offering flexible work schedules and boosting diversity, the legal profession requires interventions that address its androcentric nature, eradicate sexism, and level the playing field for women. The legal profession requires feminists, both male and female, who are prepared to use their position of authority to uplift women and challenge the attitudes and customs that maintain women's subordination.

Some key steps that can be taken by employers include:

1. Proactively support women's career progression at all stages and put them in positions of leadership until there is parity at every level. Recognize and remove barriers and implement quotas to accelerate progress.

Provide women lawyers with the tools and support they need to succeed in leadership roles, including:

a. creating a positive work environment
b. investing in measures directed at redistributing their care roles
c. taking steps to dispel common myths and stereotypes based on grounds of sex, gender, and race

Create formal processes and mechanisms to eliminate discrimination, violence, and harassment in the world of work such as:

a. conducting audits to identify the prevalence of sexism and gendered violence and its risk factors
b. introducing legal protections and measures to support victims of domestic violence at work
c. creating formal reporting mechanisms

d. preventing reprisals against those who report such incidents

Some key steps that can be taken by relevant institutions, government, and societal actors are:

1. Sow the seeds of transformation through legal education by making sure that law school curricula embody the principles of equality and non-discrimination. Encourage law students to interrogate the unequal power dynamics embodied in law and in the legal profession and recognize the gendered barriers to entry and advancement. Equip future lawyers, through continuing legal education, to become agents of change and open new doors for those who follow.
2. Support and invest in feminist lawyering and movement-building for women to collectively raise their voices against gender and sex-based discrimination and violence at a societal level. This should have a transformative purpose, so that calls for fundamental change of the legal profession, and those leading reform from within, can receive broad support.

10.3. ISSUES RELATED TO POLICING AND INCARCERATION

In the legal system, women of color confront particular and significant obstacles, particularly with regard to police and incarceration. These problems create intricate, multidimensional forms of discrimination because they are closely linked to racial, gender, and socioeconomic inequalities. Women of color's experiences with law enforcement, the criminal justice system, and the wider range of issues associated with incarceration are impacted by this intersectionality. Understanding the intricate relationships between these systems and how they disproportionately affect women of color is necessary to address these problems.

10.3.1. Policing and Racial Profiling

Womffer particular and harsh consequences as a result ofbecause of the disproportionate targeting of communities of color by American policing practices, which have long been criticized. Women of color are disproportionately stopped, searched, and arrested more frequently as a result of racial profiling and discriminatory policing tactics. Even after adjusting for behavior, studies reveal that Black and Latina women are more likely than White women to be stopped and searched. Racial biases that are deeply ingrained in law enforcement procedures are the primary cause of this disparity, and stereotypes that criminalize women of color can make them even more so. Discrimination based on gender is frequently the consequence of the intersection of race and gender in law enforcement. Racial biases can exacerbate the gender-based violence and harassment that women of color often experience.

For instance, the experiences of Black women who are victims of domestic or sexual abuse are frequently disregarded or not given enough attention by law enforcement, which is indicative of larger trends of racial and gender-based neglect in the policing system. Furthermore, as evidenced by the prosecution of domestic abuse survivors for allegedly defending themselves against violent spouses, women of color who have experienced violence may also face criminal consequences for responding to their abuse.

10.3.2. Criminalization of Survival and Economic Inequality

An additional important problem that impacts women of color is the criminalization of survival. Systemic issues like unemployment and poverty cause economic marginalization for a large number of women of color. Due to their economic disadvantage, women of color are disproportionately punished for engaging in survival crimes, such as petty theft and sex work, which are considered minor offenses. In response to these survival crimes, the criminal justice system frequently overlooks the underlying socioeconomic problems, which perpetuates cycles of arrest and incarsproportionately affect women of color.

Particular legalLegal issues arise when racial, gender, and economic factors come together. For example, women of color who work in survival sex are more likely to be arrested and face legal repercussions. Furthermore, economically disadvantaged women of color may encounter obstacles in obtaining legal counsel, which makes it more challenging for them to successfully navigate the legal system and defend their rights.

10.3.3. Sentencing Disparities and Incarceration Rates

When women of color enter the criminal justice system, there are notable discrepancies in sentencing. Women of color frequently receive harsher sentences even though they commit similar offenses as their white counterparts. Systemic injustices in the legal system and racial bias are two of the many factors influencing this disparity. For instance, research indicates that Black women frequently receive harsher sentences than White women for comparable offenses, which reflects larger racial disparities in sentencing policies.

Mass incarceration has a significant negative effect on women of color. With one of the highest rates of incarceration in the world, women of color are disproportionately represented in the criminal justice system in the United

States. This discrepancy has been exacerbated by laws like the war on drugs and mandatory minimum sentences. For example, the Anti-Drug Abuse Act of 1986 and the 1994 Violent Crime Control and Law Enforcement Act imposed harsh sentencing guidelines that disproportionately impacted communities of color, increasing the incarceration rates of Black and

Women of color face particular challenges as a result ofbecause of incarceration. Reproductive health services are frequently neglected in prisons and jails, which disproportionately affects women of color who may already encounter obstacles in obtaining these services outside of jail. Additionally, the experience of incarceration can have detrimental effects on the families and communities of women of color, perpetuating marginalization and poverty cycles.

10.3.4. Reentry and Post-Incarceration Challenges

Beyond jail, women of color confront additional difficulties during the reintegration process. Reintegrating back into society can present major challenges for women who have served time in prison, such as trouble obtaining housing, work, and social serf color may encounter additional obstacles as a result ofbecause of discrimination based on both race and gender, which makes these difficulties worse. For instance, women of color may find it more difficult to obtain stable employment and housing due to the stigma attached to having a criminal record.

Furthermore, a successful reentry can be hampered by the absence of post-incarceration support networks for women of color. Social services that are essential for a successful reintegration, like mental health and drug abuse treatment, are not easily accessible to many women of color. The way that race and gender intersect in this situation emphasizes the need for specialized support services that deal with the unique difficulties that women of color face.

10.3.5. Advocacy and Reform Efforts

Addressing the unique challenges faced by women of color in the context of policing and incarceration requires comprehensive and intersectional legal reforms. Advocacy efforts must focus on several key areas:

1. **Policing Reforms**: Efforts to address racial profiling and discriminatory policing practices are essential. Reform initiatives should include anti-bias training for law enforcement, community policing models that prioritize building trust with marginalized communities, and increased oversight and accountability mechanisms to address instances of police misconduct.

2. **Sentencing and Incarceration Reform**: Legal reforms aimed at reducing sentencing disparities and addressing the impact of mass incarceration on women of color are crucial. This includes revisiting mandatory minimum sentences, eliminating sentencing disparities, and focusing on alternatives to incarceration for non-violent offenses. Additionally, efforts to decriminalize survival crimes and address the root causes of economic inequality can help mitigate the disproportionate impact on women of color.
3. **Support Services for Reentry**: Enhancing support services for women of color during reentry is vital for successful reintegration. This includes expanding access to employment programs, housing assistance, and social services that cater to the specific needs of women of color. Providing comprehensive healthcare services, including reproductive health care, is also essential.
4. **Intersectional Advocacy**: Advocacy must adopt an intersectional approach that recognizes and addresses the compounded nature of discrimination faced by women of color. This involves integrating perspectives from both racial justice and gender equity movements to develop policies and practices that reflect the diverse experiences of women of color.m, women of color confron particular difficultiesdifficulties, especially with regard toabout police and incarceration. Complex forms of discrimination resulting from the intersection of race, gender, and socioeconomic status have disproportionate effects on policing practncing, incarceration rates, and reentry challenges. In order toTo address these problems, legal reform must take a comprehensive, intersectional approach that recognizes and addresses the unique needs of women of color. More equitable legal systems that better serve all people and advance justice and fairness can be established by putting targeted reforms into place and improving support networks.

Them that acknowledges and responds to the particular difficultiesdifficulties faced by women of color as a result of the intersection of race and gender is highlighted by the law of gendered justice. Racial and gender inequalities are often addressed in i traditional legal frameworks, which are inadequate in light ofconsidering historical and current disparities in employment, education, policing, and incarceration. A more equitable legal system that successfully advances justice and addresses the multiple forms of discrimination faced by women of color requires an intersectional approach to legal reform. Law and policy reforms that take intersectional perspectives into account can help society move toward a more just and inclusive legal system that benefits everyone.

REFERENCES

1. Anderson, C. (2003). *Eyes off the Prize: African Americans, the United Nations, and the Struggle for Human Rights, 1944–1955*. Cambridge, UK; New York: Cambridge University Press.
2. Blau, J. R., & Moncada, A. (2006). *Justice in the United States: Human Rights and the U.S. Constitution*. Lanham: Rowman & Littlefield Publishers.
3. Blau, J. R., et al. (2008). *The Leading Rogue State: The United States and Human Rights*. Boulder, CO: Paradigm Publishers.
4. Moraga, C., & Anzaldúa, G. (1981). *This Bridge Called My Back: Writings by Radical Women of Color*. Watertown, MA: Persephone Press.
5. Zoelle, D. G. (2000). *Globalizing Concern for Women's Human Rights: The Failure of the American Model*. New York: St. Martin's Press.

INDEX

D

E

F

G

H

R

S

T

FSC
www.fsc.org
MIX
Papier | Fördert gute Waldnutzung
FSC® C083411

Kolibri 360 GmbH
Ferdinand-Jühlke-Straße 7
99095 Erfurt, Deutschland
produktsicherheit@kolibri360.de